OCCIDENTALISM

Theory, Culture & Society

Theory, Culture & Society caters for the resurgence of interest in culture within contemporary social science and the humanities. Building on the heritage of classical social theory, the book series examines ways in which this tradition has been reshaped by a new generation of theorists. It also publishes theoretically informed analyses of everyday life, popular culture, and new intellectual movements.

EDITOR: Mike Featherstone, *Nottingham Trent University*

THE TCS CENTRE
The Theory, Culture & Society book series, the journals *Theory, Culture & Society* and *Body & Society*, and related conference, seminar and postgraduate programmes operate from the TCS Centre at Nottingham Trent University. For further details of the TCS Centre's activities please contact:

Centre Administrator
The TCS Centre, Room 175
Faculty of Humanities
Nottingham Trent University
Clifton Lane, Nottingham, NG11 8NS, UK
e-mail: tcs@ntu.ac.uk
web: http://tcs@ntu.ac.uk

Recent volumes include:

Michel de Certeau
Cultural Theorist
Ian Buchanan

The Cultural Economy of Cities
Allen J. Scott

Body Modification
edited by Mike Featherstone

Paul Virilio
From Modernism to Hypermodernism
edited by John Armitage

Subject, Society and Culture
Roy Boyne

Norbert Elias and Modern Social Theory
Dennis Smith

Development Theory
Deconstructions/Reconstructions
Jan Nederveen Pieterse

OCCIDENTALISM

Modernity and Subjectivity

COUZE VENN

SAGE Publications
London • Thousand Oaks • New Delhi

© Couze Venn 2000

First published 2000

 SAGE Publications Ltd
6 Bonhill Street
London EC2A 4PU

SAGE Publications Inc
2455 Teller Road
Thousand Oaks, California 91320

SAGE Publications India Pvt Ltd
32, M-Block Market
Greater Kailash – I
New Delhi 110 048

Published in association with *Theory, Culture & Society*,
Nottingham Trent University

British Library Cataloguing in Publication data

A catalogue record for this book is available
from the British Library

ISBN 0-7619-5411-2
ISBN 0-7619-5412-0 (pbk)

Library of Congress catalog record available

Typeset by Mayhew Typesetting, Rhayader, Powys
Printed in Great Britain by Redwood Books, Trowbridge,
Wiltshire

CONTENTS

ACKNOWLEDGEMENTS

This book has taken much longer to write than I had intended. In the course of it, I have been sustained by two things: the knowledge of living in an incredibly unjust and unethical world, and the encouragement given by colleagues, who, from reading odd chapters or through our many conversations, gained some idea of what I have been attempting to achieve and urged me to finish the work. My postgraduate students at the University of East London have over the years obliged me to clarify and develop what would have remained half-baked ideas. The book would have been poorer had Neal Curtis, Mike Featherstone, Chris Miles and Jeremy Valentine not read whole early drafts and made comments that have helped me avoid some serious mistakes. Other colleagues have read selected chapters or earlier versions and provided feedbacks that have fed into the much-needed rewrites. Amongst them are Phil Cohen, Tom Foot, Stuart Hall, Scott Lash, Ken Parker, Vivien Schelling, Bill Schwarz, Ash Sharma, Richard Sheldon. In some ways this book continues a number of themes first explored in *Changing the Subject*, and re-examined in the always fruitful and comradely discussions the co-authors of that book have enjoyed over the years; I owe more to Julian Henriques, Wendy Hollway, Cathy Urwin and Valerie Walkerdine than they know. Chris Rojek and Jackie Griffin, as well as Jane Evans, Justin Dyer and others in the production team at Sage, have been enormously helpful and patient. Francesca and Hari have put up with the fact that I was often cocooned in a world of my own, caught up in the obsession of reading yet one more article, struggling with yet one more puzzle. Their patience and love have helped me see the work through to the end.

INTRODUCTION

This book has been long in the making. It has been constantly interrupted by other projects that have fed into it so that it has mutated over time. One thing has remained constant through these explorations, namely, the aim of interrogating modernity from the standpoint of a postcoloniality that knows itself to be caught up in the history of modernity, inflected by its discourse, yet conscious of the need to disrupt the limits and the limitations which the modern now signifies. These limits exist at both the discursive and the historical levels, since they operate at the level of modernity's self-understanding inscribed in the discourses that articulate its intelligibility, as well as at the level of the lifeworlds that have been constituted in the course of its history. My task has been one of finding critical spaces for engaging with that reality, spaces from which the question of what is to come after modernity converges with the question of the postcolonial. The stakes in breaking out of the limitations concern the possibility of imagining radically different forms of sociality in the moment of the 'post'.

I will begin with a brief explanation of the project indicated in what I have just said. At the level of theory, two series of analyses that have framed the critique of modernity are central to my approach. On the one hand, from the 1960s the spectrum of critiques collected under the sign of poststructuralism has targeted the discourses that have authorized modernity as a project, interrogating the foundational concepts and narratives which underwrote it, like those of the logocentric subject or of History as the linear and progressive unfolding of a *telos*. These critiques, in recognizing the epistemological and ethical violences that have shadowed the institution of modernity, have increasingly been directed towards the question of the ethical basis of a post-Enlightenment ethos, particularly in the work of Derrida, Foucault, Lyotard, Ricoeur, Levinas, elaborating a number of themes which phenomenology, from Husserl, had started to bring to the surface.

On the other hand, the critique of colonial discourse and modernity which has now been assembled in something called postcolonial theory has ended up addressing the same issues about foundational and authorizing concepts that the problematic of ethics trails in its wake.[1] Stuart Hall (1996b), a pivotal figure in this convergence, whose work weaves together cultural and postcolonial studies, defines the postcolonial in terms of 'thinking at the limits', that is to say, an analytical approach which keeps 'under erasure' the concepts and theories that one must borrow from the

discourses of modernity whilst engaged in their critique. Such an attitude to
theory cannot avoid a constant vigilance about the grounds of knowledge,
and thus it cannot avoid putting into question the epistemological, ethical
and aesthetic enframing of modernity as a project.

This heretical analysis requires that, for strategic purposes, one is able to
locate oneself at the edge of existing paradigms, in an in-between discursive
space from which one may perceive the figures of the 'figurants', as Derrida
might put it. My search is thus for a way of narrating the present, a
genealogical discourse that, in its refiguration of modernity, indicates a way
out of the present. I am therefore not concerned with sociological accounts
that propose models of development that point to the structural determi-
nations of modernity – for instance, the possible structured–structurizing
relationships between the economic and the social – or analyses that trace
the mutations of modernity, by reconstructing its articulation, first, with
mercantile capitalism, then with industrial and consumer capitalisms and
the cultures affiliated with these forms. The summaries of the main positions regarding a sociology of modernity in Hall and Gieben (1992) and
Hall et al. (1992) show clearly enough the problems intrinsic to the variety
of models on offer from the classical analyses of Durkheim, Weber and
Marx to the more recent departures of, say, Giddens (1990) and Beck
(1992). It has become more and more difficult to assert directions from the
claims of structural relations. Instead, my question about modernity concerns the meaning of the 'post'-as-limit from the point of view of a narrative that changes the present.

My own path through these developments has been to establish the
specificity and uniqueness of the institution of modernity by reference to
two themes, namely, the contribution of the New World as condition of
possibility for its emergence, and, by reference to a longer genealogy of the
questions about being that the discourse of modernity addressed, arguing
that the specificity of the answers that it has elaborated is bound up with
the history of colonialism and capitalism. Occidentalism, from that point of
view, is the conceptual and historical space in which a particular narrative
of the subject and a particular narrative of history have been constituted;
these have become hegemonic with modernization, having effects throughout the world because of the universal scope of the project of modernity
and the global reach of European colonization. The book breaks with that
conceptual space, that is to say, it breaks with the privilege of epistemology,
with subject-centred ontologies and psychologies, and with the mutation of
occidentalism recently into a performative modernization underwritten by
neo-liberalism and the instrumentalisation of reason. It tries to dislodge
from post-Enlightenment philosophical discourse a number of critical elements that enable one to indicate a discourse of being which opens towards
a different postmodernity, a transmodernity, one which is the correlate of a
postcoloniality to come.

A great deal of material, developed in the course of teaching and thinking,
invisibly remains in the background of my critique of modernity. For

instance, I have over the years compiled a dossier of events relating to what used to be called the 'Third World', assembled from newspaper cuttings, specialist magazines, Amnesty International reports, and so on, letting them stand as evidence of the incredible inhumanity which characterizes everyday reality in postcolonial times. I keep it within my sight for much the same reasons that medieval scholars kept a skull, namely, as a memento, in my case, of the inadequacy of language, particularly theory, to encompass the unspeakable horror which is committed daily in the name of profit, efficiency, order, modernization, oppressive power and its maintenance. Gradually, the dossier has included events from everywhere, so that the 'Third World' could no longer be contained within the older colonial space; the relationship of the global and the local became deterritorialized. Edward Said established some time ago that colonial discourse was not just about the discursive construction of the colonized 'other' but that it was intrinsic to European self-understanding, determining how Europe and Europeans could locate themselves – as modern, as civilized, as superior, as developed and progressive – only by reference to an other that was represented as the negation of everything that Europe imagined or desired itself to be. Today, similarly, the postcolonial world is present everywhere, but it is filtered for the 'West' through the representational devices of consumer culture and the tourist gaze, or it is relocated by the conceptual suppositions of development theory and of modernization such that it can still appear outside or peripheral, either beyond the concern of everyday calculations or dispersed in the generalities of globalization theory; often the post-independence countries appear only as the place of catastrophe. A central intention in this book is to make present this presence, to demonstrate its effects at the heart of the postmodern critique of modernity.

Another corpus of material which has been formative concerns the exploration of questions of identity, widely dispersed, existing in a variety of forms, from academic writing to novels and films and music, questions which I have addressed elsewhere – for example in Venn (1993) and (1999) – but which I have had to leave in the shadow of the more general problem of subject-formation. Equally, it would not have been possible for me to focus on the point of view of historicity and temporality in my elaboration of a critical phenomenology had people like Vattimo (1988), Lacoue-Labarthe (1990), Grosz (1994), Critchley (1997), Wood (1988), Osborne (1995) and many more, gone some way in preparing the ground in their reflections on some of the key texts that I have put to work here. It goes without saying too that the collaborative work I have done with the co-authors of *Changing the Subject* (Henriques et al., 1984), excavating the ground of psychology and of psychoanalytical thought, has shaped a good deal of what appears here without being explicitly addressed. As we know, it is easier to 'think at the limits' when one knows one is simply taking a few steps further along paths that others have already cleared out.

The disadvantage in my approach is that those who have not ventured along similar roads may think that too much is taken for granted or left unsaid in my analyses. I have but two excuses for this neglect, namely, that it would have required a much longer work to do justice to the wealth of material, and that the trajectory I have indicated has led me to the conclusion that the challenge to the foundational narratives of modernity cannot avoid the focus on the core theoretical issues. The problem of the subject has appeared intrinsic to this interrogation for two reasons, namely, because what is articulated at the heart of the founding narratives of every epoch are the forms of subjectivity that it engenders, and because the problem of the reconstitution of the colonial subject has been central to postcolonial questioning, as my analysis will make clear. The focus on the question of foundation and on the question of a different theorization of subjectivity has meant that the approach in the book has taken a philo-sophical turn, even if limited to the conceptual framework of post-structuralism and selected figures.

The work of Foucault has been important in this trajectory, surprisingly so, since he has little to say directly about the (post)colonial in spite of his interest in the Iranian issue. I deal with this neglect in Chapter 4, reading it symptomatically to bring out the invisibilities in the way that the Enlight-enment formulates its problematic of the subject and its project of the emancipation of humanity, invisibilities reinscribed in Foucault's refigura-tion of the question which motivated the Enlightenment in terms of who we are in the present and in terms of a critical ontology implicating an ethics and an aesthetics of being. What is immediately relevant is the fact that his analysis of modernity directed attention to the effects of power inside the very process of intellectual labour, so that claims to knowledge could no longer shelter behind the epistemological defences of objectivity, but had to acknowledge the locatedness of knowledge within stratagems of power, and so reveal its hand. Truth in the social sciences could thus be refigured in terms of regimes of truth and of the instruments for instituting the par-ticular forms of sociality which theory theorizes. In the course of his elaboration of these problems, Foucault has demonstrated something about modernity, namely, its historical specificity and its conditions of possibility, thus its contingent character, which enables us now to stand back from it and interrogate it from the standpoint of an emergent counter-narrative, no longer seeing in modernity the inevitability of a process of historical unfolding.

Yet when one thinks about modernity in the light of recent debates, what is striking is the astonishing success of the now suspect modernist ideas about history and subjectivity, and about the mechanisms and causes of stability or development in human societies. Of course, today, it is possible to invoke the fact of European colonialism and Western imperialism and the achievements of capitalism and of technocratic reason to find, however retrospectively, reasons for the triumph of modernity, particularly in its occidentalist form. My approach is to consider a longer genealogy of the subject (and of humanity) within which to locate modernity, in order to allocate to it a different measure, one that cannot be returned to its own criteria for judgement. This requires a number of strategic discursive deterritorializations. I would begin with the argument that modernity derived its appeal from and was instituted on the promise of a solution to questions that are rather more archaic and fundamental than the objectives of the progress of reason and the advancement of society on the basis of rational calculation and planning. These questions concern the existential realities which all cultures have faced in their own way, to do with finitude, and lack and loss, and the peculiar, indeed uncanny, ungrounded character of our beingness or dwelling in the world. Before the modern period, religion, or, more generally, discourses with a claim to a sacred foundation, was the privileged terrain in which people sought to still the anguish immanent in the human condition and to anchor ontological security. The discourse of modernity, in proposing the possibility of human beings taking charge of their own destiny on the basis of secular narratives of emancipation, owing nothing to the erstwhile fateful forces of nature or to the mysteries of a transcendent divine will and a vagrant destiny, ensured that ontology and epistemology took the place of theology and metaphysics. By the time of the Enlightenment, epistemology, however troubled by Kantian hesitations, had come to be the privileged terrain upon which were displaced all the questions concerning who 'we' are and what is to be done. The age of Reason, or rather a particular understanding of the rational, became at once enshrined and validated in the success of the sciences and the technological miracles which they made possible.

Reason has another, less illustrious, but equally central, function in the story of the success of modernity. From the time of its refiguration within the Cartesian problematic of the subject, it functioned to consign the colonized and women, the propertyless and non-white peoples to the status of inferior beings, delivered to the violences of oppressive and exploitative power. This is a more complicated story than the tale told from the point of view of a hasty anti-rationalism or anti-modernity. To tell it, one needs to set the scene differently, to defamiliarize expectations. The first chapter begins this process.

The political and the theoretical problem today is that in the wake of the developments and transformations in the last twenty years or so we no longer know for sure how to make sense of the reality of the world as we find it. Some would even call into question the notion of reality itself, correctly challenging the pretensions of realist representation, but incorrectly claiming dispensation from the obligation to judge, on the grounds that the subject of knowledge is so thoroughly inscribed in the stratagems of discourse that there can be no neutral or uninvested ground for deciding between competing genres of discourse. Discourse, however, is not outside the political or the ethical. The idea that one cannot judge because we are all inscribed in discourse – or indeed because there is 'nothing outside' the text, forgetting Derrida's (1999) own strictures about the implications for relativism – is itself a legacy of the privilege of the epistemological instance in the philosophical discourse of modernity. The reasoning seems to be that of claiming that if there can be no unimpeacheable, objective ground for truth – the protocol demanded by the epistemology intrinsic to modernity – then there can be no truths in the first place. Nostalgia for epistemological certainty and a degree of abjection for the modern subject have combined to produce a self-indulgent chatter. Time was when we were accustomed to the thought that there were a number of grand truths to which we could hold on in the security of unshakable foundations. Had we not been assured that progress in every domain was possible, even inevitable? Were we not certain that 'History' proceeded according to well-understood patterns or laws, and that scientific thought would find answers to every mystery? Were we not convinced that we were the masters of our own destiny, in spite of being burdened by circumstances and by the weight of history? Later, we rejoiced with equal certainty in the death of a number of ideas, like the Subject, History, Humanism, ideas that swiftly joined others in the big cemetery of discarded transcendentals. Then we learned with some anxiety to question our own questioning, balancing anxiety with the excitement of the possibility of a ludic nomadism of identity and of theoretical practice. If in doubt, credibility could always be restored by making a certain kind of deconstruction the name of the game. In any case, playful irony could be counted upon to get us out of any uncomfortable situation.

Meanwhile, the debris of history has kept piling up, which makes us fear for the future and question our responsibility. New names of disasters, like ex-Yugoslavia, Rwanda, Cambodia, Algeria, Afghanistan, Chile, have joined those like Auschwitz and the Gulag, names of the Disappeared everywhere that have derailed the lofty ambitions of the project of modernity. Already, to reduce to the symbolism of proper names the suffering of Auschwitz and its contemporary metonymies, or the injustice of the Disappeared, damages our ability to confront the unrepresentability of the injustice done to countless named persons. To all this, one must add the list of the familiar and routine examples of inhumanity: chronic famine, abject poverty, the uprooting of those who do not fit for ethnic or economic reasons, and the extermination of tribes because they are in the way. If we were to include the damage done by every manner of pollution and the environmental destruction caused by cynical over-exploitation or ignorance, we would have a picture of inhumanity and catastrophe that should stop us in our tracks when we contemplate the wonders of the cybernetic world or the miracles promised by biotechnology, genetic engineering and nano-technology.

Furthermore, other narratives have surfaced, mutating from pre-modern metanarratives, to compete with the grand schemes which once legitimated the project of modernity as the one that should prevail universally. For example, religious and ethnic fundamentalisms make similar claims to universal validity and are as totalizing in their reach. The appeal of fundamentalism must be set against the *agon* of the 'we' – the people, the nation, and, at another level, humanity – the ideological signifiers that had functioned to authorize political action, a 'we' that the failures of the project of modernity and of 'development' reveal to have been riven by inequalities of power and wealth. The fundamentalisms of today are modern recastings of older traditional and religious discourses, preserving their mythic dimension, but conditioned by the experience of modernization, including the mass media and military technology. Indeed, fundamentalism's claims to derive its authority or legitimacy from the purity of an unblemished tradition forgets the extent to which its discourse is so conditioned. In some cases, say with Zionism and varieties of fundamentalist Christians, the authority of scientific rationality is recruited to validate claims about race or about psychological processes. Other narratives include scientistic and 'New Age' grand theorizations and visions, whether grounded in genetics and biology as in varieties of socio-biology, or in less tangible occult forces in the case of New Age discourse. They imagine an implicate and over-arching order in the world which makes sense of events and gives meaning to human existence.

It could be argued that, faced with this Benjaminesque vision of the angel of history terrified by the sight of humanity in ruins, it would be less messy to close the book outright on the episode of modernity rather than sift through the rubble. Yet if we wish to turn our face towards the future, we cannot afford the innocence of born-again post-isms that will have for-gotten the conditions that institute the present. For a start, a term like 'post' implicates a concept of periodization – as linear and developmental, proceeding through ruptures or transformations, and so on – which modernity itself invented. If every discourse finds its place in relation to a particular stream of questioning that locates its contingency and con-juncture, then there can be no privileged site, called either postcoloniality or postmodernity, from which truth can declare its authenticity. This is not simply a matter of reflexivity, which some people would like to think of as specifically postmodern; it is an aspect of the historicity of discourse. We need, in any case, to ask ourselves who will testify and bear responsibility for what has been done. What lessons should we take with us to avoid repeating past errors and excesses as we follow a new direction? Are we not inheritors of the found world and carriers of the same temptations, inscribed in that world, which have driven previous generations to seek transcendent destinies in spite of the cost in terroristic forms of sociality?

My point is that, one way or another, the discourse of modernity, with all its ambivalences, is far from being a spent force. Besides, in spite of the intimations of postmodernity, the term 'modernization', recently repack-aged in political and managerial rhetoric, still has the power to command submission to its authority or its claims to good sense. It increasingly functions in the service of goals that its own occidentalist logic decrees. By this I mean something more than what Lyotard (1984) said about legiti-mation in postmodern times. We recall that his analysis highlighted how the commodification of knowledge within an economy of capitalist exchange, together with the uncoupling of a narrative of legitimation grounded in ethical judgement from a narrative establishing claims to truth, has resulted in a self-referential, performative system for the instrumental determination of the means for and the ends of human advancement. Within this system, the criterion of efficiency, measured according to the logic of instrumental rationality, enshrined in the performativity of a technocratic and economistic *techne*, has become the norm for judgement about desirable ends. My contention is that to the coupling of a despotic reason with the logic of capitalist accumulation one must add the force of colonialism and imperialism in overdetermining the development of a hegemonic discourse of modernity which has left behind both the ethical priority in the emancipatory ideals of Enlightenment and the memory of the physical, psychological and ontological violences that have shadowed the making of the modern world. It relates to the process of the becoming-West of Europe and the becoming-modern of the world that I am calling occidentalism. Thus, occidentalism refers at once to the space of intelligibility of a triumphalist modernity and to the genealogy of the present as a history of the transformations that have in the course of time instituted the forms of sociality and the lifeworlds that inscribe occidentalism. As I indicated earlier, this book is about the disengagement from the conceptual terrain of occidentalism and the disentanglement from the discourse of modernity of a number of elements that, relocated outside occidentalism and its affiliates like egology and phallogocentrism, hold out the possibility of not repeating the violences intrinsic to it.

The triumph of capitalism coupled to the failures of Stalinism have, for the moment, silenced the narratives of a socialist alternative. A variety of social movements have appeared, like radical ecology and communitarian projects on the fringe of administered society, but they remain marginalized or subject to recuperative tactics whenever their appeal rekindles some humanitarian value, as with some varieties of green politics.[2] In the 'Third World', uprisings – for example, the Zapatista in Mexico – constantly face overwhelming military and economic power. The greatest obstacles to fundamental change exist in the form of the terroristic, semi-criminal forms of power that now operate, sometimes in the guise of the 'state', locking whole populations in cycles of exploitation and oppression. Then there are the obstacles in the mind, namely, habitual ways of thinking materialized in the lifeworld, feeding into the poverty of mass political culture. The general will today is a ventroliquist will, its autonomy is but the effect of a specular sleight-of-hand. The emasculation of 'public man' (Sennett, 1976) goes hand in hand with the priority of the private world and the privatization of fulfilment alongside the privatization of responsibility and care. A mafioso capitalism has spread, in networks and folds, recognizing no responsibility for anyone, laying claim to the future, whilst an army of apologists and 'realists' are busy working out the ways of legitimizing or living with it.

The problems that we now face require other investigations. At the theoretical level, I would indicate the critique of value, the critique of the new economy of power, and the critique of knowledge, informed by the kind of analysis of being that I shall be developing. Specific themes would concern the manner in which money has come to be identified with value, as the value by which all other values are measured. The value of time too has been inflected by the equivalence asserted by the copula 'is' in the expression 'time is money'. Time, accelerated in cyber-culture, is performatively produced through speed, so that the equivalence of time and speed and money can be assured by virtue of the conversion of time into the simulacral form of money. Within the discourse of neo-liberalism, and new governance, money, infinitely versatile, is becoming the new transcendental object, virtually infinite and total. One would need to examine the diremptions between the time that money buys, as efficient time, and as the coefficient of the rate of appropriation of value, and the time of the who, which is the time of being-in-the-world and of being-with, the time of finitude, the value of which is measured in hope and pleasures.

The critique of the new economy of power will have to address the changes in governance; the globalization of networks of power through the economy and informational and administrative technologies, for instance through NGOs like the International Monetary Fund and the World Trade Organization and new media, and through new mechanisms for instituting subjectivities and authorizing ways of being. The critique of knowledge would in part refer to these changes, taking a cue from Lyotard's analysis of the postmodern, but taking centrally into account postcolonial factors and inputs. In part it would be a way of moving away from the traditional epistemological terrain altogether, recognizing that knowing and being are not so neatly separable, and that truth is not a matter of the objective knowledge of some independently existing 'natural' world, since human beings are an intrinsic part of the 'natural' world, and since that world has been 'technically normed' by human societies for a considerable time. We now see with the eyes of all those who have been before us, so that it is a 'complex seeing',[3] which positivist science would like to simplify or rationalize, and that ethnocentric attitudes, both 'black' and 'white', wish to disaggregate and hierarchize.

The task now, after the time of modernity and the time of the gods, the time of universal being and the time of the tribes, is to give to the 'postmodern' its own temporality and its own ethos of being. If I still attach the term 'postmodern' to the time of futurity, it is because the reflections that we are able to pursue, and the discursive and material conditions that we have to recognize, as limit and as condition of possibility, are the result of this extraordinary event called modernity. No one can pretend to stand outside these circumstances or outside the differential and plural history of modernity. So, the question of settling accounts with modernity means the refusal to allow repressive forgetting to place under erasure the debts and the lessons tied up with the consequences of modernity. It does not call for restitution or compensation but for renunciation, in particular the renunciation of the oppressive and exploitative practices, like capitalism, racism, masculinism, ecological imperialism, that cause unacceptable damage to human beings and to the world.

If the project of transforming the present is to be ethically directed and motivated, it must be concerned primarily with the question of what it is good for human beings to be. There has been a widespread assumption that human beings are intrinsically driven towards the ethical – a version of a Rousseauesque noble savage. My view is that the question of becoming ethical is tied to reflection upon a history of responsibility, and that it is thus, as I examine in Chapter 2, part of a universalizing and general project, that is to say, it is a question which modernity itself has put on the agenda in the form of history as a history of responsibility. It remains an indeterminate process, since improvement is neither guaranteed nor automatic; it is a task that must be renewed every generation. My exploration tries to show that subjective and historical transformation is a complex process, working at several levels, involving reflexivity and the work of rememoration, in the sense I develop in Chapter 4, where I correlate it with the refiguration of the history of a community alongside the work of working through. I also argue that working through, in that it accomplishes the refiguration of identity, includes both a form of confronting private fears, pains, anxieties, traumas, memories, guilts, and so on, as in the therapeutic practice, as well as renarrativizations of collective memories and projects. Rememoration is the articulation of the one with the other, which means to say that it is a process that cannot privilege, or be reduced to, rational deliberation. Indeed, one of my central propositions is that the dimension of the aesthetic–expressive, understood as the space where the experience of the sublime and what is un(re)presentably present is brought to presence in the liminality of 'art', is an essential element, functioning at the level both of a critical hermeneutics and of the experiential, combining both mind and body, touching Being 'on its inside part', to borrow an expression from Toni Morrison's novel *Beloved* (1987).

Communicative rationality is certainly needed, because of the 'differends' that already exist in contemporary societies and because of the requirements of democratic politics. Deliberative politics, however, are means to an end which from the beginning, well before modernity, have concerned the fulfilment of a life. It will be my aim to establish, first, the unethical nature of any culture and any project of becoming which does not provide conditions which equalize every person's chances for fulfilment; thus, no society so far has been ethical in the sense I am developing in this book. Second, I will show that our presentness has been the indeterminate outcome of mostly irreversible changes that have instituted the lifeworld we inhabit as the ready-to-hand world which we can neither 'cleanse' nor 'forget' because it is the 'flesh' in which we dwell. Today, because of modernity, these conditions apply globally, in the old imperial metropolises as well as in the 'post-colonial' world. So, the 'to come' of postmodernity and the postcoloniality to come have become indissolubly twinned destinies. They announce either the naturalization, through the discourse of efficiency and the promotion of money to the rank of the postmodern transcendent value, of all the violences that currently amplify inequalities and injustices, or the reinvention of narratives of hope that motivate the transformation of both subjectivities and cultures. In the wake of modernity, we should now envisage the becoming-mature of humanity in terms of the becoming-ethical of post-modern or, more properly, transmodern, societies.

The rest of the book moves in that direction, beginning with a displacement of the question of subjectivity away from the terrain of the philosophy of the subject, by linking it with the standpoint of the historicity of being and of responsibility for the other, and, thus, putting the emphasis on notions of being-with and being-towards-the-other, against the solipsistic privilege of individualism. I will then examine the birth of modernity and its discourse of the subject in terms of the discursive displacements and the historical conditions which combine to establish the conjuncture in which the event of modernity appears. Again, the aim is to draw out conclusions that feed into the main project, particularly to do with the longer genealogy of the fundamental questions that have preoccupied human beings from the beginning of culture, so that modernity itself can be located and localized with respect to these questions. The functioning of the colonial enterprise in the birth of modernity will be a central issue.

There follows an interrogation of the Enlightenment from the point of view of what we may still learn by way of its critique. In particular I will explore further the dimension of the unpresentable and unrepresentable aspects of beingness that 'art' attempts to disclose, a dimension which the analytic of the sublime has sought to express, for instance in Kant's Third Critique and Lyotard's (1994) reflections on that critique. My intention is to extract from this analysis the way we can refigure Foucault's question of who we are in the present in the moment of the 'post' of occidentalism. The focus on Enlightenment discourses is premised on the recognition that it still circumscribes the political, aesthetic, ethical, epistemological, terrain that the point of view of the postmodern problematizes but has not escaped, as is clear in the efforts of figures like Habermas, Rorty, Lyotard or Foucault to redefine the project of human becoming after modernity.

My final chapter deals with the possibility of overcoming these limits. It proposes a negative ethics as regulative Idea, a non-normative, non-prescriptive ethics that transmutes notions of being-with and of responsibility for the other into the principle of respect for the time of the other and recognition of the other. It develops the idea that being-in-the-world implicates an embodied self coupled to concrete others and to the world of objects such that they establish the dwelling in which particular selves are dispersed. Both propositions relate to the historicity of the lifeworld and the temporality of being. One implication concerns the reworking of the notion of project so that it no longer refers to the realization of History, but to the becoming of being as ethical being. Within this problematic, anticipation and emancipation come to be understood as a promise arising from the recognition of injustice and the commonality of suffering – because of finitude, fragility, loss, lack, dependency – and the desire to overcome or transcend these existential conditions. The becoming-ethical of 'humanity' can thus be seen to be the result of a developmental process suggesting an apprenticeship. The latter combines the concepts of work and of instruction, that is to say, it has both an instrumental and an ethical interest – instrumental in relation to the process of transformation, to *physis*, and ethical by reference to the work one does in coming to recognize that the gift of responsibility and of time fulfils an immemorial promise inscribed in the history of being. The concept of work requires the existence or the elaboration of critical narratives that inform the process by which being questions itself as to its way of being. These narratives operate at the level of the formation of subjectivities, for instance by directing reflection, or disrupting normalizing emplotments and by telling the past differently so that one comes to locate oneself according to a different historicization of the community and of oneself. They include too the expressive domain that makes visible the liminal dimension of beingness, so that the questioning of being brings to presence an elemental passion, driven by hope and memory, seeking to be consumed and liberated in the convivial act of telling. A question that remains is that of knowing whether the gift is motivated by critical reflection or whether it is a desire that wells up in the vulnerability of the face of the other, as the enduring trace of the 'there is'. These considerations clearly invoke ways of thinking about being that transcend modernity, reaching beyond its 'posts', but that modernity rephrased in terms of secular narratives of what it means to be human. The political implications derive from the consequence that all forms of exploitation and oppression everywhere breach the condition for an ethical form of sociality. Besides, the same considerations explicitly bind the destiny of the postmodern with that of the postcolonial, for, in the wake of modernity, the world today consists of complex networks, economic, financial, cultural, technological, political, that relay and condition each other. Everything else is left open to the determination of an indeterminate future.

Notes

1 The affiliation between postcolonial and poststructuralist critiques should not surprise us since both series link up with the critique of modernity by way of the analysis of contemporary culture and subjectivity developed in cultural studies. The latter approach has been crucial to the particular manner in which contemporary philosophy, Marxist theory, semiotics and elements of psychoanalysis were recruited into the analysis of culture. The same mix of theory informs postcolonial theory. Apart from the work of Hall, one should mention Spivak's strategic use of Marxism and deconstruction to maintain a critical distance from the hegemonic discourses of modernity whilst locating her work 'inside/outside' the academic world. Gilroy (1993a) focuses on the counter-cultures of modernity, produced by those marginalized by occidentalism, exemplified in the insurrectional or subversive cultural 'texts' which inscribe their lived experience of modernity marked by displacement and doubleness. He argues that the politics of fulfilment and subjective transformation which underlies these aesthetic products requires attention to rethinking the ethical. The trajectory of postcolonial cultural critique towards questions of foundations and a critical ontology is admirably mirrored in Bhabha's work. The pioneering analyses of Said, for their part, remind us that intellectual work cannot

be separated from the politics of power/knowledge, so that it becomes a duty to speak the truth to power.

2 One needs to bear in mind the different positions, such as green environmentalism, eco-feminism, eco-socialism, deep ecology, and so on, discussed, for example, in Benton (1993) and Macnaghten and Urry (1998).

3 The reference is to the work of Bachelard. See Venn (1982) for a detailed study.

1

REMEMBERING MODERNITY

> Postmodernity is not a new age, it is the rewriting of a number of
> features claimed as its own by modernity, and first of all its claim to
> found its legitimacy upon the project of the emancipation of the whole
> of humanity by means of science and technique. But this rewriting, as I
> said, has been at work, for a long time already, inside modernity itself.
> (Lyotard, 1988a: 202)

The discourse of modernity in crisis

I will be concerned throughout this book with the question of who comes
after the subject of modernity. Immediately every kind of qualification
clamours for attention in the wake of this enigmatic intention. To begin
with, since every period is fundamentally about the institution of a particular form of subjectivity, the question of who comes after calls up that of
the forms of sociality which would inscribe new subjectivities, and thus all
the issues which have filled the agenda of postmodernity. It is not my aim
to review the relevant debates, for the rewriting that I want to develop is
motivated by the possibility of a narration of modernity which is at the
same time a critique of the present and the thread for binding the destiny of
the postmodern to that of the postcolonial by way of the to-come of
subjectivity. Clearly, in saying this, I am taking for granted that the 'post'
marks a hiatus in the history of the modern, the index of a crisis as much as
of a point of transition towards an indeterminate transmodern future. My
remarks are also meant to highlight the relation of critique to the work of
memory, for the danger today is that of forgetting the continuities of
occidentalist modernity and the risk, therefore, of repeating its violences.
The danger is all the more acute now that the restraining hold of liberal
humanism no longer deters political action in so many places across the
world, and that the ethical values inscribed in the grand narratives that
underwrote the project of modernity have become fragile. For all these
reasons, the question of who comes, as I shall establish, provokes a fundamental problematization of modern times and of the ethical.

Lyotard, in the text I cited above, argues that rewriting concerns the
'anamnesis of the Thing', and not only of what haunts the birth of
'individuals' as singular beings, but 'of what haunts "language"', tradition,
the material with which, against which and within which one writes' (1988a:
202). So, every counter-narrative of modernity makes visible in the form of

a memory the trace of what will have been written over in previous narrations, forgotten in the 'oubliette' where whatever is disavowed and silenced is consigned. Lyotard's thought gestures towards a dimension in critique that exceeds the claims of objective knowledge, and implicates subjective investments in the process such that knowing, being and desiring are seen to relay each other. It follows that while critique belongs to an agonistic space, it cannot claim an innocent space, immune from what it opposes. So, the refiguration of the subject, which doubles into a critique of modernity, must declare its own positioning, acknowledging the provisional character of its claims, and the fact that the concepts that one may put to work in a different narration of (post)modernity are 'under erasure', as Hall (1996b) once put it.

Another point I want to signal about the historicity of the process of critique is the fact that it is modernity itself, as event, which provides us with the conceptual tools and the archive upon which we rely to refigure its history, and to thus reconstitute our understanding of 'who we are in the present', to recall Foucault's (1984c) way of rephrasing the question of what is enlightenment. All events shed light on themselves in this way, that is to say, they retroactively configure for us the points of reference whereby we are able to narratively join the past and the present and locate ourselves along a line of dispersion from them. Every event can thus be thought as a breach in history which the event itself opens up, thereby making history, that is, announcing a different future. Clearly, every event has its conditions of possibility that a genealogy may reconstruct. The points I wish to make concern the retroactive manner in which the event is designated as inaugural, the degree of indeterminacy which attaches to events and the irreversible effects they have for history. In rephrasing the question of modernity and of subjectivity in the form that Foucault gave it, I wish, like him, to direct attention to the three central issues that modernity had both constituted and problematized. Modernity invented a heroic subject, raging against the storm of finitude and loss, urged on by narratives of universal and subjective emancipation to accomplish incomparable deeds, yet reduced to almost nothing in the machineries of modernization and the abstractions of systems, now contemplating the ironies of just gaming among the bright lights of the postmodern world. As for the 'we' which was supposed to authorize the project of the progressive development of all, standing for the will of the people, it is now pluralized and dispersed according to the heterogeneity of goals and political constituencies. Increasingly, the we of the people survives in a virtual form through the ventriloquism of a mediatized political culture. Humanisms, since the Enlightenment, had promised the realization of a cosmopolitan we, a *sensus communis*, secure in the ability to determine the future on the basis of consensus and reason. Modernity has failed to deliver on this and other promises, unable to reconcile the diversity of cultures, for it could not separate its avowed goal of universal emancipation and liberation from its own history of subjugation. Lastly, the idea that the present is a point of transition, at the edge of the new, located in relation to the historicity of events, and thus circumscribed by inevitable limits, belongs to a narrative of history – linear, progressive, driven by a *telos* – that modernity itself inaugurated. The discourse about the meaning of the present is now in crisis, abandoned to the eschatology of endings: of history and of grand projects. In these circumstances, the questioning of who we are in the present should encourage us not only to challenge the narrative of a hegemonic modernity and its foundational discourses, but to endeavour to transcend the limits that seem imposed on us: a paradoxically modern gesture.

This aspect should alert us to be vigilant about the constraining habits of thought which have reduced the stakes in the debates regarding (post)modernity to a question of being for or against particular doctrines and positions, for instance for or against the project of the Enlightenment, or, indeed, for or against modernity itself. One could add to the list of habits a number of familiar dichotomies, particularly those of the individual versus the social, the natural against the human, and all the suppositions and distortions which are collected in the opposition between the modern and the traditional. For instance, the eruption of apparently archaic violences recently – ethnocides in Eastern Europe, in Rwanda, in East Timor, fundamentalist brutalities everywhere – combine with very modernist technologies and interests to remind us of the similar violences that have shadowed the development of modernity from the beginning, certainly in its occidentalist form. Equally, one must refuse the temptation of simplifying the complications associated with the moment of the 'post' by attributing them to the effects of the latest transformations in capitalism or to the plural sites of resistance to the totalizing and globalizing imperatives of a rationalist administrative order. Such an option, however appealing, is too limiting since it already assumes the validity of positions which a break with the conceptual structure of modernity obliges us to suspect.

One of my aims in this book is to deal with this inheritance, interrogating it from the standpoint of a postcoloniality that does not allow itself the comfort of an unblemished marginality. It has been argued that there are other spaces outside modernity, or not inflected by it, upon which the basic questions of human well-being can be, and have been, posed. I initially thought that it might be possible to figure the 'post' of the postmodern from the standpoint of postcoloniality, seeking in that space the distantiation and the discomfort of an 'in-between' position. The problem, once more, is that the terms of this postcolonial interrogation cannot escape the kind of circularity I have just noted, for instance the fact that a concept like 'post' already belongs to a particular, namely, modern, idea of periodization.

So we have to temper the good intentions of radical breaks with the recognition that we neither have the luxury of a blank slate upon which to relocate analysis, nor can we load the dice of critique by claiming the authority of marginal belongings, for instance in the name of women or postcoloniality or Blacks. Nevertheless, without the provocations to rewrite the history of modernity which feminist and 'postcolonial' challenges to the established narratives of modernity have encouraged, and without the interrogations of the philosophical foundations of the discourses of modernity from within the critical spaces interior to it – today, one could call them deconstructive or poststructuralist – it would not be possible for anyone to think of the possibility of a radical or critical postmodernity. It would clearly not have been possible for me to formulate the problem in the terms that I have been employing, or even to think that there is a problem to worry about at all.

The drift in my line of argument might suggest that the political and theoretical problems we face today are the consequences of modernity. But my intention in this book is far from engaging in yet one more exercise in allocating blame or in wondering what 'went wrong' with the project of modernity. Instead, my task is that of a renarrativization which attempts to establish a new scale for judging the present, for sure informed by the many concerns which have surfaced in the critiques of the present, but focusing on the point of view of the historicity of events in the sense that the past and the future are relayed by way of how the work of memory and history, in narrating the past in a particular way, reorganizes our anticipation of the future. In relation to the 'post' of modernity, I have in mind the possibility of a future which would no longer be fixated by the traumas induced by the events which, in an important sense, began with 1492. Posed in this way, that is to say, by reference to the question of founding narratives and by reference to the point of view of promise and of a possible or desired emancipation, the question of the narration of our epoch entails a discourse of being which prioritizes an idea of justice and of responsibility, and a memorization which activates the relation of debt and of gift to what has been in history.

Already the stakes which appear in the agenda that I am developing signal a desire to break with the privileged terrain – of epistemology and of a logocentric subject, against the ethical and the aesthetic dimensions of being – upon which the interrogation of the conditions of (post)modernity has often been reinscribed.

On the uniqueness of modernity

I think it is fruitful to start with the familiar claim that modernity has been a unique period in history characterized by the institution of a radically new form of sociality and of subjectivity. Let us consider three claims that I think characterize this uniqueness and epochality. First, no other period has had as fundamental and widespread an effect as modernity, operating right across the whole world. Nothing has been left untouched in its wake, and there is much that has been irreversibly changed, for good or for ill, directly or indirectly. The interesting point, however, is that the world is irrevocably different not just by reference to the obvious, visible material or spatial level of transformation, like the technological metropolises that have sprung up in all countries, constructed out of metal and glass and by-products of the petro-chemical industry like plastics, equipped with electronic and electrical systems of communication and forms of energy, disposed in a spatial organization that they make possible and that the modern subject inhabits as its dwelling, a world made up of a multitude of everyday objects which could not have existed before the modern period. It is not possible to account for human capacities and action without that range of technologically constituted and normed objects. Besides, the modern world is different just as much because of the less visible dimension of transformation, to do with what we are able to think and do, the changes in our perception of ourselves arising from the accumulation of knowledges and memories, their sedimentation in the lifeworld, a whole history of conceptual mutations which makes us different. The event called modernity has altered the future, and there is no way back – not even through the most violent forms of 'cleansing'. It is, like other events, a signifier of the relation to time.[1]

Second, modernity is the first historical period to be legitimated on the basis of narratives that are secular in their foundation. I noted earlier that all complex cultures – complex enough to have left traces – have invented narratives in answer to the 'big' questions, to do with the meaning of existence, gathered around the themes that prowl in the shadow of the anguish of finitude and loss and the mysteries of an imponderable destiny. I think that all these questions fundamentally relate to the recognition of the temporality of being (see Osborne, 1995). Before modernity, such narratives appealed to a notion of a transcendent being or entity, imagined in the form of a deity or a divine or supra-human force, independent of human will, yet active in the world in fashioning individual and communal destinies. The discourse of modernity breaks with this metaphysics and onto-theology, that is to say, it breaks with the discourses which refer the problem concerning the meaning of being to a basically religious and mythical imagination. Modernity refuses the prioritizing of religious discourse in deciding about truth and value, though it does not quite abandon religious or mythical thought. Modern philosophical discourse operates a distance from the ground of religion through the displacement which relocates historical agency and will in the concept of the logocentric subject, that is, the subject whose constitution is understood in relation to the privilege of *logos* or the cognitive dimension and to the autonomy of the subject. The notion of metanarrative as understood by Lyotard helps us understand the difference. He says that the metanarratives of modernity promise the 'progressive emancipation of reason and of liberty, progressive or catastrophic emancipation of labour, enrichment of the whole of humanity through the progress of capitalist technoscience' (1988b: 31). They are not necessarily opposed to the Christian narrative of the redemption of souls through sacrificial love. They share with myths the function of legitimation, but unlike myths, 'they do not look for this legitimacy in an originary founding act, but in a time to come, that is to say in an Idea to be realised' (1988b: 32). The universal character of this Idea grants to modernity 'its characteristic mode: the project' (1988b: 32). So, unlike other metanarratives, those which appeared with modernity engender the future: by circumscribing the future within the problematic of the becoming of modernity and of its subject, proceeding according to the logic of 'History'. The vexed question of the displacements which construct the discursive space of modernity, and of the concept of the subject as the agent of History which modernity puts in place, will be a central theme in my critique.

Third, the epochality of modernity is specified by the unique conjuncture characterized by the co-emergence of 'rational' capitalism, European colonialism and modernity. This means that the specificity of each must be understood in terms of the relation of co-articulation between them, a relation which is complex and uneven, irreducible to the model of mechanistic determination. The intertwined histories of these three processes map out the history of the modern period. The conjuncture, therefore, has functioned as event, in the sense of rupture and beginning that I introduced above, announcing the undecidable but conditional future.

I use the term 'occidentalism' to qualify the specificity of the history of modernity in the light of that conjuncture. Occidentalism thus directs attention to the becoming-modern of the world and the becoming-West of Europe such that Western modernity gradually became established as the privileged, if not hegemonic, form of sociality, tied to a universalizing and totalizing ambition. Occidentalism indicates a genealogy of the present which reconstructs a particular trajectory of modernity, inflected by the fact of colonialism and of capitalism. I relate it to the imperial form of governmentality which begins to appear from the early nineteenth century, and which becomes institutionalized in technologies of the formation and disciplining of subaltern populations, with effects for the process of subjectification/subjection. Occidentalism has culminated today in the establishment of global forms of regulation and of the exercise of economic, political, cultural and military power, instituted in apparatuses and NGOs like the World Bank, the IMF, the United Nations, and networks of expert knowledges supported by international bodies, journals, and so on, enframed within its discursive space. Clearly, it is important to recognize that it exists in an agonistic space in which occidentalism, non-Western narratives of existence and what one could call an an-archic discourse of modernity struggle for an emancipatory ideal. Postcolonial critique is located inside that space.

In the background of the approach I am sketching for the analysis of modernity lie some more fundamental issues, opening towards a critical phenomenology, secular in orientation, the elaboration of which is pursued throughout the book. I will, however, give an inkling of what is involved, since it helps to signal the tactics I am employing to operate a distance – to the extent that this is possible – from the discursive perimeter of modernity. Earlier, I proposed the idea that it is the recognition of the temporality of being which itself grounds the questioning of being in terms of a relation to meaning. This recognition, I would suggest, inaugurates a properly human history, and motivates the narration of that history as that of beings who know themselves to be finite entities, a spark in the night of an infinite duration. Several terms come into play that require clarification. Following Heidegger, I understand being as the entity who questions itself as to its way of being. Being is also the only living thing who experiences death as death, that is, as an anticipated end to the conscious self; death is more than simply the black hole of existence from which there is no exit, the place whence the future is cancelled for every sentient thing. It is the fact that one knows in advance its inevitable coming which marks out the specifically human experience of death. With Heidegger, the anticipation of death is tied with the faculty of speech, so that an essential relation exists between language and death.[2] In his discussion of this relation, Agamben argues that it leaves us 'open to the possibility that neither death nor language originally belongs to that which draws man into its concern' (1991: xii). Whilst he attempts to clarify the relation by developing a notion of negativity, I will suggest instead a connection with the emergence of consciousness.

It could be argued that the birth to consciousness was also a birth to conscience, implicating the co-articulation of the temporality of being and the primacy of the relation to the other, suggesting the dynamic inter-relationship of language and the ethical. The manner of this birth would correlate the excessive anguish of the recognition of loss and lack and finitude, associated with the emergence of being as a being in time, with the experience of the abyss, and with the motivation to fantasize a God who could vouchsafe the possibility of an emancipation from the insufficiency of being on condition of obedience to the Law. The concept of the divine, by the same token, founds the Law, and functions as the transcendent guarantor of the unity of the collectivity or 'tribe'. On the one side of this early ontology would be the idea of a God, as the perfect, omniscient, infinite being, that is to say, everything that human beings wish themselves to be in order to still the anguish of ontological insufficiency; and on the other side the feeling of an original imperfection, expressed in, or correlated to, concepts of fallenness, lack, loss, incompleteness. In religious discourse this idea of an original imperfection is refigured in terms of narratives of the destiny of human beings as a journey in search of redemption or salvation: an emancipation from the conditions which provoke suffering. This religious economy in turn would have connected the idea of sacrifice with the promise of salvation.

Let us juxtapose at this point the proposition, developed by Vygotsky (1986), Luria (1982) and Volosinov (1973), that consciousness is profoundly social in character, in that it is the effect of an in-folding of an exteriority into an interiority by way of the development of inner speech, and the interiorization into the mind, through inter-subjective activity, of a cultural matrix of meaning. Both action and language are necessary for the emergence of consciousness, and both are oriented towards an other. In an important sense, the social character of consciousness and the history of consciousness are entwined. Let us add Ricoeur's theorization of 'self', or the 'who' of action and speech, which he has elaborated in terms of the concept of narrative identity, which I discuss fully in the next chapter. Simplifying, one can say that, basically, it is the idea that a self is a narrated self, constituted as an identity by the stories that a person tells about herself, and are told about her by others, and that this narration functions to knit the past of a life to the present and the future, according to culturally located scripts or emplotments of action that help figure and refigure each self.

An implication is that we can correlate the emergence of consciousness with the perception that time is lived as a passage from a remembered past through the immediacy of the present and the anticipation of a future; these are the moments of temporality that are joined in the form of narratives. Language, thus, is the mode in which temporality as lived is brought to consciousness, and communicated. A further implication is that language, in the broad sense of a signifying system, is bound up with the recognition of temporality. It follows that language and, therefore, culture are intrinsic to the process whereby individual and communal lives are woven together. I am suggesting that the relationship between language, consciousness and the recognition of temporality is both actual and developmental/ontogenic, synchronic and diachronic. We would have to assume that the processes involved in these conjoined emergences are dynamic and dialogic, and that they adapt and change in response to alterations in the 'environment' in an autopoietic fashion.[3] I think that the stability of language and sociality suggests that the mechanisms are more complex, involving self-creative and self-repairing functions, that strive for order against disorder – though not by abolishing the latter, for then there is no freedom and no creativity (see Deleuze and Guattari, 1994). These thoughts bring intentionality and memory into the equation.[4] The nodal or relay point which sutures them – the emergence of language, the emergence of consciousness, their imbrication in the inter-subjective reality of culture – is the human being. Language, to that extent, is the most central mechanism in the story of formation and development of the human being, tied to duration in Bergson's sense, or what I am calling historicity.[5] My account of subjectivity is consistent with the idea of 'the immanence of intelligence to things . . . [recognizing that] "Man" is but a sophisticated knot' (Lyotard, 1988b: 35–6) in the web which constitutes the universe.

At the level of discourse, the little narratives which constitute named individuals are relayed to the beliefs, myths, sayings, histories which are inscribed in the more general narratives that bind a community into a whole, and make it a community. These narratives acquire authority in the form of a tradition, grounded, as I noted, in some form of religious discourse that has a transcendent value for truths and meaning. For example, for the religions of the Book, the Scriptures, the Qur'an or the Talmud act as final court of appeal in matters of justice and value, and function as guide and rule book instructing the faithful regarding how one is to conduct one's life. Before modernity, ontological security for every person and social stability and order for the community were secured in foundational narratives of this kind, and not just in Europe and the Middle East. The discourse of modernity breaks with this metaphysics – or claims to do so, for the opposition between tradition and modernity is something that the discourse of modernity itself invents or specifies, and the traces of metaphysics, as Levinas and Derrida have shown, are not so easily erased. It operates a distance from the ground of religion and metaphysics through the displacement which relocates historical agency and will in the concept of the logocentric subject.

My argument so far has been to establish that it is possible to refigure the specificity of modernity by reference to narrations of being which transcend, but do not exclude, those grounded in the grand narratives of modernity. The point is that it would be possible then to think the future not by reference alone to the parameters established in these narratives, but just as much by reference to the longer history of the self-reflexive questioning of being which makes us specifically human. This questioning could not have emerged without the consciousness of temporality and without the development of language, neither of which can be understood by reference to single individuals or to the notion of the unitary, rational subject of the discourse of modernity.

Modernity redux? Or the end of great expectations?

I indicated in my introduction that the problems underlying the question of futurity, once we have abandoned the privilege of epistemology, spill onto the terrain of an ethics. The cognitive is not the ethical and the ethical is not the political; however, there are relays between them. The problem for the discourse of modernity has been to avoid reducing the one to the other, or to imagine a universal element, like reason, that would enable their reconciliation. The functioning of aesthetics in this process is a central issue that I will explore in Chapter 4. Habermas (1996) has reformulated the problem in terms of a shift from the standpoint of steering mechanisms to those of the normative criteria for desirable forms of sociality, from the rational calculations of instrumental and solipsistic interests to the ethics of communicative action in search of consensus. Lyotard's differences with the Habermasian project rest on the argument that there can be no common ground on which could be reconciled the different regimes of phrases that separate communities from the point of view of political action and ethical judgement. One implication is that the search for consensus as the goal of rational deliberation necessarily suppresses or excludes certain regimes and thus constitutes a form of violence and injustice. The dilemma is that already existing differences of power and of access to political instruments

deny the assumptions of a 'level playing field' which consensual politics
requires. The debate clearly goes to the heart of the problem of the grounds
and the narratives of desirable futures which could be reconstituted after
modernity.

My reason for addressing the issue of foundational principles derives,
besides, from the conviction that no society so far has been ethical in the
sense that I shall be developing throughout this book. Part of the reason is
that before or outside modernity, the question of ethics and of being has
been posed on the grounds of religion, whereas I am searching for secular
principles to guide the questioning of being as to its way of being. This
means that all existing terrains are suspect, so that once again the situation
demands that one constructs a theoretical jetty from which to imagine a
new beginning. It follows too that there are no models which one can use as
a measure, although, clearly, the point of view of historicity indicates that
we cannot avoid drawing lessons from previous discourses and practices
and their effects, nor escape the limits that historicity imposes upon our
thinking. A number of interrogations exist, however, which I will indicate
below, that will provide me with the elements for displacing the issue
towards a post-occidentalist reformulation, and for finding a different
measure for judging what is to be done.

There are, of course, other fruitful approaches, for instance in relation to
the idea of reflexive modernization as developed in the work of Beck,
Giddens and Lash. The key ideas that I would pick out from Beck (1992,
Beck et al., 1994) are: the unseen and unwilled consequences of modernization; the emergence of new types of agents; increasing individualization;
a focus on intimacy; the era of side-effects; risk society; disavowal of
responsibility. In Giddens (1990, 1994), I would focus particularly on his
analysis of the global scope of modernization; manufactured uncertainty;
institutional reflexivity; de-traditionalization; dis-embedding and re-
embedding; expert systems versus lay and alternative cognitive knowl-
edge-claims and interests; dialogic democracy. In Lash (1994), meanwhile,
we find an elaboration of the aesthetic and hermeneutic dimension of
modernity, and the development of ideas of informationalization, sign-
economy, post-traditional creation of active trust, heterodoxy. It is clear
that these positions are concerned with the 'this-sidedness' of the world we
inhabit, so that it is a matter of diagnosing what has changed and of
thinking about what is possible. These writers eschew grand narratives and
projects without being cynical, keeping alive the goals of a social justice. In
this, they join with other writers like Laclau, Mouffe, Jameson, even
Habermas, who have tried in their different ways to face up to the resilience
of capitalism and the failures of the older socialist project, recognizing the
complexity and plurality of the new forces at work in modern times, to do
with new technologies, aspects of 'globalization', new social movements
around issues relating to the environment, ecology, sexuality, and so on,
and shifts in the forms of governance. Perhaps the question in the background concerns what one is to do with capitalism and the structures we

have inherited, including those that institute contemporary subjectivities. Claims of the kind I have just listed will figure as background knowledge in the analysis I am pursuing.

I think it is possible to enter the dispute about the grounds for judging modernity by starting with the proposition that the defining moment of modernity consists in the shift from the mode of being and thinking which posits the dispossession and fallenness of being by reference to an infinite, all-powerful and unknowable God to one which proposes the possibility of an 'I' who could tame the world of things, including the self, and take possession of 'his' destiny. The destination of being turns away from the after-life towards the realization of the subject by way of the historical project of the realization of Reason or Mind. The institution of this subject of modernity desires the recuperation of a 'stolen' *jouissance* and lost plenitude; it envisions the organization of human and universal time into a project which aims to guarantee the progressive realization of autonomy, of universal liberty and the redemption of 'humanity'. I will argue, in the third chapter, that the attitude to nature implicit in this project, together with the allied alignment of knowledge with possession and dominion, was complicit with the 'knowledge that kills' (Todorov, 1992) that marked Europe's encounter with its 'others' at the beginning of the colonization of the New World in the modern era.

The recuperation of the idea of a project is constant in the work of Habermas since the 1980 lecture, suitably titled 'Modernity – an incomplete project' (Habermas, 1983 in Foster, 1983), and the series of examinations of key positions (for instance in Habermas, 1987) which he undertakes to chart the path of the philosophical discourse of modernity that has led to what he sees as a politically debilitating impasse in the work of the 'neo-conservatives' and post-structuralists, the heirs of Nietzsche and Heidegger. Habermas agrees on many counts with the radical critique of reason and the rejection of the 'philosophy of the subject', which have been important objectives for the Frankfurt School. The problem for Habermas seems to be the danger of throwing out the baby of truth, justice and reason with the bath-water of logocentrism, historicism and transcendentalism. The continuity of the ideals of modernity has become a challenge: how to draw from the counter-discourse of modernity the elements that would enable one to reformulate a project that would have both universal and local validity and would indicate the possibility of a non-coercive intersubjectivity based on reciprocal recognition and understanding arrived at through rational deliberation. It is a matter for Habermas of steering a course between the Heideggerian privileging of Being and its inner-worldly 'destining' – whereby Heidegger ontologizes radical historical thinking – and the deconstructivist privilege of the poetical and rhetorical functioning of language in disclosing aspects of the world previously invisible or immanent, and its aim of showing the world's openness to the indeterminacy of futurity. The gain, for Habermas, is the possibility of preserving a dialectical relation between the general and the concrete, the universal and the context-specific, so that the practice of everyday life can be submitted to the critique of an enlightened and general reason and thus kept open to transformation, whilst communicative reason inscribed in the everyday can inform theory.[6]

Habermas's reconstruction of the philosophical discourse of modernity draws out from Weber the key words that now function as the apparently neutral coinage for analysing the 'bundle of processes' called modernization. He points to the process of rationalization whereby society has been transformed into secular and bureaucratized systems; he rehearses the argument that legitimating discourses have become differentiated, with the growth of the culture of the experts, into the three value spheres of the theoretical or cognitive–instrumental, the aesthetic–expressive and the moral–practical. Values and norms have been colonized by standards of rationalization appropriate to instrumental reason, displacing the communicative rationality inscribed in the inter-subjectivity of communicative action; from the point of view of legitimation, this leads to Weber's 'warring gods' situation. Furthermore, Western rationalism, through the implantation of modernization worldwide, has grown into a self-motivating, autonomous process, cut off from cultural modernity, that is to say, cut off from the Zeitgeist. The Zeitgeist, as understood by Hegel, was what provided modernity with its orientation; it is inscribed in 'the expectation of the differentness of the future' (Habermas, 1987: 6), a principle by which every new age would distance itself from the period that preceded it. Lyotard too talks about the impulse in modernity to repeatedly 'set the clock back to zero', and thus break with, but also 'forget', that from which it arises. It is significant that, for someone like Baudelaire, the Zeitgeist of modernity is more clearly discerned in the aesthetic experience, directing us to locate the modern consciousness of time in the space of a liminal, poetic dimension, lodged in the gap between the 'space of experience' and the 'horizon of expectation'; it has continued to provide one of the key themes of the discourse of modernity. Habermas uses Benjamin's theses on the philosophy of history to point to the dynamic relationship which 'effective history' establishes between the present, the past and the future. Benjamin proposes that 'the anticipation of what is new in the future is realized only through remembering a past that has been suppressed' (Habermas, 1987: 12), and thus draws the process of memory into the elaboration of both the present and the future. His reversal of the relation between the space of experience and the horizon of expectation enables him to move away from the kind of temporalization of the present and the future which preserves or appropriates the past only with an orientation to the future, a view which runs the risk of either erasing the pastness of the past (seeing in the past only the signs announcing the future to come), or else preserving it in the form of the happening of tradition in the present. For Habermas, Benjamin's argument about a horizon of unfulfilled expectation in the past and the presencing of the past through remembering leads to the 'insight that ethical universalism also has to take seriously the injustice that has already happened . . . that there exists a solidarity of those born later with those who have preceded'

(1987: 14), a solidarity enacted in acts of remembrance. The remembrance of things past has to do with the purging of a guilt, through extending the responsibility we have in the present to both the past and the future. Habermas adds that 'the anamnestic redemption of an injustice . . . ties up the present with the communicative context of a universal historical solidarity' (1987: 15). It must be admitted that there are so many parallels in this line of argument with points made by Derrida and Lyotard in relation to historicity and responsibility, which I discuss in the second chapter, that the quarrel with the 'poststructuralists' seems excessive sometimes.

Habermas, however, tends to tar everybody with the same brush in his criticism, for it is clear that the radical critique of reason does recognize the ambivalences in the discourse and the artistic work of modernity. He also notes that these critiques have no place for everyday practice, which is certainly not the case with Lyotard when he counters the excessive totalizations of the grand narratives with the 'little narratives' of the people embedded in the local and the everyday, as we shall see. But let us pass on, for the main issue in the dispute is about the possibility of putting to work certain critical elements, introduced in the discourse of modernity, in the hope of re-establishing confidence in the idea of an emancipation to come – a worthy aim. For Habermas, this aim cannot be accomplished unless one avoids the totalizing tendencies in both instrumental reason and inclusive reason, by counterposing totalization with the idea of a communicative reason that would operate in the 'risky' search for consensus whilst preserving the normative content of modernity. The reason for staying within the normative framework of modernity derives from his view that the critiques of reason developed by negative dialectics (Adorno), by genealogy (Foucault) and by deconstruction (Derrida) have avoided the question of the grounds of their own critique by locating themselves outside the established disciplinary sites of the value spheres. This argument of Habermas underestimates other dilemmas in the philosophical discourse of modernity which have reappeared and deepened in postmodern critiques of *Logos*. Gillian Rose characterizes this shift – more visible in the work of Jewish philosophers like Levinas, Derrida, Adorno, Arendt, Benjamin – as a reworking of the symbolic divide between Jerusalem and Athens, that is to say, between 'the hearing of the commandments against the search for first principles, for the love of the neighbour against explanation of the world, and for the prophet against the philosopher' (1993: 1).

These critiques, which irritate Habermas, cannot be reduced to a matter of standing outside the disciplinary terrain of philosophy, nor can they be condemned on the grounds of a flight into postmodern theology, as my analysis in the earlier part of the book shows. The quest that underlies them is a new inquiry into the establishment of justice, outside the philosophy of *Logos*, an aim that Habermas shares too. Habermas, however, seems to think that his opponents proceed in a self-referential manner, yet appeal to 'normative intuitions' that appear to derive from the modernity they reject. The values they defend are drawn from the contents of aesthetic experience, namely, 'the values of grace and illumination, ecstatic rapture, bodily integrity, wish-fulfilment, and caring intimacy' (Habermas, 1987: 337); they suggest forms of subjectivity revealed in the experience of modernity, but they cannot substitute for the moral grounding that an ethical post-modernity requires. Habermas seeks to preserve an idea of 'subjectivity as an unredeemed promise' (1987: 337), holding out the hope that the self-determination of all could be in solidarity with the self-realization of each. Such a project must maintain the distinction between 'emancipatory–reconciling aspects of social rationalization and repressive–alienating aspects' (1987: 338), a distinction that the repudiation of modernity blurs, especially in its failure to recognize the ambivalent content of cultural and social modernity.

Against what he sees as the shortcomings of the 'postmodernists', detailed in the course of the *Twelve Lectures*, Habermas proposes 'the concept of a communicative reason that transcends subject-centered reason' (1987: 341). The development of this position takes the line of explaining why modernity has stifled or undermined the possibilities for emancipation immanent in modernity. The first consideration moves away from the categories of social labour, as it functions in Marxian social praxis, using instead the categories of lifeworld and communicative action to maintain a separation in the process of human self-realization that cannot be reabsorbed into a 'higher unity'. In the 'balanced and undistorted repro-duction of the lifeworld' (1987: 344), the difference between lifeworld and communicative action is tied to the interpretative performances and the cooperative actions of participants. The lifeworld itself can be considered to consist of culture, society and persons. It functions as a resource enabling participants to utilize the store of knowledge in a culture to constitute groups based on solidarity and consensus. These linkages occur through communicative action, so that the lifeworld itself is bathed in symbolic action whilst belongingness takes the form of a metaphorical location. Under conditions of change and with the growth in reflexivity, universalism and self-directed individuation in the ideal speech community are mediated through the processes of cultural reproduction, whereby the consensus needs of everyday practice are ensured through the adjustment of tradition and new knowledge to enable people to deal with both change and continuity. This involves social integration, instituted by means of the legitimate regulation of interpersonal action, and socialization, whereby members acquire the kinds of capabilities and attitudes that ensure the harmonious constitution and reconstitution of identities.

The problem is why this has not happened; why, instead, we have ended up with conditions of 'distorted communication'. Habermas points to the rationalization of the lifeworld directed by the needs and forces of the capitalist market and a bureaucratized state, so that money and power have acted as the steering mechanisms to produce an 'administered' lifeworld and the 'reification of everyday practice'. The result is a variety of 'social pathologies' (1987: 348); in other words, it seems that Habermas's analysis wants to convince us that what is wrong with modernity is that it is sick, but not fatally so. What is needed is for 'Europe'[7] to realize that the illness is self-inflicted, aggravated by bad theoretical prognoses in conditions of unfettered capitalist development, and that 'Europe could draw from *its own* traditions the insight, the energy, the courage of vision' to cure itself (1987: 367, original emphasis).

Amongst the ills, Habermas (1992) picks out metaphysical assumptions that underlie both the search for the grounds for validating truth and the elaboration of a universalist ethics. He argues that one can avoid these problems by relying on the structure of communication, given that, for him, the goal of communication is mutual understanding. A further assumption is the universality of reason, that being necessary for the validity of claims to truth to be based on consensus (Habermas, 1996). But the focus on Europe is problematic when we consider his claim that consensus on normative issues can be achieved. In spite of all the stress on the inter-subjectivity of a discursively mediated lifeworld, it is not clear what values one could appeal to in order for example, to persuade ethnic groups in ex-Yugoslavia to put an end to 'ethnic cleansing', or to encourage Jews and Arabs to resolve the *'différends'* separating the different communities in Israel/Palestine.

Or consider an apparently more straightforward case, where the problems of appeal to universals are more starkly visible, but where the legacy of occidentalism cannot be discounted. I refer to the case of the customary sexual mutilation of girls in many Muslim communities, carried out by avowedly caring parents, whose declared intention is to make them suitable and desirable candidates for the marriage market. Would Habermas condemn the practice, embedded in the everyday lifeworld, either on the grounds that it is traditional, not open to change through the kind of deliberative process that he envisages, or on the grounds that it offends a universal ethics, that is, on the grounds that it should be possible to reach universal consensus about values applicable to local contexts? Would its rationality, inscribed in the practice, and which participants can make explicit in discussion of its justice or rightfulness, be considered defective by comparison with the ideal rationality of a liberatory modernity? Is it a case of 'pathology' or is it a case of an incommensurable 'differend', as Lyotard might put it? And is the standard of what is acceptable necessarily European? Are there, on the other hand, no grounds for intervening in such situations, except in the name of an oppressed category, like women? I use this example, to which I will return below, to indicate the range of problems left in abeyance by Habermas's analysis of modernity, and systems theory approach generally. The assumption that participants in a dispute will consider it reasonable to proceed by appeal to rational deliberation to resolve problems arising from different perceptions of interest and different orientations to the future must assume that the participants are already convinced about that procedure and agree already about what constitutes rationality in concrete situations. Communicative rationality must deal with the dilemma that the understanding of rules is grounded in a hermeneutic circle, a dilemma repeated in the option, for theoretical analysis, between appeals to either prior 'socialization', and to universal ethical principles, or to incommensurability. Thus, in the case of sexual mutilation, one would have to assume that it is possible to appeal to some notion of justice that transcends local criteria, or that identities can be changed through a form of 're-education'.[8] Furthermore, the distinction and differences between particular, context-bound rules of legitimate action and universal principles that can act as a foundation for them refer, at another level, to the distinction between the concrete and the generalized other, which I shall examine below after further explorations of the question of legitimation and of differends.

Lyotard's understanding of modernity will serve as a staging point for moving on from Habermas because elements in his analysis are consistent with my line of inquiry, though his discussion of modernity focuses on the problem of legitimation, thus on the problems of the narratives that ground and authorize its project. One of the many versions of Lyotard's understanding of the metanarratives of modernity explains that they are the 'progressive emancipation of reason and of liberty, progressive or catastrophic emancipation of labour, enrichment of the whole of humanity through the progress of capitalist technosciences . . . redemption of creatures through the conversion of souls to the Christian narrative of sacrificial love' (Lyotard, 1988b: 31). The addition of capitalism, technoscience and Christianism to an earlier version which referred to 'the dialectic of Spirit, the hermeneutics of meaning, the emancipation of the rational or working subject, or the creation of wealth' (Lyotard, 1984: xxiii) is his way of concretizing and historicizing the grand narratives, giving them a content which adds something different to the system-theoretical focus on the logic of particular rationalities working through processes of administration, production, normalization and regulation. As with myths, these narratives have a function of legitimation, but unlike myths, 'they do not look for this legitimacy in an originary founding act, but in a time to come, that is to say, in an Idea to be realized' (Lyotard, 1988b: 32). This idea thus grants to modernity 'its characteristic mode: the *project*' (1988b: 32, original emphasis). There is agreement with Habermas on this point at least. The problem comes with the analysis of legitimation and the grounding of authorizing narratives.

In *The Postmodern Condition* Lyotard was keen to emphasize the centrality of the narrative form of knowledge in order to then examine how the way in which these narratives are grounded gradually shifts towards the performative instantiation of truths. In the discourse of the Enlightenment, the claim of scientific knowledge to be the basis for authorizing particular norms and conduct, that is to say, their functioning in constituting the normative and prescriptive rules for social action, rested on a discourse outside of the sciences, namely, a philosophy establishing the proper, that is, the ethical and political, ends of 'man'.[9] From the nineteenth century, the interweaving of the domain of the state and that of the sciences has become more systematic, whilst at the same time the affiliations of the sciences with the aims of capital have grown in strength.[10] The result is that the separation between the various language games has become blurred, and '[a]n equation between wealth, efficiency and truth is now established' (Lyotard, 1984: 45). Science now 'plays its own game . . . it is incapable of legitimating itself' (1984: 40). The hegemony of the technosciences means that the criteria for judging a 'good' move have shifted from the ethical, aesthetic or political to those of efficiency. A 'generalized spirit of per-formativity' expressed in input/output relations (1984: 45) now determines the choice between options, whilst the only credible goal is power. The consequences for remaking the relationships and distinctions between force, right and wisdom are crucial for the fate of modernity and its legitimizing ideals. The performance criterion confers upon itself the normative status of law, reinforcing the autonomous working of power:

> Power is not only good performativity, but also effective verification and good verdicts. It legitimates science and the law on the basis of their efficiency, and legitimates this efficiency on the basis of science and law. It is self-legitimating. . . . Thus the growth of power, and its self-legitimation, are now taking the route of data storage and accessibility, and the operativity of information. (1984: 47)

So, according to Lyotard, the victory of capitalist technosciences has fundamentally undermined the project of modernity by intensifying the process of delegitimization. I should add that the coefficient of efficiency is increasingly measured in monetary terms, determined by the accounting practices that have become universal across the apparatuses of adminis-tration and regulation of the social; the transitivity of accounting practices joins every social practice within the same economy of production, for instance, in educational institutions. Money and efficiency refer to each other, eliminating other values or reducing them to their measure, closing off the horizon of the ethical.

These are the broad lines of a too brief summary of the familiar argu-ments that Lyotard advanced in *The Postmodern Condition*. He now accepts that he exaggerated the importance of narrative form, since knowledge, he says, cannot be reduced to narration (1988b: 34). Besides, although the technosciences may appear to provide humanity with the means to accom-plish the project of control and possession over nature, it 'fundamentally destabilizes' this project because

> under the name of 'nature', one must include equally all the constituents of the human subject: its nervous system, its genetic code, its cortical computer, its visual and auditory apparatus, its system of communication, particularly lin-guistic ones, and its organizations for communal life, etc. Finally, its science, its technoscience, is itself part of nature. (1988b: 35)

It is a position which recognizes the 'immanence of the subject to the object that he studies and transforms . . . [such that] man is but a sophisticated knot' (1988b: 35, 36) in the web which constitutes the universe. Later in my elaboration of a critical phenomenology of the lifeworld, I will relate this proposition to the work of Merleau-Ponty in *The Visible and the Invisible* (1968), and to Haraway's (1991) theses about the analytical poverty of holding on to the dualities of nature and culture, the human and the machinic.

Lyotard's exploration follows two strategies, aiming, on the one hand, to come to terms with modernity, that is, its loss and its legacy, and, on the other hand, to refigure the question of the future in terms of what we are able or competent to do now, and by reference to what we ought to do. There are two kinds of losses which the experience of modernity obliges us to face up to. There is the loss associated with everything that the process of modernization destroys or leaves behind in its repeated gesture of breaking away from the past to venture into the newness instigated by a progressive history. This loss is bound up with the 'forgetting' of repressed knowledge – for example, of the (sacrificial) violence done to others in the suppression of the colonized and their exploitation. This forgetting short-circuits the process of coming to terms with and learning from the past without which one gets caught up in cycles of repetition and compulsion, particularly (for late modernity) of the violences intrinsic to totalizations on the side of instrumental reason.

The other loss is that of the promise of universal emancipation, the loss which the postmodern condition reveals. One possible way of mourning such a loss, as Lyotard points out (1988b: 43) is a retreat into secondary narcissism,[11] when it is possible for those with the means – that is, those with power or money – to seek their own satisfaction and to pursue their *jouissance* at the expense of others. The result is another form of terror: 'that of "our" satisfaction, the satisfaction of a we limited to its own particularity' (1988b: 44). It is possible, of course, to do the work of mourning through the kind of 'working through' which is meant to occur in analysis. However, if the consequence of 'working through' is meant to be a refigured narrative of what has been the history of modernity so far, and a new understanding of the goals to pursue now, then the psychoanalytic model is conceptually limited since it cannot provide the explicit narratives of emancipation and liberation which historical and subjective transformation requires.

Questions of method

I think it is time to indicate the corpus of work from which I have borrowed to knit together the analytical apparatus that I am developing throughout the book. Levinas, Derrida, Foucault, Ricoeur and Lyotard are the names most often invoked, standing in for critical positions inside/outside the philosophical discourse of modernity. It might appear that nothing much is held in common among these figures,[12] except that they have explored a particular way of doing philosophy, namely, of thinking being or the subject at the limit of what it is possible to think, and so, at the same time, of thinking the 'end of philosophy'. My selection has to do with a number of affinities and affiliations in their thought that I am reconstructing. The first observation is that although they recognize the specificity of modernity as a period, they have all problematized the foundations upon which the grand claims of modernity rest. Let us remind ourselves of the important elements, at least from the point of view of their contribution to a critique of occidentalism. They concern the Levinasian project of breaking with the privilege of epistemology which shapes most of modern thought, replacing it with 'ethics as first philosophy'; Derrida's task of using concepts like the metaphysics of presence or like *différance* and trace, and so on, to undo the certainties of the logocentric subject; Foucault's analysis of the specificity of modernity and its subject by pointing to the specificity of the conditions which made possible the discourses and practices that constituted them, conditions which may now be disappearing; Ricoeur's refiguration of the temporality of being which recalls us to an immemorial debt and to responsibilities that the narrativization of history and of selves ought to make visible; and, finally, Lyotard's invocation of generalities applying beyond modernity concerning knowledge and value that open up the aporetic and indeterminate character of the criteria that we may use to judge the validity of truth-claims and the dispensation of justice. In these different ways they have tried to find a measure for judging modernity which urges us to a reflection on our condition that encompasses the whole history of humanity. It could be argued that to speak of humanity in the singular returns us to the suspect universalist assumptions and the mis-recognitions and pathologizations of difference of which the discourse of modernity stands accused. I shall take up this view below when discussing the stakes in the position I am advocating. My point, at this stage, is to signal that these figures have been able to undermine the foundations of modernity only by taking a position within philosophy which makes visible again the general form of a questioning about being, and so recover the stakes in this reflection concerning emancipation and liberation posed on the secular terrain which modernity introduced.[13]

Another reason for allowing the work of these figures to inflect my interrogation comes from the interesting trajectory in the development of their thought which passes through the work of Heidegger – clearly, differently for each – and reconstitutes a phenomenology; the two, in any case, pour into each other. On one side there is the road through Heidegger, the paradoxical figure at the centre of the Western questioning of being, who develops and brings to an end a line of thought about ontology which begins with Plato and, after the Augustinian Christian meditation, is modernized in the form of Cartesianism. It mutates in the Husserlian critique, though without, in this case, escaping reliance on a transcendental dimension, before overflowing into existentialism, critical theory and post-Husserlian phenomenology. Heidegger inherits the accursed share of Western philosophical tradition, one that still dreamed of a will to power that would liberate 'man' from the dispossession of the self by God or gods.

This share secretly desired the mythology of presence redeemed, grounded in some new home: *Heimat*, the Community, the great State (see Lacoue-Labarthe, 1990, for an instructive discussion). The affiliations of this tradition with European imperialism and its 'worlding of a world', and thus with the idea of occidentalism that I am developing, have been important considerations in my selection of the figures. A further significant reason concerns the manner in which they have had to engage with the fissures in this tradition, and overcome the totalizing and totalitarian temptations it harbours. In some cases, as with Foucault, the engagement with colonialism and imperialism has not been as thorough or enlightening as one might have wished, as I will show in Chapter 4.

The other side of the trajectory to which I am drawing attention brings up the encounter with phenomenology's attempt to ground subjectivity and knowledge in the domain of the experiential and the concrete, to cut the theorization of being adrift from the grounding in transcendental a priori. It develops a space against psychologisms and against epistemological certainties and closures in order better to understand the world of objects in its givenness. It is not my aim to review the different strands in the web of phenomenology, nor provide a critique. I am simply borrowing from that problematic a number of propositions concerning the following: the recognition of the provisional character of all knowledge; the problematization of the dichotomy between the corporeal and the mental; the point of view of the constructedness of subjectivity and forms of sociality; the challenge to logocentrism; the opening toward the recognition of an unrepresentable or unpresentable dimension in our apprehension of the world and of ourselves (against pragmatism's reduction of phenomena to a system of effects). Much of this appears in one guise or another in the later work of Merleau-Ponty, a key figure for the development of Foucault and Lyotard, and many French intellectuals in the 1950s.

What is helpful for the kind of critique I am trying to develop here is that Levinas, Derrida, Foucault, Ricoeur, Lyotard, have all tried to subvert the conventional opposition between a philosophy of experience and a philosophy of the concept, between the standpoint 'Husserl' or 'Merleau-Ponty' and the standpoint 'Bachelard' or 'Canguilhem' (see Kearney, 1988; Macey, 1993). This subversion opens up a way of refiguring historicity by reference to several elements. First, the materiality of the world we inherit and inhabit and transform. We come into a world which is always-already constituted before we encounter it, so that we are hostage to it, both its materiality and its sociality, that is, from the beginning we experience the lifeworld as a way of dwelling in the givenness of the world that operates as our habitus. In learning to inhabit that world, we rely on the hospitality of those closest to us and on order in the surrounding world, the regularities of which we can learn through an apprenticeship. Language is central in this process and thus inter-subjective action, and thus, crucially, the relation to the other. This involves both the culturally normed mode of this relation and what Levinas calls the face relation, that is to say, the immediacy and vulnerability of the other in the moment when the other presents itself to us as face, as this alterity that is offered for recognition (or erasure). What I am trying to say is that an ethical relation to the other, from the beginning, is triggered by our beingness in the world, anterior to any normative rules, unconditioned by calculations of duty or obligation, and so on.[14] Clearly, because of the concrete reality of the face, and the embodied character of inter-subjective action, the materiality I am describing is made up of bodies as well as the (socialized) matter of the objects of the world.[15] So apprenticeship involves a way of learning to be ethical beings, at the same time as one learns to be a particular subject and to act on the world according to particular technologies of transforming and appropriating the world, that is to say, apprenticeship instructs us into the ways of coupling with the objectal and inter-subjective worlds in which we dwell.

Second, I have introduced the face relation in order to add another dimension to the point of view of the grounded character of our beingness in the lifeworld, namely, that referring to the ungrounded element in the manner of our dwelling in the world. I say 'ungrounded' rather than use the more familiar term 'groundlessless'; the latter relays a discourse about being that too easily or too quickly slips into a metaphysics and towards presuppositions of a transcendental domain, whereas the term 'ungrounded' recognizes the liminal side of the experiential without detaching such an experience from the ontic or phenomenal character of beingness. The ungrounded character besides refers to the unpresentable and unrepresentable dimension activated in the face relation. A different language is required in addressing this element of subjectivity, a poetics invoking fragility, lack and loss, suffering, giving expression to the dehiscence of being, and calling up concepts like hospitality, friendship, responsibility, gift, which I will develop in my last two chapters.

My particular approach to the problem attempts to relate the referent in the notion of the ungrounded to the 'almost nothing of the unpresentable' (Derrida, 1995a: 83), which conceals the desire for presence, tucked away in the trace. This 'almost nothing' is thus revealed to be everything, since 'desire for presence . . . is desire itself' (Derrida, 1995a: 83). If we were to think of the space which relays desire and presence as the space of *jouissance*, and if we bear in mind the liminality of the three terms I am relaying, then the idea of the ungrounded dimension of being refers, at the ontological level, to the face relation, or to what is activated in it; the concept of the ungrounded ground thus opens towards a problematic of the ethical which invokes concepts of love, filiality, responsibility, alongside the problematic of the aesthetic, which calls up concepts of ecstasy, epiphany, the sublime, embodiment, transfiguration. Although the idea draws in part from Levinas, I am adding to the discussion elements from other, mainly secular, reflections about being – for instance, in Walter Benjamin – which have been trying to escape occidentalism.

Different cultures and different periods have invented different languages to deal with the range of philosophical and theoretical issues implicated in the question of the ungrounded dimension. My point is that there is nothing natural or originary in the recognition of this dimension of being-in-the-world, even if the feelings which motivate its narrativization may be immanent to being. For instance, the idea of ethics as fundamentally the discourse theorizing the relation to the other, or any other idea of how to conceptualize and found the ethical, is in a sense conventional, located within specific traditions. What is important is that all such conceptualizations have conditions of possibility that locate them by reference to a genealogy and definite historically located practices. For instance, the Kantian problematic of ethics could not have appeared at the time of Augustine or outside modernity or within Buddhism. So both the grounded and the ungrounded aspects of being in the world can be examined by reference to the historicity of particular lifeworlds and the discourses of being inscribed in them. Apprenticeship includes learning to deal in culturally specific ways with both the liminal and the material side of beingness, so that we learn to figure and refigure our experiences, and so give meaning to them, in terms of a whole set of rules and stories, beliefs and values inscribed in performative as well as in reflexive practices of becoming instituting particular subjectivities.[16]

The third opening which I have in mind concerns the locatedness of the social and subjective dimension in the constitution of knowledge so that the interrogation of the world is at one and the same time a problematization of who we are and a recognition of the historicity of that interrogation. A number of examples will establish the point of departure. A question like how fast light travels could not be, and had not been, thought before the transformations in the concept of light – wave and particle theory – which allowed the mind to think of light as something that could travel and that its speed could be measured. Previous conceptions made such a question unthinkable. Equally, previous techniques and apparatuses for measuring speed made unthinkable the possibility of measuring the speed of light. The two sets of development, that is, the conceptual break and the technical innovations, were necessary conditions, themselves conditioned by specific changes in scientific knowledge and concepts of nature. Or take Darwin's concept of natural selection. Without the developments that were at once cultural and technical and scientific, the evidence for such a concept and the conceptual framework within which it has been formulated could not have appeared (see Venn, 1982, for details). For instance, it is the fact of the British empire and its interest in the systematic classification and census of species throughout the world that made possible the financing and feasibility of scientific expeditions like that of the *Beagle* and countless others and of the collection and transport of species, leading to the kind of accumulation of knowledge about the distribution and variations in species that was a key part of the theory. We must add a number of crucial other components like developments in geological knowledge – the work of Lyell and others – and the support for evolutionary theories in the field of language, behaviour, culture, civilizations, which Darwin discussed in his *Notebooks*. There is, furthermore, the political radicalism of Darwin and his intellectual circle which disposed him to countenance a theory, namely, the evolution of species, which he knew would offend many. So a concept like natural selection appears in quite definite historical circumstances, at a particular point in a series of other developments that provide the (necessary but not sufficient) conditions of possibility for it – wider than the conditions examined in the context of discovery and the context of validation.

Another example, this time from the social sciences, could be Marx's theorization of capitalism. It is well known that the conditions of possibility included the work of political economy and the fact of political radicalism in Europe when Marx was developing the theory, as well as the Enlightenment's view of systematic progress in human society, and Hegel's systematization of the mechanism in terms of the (conjectured) intrinsic laws of development of history and the logic of the dialectic. Not only have these conditions acted as limits, but a particular concept of reason thereby wormed its way into the Marxian theoretical edifice, overdetermining the extent to which Marxism became mortgaged to the assumption of necessary structural relations that became privileged. Additionally, it could be argued that the privilege of labour as the determining category has something to do with the fact that in the nineteenth century it was effectively and explicitly the main target for disciplinary power and theoretical elaboration in the social sciences and the determining element in people's lives. Yet, today, we can conceptualize the development of modernity and of capitalism in quite different terms, away from the assumptions of necessary structural relations privileging the economic instance or the market. Instead, we can, for instance, examine the economy by reference to contingent arrangements and steering mechanisms which a genealogy is able to reconstitute, namely, in terms of the slow but deliberate or reasoned assemblage of a complex network of apparatuses, together with the constitution of appropriate subjectivities congruent with capitalist practices and the establishment of a legal framework that authorizes or compels conformity to its rules. The interesting point is that the structured–structurizing aspect of the system owes as much to the practical consequences of the theoretical assumption about it being a structure, as to the pragmatic calculations that have gone into its institution as a system.[17] By reference to consumer and cybernetic capitalism, the main categories may well now be that of the symbol and the sign-commodity, calling for a different theorization of capitalism.

A general point to note is that in the natural sciences, theory makes possible the construction of a theoretically normed environment – the apparatuses, the problematics, the paradigms, the community of practitioners, the forms of communication, in short a 'technical city', as Bachelard called it; it is within this environment that properly scientific questions arise or make sense, and particular research programmes can be pursued. In the social sciences, the knowledge produced, besides being inscribed in definite power relations, or having definite effects for the exercise of power, is the result of processes that are in part contingent and in part structured–structurizing, tied to calculations and intentions that are reflexively relayed through agents and agencies within the context of the institution of particular forms of sociality.

The arguments above support the view that the historicity of lifeworlds refers not simply to the recognition in consciousness or in discourse of the historical specificity of cultures, that is, it is not simply the idea that we need to understand cultures in relation to a genealogy that acknowledges their contingency and specificity. I mean historicity to indicate, additionally, several recognitions: the process of the material constitution and investment of the world we inhabit such that its physical characteristics and its symbolic meanings are the accumulated result and sedimentation of past events and human activity; a monument and the living archive to the having-been of a community; the making-present of the events inscripted – both inscribed and encrypted – in the everyday as a repository of deeds and as the evidence of history, legible still, provided we know the codes for deciphering the traces; our own inscription in this complex world so that we are coupled to it. Historicity, then, as archive and as monument, combines temporality and spatiality; it is the space of memorization and remembrance, and the home, or *domus*, in which being dwells.[18] Not only is history preserved in the materiality and the signs around us, our own action in the present is conditioned and limited by the contingency of living history. Historicity, thus, points to the accumulation of the technical and discursive means, as the 'ready-to-hand', for enacting the world that we encounter as an inheritance and a given lifeworld, into which we have to be instructed. This sense of history 'as lived' in the everyday is what Jean-Luc Nancy understands as 'finite history', that is, the history that

> does not belong primarily to time, nor to succession, nor to causality, but to the community, or to being-in-common . . . community itself is something historical. Which means it is not a substance, nor a subject; it is not a common being, which would be the goal or culmination of a progressive process. It is a being-in-common which only *happens*. (1990: 149, original emphasis)

With this sketch of these methodological considerations and theoretical preambles about the possibility of a critical phenomenology and about the consequences for analysis of the point of view of the historicity of the social world, the ground has been prepared for two further elements. They have centrally to do with the question of the displacement which is implicated in my refiguration of the history of modernity in terms of the hegemony of occidentalism. This displacement has a counter-hegemonic interest. The logic of my thesis about occidentalism is that it makes little sense to segregate the analysis of (post)modernity from the analysis of the (post)colonial, since the one functioned, and functions still, as a condition of possibility for the other. In order to develop further the theoretical apparatus for the task of countering occidentalism, I will clarify the standpoint of the heteronomy of the subject and of postcoloniality as a critical space from which to interrogate modernity. This will enable me to establish the reasons for thinking that the critique of occidentalism and the modern subject have lessons for the postcolonial world.

A brief history of the subject

The first displacement I want to operate concerns the 'who' in the theme I introduced via Foucault earlier, the clandestine being and agent smuggled in the question of who 'we' are in the present and of who comes after the subject of modernity. I am pursuing the thought that the question of who we are inevitably calls up that of who we have been and who we desire to be in the future, so that the problem of subjectivity overflows the space of the present and of singular beings to be relocated within the archival space of the institution of subjects, tied, at the level of language, to a narrative of the history of the collectivity: the community, the people, humanity. The idea of a correlation between the wider historical dimension and the level of the personal or private drama of subjective becoming finds support in the focus on questions of identity today, prompted by the dislocations provoked by postmodern conditions.This correlation, one could argue, indicates already that the proper ground for an understanding of the processes involved in the constitution of subjectivities is that of the temporality of being and of the historicity of the lifeworld generally.

The immediate implication of this proposition is a shift from universalist assumptions that essentialize the subject, for instance in terms of concepts of reason, gender, genetics or race, all of which presuppose invariant characteristics. The concept of the subject has admittedly appeared relatively recently. Yet we have become so accustomed to thinking about subjectivity within the perimeter of the discourse of modernity that it requires an adjustment of perspective to recognize what it means to say that the subject is a recent invention, and thus that it has a genealogy, and that such a standpoint undermines all the universal categories that are usually deployed in its theorization, as, for instance, in psychology or psychoanalysis. Take, for example, the idea of an interiority that each of us is supposed to have, often commonly assumed to be some authentic or true self, with which we are supposed to 'get in touch' or which we are meant to recover from the fragmenting and distorting effects of everyday living. As soon as we recognize that this idea of an interiority is of relatively recent birth – for it is a phenomenon associated with the early modern period, evidenced in the discourse of self-fashioning in the texts of, for example, Montaigne or Shakespeare (Greenblatt, 1980) – we begin to attend to the conditions that generated it and to analyse its specificity, as I shall do in Chapter 3. New questions then surface, for instance regarding whether, or in what manner, its genealogy is bound up with the idea of conscience in the Christian narrative of being, already signalling the European and Western provenance of the concept. And other issues further down the line, such as whether we would need to historicize a concept like that of the unconscious – and what would be left of Freudianism then?

The first thing to note is that the questioning of the subject from the point of view of its historicity shows the impossibility of separating out this line of interrogation from an interrogation of modernity as a period and from recognizing that the questions, and the form of questioning, are themselves already conditioned by the history which has brought us to this point. To that extent, the genealogy of the subject leads us to begin with the breaks that inaugurate the modern narrative of a unitary, rational, self-sufficient subject, and to chart the shifts that attended its trajectory to the present. I suppose most approaches would begin with the work of Descartes, and the way he splits up the older notion of 'conscience' into an emotional and a cognitive component, privileging the latter, and founding it in the *cogito*, as we know. In that gesture he appears, for modern philosophy at least, to cancel the dispossession of the subject which the idea of a transcendent God implies.[19]

My way of putting it already runs ahead of itself, for such a declaration does not make sense without a number of assumptions about the place of the concept of conscience in Christian onto-theology. I will develop this thematic of subjectivity before modernity in Chapter 3. The point I want to make is that the genealogy of the subject of modernity can only avoid a repetition of what the discourse of modernity already claims about the subject if it re-examines that discourse from the longer *durée* of an archaeology. It is this wider perspective that reveals the place of conscience, as well as the point of view of dispossession. Both have effects on how we are to refigure the displacement concerning agency and foundation that are central themes in the critique of the metaphysics of presence and of the logic that sustains logocentrism.

Another perspective which the longer history of the subject reveals concerns the transmutation in the narrative of human existence imagined in pre-modern times in terms of a journey which every human must undertake in search of an eventual or anticipated emancipation and salvation. Instead of the idea of the redemptive journey of the pilgrim in the course of which the Christian becomes worthy of salvation,[20] the discourse of modernity transforms the idea of journey into the progress of reason, at first in search still of an emancipation from the insufficiencies bound up with the human condition and with the idea of fallenness. The modern journey no longer required the purification of the soul but that of reason, the faculty guaranteed by God for the subject's own search for truth and emancipation. Descartes proposes a method for this progress which already grants to the subject the autonomy of a self-sufficient being, and thus also responsibility for success or failure.

Kant, as we know, further distances the process from divine intervention or design, and redefines the purpose of the journey in terms of the coming to maturity of humanity as a whole, making of modernity a universal and universalizing project. The subject becomes the agent of the project, and thus the agent of its own process of becoming. This shift is made even clearer with Hegel. The Hegelian phenomenology historicizes the process by way of the working of the dialectic, when mind or consciousness becomes the object and subject of History, propelled by its own, immanent, *telos*. Marx changes everything and too little: he introduces the political at the heart of the system, and finds a collective agent for history, but he keeps the Hegelian logic, and thus the totalizing ambition and temptation inscribed in it; when aligned with the imperatives of instrumental reason, this position produces the imaginary we know as Stalinism.

The history of the subject after Hegel is the history of crisis and triumph. On the one hand, it is marked by the accomplishments of an imperialist modernity, in its occidentalist form and in alliance with capitalism, in transforming the whole world, materially and culturally, in the nineteenth century. The project of modernity and of Enlightenment imagined it could authorize a civilizing mission, the goal of which was supposed to bring the law to all other peoples (Kant, in Derrida, 1997: 27). On the other hand, one must place alongside this exorbitant ambition the awareness of a sadness at the heart of the Zeitgeist. This is evidenced in some of the reservations of radical Enlightenment thinkers like Diderot, the questioning of subjectivity by German Romantic thinkers like Schelling and Schleiermacher (Bowie, 1990), or in the meditations of a Baudelaire and the critique of the foundations of modernity by Nietszche.[21]

It is with the critique of Cartesianism by Husserl (1960) that an interrogation is inaugurated of the foundations of the subject of modernity, developed later on by Heidegger, and those who have been instructed by a reading of his work since, in particular the authors to whom I have drawn attention earlier. The basis for rethinking what and who comes after modernity must draw from that critique.

Elements: towards the heteronomous I

A different theorization of being begins to emerge with this fundamental interrogation, within an agenda that looks to a postmodern or transmodern becoming of the subject, drawing from two sets of reflections. On the one hand, we find the recognition of the embodied, inter-subjective and mobile character of subjectivity, so that the subject is 'always in process', the indeterminate result of the 'complex transactions between the subject, the body and identity' (Hall, 1996a: 14). Questions of the effects of power become central in this approach, so that the constitution of identities is bound up with the 'discursive construction of a constitutive outside and the production of abjected and marginalized subjects' (Hall, 1996a: 15). The theorization of subjectivity, in this way, is seen to be open to a historicization whereby issues of difference – gender, race, and so on – and of the specificity of conditions, for instance the colonial context of the process of subjectification, must be brought within the frame of analysis of how the psychic, the social and the discursive come to be folded in the constitution of the 'interiority' of a self. This theorization points towards an heteronomous I for whom the relation to alterity is primary. Significantly, some of the voices which have begun to problematize the egological paradigm come from the 'unhomely' space of a critical theory that locates itself in the in-between space relative to Western thought and the 'jetty' of the postcolonial. Bhabha (1996), for example, indicates that the other is not necessarily an adversary, or that in opposition to which the subject understands itself. Instead, with a clear reference to Levinas, he proposes that the 'subject is inhabited by the radical and an-archical reference to the "other"' (1996: 58). Furthermore, Gilroy's (1993a) analysis of modernity in relation to subordinated subjects highlights the disjunctures of time, arising from the different temporal routes that different belongings, or different roots, produce. Together these explicit and implicit critiques of the occidentalist subject redirect attention to questions of the inscription of historicity in the lifeworld and the processes whereby its effects shape identities.

On the other hand, in refiguring an other history of the subject that would at the same time be an other history of modernity, we encounter an older narrative of being in which the theme of becoming is tied up with issues of responsibility, debt, sacrifice, gift, the gaping and trembling of being (Derrida, 1995a; Lyotard, 1993). Let us make sense of this way of speaking about the subject by turning to a prior question, addressing the ontological problem of what being is, which Heidegger had expressed in the view that being is the entity which questions itself as to its way of being. This questioning itself is inseparable from the recognition that we exist as beings in time, conscious of temporality and of the inevitability of finitude, and inseparable also from the recognition of the inter-subjectivity of existence.

I will show later, in the course of the book, that it reveals being as *epoché*, that is, as trace and event, or as the space of the happening of being, and not as punctum or as *arche* or origin. We know ourselves to be fateful and fatal beings, measuring our presentness by reference to the trace and spacing of time, that is, by reference to duration understood as the space of becoming. I draw attention to becoming because I want to stress the need to move away from any thought of being as presence, or as present to itself without borders. It is a break with traditional ontology's assumptions about the horizon of being which grounds the self-sufficient subject of Cartesianism. Instead, I am indicating a sense of temporality in which we live the now as a movement from a becoming-past to a coming-towards so that the consciousness of the present always leaches into the memory of the having-been and the anticipation of a to-come. The point, basically, is that temporality is a fundamental dimension of being, as I will demonstrate in the next two chapters. The way it is lived is tied to loss and lack, namely, of what has been (or to what cannot be appropriated as sign), to the anticipation of the to-come as a time of emancipation and redemption, that is, as a time of the recovery of (fantasized) presence, and to the intimation of some un(re)presentable, liminal aspect of beingness in experiences of a sublime feeling: in ecstasies and epiphanies of the subject.[22] My argument is that the unity, or seeming unity, of the subject – and of the community – is a projected unity, beholden to an imagined ideal subject, awaiting its realization. Thus, Foucault's question: 'Who are we in the present?' is a question that exceeds genealogy, since the subject is located by reference to a memory, as well as to a narrative of emancipation, that is to say, to a sense of an imponderable to-come. The notion of the subject as presence, that is, as a self-present, egocentric consciousness, as in the modern, logocentric concept of the subject, has the effect of erasing this fundamental historicity of beings.

My next point repeats the proposition that the way in which, and the means by which, being questions itself as to its way of being is through language. Narrative is the form in which being comes to know itself as a being in time, for time is not a thing, it cannot be directly represented or possessed, but is indirectly communicated and experienced in the form of narrativity. Narrative, in that sense, is 'the guardian of time', as Ricoeur (1988) puts it. Specifically, the existence of a self as a temporally circumscribed entity takes the form of a narration. Thus, every self is a storied self. And every story is mingled with the stories of other selves, so that every one of us is entangled in the stories we tell, and are told about us. The understanding of subjectivity cannot be separated from the way selves are narrated. The who is a narrated identity.

It follows from the above that the entanglement of subjectivities and identities means that every subject exists as a relation to an other or to others, that is, every subject is intricated in an inter-subjective web: 'An I by itself does not exist,' says Ricoeur (1992: 18). Our inscription in language, and the narrative character of identity, instantiates the inter-subjective ground of subjectivity; it signals the primacy of the social in the process of constitution of subjects.[23]

The embodied and performative character of human relations amplifies the standpoint of the subject as an heteronomous, rather than an autonomous, I. The world of other bodies and the world of objects constitute the 'dwelling' for subjectivity. It is not enough to say that the self or the *cogito* emerges in relation to or in opposition to an other, for instance in Lacan's metaphor of the mirror stage, implicating separation from the Other in the formation of the ego and the recognition of the difference of the other as an other (and the specular misrecognitions which, for him, are intrinsic to the process). I am stressing the idea of the self as more than one but less than two, as Irigaray (1984) would put it. This understanding cashes out the idea of being-with and being-in-the-world. It is instantiated in the notion of choreography, by which I understand the co-emergence or compossibility of a subjective dyad, as in the mother–infant dyad, whereby each element produces the other in terms of activities marked by hospitality, generosity, pleasure, attachment, mingling the time of the body with the 'time of the soul' (Ricoeur, 1988).[24]

The models for the emplotment of experience already exist in the culture, inscribed in practices of the everyday, dispersed in tales, novels, films, parables, stereotypes, and so on. In other words, the plots and scripts and models which provide the vocabulary that we use to make sense of our experiences exist as a given in a culture; we do not invent them from scratch, or choose them as 'free' agents. The authority of the narratives of identity depend on the cultural forms of validating stories, from appeal to their basis in science, as in socio-biology (however invalid the arguments may be), to reliance on the charismatic authority of 'personalities'. Increasingly, print media, television and film have become the vehicles and the sites for the emplotment of experience. They include the narratives that construct the horizon of expectation, instructing us about what we should anticipate and desire. Culture, therefore, delimits the space of experience and the horizon of expectation. The force of these plots for subjectivity is that not only do they provide the models for the configuration of experience, but they circumscribe the discursive and 'textual' world from which we draw in order to question ourselves regarding the meaning of our experiences, and to rectify our 'selves', since the subject is always in process. The process of figuration and refiguration of identity describes an apprenticeship. It is in part a way of appropriating, of making one's own what belongs to the inter-subjective dimension of culture, a way of folding the outside inside ourself, a folding that changes the self. I will argue, in Chapters 2 and 4, that apprenticeship and refiguration involve an ethics and an aesthetics of the self, tied to an 'hermeneutics of desire', but without the volitional slippages in Foucault.

At the analytical level, the interweaving of the space of experience with the horizon of expectation refers to the process whereby the historical dimension of narration is co-articulated with the biographical level. Two forms of temporalizations cross each other to constitute a particular subjectivity at the point of intersection. A who or self 'happens' at the relay point where the history of a culture, sedimented in its stock of knowledge, its narrations, its texts, joins with the history or biography of a named person. In this way every self is sutured in history. I understand the historicity of subjectivity to refer, amongst other things, to this double inscription of subjects by reference to time. In the next chapter, I shall discuss these propositions in detail and consider some cases.

Postcolonial provocations

Defining the postcolonial

The methodological issue which remains to be examined concerns whether a standpoint located in the space of the postcolonial enables the distantiation necessary for breaking with habits of thought that prevent the emergence of the new. I suggested earlier that the view of the postcolonial which I am proposing is that of an imagined space, the space for imagining the 'post' of modernity, a space beyond occidentalism, and, thus, the space of emergence of futurity. It is clearly, therefore, not a reference to the state of affairs after the formal ending of colonialism, that is to say, it does not mark a periodization, it is not the same as post-independence. It is not possible in any case to think that the ending of the old imperial order put an end to the relations of power and to the forms of oppression that had been put into place since 1492. The reality of the world after the age of empire is one of continuing exploitation and inequalities in more complex forms, indeed their intensification. New apparatuses and networks have appeared – the World Bank, the International Monetary Fund, the United Nations, and so on – that now regulate and discipline a transnational system of production and exchange for a largely capitalist global economy. The old centre–periphery divide may now appear overtaken by the growth of the Newly Industrialized Countries (NICs) and by the shifts in the balance of economic power, for example with the increasing importance of the Pacific Rim. Recent crises in the once 'model' economies of, for example, Japan, Hong Kong, Indonesia, counsel a note of caution before proclaiming the end of long-standing power relations. One need only examine the complex network of corporate transnational conglomerates, and look into the details of their strategies regarding the transfer of technology, or concerning 'development aid', or pay attention to the effects of licensing policies, franchising, patenting and tariffs, or, more obviously, inspect a list of the burden of debt between the countries of the old centre – ironically called donor countries – and the post-independence countries to verify the continuities in new forms of the older relations of power. Additionally, as I will discuss below, the continuing effects of the apparatus of imperial governmentality, put into place in the nineteenth century, bind the 'Third World' to the imaginary of occidentalism.

Similarly, the data concerning the global flows of investments and the distribution of income and wealth, the process of 'unequal exchange', access to basic necessities like telephone, electricity, safe water, medical services, will confirm the extent to which the term 'postcolonial' would be seriously misleading if it were meant to signal a radical break with the old regimes. That there have been changes is undeniable, and not only in the context of increasing globalization. The problem is not the recognition of independence and what it has brought; it is about the limits that geo-political and economic interests impose on possible development. For example, a country like Tanzania, which technically became free to experiment with different models of development appropriate to the conditions and the culture prevailing at the time found its efforts undermined by systematic sabotage. If one were to focus on the catalogue of military, economic, technological and cultural interventions in the post-Second World War period it would be easy to find evidence supporting the view of neo-imperialism. Matters are more complex and more intractable than this, though, for even imperialism was a complex, uneven process, as several recent studies reveal.[25]

I think the recognition of the differential character of the process of colonial subjugation enables one to distinguish distinct trajectories and genealogies regarding the economy, the political sphere and ideological mechanisms, that is, the variations in the relationship between economic domination, political power, and the mechanisms of subjectification/subjection in different parts of the 'Third World'. The implications for the study of the cultural and social dimensions of colonialism and imperialism would need to be checked out concerning the claims of a more generalized system of exploitation, as in the work of, say, Immanuel Wallerstein (1980, 1984, 1991), against the claims of a relatively indeterminate and contingent co-articulation of the different processes and systems. I note these theoretical problems because they have had a knock-on effect for the theorization of the postcolonial. In particular, some of the disputes about the fruitfulness of using a term like the 'postcolonial' have centred on the fact that it can appear to homogenize the different processes and levels, and so, like the popular term 'globalization', it can suffer from the kind of problems of over-generalization and glossing over differences and historical specificity which are endemic to system-theoretical approaches.[26]

I am going to refer my analysis not to economic and political developments, for which the term 'post-independence', if not 'neo-imperialism', may be more appropriate from the point of view of periodization, but to the task of establishing a different problematic of culture, specifically, the culture of modernity and the question of subjectification/subjection. In that sense the year 1492 can function as both limit and point of origin, if we bear in mind that the origin is only retroactively named, acting as the myth of the beginning. Equally, between the limit of the old and the beginning of the new is the gap which the event of the beginning fills, marked by the violence of the originary moment. '1492', then, functions as the point of catastrophe, and as 'hymen' (Derrida, 1982). It designates the violence of the birth of the West; the New World paying for its newness and the becoming-West of 'Europe' with the destruction of its old existence, its bride-price. The history of the transformations that followed, and that has accomplished the 'worlding of a world', as Spivak (1985: 128) has put it, is the history of the inscription – at once an inscription and an encryption, as burial and encoding, the memory buried in the monument of the 'there is' – of the events that since 1492 have produced the postcolonial world. It is from this point of view that I consider the question of the postcolonial to refer to the analysis of the becoming-West of Europe and the becoming-modern of the world. The postcolonial is the critical space that is itself modified in the course of the kind of critique that I am proposing. It designates the to-come of postmodernity – if we bear in mind that all the terms are under erasure in the problematic that I am suggesting. Additionally, it is my intention to show that such an understanding is not separable from the questions that have now surfaced about breaking with what ails 'modern civilization' (Derrida, 1995b).

So, how to understand the postcolonial? At this stage, my concern is to limit myself to a sketch of its analytic space by reference to the concepts of 'jetty', heresy, virus and '*pharmakon*'. Derrida (1990), noting the open and non-unified state of theoretical activity in the wake of all the isms – principally: structuralism, poststructuralism, historicism, post-Marxism, postmodernism – and the instability which makes their totalization impossible, uses the concept of theoretical jetty to point to the functioning of theory today. Theories, he argues, constitute a field of forces that we may call libidinal, political–institutional or historical–socioeconomic, which inscribes concurrent forces of desire and power: '[I]n this field of forces . . . there are only theoretical jetties' (1990: 65). Whilst there is competition between them, they are not necessarily antagonistic, since each theoretical jetty 'claims to comprehend itself by comprehending all the others – by extending beyond their borders, exceeding them, inscribing them within itself. . . . Each jetty is structured, constructed, designed in order to explain and account for all the other jetties' (1990: 65, 66). Each species of jetty 'constitutes its own identity only by incorporating other identities – by contamination, parasitism, grafts, organ transplant, incorporation, etc.' (1990: 66). For example, the field called Marxism develops by incorporating elements of other 'jetties', like psychoanalysis or poststructuralism, which might appear to oppose Marxism in the way they constitute certain theoretical objects or stakes. Each jetty concurrently extends beyond the whole field of forces yet folds back into it, seeking to appropriate other jetties and speak in their place.

Postcolonial theory cannot escape this strategy and location. If we look at the kinds of methods that structure its discourse, the concepts that are at work in the way it problematizes a field like colonial discourse, or if we question it as to its questions – difference, modernity, globalization, dissidence, revolution, historical specificity, identity formations, and so on – there is no doubt that postcolonial theory could not have been con-stituted without the 'jetties' called poststructuralism and Marxism, historicism and psychoanalysis. Of course, it is possible to object to post-colonial theory altogether precisely on the grounds that it relies on such theories and must import into its way of thinking Western canons and paradigms that cripple it from the point of view of radically oppositional theorization or from the standpoint of informing resistance. But such a view rephrases the dualism of us and them and dichotomies of colonizers and colonized that ignore the extent to which the process of colonialization and imperialism has made it impossible to return to a pure uncontaminated space of authentic experience or thought from which the West can be expunged. Similarly, the discourse of modernity generally and, more explicitly, the recent developments relating to the critical moment of the 'post', owe much to the colonial moment, as in the work of Derrida, Lyotard or Cixous. My borrowing of the term 'jetty' is meant to signal this system of mutual conditioning and borrowings and grafts, and the tendency to bring a wide range of historical events and culturally diverse practices within the orbit of postcolonial theory. At the same time I want to signal through the term 'jetty' the sense of being attached to a theoretical territory yet looking outwards into an uncharted territory, in search of a discursive and political space from which dissent can be articulated and alternative imaginations grounded. Equally, the looking outwards obliges the intellectual to engage with another aspect of the 'outside', namely, 'native' realities and limits.

The provisionality of the postcolonial as limit is nicely established by Stuart Hall in his challenge to the binary form of representation of the colonial encounter where he talks about the need to 're-read the binaries as forms of transculturation, of cultural translation, destined to trouble the here/there of cultural binaries for ever' (1996b: 247). We are instead forced to recognize a 'double inscription', disrupting the inside/outside demarcation so that we 're-read "colonization" as part of an essentially transnational and transcultural "global" process – and it produces a decentred, diasporic or "global" rewriting of earlier, nation-centred imperial grand narratives' (1996b: 247). This rewriting is part of the task of postcolonial thinking. It includes the recognition of the colonial process not as peripheral but as a 'ruptural world-historical event' (1996b: 249). The post-colonial 'retrospective re-phrasing of Modernity . . . marks a critical interruption into the whole grand historiographical narrative' shared by liberal as well as Marxist historiography (1996b: 250). Such a postcolonial refiguration of modernity takes account of the transverse linkages across nation-states and the global/local system of relationships involved in the institution of the 'always-already diasporic' and 'hybridized' (1996b: 250) cultural and socio-political spaces of the 'Third World'. It involves the reconfiguration of the power/knowledge fields in terms of their inscription into the system of formation and regulation of a globalized world, as well as through a critical interrogation of the epistemic enframing of knowledge and experience that have located cultures and histories within a Eurocentric temporality and spatialization. This interrogation must engage with the discourse of the Enlightenment to the extent that it brought differences within 'the universal scope of a single order of being' (1996b: 252), fetishizing and pathologizing difference. Hall argues that the postcolonial critical enterprise must consider the concepts it borrows as operating 'under erasure', in the sense Derrida gives to the idea. The postcolonial, to that extent, is a way of 'thinking at the limit', attempting to go beyond the colonial and eschewing the disavowals of the presence of Western categories of thought within this thinking. It is clear from the language of Hall, the range of concepts put to work – selected from poststructuralism, Marxism, psychoanalysis – and the recognition of double inscription, that it fits well Derrida's idea that, in the moment of the 'post', critical theory operates as jetty.

Equally, we could look at the work of Trinh Minh-ha, crossing the conventional lines of demarcation between theory and expressive modes of exploration like photography and film, allowing the one to disrupt and inform the other so that a new way of writing the postcolonial may appear, subverting the effects of power for subjectification, given that 'language is one of the most complex forms of subjugation, being at the same time the locus of power and unconscious servility' (1989: 52). She points out that although the postcolonial intellectual, belonging to hyphenated cultures, gets tired of hearing terms like hybridity, border, in-betweenness, terms that are ever open to being co-opted, s/he must nevertheless rely on them, bending and redefining their meaning so that they may function as tools in the mobile struggle for the counter-appropriation of one's history and identity from the appropriative grasp of 'master-discourses' (1989: 43). For women especially, 'writing the body' has become an essential part of reclaiming women as site of difference and for politicizing everyday life. This is no one-sided matter, however, for 'no writing can ever claim to be "free" of other writings' (1989: 21); nor is it a simple claim to autonomy, since, for her, the kind of writing she wants to develop fashions the space for 'listening to the other's language and reading with the other's eyes' (1989: 30). Which means to say that it is a writing that welcomes the other. So whilst one must disengage from the master discourses of the West and the monolithic ambition of Western categories, one must beware of reinscribing dualisms and tying oneself to the double-bind of 'otherness'.

There are reasons for considering postcolonial theory to be engaged in a reflection which is more ambitious and more challenging to the foundations of modernity than other postisms. Already, the work of Homi Bhabha, Paul Gilroy, Stuart Hall, Edward Said, Gayatri Chakravorty Spivak, has prepared the grounds for moving beyond simply oppositional discourses or the recovery and legitimation of marginalized memories and existences. The interruptive strategies of postcolonial intervention aim to change the material and discursive world we inhabit. The rhetoric of postcolonial politics may strategically, or wishfully, claim to exist on the border, in the in-betweenness of the temporalities and spatialities that colonial and 'neo-colonial' discourses have constructed, but in truth, the postcolonial critic inhabits the 'structures of violence and violation' (Spivak, 1990: 72) as much as do those – that is, 'local' or 'native', non-diasporic intellectuals – who imagine they are outside of them. To that extent the deconstruction of the 'master discourses' and the rewriting of the history of modernity has a heretical thrust. The heretic, it is clear, is not someone outside the city of believers but one who challenges the authority of the priesthood; the heretic is the believer who elaborates a principled dissidence. Postcolonial theory as heresy intends to operate a difference and make a new departure through the rupture of what has become institutionalized or normalized as tradition or convention, for example, in the case of medical practice where definitions of development and modernization have become instituted in forms of the regulation and disciplining of the social and in apparatuses of governance in post-independence states. Heretical discourse must be motivated by a responsibility, a problematic responsibility to be sure, for it must claim to be on the side of truth and the ethical, and thus it must engage with language games played according to the rules of the discourses that already lay claim to the terrains on which is fought out the *agon* of the authoritative speech determining truth and ethics.

This is one of the main reasons why postcolonial 'thinking at the limit' cannot confine itself to theory, for it engages with a way of being at the limit. If we were to ask what should be the principal target of postcolonial theory, the answer indicated in my analysis so far must be: the form of life called occidentalism and the being inscribed in it. But this being is not circumscribed within philosophical discourse alone, though its founding narratives are to be found on the terrain of philosophy, in the ontological, epistemological and metaphysical discourses that ground the philosophy of the subject and that struggle with its aporias. Modernity, through imperial governmentality, and now additionally, through, the complex apparatuses of subjection/subjectification which have emerged around new media and forms of representation, has been implanted in every corner of the globe, instituted in the invisibility of the taken-for-granted, subject to partial resistances certainly, but promoting ways of life and an ethos that remain in thrall to occidentalism. An invisible occidentalism in the guise of a modernized lifeworld and the values and ideologies routinely inscribed in it sets limits to one's understanding and vision. These limits continue to apply in those spaces once subjected to the imperial project of Europe. When we examine the range of intellectual activity which has been recruited for the field of postcoloniality, it is important to recognize the contribution that artists, novelists, poets and musicians have made as producers of the critical and dissident culture which brings occidentalism to crisis.[27] It can be argued that this kind of work, entering into the system of production of the culture of modernity generally, as a counter-culture of modernity, acts, and has acted, as virus, infecting and changing modernity from within, making visible the lines of fracture, precipitating the kind of self-questioning that undermines its authority and self-assurance.[28] Postcolonial critique must include the non-theoretical work, produced outside the 'teaching machine', without which it would run on empty, theory lacking the vigour and fury of the 'lived', expressed in the arts of resistance.

Is there not another side to this functioning of the 'Black Arts', the side of their positivity, standing for the demonstration of the humanity of Europe's 'others', and which thus acts as remedy, not so much to cure Europe's ailment, but to heal the wounds that the violences of occidentalism inflict, turning the poison of oppression against itself? Derrida, playing on the notion of *pharmakon* in *Dissemination*, develops precisely the double-edged characteristic of the kind of discourse that remedies but, in the wrong measure, could equally poison. He cites this passage from Phaedra in order to reconstruct the chain of signification which the term *pharmakon* solicits in the discourse of Plato: 'Here, O King, says Theuth, is a knowledge which will have the effect of making the Egyptians wiser and more able to remember themselves: memory as well as instruction have found their remedy (*pharmakon*)' (1972: 109). Derrida picks on the ambiguities in the meaning of *pharmakon* which diegetic consideration of the text discloses, so that *pharmakon* invokes at another level the sense of poison.

Thus, in its inversion, it functions as the 'dangerous supplement'. It is tied to a knowledge, to a game of truth:

> The inverted *pharmakon*, which puts to flight every image of dread, is none other than the origin of the episteme, the opening towards truth as the possibility of the repetition and submission of the 'fury to live' to the law (to property, to the father, to the king, to the leader, to capital, to the invisible sun). (1972: 140)

Knowledge can prove to be the best medicine, provided one wishes to cure the whole person, both body and mind. The chain of signification which Derrida brings out links up knowledge, truth, memory, philosophy or critical thought with the idea of remedy and antidote, in other words, with the idea of a wise judgement of differences: '*Pharmakon* is the movement, the site and the play of (the production of) difference. It is the *différance* of difference' (1972: 146).

The thought which these reflections of Derrida prompts concerns the possibility of a knowledge, a critical practice activated inside/outside the discourse of modernity that would counter the poison secreted by the epistemic and ontological violences associated with the totalizing discourses of the modern form of subjugation, a practice which works by way of a rememoration. Aside from counter-hegemonic discourses, indeed as their other side, I have in mind, for example, the process of rememoration evoked in Toni Morrison's *Beloved*, which I will discuss in relation to the transfigurative effects of the work of art, in Chapter 4. Morrison has examined this process by reference to the role of music in particular, when she argues that 'Black Americans were sustained and healed and nurtured by the translation of their experience into art, above all in the music' (in Gilroy, 1993b: 181). She stresses the connection between the responsibility of the artist/intellectual and a language that preserves yet refigures through a rememoration the history and the experience of oppression. The turn to history is a responsibility as well as a way of coming to terms with the past which she describes as 'learning to grow' (in Gilroy, 1993b: 179), implying that it is a form of enlightenment. One can extend this argument to include a great deal of other works which have this effect of a curative renarrativization of what has come to pass – clearly, not just for the 'postcolonial'. In this sense, the postcolonial is a *pharmakon*, acting as poison or cure, depending on the circumstances and the target, obliging us to attend to the judgement of the just measure. It indicates the space of a cultural practice that participates in 'decolonizing the mind', that is to say, in the work of refiguration and transfiguration. The subjective level of this process allows us to think of the connections which can be made to the point of view of narrative identity, so that the question of social transformation and agency cannot avoid passing through the question of the who of action. Our attention is thus directed to the problem of subjectivity, and, further down the road, the issue of political culture and narratives of emancipation and the idea of justice.

The postcolonial, then, is also an attitude and a point of view, inscribed in a critical intervention in the disjunctive cultural spaces of modernity, seeking the reformulation of the grounds informing the idea of the future as the becoming-ethical of human societies.

Colonial and imperial governance

One of my aims in this book is to try to theorize modernity in a way which fully includes the encounter with the regions colonized by Europe and breaks with the Eurocentric and occidentalist presuppositions which the focus on the conventional discourse of modernity otherwise imports into the analysis; one can then think the 'post' of the postmodern by reference to a postcoloniality. There are risks that have to be taken, particularly that of appearing to dissolve the differences which have existed and which continue to have effects on the history of the different regions involved. It is clear, for example, that, today, the ethnic conflicts in India are quite distinct from those in Nigeria, and that the history of modernization in these two regions has been significantly different. Similarly the initial conditions in the variety of places which Europe colonized – relating to cultural, religious, economic, social and political specificities, and the power relations and relations of oppression inscribed in them, and relating also to geography and time – mean that the effects of modernity across the world show mutations that invalidate certain kinds of generalizations. Nevertheless, there are aspects of the process that enable one to look for common features and trends. The fact of capitalism as a force acting globally, and the interest of colonial domination, have amplified the common elements which validate the standpoint of plural modernities, each related by what they have inherited of the fundamental parameters of modernity as an epoch. The case of imperial governmentality will clarify what is at stake.

The reason for examining the genealogy of an imperial governmentality derives from the postcolonial reality that the technologies for constituting the social which began to emerge with imperial governmentality, then spread to Europe with the sciences and technologies of the social to form the modern apparatuses of formation, disciplining and regulation, have become more widely established and more deeply embedded in the machinery of postcolonial governance. The result has been to naturalize the rightfulness or assumed superiority of certain knowledges, know-how and practices, for example, to do with modern medicine and administrative systems. These apparatuses inscribe the authority of particular knowledges, for example those produced in the natural sciences, or the legitimacy of particular laws and rights, for instance regulating the ownership of property and labour practices, or the legislative system and the system of representation, as in parliamentary democracy.

This naturalization and normalization is pursued under the guise of modernization, mostly seen as an intrinsic good, especially by those formed

by Western education. This is probably the most significant basis on which
something like a Western hegemony is reproduced. It works not just on the
strength of authoritative discourses but because of several other elements.
First, there is the alliance with local owners and managers of capital
validated in the agreement to play the game according to the rules of global
capitalism, policed by transnational institutions like the World Bank, the
International Monetary Fund, existing international laws, for example
about patenting and licensing, the workings of the stock markets, and
diplomatic, economic and military incentives and threats. The history of
post-independence Tanzania or of Chile under Allende are good cases of
how neo-imperial policing and geo-political interests operate to prevent
developments that breach the rules.

Second, the narratives that authorize the idea of modernity as a project
of the planned and possible social and ethical progress of humanity as a
whole are either not properly understood or left out or rejected as belonging to Western strategies for cultural hegemony, except amongst an elite
of intellectuals. The loss of faith in the great political doctrines which
expressed these narratives, namely liberalism and Marxism, has altered the
historical basis of the legitimation of power in modernity. The relationship
between modernity and modernization has become one of performativity:
modernity is what is effected through modernization. No other criteria are
brought to bear in judging the rightfulness of decisions and the direction of
development. Added to the existence of a thin or *de jure* nationalism – and
the consequent fragile or simulacral character of the we who authorize state
power – and procedural but ineffective democracy in many ex-colonies,
modernization takes the form of the improvement in the technical and
economic efficiency of existing practices, increasingly framed by neo-
liberalist thinking. This dystopian modernization cannot challenge the
status quo since it cannot articulate the basis for such a challenge.

Third, one needs to add the effects of the mediatization of practices of
signification and representation and their globalization, itself consistent
with the historical thrust of modernization and capitalist rationalization.
To the extent that these practices inscribe existing relations of power, both
local and between states, public culture and political culture are reduced to
the workings of these new machineries; everything else is effectively disempowered, either through repression or marginalization.

Perhaps the most important effect of imperial governance concerns the
continuing effects of the disjunctures produced at the level of political
culture, the economy, the community, the legitimation of power which its
operation instituted and institutionalized.

Imperial governmentality

Let us contrast two conclusions regarding the constitution of a properly
modern economy of power. To begin with, Michel Foucault's genealogy of

the emergence of a new technology of government, a 'governmentality' characterized by the articulation of three elements: 'The pastoral, the new diplomatic and military techniques and, lastly, police: these are the three elements that formed the basis for the production of this phenomenon, fundamental in Western history, of the governmentalization of the state' (Foucault, 1979: 21). Foucault's analysis of modern governance is vital for an understanding of modernity, yet his analysis hardly mentions the fact of colonization as a central feature of the conditions in which a new, modern form of government appears in Europe.

If we turn to Edward Said's (1993) analysis of the relationship betweeen culture and imperialism, we find him interrogating classics of Western literature like Jane Austen's *Mansfield Park* (1814) to establish how the values and ideologies operating 'outside' in the plantations of the English empire come to constitute the 'inside' of the English upper-class household in the form of a 'disposition'. He tells us that Austen

> synchronizes domestic with international authority, making it plain that the values associated with such higher things as ordination, law, and propriety must be grounded firmly in actual rule over and possession of territory. She sees clearly that to hold and rule Mansfield Park is to hold and rule an imperial estate in close, not to say inevitable association. What assures the domestic tranquillity and attractive harmony of one is the productivity and regulated discipline of the other. (1993: 104)

I have contrasted these two positions not simply in order to point to the 'forgetting' of the moment of colonialism in the institution of modernity or the neglect of the colonial dimension in Foucault, symptomatic as this is (see Bhabha, 1994: 171–97). My aim is to use this disjunction to explore what this and other forgettings might have to tell us in refiguring a history of modernity, and in refiguring it in relation to colonial and postcolonial subjectivity.

Foucault's analysis of power belongs to the broader analysis of the specificity of modernity as a period. His genealogy of governmentality picks out the mutations in the discourse of the state from the Middle Ages, highlighting the shift from a concern with the proper conduct of the prince to the development, from the sixteenth to the end of the eighteenth centuries, of an 'art of government' when the concept of government becomes the focus of a problematization that ranges over questions to do with: 'How to govern oneself, how to be governed, how to govern others, how to accept him who is to govern us, how to become the best governor, etc.' (Foucault, 1979: 5).[29] For Foucault, two processes enframe the development of the new economy of power, namely, that tied to the dissolution of the feudal state, and the process concerned with the question of spiritual conduct and salvation. The new problematic of government is formed at the intersection of these questions. One text, Machiavelli's *The Prince* (1532), is central to these debates, whether as the negative point of reference for those opposed to Machiavelli's view, or as the politically realist text that sets out the pragmatic rules for maintaining power. The main bone of contention, from the point of view of those who objected to the relationship of externality that the Machiavellian prince establishes with respect to the governed, seems to be centred on the absence of the relation of care that the (Christian) sovereign is meant to have for his subjects. The Church, as we know, underwrote the moral and political authority of the sovereign in the long-standing affiliation of Church and state. The reconciliation of the idea of a Christian order and the secular administration of things gradually emerged in the idea of pastoral power. According to Foucault (1982), from around the eighteenth century the principle of a Christian responsibility for salvation becomes inscribed in the form of a pastoral power, working at the level of a whole community as well as targeting individuals.

The problem that immediately arises concerning colonial and imperial power is the different genealogy that charts the passage from the Machiavellian power exercised in the period of conquest, and of rule by terror (see also Taussig, 1987), to the Enlightenment variation of pastoral power expressed in the ideology of a European 'mission civilisatrice' cashed out in the form of a tutelage. From the nineteenth century, imperial governmentality invents the new, modern technologies of the social, yet combines it with pre-existing strategies of power to constitute hybrid regimes that are locally specific. Colonized populations are reconstituted in terms of segments that function differently with regard to the exercise of power, for instance either recruited as strategic allies in the case of amenable local elites (for example, the Indian elite), categorized as adversaries to be eliminated (for example, Native Americans), or chosen as a potential source of labour to be domesticated (peasants throughout the colonies). This has important consequences for the analysis of postcoloniality and of the implantation of modernity, as we shall see.

First, I need to spell out elements of Foucault's analysis of the emergence of the modern form of state power that will enable me to examine these hybrid regimes. His genealogical reconstruction of governmentality distinguishes two thresholds in the shift from an art of government based on moral principles and the model of the family to a governmentality founded on rational principles intrinsic to the state, based on the model of political economy, that is, based on the principles of contract, natural propensities and inclinations, general will. The first is mercantilism, entailing the development of 'a savoir which pertains to the state and can be used as a tactic of government' (1982: 15). It does not yet mark a shift from the idea of sovereign power since it utilizes laws, decrees, regulations, that are the traditional instruments of sovereignty.

The next threshold, coinciding with the demographic expansion of the eighteenth century, sees the emergence of a concept of population as the 'ultimate end of government' (1982: 17). The population is brought within the sphere of the economy by means of the new instruments of statistics which establish its regularities and tabulate its characteristics, for instance its rate of mortality, its birth rate, its geographical distribution, its habits of consumption, and so on. Gradually, the purpose of government is seen to be that of ensuring the welfare of the population by attending to the means for improving its productivity, its wealth and its health, and, more generally, its well-being and its security. The development of the notion of 'police' is a central element, addressing problems of poverty and pauperism, health and hygiene, public morality and public order, the security of the physical environment (see, for example, Procacci, 1978).

I think it is important to point out another set of intersections omitted by Foucault, notably: between an economy of the soul, which has a basis in the Calvinist organization of the social, as in Geneva from 1541; an economy of labour, on the model advocated by William Petty, co-founder, with Robert Boyle, of the Royal Society (1662), organized around a strict division of labour and the hierarchization of productive activity consistent with Baconian rules of rational and mechanical planning; and a political economy based on the principles of management pioneered by the same Petty in the course of his colonial survey of Ireland – the Down Survey – and which he systematized in his *Political Arithmetic* of 1682. One objective and incentive for the Down Survey was the redistribution of Irish land to English colonizers. Thus, from around the middle of the seventeenth century, colonialism, capitalism, the new science and the new form of government are tied in a relation of co-articulation. The new economies which emerge occupy the terrain of a new order which a mathematization attempts to universalize and which characterizes the discourse of early modernity. Curiously, the functioning of a *mathesis* in the 'classical episteme', alongside a *taxonomia* and a genetic analysis, is something that Foucault himself has explored in *The Order of Things* (1970).

In spite of these 'forgettings', the benefit of Foucault's analysis of governmentality is the idea that a disciplining power puts in place mechanisms that individualize its exercise – that is, it operates as subjection and subjectification. The notion of governmentality enables us to examine the process of the formation of subjectivity in relation to the more globalized forms of power that emerged with modernity. It also, paradoxically, enables me to do two related things: to add a dimension to the analysis of the conditions of emergence of the modern period that the neglect of colonialism and of imperialism has obscured; and to reconstruct the different apparatuses of subjection/subjectification instituted on colonial soil, such as through the work of the missions, the introduction of European education and pedagogy, the shaping of the social through legal and administrative tactics, the elaboration of a '*savoir*' in colonial discourse that supported and authorized the 'worlding' of the colonial world that we now have to deconstruct. One of the points I would like to establish is that imperial governmentality itself functioned in the place of hegemony, that is to say, that a form of governance emerged with imperialism that combined elements of what Foucault calls governmentality with the visible deployment of military force and with indigenous structures of power founded on different, traditional mechanisms of legimation. One important aspect of imperial governmentality is the extent to which the relation of power to the population as a whole remained largely one characterized by externality. There are important lessons to be drawn from this in accounting for conditions in the period after formal independence, for instance concerning the continuing effectivity of these technologies, and the often lethal break-up of former colonial territories, once colonial authority no longer hold together the often arbitrary territorial aggregates that had constituted colonial states, as has happened in India, Nigeria, Sudan, Rwanda and many more ex-colonies.

Let us try to use Foucault's analytical concepts as a check-list to examine the main elements of the imperial technology of power. One initial distinction that I would like to signal is that between colonialism and imperialism, both as a system of subjugation and in terms of periodization. I agree with Said's view that imperialism should be located not towards the end of the nineteenth century – for example, with the 'scramble for Africa' from the 1880s – but with the emergence towards the end of the eighteenth century of the project which aimed at the 'complete subordination of colony to the metropolis' (Said, 1993: 108). Said's argument is worth repeating because it also points to the correlations with several other developments that provide key parameters for understanding the specificity of modernity as a world-historical and world-transforming project. He says:

> A closer look at the cultural actuality reveals a much earlier, more deeply and stubbornly held view about overseas European hegemony; we can locate a coherent, fully mobilized system of ideas near the end of the eighteenth century, and there follows the set of integral developments such as the first great systematic conquests under Napoleon, the rise of nationalism and the European nation-state, the advent of large-scale industrialization, and the consolidation of power in the bourgeoisie. This is also the period in which the novel form and the new historical narrative become pre-eminent, and in which the importance of subjectivity to historical time takes firm form. (1993: 68–9)

The point of the distinction between a colonial and an imperial regime is to suggest that it is possible to relate Western imperialism to the shifts that Foucault explores in terms of the form of power he characterizes as governmentality. The advantage is that the relationship with the project of the Enlightenment can be differently conceptualized. In particular, the affiliations between subjugation on a global scale and the universal reach of the Enlightenment project is opened up for an interrogation in terms of the translation of the ideals of the Enlightenment into the ideology of a civilizing mission. We can then explore how far the new government of the soul, and the ontology of being with which it is bound, become part of an imperial imaginary and are implanted in the colonized world. For instance, by reference to the idea of occidentalism that I am developing, the project of subjugation comes to be framed within a 'Manichaen aesthetics', as JanMohamed (1983, 1986) has argued; it is an idea that has implications for Western and colonial subjectivity.

In the third chapter, I establish the grounds for claiming that Europe's encounter with the 'new world' is the inaugural event of modernity.

Todorov (1992), for instance, in his admirable narrative of the conquest of America, considers 1492 to 'mark the beginning of the modern era', for the conquest 'heralds and establishes our present identity' (1992: 5). It is so because the conquest of the New World is an event of the othering of that which is not Europe which at one and the same time refigures Europe's identity. The story is a complicated one, irreducible to single events, or simple periodization. It is also a totally unique historical moment because it is an encounter with what had not and could not be imagined before, and because of the degree of cruelty with which the peoples of the New World were exploited and destroyed. Todorov writes it as a history of the present, his interest being that of the moralist rather than that of the historian, so that his underlying concern is the ethical question of 'how to deal with the other?' (1992: 4). There are some interesting juxtapositions with Foucault to the extent that Todorov describes the details of the barbaric calculations and dealings that the early colonizers made in conquering that world and putting it to the service of creating wealth for Europe without the slightest regard for the well-being of the Native Americans. Cortés, the Conquista-dor, proves to be the Machiavelli of the New World, for instance in his employment of a tactical combination of force, subterfuge, terror, auth-ority, trickery, in subduing the Aztecs at the beginning of the sixteenth century. The relationship is one of pure externality: the Native Americans are construed as a satanic offence to the Christian God, reduced to the status of objects, deprived of humanity, indeed, considered less than beasts and treated accordingly. Even so, there is an effort to know this other, but it is an 'understanding-that-kills', locked into the logic whereby 'destruction becomes possible because of this understanding . . . [and] . . . grasping leads to taking and taking to destruction' (1992: 127). One of Todorov's conclu-sions is that massacre is symptomatic of this phase of colonization; it is the consequence of conceptualizing the other as utterly different, and of the eradication of all bonds of responsibility for one's others in the colonial context.[30] The Nazis, in reconstituting the ethnic identity of the Germans in terms of the 'master race', operated within that same imaginary, reducing its others to the category of degenerate sub-humans who could be exter-minated like vermin. The judgement of Todorov is that '[t]he barbarity of the Spaniards has nothing atavistic or bestial about it; it is quite human and heralds the advent of modern times' (1992: 145). The view expressed here is the relation drawn between modernity and terror, modernity and death, which reappears in different guises in the discourse of the Enlightenment. Taussig (1987) has amply demonstrated this relation concerning the Native Americans, a relation that persists in the frequent episodes of massacre which occur to this day in Latin America, as the case of the Chiapas reminds us.

For now, a question surfaces that brings me back to the issue of how the colonized 'other' of Europe came to be constituted as internal for Western culture, when, according to J.S. Mill, a country like the West Indies could be regarded as a place where England finds it convenient to carry on the production of sugar, coffee and a few other tropical commodities. All the capital employed is English capital; almost all the industry is carried out for English uses; . . . [The] trade with the West Indies is hardly to be considered an external trade but more resembles the traffic between town and country. (*Principles of Political Economy*, quoted in Said, 1993: 108)

Equally, Adam Smith (1812 [1776]: Book 4, chp. 7) could put the benefits of colonialism in the equation for calculating the wealth of nations and in arriving at the conclusion that the internal economy of a (European) country is inextricably bound up with the extent to which it is able to maximize profits from its colonies. The question concerns the form of rule and the form of power exercised in the colonies before this time of integration into one administrative and economic unit, that is, before the time of empire; the latter is also the time when the imperial countries reconstitute the notion of nation – for instance Englishness – in terms of an idea of empire, that is, by reference to something exterior to it but over which it exercises a dominion that becomes constitutive of its own identity.

It is important to emphasize at the outset that we are talking here about different durations, different conditions and different strategies, as for example between the Americas and India or Australia, and between the French and the English. Yet it is possible to propose that the form of power is closer to the model of sovereignty discussed by Foucault. We should not forget that the aim of colonial power was to take possession, to accumulate land, to put the people and the resources to work for Europe, to establish the authority and rights of the new owners. It is a power over life, exemplarily exercised on the slave plantations, where the master had complete power over the slave's body and could decree death as an expression of his will. There is nothing pastoral in its conception. The support that colonial regimes provided for the Christianizing mission worked so well as ideological cover for genocide and dispossession, and in grounding the moral authority of the new masters, that one cannot accept the argument that evangelization was the main motive for conquest. The arguments advanced by some church authorities to legitimate war against a people which had presented no threat functioned admirably in demonizing the colonized and in precipitating their subordination, as demonstrated by the debate between Sepulveda and Las Casas at Valladolid in 1550.[31] The universal claims of monotheism, that all are equally children of God, only succeeds in erasing the difference of the other by refiguring the other within the conceptual framework of the philosophy of identity; the other can only be saved by becoming Christian, otherwise s/he remains a 'barbarian outcast', outside the family of man, or, indeed, the vessel for the work of the Devil.

What conditions made possible the emergence of a properly imperial governmentality, that is to say, one that takes as its object a population as a whole that it in fact constitutes at the level of both the collectivity and the individual subject, and whose conduct it seeks to normalize? How far does it depart from Foucault's model? To start with, I should note that Foucault, in differentiating between the modern form of power and other forms, does not propose either a progression from one to the other or a system of mutually exclusive forms and interests. Struggles against forms of ethnic domination, against exploitation and against forms of subjection tend to co-exist. However, because of the emergence of pastoral power, he believes that the struggles against forms of subjection have become increasingly the mode in which in contemporary times we live the effects of the mechanisms of power, although he does make the point that 'the mechanisms of subjection cannot be studied outside their relation to the mechanisms of exploitation and domination' (Foucault, 1982: 213).

It is clear that the focus of Foucault in analysing the modern technology of power derives from his assessment of the apparatuses that have started to appear since the Enlightenment which seek to institute the modern social order primarily by constituting particular subjectivities The machinery of disciplining, regulation and normalization requires a knowledge of 'the inside of people's minds. . . . It implies a knowledge of their conscience and an ability to direct it' (1982: 214). In that sense the new pastoral power is a 'government of the soul', as Nikolas Rose (1989) has suggested, operating through bodies and behaviour, ensuring the worldly well-being of the individual. In its contemporary form, it is encapsulated in the promise that, in exchange for conformity to the norms of good order and for self-discipline, the welfare state will care for the citizen 'from the cradle to the grave', as William Beveridge put it.

I think the context of the Enlightenment is important for other reasons when analysing imperialism. I noted at the start that Foucault (1984c) rephrases Kant's question about the Enlightenment in terms of who are we in the present, thus displacing the question onto the terrain of ontology, specifically of a 'critical ontology'. We know that Foucault would answer the question by proposing an ethics and an aesthetics of existence, which I will interrogate in Chapter 4. Kant's emphasis draws attention to 'man's release from self-incurred tutelage' (1992 [1784]: 90) and the primacy of freedom: 'For this enlightenment, however, nothing is required but freedom, and freedom of the most harmless sort among its various definitions: freedom to make public use of one's reason at every point' (1992 [1784]: 92). The terms 'freedom' and 'tutelage' are significant when we think of the age of slavery and of the subjection of colonized peoples in which Kant's reflection appears. Derrida has perceptively remarked that Kant naturalizes European hegemony through a

teleological ruse of nature [whereby] Greco-Roman Europe, Western philosophy and history, I would even venture to say continental philosophy and history, play a determining, central, exemplary role, as if nature, in its rational ruse, had given Europe responsibility for this special mission: not only to found history as such, and primarily as science, not only to found philosophy as such, and primarily as science, but also to found a rational (non-romanesque) philosophical history and to 'one day give laws' to all the other continents. (1997: 26–7)

Another juxtaposition will introduce a dimension to my analysis of imperial governance that might otherwise obscure the complexity of the conditions of its emergence and make us miss the link to the question of subjectivity, or, rather, make us read the question of subjectivity in terms of a process of constitution by reference alone to the externality of the mechanisms, that is to say, by reference to how an outside comes to be inscribed as, and occupy, an inside.

Toni Morrison (1992), reflecting on the formation of the American imaginary in the period of the Enlightenment and American independence, points to the contrast between, on the one side, the Old World of poverty, oppression and the limitation to freedom and, on the other side, the New World of possibilities and dreams. In particular, for the colonizer escaping from Europe, '[p]ower – control of one's own destiny – would replace the powerlessness felt at the gates of class, caste, and cunning persecution. One could move from discipline and punishment to disciplining and punishing' (1992: 35).

Can we not detect in the priority accorded to freedom and autonomy in Enlightenment discourse the projections of a troubled and beseiged consciousness? Can we not also see in the emergence of an idea of a universal project that would liberate humanity from tutelage and limitations, the desire to take charge of one's destiny and align it with a world-historical transformation that also becomes the destiny of Europe? Its exorbitant expression is to be found in the idea of 'manifest destiny' that, in the nineteenth century, underwrote white America's appropriation and transformation of the Native American lands, renamed the 'West', in the name of a divinely sanctioned progress.

In contrast with the enlarged view of the emergence of modernity that I am reconstructing, the conventional history of the Enlightenment tends to attend to the ideas themselves that tried to establish the principles of a new, rational order, an order constructed in accordance with the knowledge which the methodical exercise of a reason freed from the shadows of myth is supposed to deliver.[32] I have in mind a broader picture in which to cast Kant's reflections of 1784. Let us remind ourselves that the greater part of the eighteenth century covers the beginning of industrialization, the growth of towns, the consolidation and expansion of trade, banking and insurance, the setting up of quasi-governmental companies like the East India Company and the Compagnie des Indes that undertake the colonization of the East, the growth in the power of an emergent bourgeoisie whose bases of power extend throughout the colonies. Most of the major European countries participate in the colonial enterprise, except for Germany and Italy, precisely the countries without overseas empire tempted later to join the club and to construct the great nation-state through National Socialism, making race = nation = identity the principle in which to seek the becoming of the people.[33] This period saw the most extraordinary flowering of the arts, the sciences and technology, alongside the transformation of nature which occurs with the extensive development of new modes of transport and communication, agricultural revolutions that altered for good the lands and landscape throughout most of the world. The great migrations and forced displacement of peoples across continents set in motion a process of hybridization more intense and widespread than at any other period in world history.

The drift of my analysis is to draw from the history of colonization in order to point to the actuality of a universal, global, world-transforming project undertaken at first with nothing more in mind than loot, adventure, the craving for riches, the winning of a longed-for freedom, but increasingly organized according to a vision of Europe as the chosen vessel for the 'sure march' of humanity towards maturity. It is not only the ideas of, for instance, a *mathesis universalis* (Leibniz, in Horkheimer and Adorno, 1979: 7) or the possibility of a rationally ordered social order that motivate and confirm the soundness of the vision. It is the reality of what, by the mid-1750s, had already been accomplished, the new knowledges produced – of peoples and cultures, of geography and plant and animal species, of new materials and products, of government – the new wealth created, the supremacy assured in the New World and, less securely, in parts of Asia. Europe learned to depict and to shape the world into the image of its fantasy of itself and to make it serve its ends. That representation is an intrinsic element of the history of the becoming-West of Europe that I call occidentalism.

This greatest period of change is also increasingly the age of radical conflicts on the political and cultural terrain alike; it is an age of revolution, as Hobsbawm (1962) has characterized it in his analysis of the century from the 1750s to just after 1848. The rumour of revolution comes from the discontented masses or the 'dangerous classes', whose existence remained as wretched as ever, and from those intellectuals who regard freedom and liberty to be inseparable from the exercise of a secular reason and who envisage the ends of social progress to be consistent with an egalitarian justice. For instance, Rousseau, Diderot and Herder, for different reasons, condemn colonialism and slavery, as did many other intellectuals who belonged to the age of Enlightenment.

The conditions of possibility of the modern form of governance include both the fact of resistance and rebellion, in Europe and in the plantations and estates in the colonies, and the search for the mechanisms of the disciplining and rational administration of people. What emerges from this period is a new notion of the social, as a domain amenable to normalization and regulation through the exercise of power. I am going to argue that the notion of the social constituted in the colonies is quite different from that which emerges in the nineteenth century in Europe and sections of America. To begin with, I think the idea of a pastoral power does not have the same force, even in the form of a civilizing mission. Imperial power remains external to the social body. It targets different groups differently, it makes an accommodation with existing elites, as I have noted, leaving in place existing mechanisms of power. Westernization is a tactic for forming an administrative and military cadre with limited access to the machinery of power. Other groups and communities are not drawn within this orbit, but are left to renegotiate their position relative to the elite (see Chakrabarty, 1988). Customs, old relations of power and privilege change little, except that the former elites now derive their authority from both traditional and colonial narratives and devices of legitimation. Dangarembga's novel *Nervous Conditions* (1988), admirably illustrates the legacy of this feature of colonial power. The subaltern in the colonies is a divided and fractured combination of traditional social groupings to which have been grafted the new class of traders and petty state functionaries and a growing industrial working class. The colonial state itself is often made up of contingently annexed territories organized in an administrative unit. In the circumstances, the imaginary community of this nation-state is a very unstable artifice united only as a performative device for administrative and accounting practices; in the imaginary of the oppressed, it often functions as a virtual community, or a legal fiction.[34]

The absence of a pastoral form of power, or its existence in the form of a tutelage, and the absence of a sense of a contractual obligation undertaken on behalf of the represented means that imperial governance is primarily concerned not with constituting the social, but with the partial constitution and management of a segment of the population for its own ends. The relation of externality of government with respect to the governed marks the exercise of sovereign power which suited imperialism.[35]

However, imperial governance develops elements of the form of power Foucault calls governmentality. This concerns the mechanisms and strategies of power directed at the section of the colonized population which could be reconstituted as a local bourgeoisie and an indigenous administrative cadre, functioning as vassals. The apparatuses for this subjectifying process include the educational system, the legal system, the process of training and recruitment into the lower echelons of the administration and the army, the disciplining of a labour force for the new industries like mining and new practices of production. The effects of these mechanisms are paradoxical, for the same process also produced resistance to it and formed the many Westernized intellectuals who have led the liberation movements throughout the European empires, leaders who belonged to both cultures, though often living their split subjectivity in the form of a double-consciousness, as Du Bois and others have explored (see the analysis in Gilroy, 1993a).

So how does disciplining work for the colonized? The first thing is that the mechanisms target a subject categorized as other. It is an other that the process of formation would transform into more or less the same as Western man: that is to say, make into 'white-but-not-quite', as Homi Bhabha (1994) has put it in his analysis of mimicry. It is a process fraught with ambivalences and anxieties. Clearly, mechanisms for othering the other were already in place, inscribed in colonial discourse and in systems of colonialist exclusion in existence well before the nineteenth century. In any case, subjectification requires that one must know, or presume to know, the other in order to transform or re-form 'him'. From the beginning, in 1492, as Todorov (1992) has shown, there is a massive production of discourse about the colonized and their world; it was part of the process of taking possession and subjugating.

By and large, much of colonialist knowledge of Europe's others was framed within the axis described as a Manichean allegory by Abdul JanMohamed, that is, 'a field of diverse yet interchangeable oppositions between white and black, good and evil, superiority and inferiority, civilization and savagery, intelligence and emotion, rationality and sensuality, self and Other, subject and object' (1986: 82). This binarism was more clearly operative in the common-sense idiom of Europeans. A more complicated, and more unstable, narrative of the colonized emerges when we consider the radical discourse of modernity and the fiction that narrativizes the encounter between Europe and older civilizations like those of India and Egypt. Suleri, analysing English India, emphasizes how much colonial facts 'fail to cohere around the master-myth that proclaims static lines of demarcation between imperial power and disempowered culture', but instead belong to an 'unsettling economy of complicity and guilt' (1992: 3). This economy becomes clearer when we pay attention to the machinery of governance, and to the paradoxes and ambivalences in the Enlightenment discourse of rights, liberty, equality, freedom and justice.

We should also remember the quote from Balfour's speech to the House of Commons in 1910 that begins Edward Said's interrogation of Orientalism, in which Balfour rebukes those who would speak simply in terms of superiority and inferiority when it comes to once 'great races' like that of Egypt; yet he goes on in the speech to support England's self-appointed role of absolute government over Egypt on the grounds that it would benefit both them and 'the whole of the civilized West' because 'We know the civilization of Egypt better than we know the civilization of any other country' (in Said, 1978: 32). The central Baconian theme of knowledge and power is clearly stated there, Said tells us. More specifically, the legitimation of domination on the grounds of superior knowledge draws attention to the analytique of power/knowledge, a standpoint which returns us to the question of the discourses and the technologies in which modern forms of power are exercised and which participate in instituting the social.[36]

If the model of pastoral power does not quite fit the form of power in imperial governance, what modifications of Foucault's notion of governmentality are needed and which missing bits should we add? I want to point to two fundamental elements. First, I think that the explicit or implicit functioning of a notion of contract or deal is vital in elaborating a more complete picture. Whilst contract and constitution underwrite the legitimacy of power in nineteenth-century England or France, they do not operate in the imperial situation. The notion of a civilizing mission is a decidedly one-sided and paternalistic aim. The absence of contract, and a national community based on shared and agreed interest, has meant that post-independence states had to invent constitutional arrangements that often rested on weak or thin nationalism, or, in some cases, copied or grafted inappropriate Western models. Such arrangements only reinforce existing relations of power and divisions.

The other important factor in analysing the mechanism for instituting the social, concerns the notion of community, and the concomitant relation of community to nation and to the modern state, expressed in the phrase authorizing power: 'we the people'. In Enlightenment discourse, the ideal of community is posited in the notion of a *sensus communis* that Kant notably developed. With Foucault (1982: 220), it is implied in the boundedness of a population targeted and normalized by power, since such a population is constituted by all those whose action power recognizes, that being a condition for power to have an effect on their conduct. One must think of community in the sense also of an historically constituted unity of a people because, if, as Foucault explains (1982: 214), pastoral power is the mutated form of the ecclesiastical function of the Christian pastorate, then we need to take into account the fact that one of the essential aims of the pastorate was to build a Christian community in the form of a collectivity or flock, that is, in the form of an ethical community. In the condition of imperial governance, the will of the people is a deferred one, that is, it is the will imputed to the people in a time to come, if and when the colonized become sufficiently 'developed' to recognize that the tutelage of the 'mother nation' was in their best interest: it is what they would have wished. In the imaginary of the colonizer, the representative of the community is ideally the 'educated' elite: the 'good', because respectful and Westernized, colonial. So imperial governance does not constitute communities. The colonized did so themselves, instituted through practices of the everyday, and, later, in the course of the struggle for political autonomy. Differences were often buried which reappeared later, incited by exploitative forces operating locally and globally.

I would add to this analysis the fact that the unity of community has the character of narration, sedimented in a history of the community and in a memory. To the imagined dimension of the narration of a people must be added the materiality or worldliness of a constituted lifeworld in which embodied subjects enact the inter-subjective density of real communities. The lifeworld is an historically particularized entity. The past of the community, its achievements, the transformations it has wrought to its environment and landscape, the meaning it has constructed and recon-structed of its history, the sedimentation of deeds, events, biographies, in the living memory of language, tradition, customs, sayings, stories, monuments, music, art and writings, the history that dwells in the material world that enframes it and the capacities locked there, the institutions produced in the course of its self-formation, all of this determines a community's 'coming into being' and its specificity as a collectivity. For example, it is this range of mechanisms and cultural objects, activated in the 'practices of everyday life', that give a people their sense of locality and belongingness; it is the archive we must examine to figure out, at any particular point, the Englishness of the English, the Frenchness of the French or the Indianness of the Indians. Clearly, in the period of modernity, the concept of nation operates in this field, gathering to itself in its swollen symbolism the 'social and textual affiliations' (Bhabha, 1990: 292) that weave the space and particularity of the imaginary to constitute a fantasized zone for cultural and subjective identifications. Retroactively, the time of the making of the community is projected into the archaic and timeless idiom of myths, so that it appears as if the community has always been like this, equal to itself in an authentic moment of inauguration.[37] Individual lives are woven into the fabric of the community, which, in a process similar to narrative identity, grows and changes yet remains imaginatively the same.

Historically, the imperial nations of Europe have aligned the concept of nation with metonymies of race, purity, strength, authenticity. Power legitimated itself on the basis of a promise of the prosperity and well-being of the nation, for which discipline and sacrifice were required. Good order and discipline were not themselves the ends of power but the means and conditions for the prosperity and happiness of the people or the citizen. For example, the notion of police in the eighteenth century was tied to the increase of 'public happiness' in the discourse of public administration (see Pasquino, 1978: 44ff.).

Furthermore, the modern imperial Western nation was constituted in relation to empire, both discursively by reference to subjugated subjects which were constituted as other, and in terms of a mastery exercised over other worlds and other peoples in which citizens could recognize the validation of transcendent goals that subsumed individual projects under the greater goal of collective ideals. The building of empire added an extra dimension to individual goals, by making it contribute to the greater, collective objective.[38] For example, the French reconstituted colonial lands as elements of the French Empire, in the form of overseas departments. The strategy of governance was directed at the assimilation of the colonies into French culture and nation-state. Even today, the French have difficulty, administratively, in acknowledging and dealing with cultural difference because of the erasing of difference in the notion of French citizenship and what it means for the relation of the individual to the state. For instance, because the recognition of cultural difference would imply the differentiation of the citizen into different legal categories, and thus fundamentally undermine the juridical status of each citizen and the whole constitution, there has developed no multicultural policy in France.[39]

One example will illustrate the nature of the problem of imperial power in relation to the constitution of subjectivity, and thus in relation to the question of ideology, namely, the role English literature was made to play in supporting British rule in India. I shall draw mainly from Viswanathan's subtle and insightful study of the way in which the development of the Anglicist curriculum, driven by the 'motives of discipline and management

. . . served to confer power, as well as to fortify British rule' (1989: 167). Viswanathan is clear from the outset that the (ideological) work performed by English literature is to cover the 'sordid history of colonialist expropriation, material exploitation, and class and race oppression' (1989: 20) under the 'exalted image of the Englishman as producer of the knowledge that empowers him to conquer, appropriate, and manage in the first place' (1989: 20). To that extent English literature performed rather different, though related, work in the colonial as against the metropolitan situation.

One of the earliest questions concerned the choice of the literary texts that would be appropriate for the task assigned to literature. This task consisted in the twin goals of moral and intellectual education that would dispose the native to look up to the colonizer with the respect and admiration due to a superior intellect and culture. Decisions about the literary canon were enmeshed in judgement of the literary as well as the moral worth of the texts. The moral interest complicates the history of the implantation of English in India, for the secularizing and humanizing orientation of the literature curriculum was often in conflict with the aims of the missionary movement and with the interest of commerce. As Viswanathan explains: 'the introduction of English represented an embattled response to historical and political pressures: to tensions between the East India Company and the English Parliament, between Parliament and missionaries, between the East India Company and the Indian elite' (1989: 10). The English model was therefore inadequate for transplant; new models had to be worked out, guided by the official discourse instituted in the 1813 Charter Act and in the 1835 English Education Act. Thomas Macauley's 1835 'Minute on Education' expresses the bottom line of the policy: 'to form a body of well instructed labourers, competent in their proficiency in English to act as Teachers, Translators and Compilers of useful works for the masses' (quoted in Bhabha, 1994: 106).

These conflicts indicate a more interesting story than the one Foucault tells about the relationship of the pastoral power of governmentality to the Christian Church's aim of salvation. Imperial governance shows the longer history of the displacement from the moral economy of a Christian pastorate to the moralization grounded in the humanist but secular principles of the Enlightenment. Discipline is caught between these two foundations, both in the colonies and in the metropolis, whilst keeping its sights on the more Machiavellian interests of subjugating power.

The actual process of instituting new forms of constituting colonial subjects reveals a somewhat more messy and undecidable state of affairs, for the colonial stage is the place where several fundamental ambivalences in the discourse of the West about itself and its 'others' are worked out, for instance in the conceptualization of the other as both other yet amenable to the same in the suppositions of the universality of the subject, and the other as the abject incarnation of danger, yet also the object of desire. The colonial stage is equally the place where the subjugated ward off the stratagems of the dominating power through camouflages and subterfuges that deflect the mimetic effect of colonial subjectification into the disruptive semblance of the 'not-quite', to repeat one of Bhabha's *bons mots*. Calculations of gains and losses, manoeuvres of escape and capture, plays of desire and loathing, cross each other to ensure that the state of emergency provoked by oppressive power is never lifted: the subjugated is never sure where she stands.[40]

Let us see how this works out. Viswanathan's account details the conflicting pulls of religion and a secular pedagogy focusing on the development of a 'critical sense', highlighting the stakes in this conflict between a policy of alliance with the traditional ruling class and a concomitant respect for Oriental learning – Warren Hastings, Wellesley, Wilberforce (1989: 20), versus the more impersonal bureaucratized and judicial form of administration advocated by the Anglicists – Cornwallis, Macaulay – and, partially overlapping with the Christianizing policy of the Evangelists – Wilberforce, Grant, and others (1989: 36). The period up to 1835 marks the 'historical moment when political philosophy and cultural policy converged to work towards clearly discernible common ends . . . [namely] . . . questions of administrative structure and governance' (1989: 34). This convergence paves the way for the introduction of European knowledge into the curriculum, taught in English, with the aim of producing 'useful learning' (John Stuart Mill). English literature functioned as a mediating device in providing the means for the secular, rational development of a critical sense that prepared the learner for the whole range of European knowledge and the acknowledgement of its authority without appearing to reject the value of education as a moralizing force, for literature could still be seen as 'a secular reinscription of ideas of truth, knowledge, and law derived from the sacred plane' (1989: 95). At stake in this was the emphasis on 'the legitimacy and value of British institution, laws, and government' (1989: 95) and thus the authority of British rule. By the time of Balfour's speech to Parliament in 1910 quoted by Said, authority, power and knowledge have become concepts that refer to each other within the conceptual grid of both imperialism and modern governmentality. But this authority, if it existed in the minds of policy makers and in official discourse, was ever under siege.

I have inserted a rather lengthy survey of the colonial and imperial moment into the analysis of modernity in order to uncouple it from its mooring in the familiar terrain of Western philosophy and social science, to show that it is a mistake to consider the colonial moment simply as context. The history of modernity would have been entirely different without it, as will become even clearer in my account of the birth of the modern subject in the third chapter. It should be clear too that the destiny of the postmodern and the postcolonial have become bound by that same history.

Notes

1 One could think the event called modernity by reference to unconventional examples like Wounded Knee or Amritsar or the Long March, rather than the more familiar French Revolution, that is, the events that have become the proper names for a (marginalized)

community, acting as the signifiers for telling a community's memory in a way that reconstitutes for it, its understanding of itself. It is in that sense too that the event is a signifier of the relation to time.

2 The point is made by Agamben (1991: xi) in his analysis of Heidegger's *Nature of Language*.

3 It would be interesting to explore how far they behave according to the model of dissipative structures; a dissipative structure, like the weather system or the turbulence produced when a liquid flows in a duct, describes a system in a far from equilibrium state, in dynamic interaction with its environment such that adaptive and self-regulative mechanisms operate to reconstitute temporary states of equilibrium. The mathematics of chaos and catastrophe theory provide models and analogies for their conceptualization. (Prigogine and Stengers, 1984; Capra, 1976; Watson, 1998).

4 As an aside, one could note that sociobiologists, in attributing intentionality to things like genes, stray into the domain of metaphysics, while mistakenly believing themselves to be 'scientific'. My suggestions about the co-emergence of language and consciousness are far from the terrain of those who reduce these problems to biological and cybernetic models. (For a critique, see Rose, 1997.)

5 Duration in Bergson is one of the two elemental dimensions which are combined in our experience of the concrete, namely, the spatial and the temporal dimensions. For him, the spatial element is homogeneous in kind, though made up of differences of number, size and quantity, whereas duration refers to quality; it is continuous and mobile, changing into differences of kind. Qualities exist in both our perception of things or consciousness and in things themselves. Duration thus has a psychological as well as a real existence. Bergson also believed there was an absolute ontological duration, or pure duration, which could not be destroyed, and was a dimension of Becoming. (See Bergson, 1991.)

6 Does this view mean that Habermas remains on the terrain of (neo)praxis philosophy, after its deconstruction?

7 This is a revealing slip, consistent with his neglect of difference. Not surprisingly, critiques of occidentalist modernity from other dissident voices, especially from the standpoint of feminist and 'postcolonial' theory, do not merit consideration in his work. For instance, there are but two references in his critique, one to Nancy Fraser's point about the absence of normative criteria for judgement in Foucault, and another to Mary Louise Pratt's early work on speech-act theory which he uses to beat Derrida with. There is no recognition in his analysis of the mutations in modernity in the context of its implantation in the colonies and the varieties of modernity that have developed today.

8 The horrors of re-education in Cambodia in the years of the Pol Pot regime come to mind, and other instances besides.

9 Lyotard gives the example of Humboldt and Kant in his discussion (1984: 32).

10 Canguilhem's work demonstrates the way in which specific material conditions, including the interest of production, have effects for the development of scientific concepts (see Venn, 1982, for details).

11 The distinction between primary and secondary narcissism is that the former is related to the stage before the appearance of the ego, whilst the latter can be related to the mirror stage, thus to the stage of formation of the ego, and the internalization of cathected objects. Secondary narcissism, on this reading, would be the withdrawal of libido from love objects and its redirection to the ego. The aestheticization of the everyday intrinsic to consumer culture feeds that form of narcissism.

12 Some would say, 'Ah! They are all French!', and take comfort in the familiar accusations directed at poststructuralism and the deconstructive turn.

13 We should remember, of course, that Ricoeur and Levinas do not abandon the religious space, though they have tried to remain vigilant in separating the two when engaging with the foundational issues relevant to the analysis of modernity.

14 For the infant, the fact that the other is principally the parent has much to do with the dynamic imbrication of this relation for the process of constitution of subjectivity through identification and so on, a process which is not reducible to the scene of sexualization as in

Freudianism. It is interesting that Winnicott (1963), in his study of the emergence in the infant of the faculty for concern – which we can affiliate with the Heideggerian 'care' – emphasizes the crucial role of the environment-mother, that is to say, the mother who is able to contain the 'aggressive' impulses of the infant and to remain as a source of security and trust, performatively enacting in her action what is meant by concern. Psychoanalysis is limited by the presuppositions about 'normality' in its account of the process of development of subjectivity that harbours elements of individualism, whereas I would emphasize the aspect of apprenticeship, and thus the profoundly inter-subjective and cultural dimension.

15 Regarding socialized matter, see Grosz (1994).

16 For instance, regarding the place of sexuality in the undertanding of the self, we would need to take account of the physical experience of sex, the norms of sexual conduct inscribed in the culture, as well as the broader, more theoretical or philosophical claims made about the relationship of particular sexual activities to gender and kinship, and so on, for example the claims made in psychoanalytic theory or in Christian doctrine.

17 The capitalism that Adam Smith was trying to institute did not match the existing economic practices he was examining, and does not correspond to the state of capitalism today. Another example: a bandit capitalism (its pure form?) has been able to become quickly established in Russia because the previous regime had not put into place the regulating apparatuses, the steering mechanisms, the checks and the institutionalized conduct of agents which elsewhere, at least in Europe or the USA, had ensured that capitalism developed in a particular manner, responsive in decisive ways to publicly defined goods and goals, to do with accountability, redistribution, legal responsibilities, contractual limitations, and so on.

18 Communities may decide to preserve, transform or destroy these traces, although, in any case, they leave traces of traces. A small example: the winding country road we follow traces the course of the path that over long years had shaped the land in particular ways, joining habitations that still exist or have left mementos of their existence in ruins, mounds, the lie of the land, the flora and fauna. The activities of those who have lived there have left the aura of their presence through the things that remain, and the disposition of the 'natural' world, marking the ways in which the environment has been used before and the changes the generations have wrought. The givenness of that world inscrypts a history of activities and attitudes that we appropriate as the ready-to-hand. For instance, I must follow the paths already laid down, though my own activity may result in mutations that in turn will exist, and be experienced, as the givenness of that world. The country lane is a trace of the having-been of whole communities. It belongs, or should belong, to all, as inheritance and condition of possibility.

19 Descartes wanted to eat his theological cake and still have it, saving the principle of salvation for the inevitability of finitude. The discourse of modernity cheats, and has been playing this game of the disavowal of finitude – and of the other, and another kind of dispossession arising from that relation – ever since. Derrida tried to reveal this subterfuge through the analysis of the metaphysics of presence.

20 The archetypal figure of *Homo viator* is Bunyan's Christian in the *Pilgrim's Progress*.

21 Nevertheless, Nietzsche is the last of the modernists, for, although he breaks with the idea of a project grounded in reason, and rejects the *telos* of modernity, he is unable to break away from the solipsistic privilege that self-presence grants to the subject: the *übermensch* still hankers after the divine status of the 'uncaused cause', he is the ultimate autonomous being who owes nothing to anyone or anything. In disavowing finitude, he cannot escape the metaphysics of presence.

22 Fantasized, if we associate presence with plenitude and *jouissance*, the moment of the recovery of lack and loss, overcoming the insufficiency of being.

23 It could be noted that the idea of the primacy of the social is reinforced in the (neglected) work of people like Vygotsky (1986), Luria (1982), Volosinov (1973), Bakhtin (1981), concerning the development of language and consciousness.

24 So, it is not just good and bad objects, but dynamic relations that already fill with content the liminal and sublime dimension of beingness; both, of course, refer to the economy of desire.

25 The unevenness concerns differences in local cultures as well as the degree of colla-boration with local elites and the different degrees to which particular economies were transformed into satellite economies, for instance conditions in the 'banana republics' contrasted with the more complex situation in places like India or Brazil.

26 In her polemical survey of the ambiguities and prevarications of postcolonial analyses, Benita Parry (1997) has criticized the kind of postcolonial work which ignores the effects of the new forms of colonialism and imperialism, and too readily celebrates a diasporic or exilic existence at the expense of the work of the dislocation of the machineries – discursive and material – that were put into place in the period of colonialism and imperialism and that continue to inscribe relations of power that it should be the point of postcolonial critique to disrupt.

27 A short representative list would have to include writers like Salman Rushdie, June Jordan, Ben Okri, Derek Walcott, Toni Morrison, Aimé Césaire, many blues and jazz and 'rock' musicians, populist art, such as the Latin American forms of the memorialization of the 'Disappeared', a large number of 'radical' 'Third World' film makers – see Shohat and Stam, 1994 – and so on.

28 Dissident culture may have equivocal effects in the context of a consumer culture which in some circumstances is capable of ingesting everything, including that which threatens it. It is a new form of cannibalism. Yet without these oppositional voices, the narratives that inform and sustain resistance would not exist.

29 Regarding this period, I think it is worth noting the relationship which Elias (1982) has tried to establish between the interest in disciplining one's passions and impulses as part of a project of self-governance and the process of the monopolization of the legitimate use of violence by the state; an apprenticeship into a form of civility is implicated in this 'civilizing process' whereby non-violent rules of encounter between adversarial parties emerge and the state becomes the ultimate juridical arbiter in disputes and conflict amongst citizens. It must be added that one effect of this development has been to exteriorize violence, directing it against those who do not belong to the state, and who are thus put in a category to which the rules of moral conduct no longer apply. The evidence for this is clear in the process of colonialism.

30 Massacre, it must be admitted, is not unique to the New World; the Romans as well as conquerors the world over made terror into a virtue in colonization.

31 I establish this in detail in the third chapter. (See Todorov, 1992: 151–4.)

32 The discussions of the Enlightenment by Horkheimer and Adorno (1979) and Hulme and Jardanova (1990) reveal the epistemic and ontological oppressions inscribed in such a philosophy.

33 National Socialism is thus not a national project projected outside the nation; it is not the possibility of measuring the greatness of the nation in the scale of empire and mastery over colonized others. It must instead find the proof of salvation and validate its worth inside the nation itself and its every authentic member, though clearly the early victories are read as signs of the greatness and superiority of the German race. The race-nation becomes the intrinsic good that must be purified and developed. Its logic leads without mystery to the Holocaust and the policy of the extermination of 'inferior races' on the Eastern Front.

34 Counter-imperial struggles helped to forge a reality of community that, unfortunately, has become disrupted because of the failures of the national bourgeoisie, a 'narcissistic, ignorant, cynical' class of intermediary agents for capitalism, as Fanon (1967) once put it. The postcolonial period abounds in examples of the failure to constitute a stable imaginary community.

35 As I said above, imperial power combines this form of governance with older, more visible forms of enforcing sovereignty, operating through laws, interdicts, military campaigns, terror, as well as the dividing practices that draw from a longer history of the tactics of subjugation.

36 When we examine this system, we find that the new apparatus of formation is at first mainly that of pedagogy, aiming for assimilation (the French strategy), conversion (the missionary approach) or acculturation (the English aim), centred on the introduction of the humanities curriculum in the empires. The analyses carried out by Bhabha, Viswanathan,

JanMohamed, Spivak, Suleri, sufficiently detail the questions of ambivalence, subalternity, instability and exclusion, and the problem of the stratagems of resistance to what this power/knowledge aims to effect. It is also the case that the strategy of consolidating colonial sub-jugation by means of a process of constituting subjects did not penetrate as thoroughly into vernacular cultures as one might assume, a point that Appiah (1992) makes in relation to Nigeria.

37 See the work of Jean-Pierre Faye (1972) regarding the functioning of myth and narratives in grounding the authenticity of the community, or the example of the tropic work which the proper name 'Gandhi' performs as signifier of nation and its authenticity in enacting India as postcolonial nation. I have explored this elsewhere (in Venn, 1993, 1999).

38 It would be interesting to examine the differences which separate and distinguish other, non-modern, empires – the Roman, Ottoman, Chinese, Japanese, Inca, and so on – parti-cularly from the point of view of a project which defines the progress and advancement of the community, the well-being of the people according to secular, universal terms and principles.

39 Though that is probably not a bad thing, given that most multicultural policies are tactics of governance, directed at the management of difference by routinizing or normalizing it.

40 The representation of Indians as 'other', that is, as morally depraved and intellectually deficient, in need of improvement, yet also inscrutable, unpredictable and irrational, fractures the mode of address, provoking the ambivalences that enables a 'sly civility' to deflect or contest the authority of the colonial master (Bhabha, 1994). From the point of view of the determination of imperial policy, the situation was resolved by emptying the other of historical specificity, denying cultural difference and conceptualizing the other as the dehistoricized empty slate to be reinscribed into civilization. This view of the subject, consistent with the technocratic impulse in the positivist discourse of modernity, operates in the discourse of 'man' that appears in the nineteenth century, as Foucault thought. However, as Bhabha points out, 'by disavowing the colonial moment as an enunciative present in the historical and epistemological condition of Western modernity' (1994: 196), Foucault is unable to recognize the part played by the colonial text in founding modernity's self-understanding.

2

HISTORICITY, RESPONSIBILITY, SUBJECTIVITY

As we look back at the theoretical and political transformations that have shaken modern times, it becomes clear that two forms of interrogations have profoundly disrupted the convictions and visions upon which we had relied for a long time to make sense of ourselves and of the world. The first set of questioning has its roots in the aporias of the narratives that have authorized a particular conceptualization of being and of agency in the discourses of modernity; it has excavated the fault-lines beneath the foundations that underpinned the view that the narrative of being could be figured in terms of one history, one humanity, one subjectivity. The second challenge comes from those denied agency and authority, inscribed as they are in the margins of the triumphalist history of the subject, those who have sought to dismantle the foundations from a standpoint located in the in-between or border or undecidable terrain of subordination and margin-alization. The interpenetration between the two lines of interrogation, for instance the degree to which something called 'postcolonial' theory borrows from or assumes a corpus of claims and statements established within something called poststructuralism, is not so much the sign of complicities and forgettings at the moment of the 'post' as it is an indication of how the world has been altered by modernity in ways that we are only beginning to understand or come to terms with.

The question that at first I want to tease out of these disjunctions can be posed in the form that Foucault gave to it: 'Who are we in the present?' It is a formula that combines the ageless anxiety of being confronting its constant dissolution and its finitude with the recognition of the historicity of that interrogation. In a sense it is also an eminently modern formulation of the problem of history and of subjectivity enclosing two themes central to the questioning of the foundations of the discourses of modernity. It recalls Ricoeur's and Heidegger's understanding of being as the entity that questions itself as to its way of being and, like them, emphasizes the dimension of temporality, since the presence of the present at the heart of Foucault's formulation signals how much this questioning is bound up with the consciousness of ourselves as beings in time (Lloyd, 1993). It recalls too the experiential or ontic dimension of temporality and self-reflexivity, foregrounded at the beginning of Marshall Berman's analysis of modernity where he says that:

To be modern is to find ourselves in an environment that promises us adventure, power, joy, growth, transformation of ourselves and the world – and, at the same time, that threatens to destroy everything we have, everything we know, every-thing we are. . . . [Modernity] is a paradoxical unity, a unity of disunity: it pours us all into a maelstrom of perpetual disintegration and renewal, of struggle and contradiction, of ambiguity and anguish. (1983: 15)

I evoke this particuar passage because it captures so well the underlying themes that the experience of modernity has provoked in the different forms – philosophical discourse, fictional narrative, artistic works – in which that experience of living at the limits, of pushing at the limits, has been expressed. So many of those who have addressed the experience of modernity convey the restlessness of spirit, the pervading anxiety that troubles even the steadiest of minds, like Kant when speaking about the sublime and about judgement. Indeed, behind or beneath the panache of logocentric certainties, which a certain critique deems the overwhelming characteristic of the discourses of modernity, we find the disquiet of the Rousseau of the *Confessions*, the anxieties of Hegel at Jena, the hesitations of Schelling, or of Freud in his correspondences, we pick up on the pathos in the works of a Dostoevsky or Sartre or in Beethoven's *Eroica*; closer to home, we share the torment of a Samuel Beckett and the ironies of Salman Rushdie. Modernity, from the beginning, has been a fractured dream, yet driven by an immense energy and an arrogant confidence that has transformed the world to an extent that no other period has ever accomplished. Nothing of the social and the physical habitat has been left untouched. It follows that a condition for overcoming the limits of modernity is that we must refigure this event as we wonder again who we are in the present.

It is possible that modernity simply provided conditions that amplified an existential anguish that all cultures have shared for a considerable time, an anguish that gripped the spirit as soon as human beings became conscious of themselves as finite beings who could measure their constant fading and envisage their inevitable ending against the longtime of history. The coming-to-consciousness is at once a coming to self-consciousness and the emergence of conscience, the discovery that one comes naked into the world, abandoned to a fragile freedom and to responsibility for one's actions and one's destiny. One of the most powerful myths of origin, the Judeo-Christian story of Adam and Eve could be read as a parable on the dilemmas of freedom and of the knowledge of finitude, the realization that to know is to be responsible, and that freedom is a responsibility. Knowledge and responsibility have come to refer to each other, in the discourse of religion as much as in that of the Enlightenment narrative of the progress of Reason and the possibility of emancipation. What being comes to know is the openness of the future, that is to say, the historicity of being, so that responsibility is responsibility for the present and for what might come in the future. Equally, the genealogy of the 'subject' brings out the extent to which from the beginning profound correlations emerged between the experience of the abyss and the anticipation of *jouissance*, between finitude and the exhilaration of risk, between lack and loss and desire.

Let me pursue this line of thought by engaging with the connection between responsibility and historicity and the transmutation of historicity into the promise of emancipation. The idea I want to examine is that the grand narratives of modernity are but the refigured and secular form of a more archaic search for a principle of hope born out of the foreknowledge of the possibility of pleasures renewed, and, on the dark side, the anguish of contingency and death. The promise of joy, figured as a narrative of redemption or a narrative of emancipation or the imagined fulfilment of desire, is premised on this recognition of finitude and the wound of loss and lack. Additionally, as I will demonstrate in the next chapter, the specificity of the modern narrative of being and of the history of modernity and of how *its* subject is bound up with the history of modern colonialism and of capitalism.

I would like at first to examine what Derrida (1995b) has called 'the gift of death', to ask what is given with death, that is, the sense in which this original violence is also a gift, that is, it enters the relation between the economy of the gift and the economy of sacrifice whereby the trembling of being is tethered to the secret of some ulterior and unfathomable destiny. In his reflections on the thought of Jan Patocka which generates the text of *The Gift of Death*, Derrida reminds us that the stakes in Patocka are defined as 'the birth of Europe in the modern sense of the term' (1995b: 3), and an exploration of what 'ails "modern civilization" in as much as it is European' (1995b: 3). Already, the question of Europe and of modernity is tied up with the more general question of historicity. I note this context because my own analysis includes the understanding of the becoming-West of Europe and the becoming-modern of the world as conjoined processes, that is, the understanding of the conceptual space of occidentalism.

Now, if we add the connection between responsibility and historicity to the equation about occidentalism, a number of themes begin to emerge, adding to those I have introduced earlier, that are central to the deconstruction of the discourses of modernity and vital for the reconfiguration of the future after or beyond modernity. Derrida's development of the relationship between historicity and responsibility is to argue that religion is the first form of 'a passage to responsibility' (1995b: 2) and the birth of an ethical conscience. But the Christian tradition finds it difficult to acknowledge this relation, preferring to imagine that the origin of responsibility proceeds from an unconditioned desire, interior to the soul of human beings, to seek the good. Recognition of the historicity of responsibility would break the link to faith, and to the gift, thus to a secret or mystery, namely, 'the *mysterium tremendum*: the terrifying mystery, the dread, fear, and trembling of the Christian in the experience of the sacrificial gift' (1995b: 6). This gift is that of death, at first given with the banishment or fallenness of Adam and Eve, then demanded of Abraham in the sacrifice of his son Isaac, himself a gift to Abraham from God, and finally, I should add, the gift of the death of Jesus to humankind, the redeeming sacrifice, which also works as the pledge that secures faith and trust in God. The interesting difference in the Christian scene is that the gift of death is transmuted into the promise of immortality, that is to say, the cancelling of finitude for all Christians. Equally, I would point to the transmutation of the trembling of being into the experience of an immortal interiority, attuned to the discipline of a care or solicitude for death: 'a vigil over the possibility of death', as Derrida puts it (1995b: 12), the anticipation of its proximity turned into a relation to the self, a care of the self, the theme that Foucault famously developed. The birth of a discourse of an individualized, interiorized soul and subjectivity can be inferred from this line of analysis, describing a 'subjectivizing interiorization, the movement of the soul's gathering of itself, a fleeing of the body toward its interior where it withdraws into itself in order to recall itself to itself, in order to be next to itself, in order to keep itself in this gesture of remembering' (1995b: 13, original emphasis). Derrida here rewrites the passage in Plato's *Phaedo* relating to the assembling of the soul into itself, which also can be read as the recognition of the self's relation to death and finitude, as does Levinas in his commentary on the same passage. An underlying theme in the Heideggerian problematic of being surfaces here, figured in terms of an 'egological subjectivity', linking in its make-up 'care, being-towards-death, freedom and responsibility' (1995b: 19). Indeed, the surprising element in the way I am recasting a genealogy of subjectivity is the extent to which even the Heideggerian attempt to break with a particular metaphysics and a particular ontology can be seen to remain attached to a more archaic, traditional thematic of being with its root in religion and in Plato, that is, in the crossing of the Judeo-Christian narrative of being and Greek thought. I shall have occasion to return to this fateful/fatal crossing in my examination of the birth of modernity and the modern subject. I should note at this point a thought of Levin, which keeps visible the position that sets the pessimism anchored in the soil of *Thanatos* or being-towards-death against the ecstasy of Being witheld within the 'unrealized power of *Eros*. For *Eros* is, in truth, an immortal aspect of *Physis*: its sheer energy and ecstasy of Being' (1985: 2). The body's remembrance of Being is the key for a new task: 'the *humanization* of our sensibility and the *culture* of our capacities for perception' (1985: 31, original emphasis).[1]

One might well wonder then what displacements and what disavowals inaugurate the modern discourse of subjectivity. And what has been the history, or cryptology, as Derrida would put it, of the secrets buried with the forgettings, particularly of the relation to the other and the difference of the other, forgettings which produce the singularity and interiority of the egocentric subject? History, however, 'never effaces what it buries; it always keeps within itself the secret of what it encrypts' (Derrida, 1995b: 21); traces are left that genealogy can uncover. But where does one look, and what are the questions to ask of the texts that authorize occidentalism?

Emancipation

In a surprising coincidence – but why should it surprise us? – Lyotard, reflecting on precisely the same events and paradoxes that Derrida explores in *The Gift of Death*, comes to this conclusion:

> With the modern thinkers, since Paul and Augustine, the promise of emancipation was what ordered time along a history or, at least, according to a historicity. For promise required setting out on a journey of education, the emergence from a condition of prior alienation, in the direction of a horizon of a legitimate *jouissance* [*jouissance du propre*] or of a liberation. Duration acquires the sense of an orientation filled with waiting and labour. (1993: 11)

The idea of the human condition as something motivated by the expectation of an emancipation is not specific to the Semitic religions alone. The same underlying idea reappears in all the major cultures the world over, for instance in the notion of a journey towards Nirvana through a series of reincarnations, or in the idea of the getting of wisdom by reflection and through suffering and learning, a wisdom that necessarily liberates us from whatever mortifies us. The model of a journey from infancy towards adulthood is precisely the model that we encounter in Kant's (1992 [1784]) definition of the Enlightenment as the passage of humanity from its state of immaturity towards its maturity and autonomy, charting a process of liberation from dependency and ignorance.

All these narratives speak of a difficult journey of discovery in the course of which the individual must renounce the wants and interests that shackle us to suffering and lack. Christian thinking defers the denouement, to the next life, routinizing sacrifice into the daily effort of the pilgrim to deserve the reward of an eventual emancipation.[2] For Lyotard, sacrifice and deferral create an ethical tension into which modern philosophy 'grafted . . . the eschatology of a knowledge [*savoir*] which is at the same time a will for the emancipation of meaning, always in process' (1993: 11). He points out that contemporary thinking shortens the delay, thus abolishing the historicity of emancipation. It also thereby abolishes the sense of an initial or original lack or loss which drives the desire for emancipation. The discourse of modernity emerges out of the break with the Judeo-Christian idea that emancipation could only be pursued through a listening to the proper, authentic authority, recorded in the sacred texts that one must learn to interpret. The good interpretation came out of a process of learning how to listen and how to read; it is an hermeneutics that prepares us for the coming to wisdom or to grace. Modernity sought to achieve its emancipation by itself, requiring no other help or means save its own effort and its own decision, gradually extending its power over whatever stood as obstacles to the exercise of a dominion that conditioned autonomy, and the exercise of a liberty that itself appeared as the proof of emancipation. Today something inadequately called the postmodern has emerged which completes the disappearance of historicity, this completion itself standing for the sign of postmodernity. Of this flight into an absent-minded future,

Lyotard says: 'it is as if a paganism without Olympus and without the Pantheon, devoid of *prudentia*, without fear, without grace, recognizing no debt, and *desperate*, was being reconstituted' (1993: 15, original emphasis).

One can understand this orientation in the modern project by refiguring the meaning of the hyphen which separates yet joins Judaism and Christianity and, I would add, the silent hyphen which attaches the Judeo-Christian discourse to that of modernity. Like Derrida, Lyotard finds a point of departure in the episode of the sacrifice of Isaac by Abraham, the trial or temptation of Abraham, to test his faith and his submission. Lyotard derives from this story the sense of a dread at the heart of the anticipation of salvation, even *in extremis*, which the faithful expects from God: what if God does not provide (the ram, in the case of the Holocaust of Isaac)? A dimension of secrecy is inscribed in this not knowing: God's will is the *lettre de cachet* that only the future reads; we only know afterwards, and must ever act without knowing. Perhaps a distinguishing feature of fundamentalism – whether based in religion or in a science – is the claim to know in advance, the claim to certainty, whereas there must always remain an element of doubt. Sacrificial faith demands that faith be absolute: for instance, in the civilizing mission of imperialism which envisaged the sacrifice of whole cultures to the promise of an occidentalist future; in Stalinism and its justification of the wholesale liquidation of categories of people, as in the Soviet Union or in Cambodia; or in monetarism and its sacrificial policies today (when it is not merely political cynicism).

Let us return to the text of Derrida, who directs us to another lesson about responsibility. For one thing, he tells us, Abraham is free to refuse, and he must face the paradox of duty and absolute responsibility, having to decide in secrecy, that is, by himself, without guidance, which is the highest duty or responsibility: the duty owed to his son, or that owed to God and responsibility towards the community. Secrecy and transcendence are 'essential to the exercise of this absolute responsibility as sacrificial responsibility' (1995b: 67). For Abraham, to speak about the command, to share with others the responsibility by allowing them to guide his decision, would betray a lack of faith, in wondering if God's commandment should be carried out. The relation to the absolutely transcendent Other must be absolute, and must remain secret, that is, uncommunicated and unknown.

There is another paradox concerning the problem of responsibility. Prompted by the work of Levinas, which aligns the question of responsibility to the problem of thinking the relation to the other, Derrida says:

> As soon as I enter into a relation with the other, with the gaze, look, request, love, command, or call of the other, I know that I can only respond by sacrificing ethics, that is, by sacrificing whatever obliges me to also respond, in the same way, in the same instant, to all the others. I offer a gift of death. I betray. (1995b: 68)

I think there are two aspects concealed in this impasse; on the one hand there is the implication that the call to a responsibility for the other cannot be answered because as soon as I respond to a particular named person, I abandon all others, which is the implication that Derrida is pursuing. I think Derrida's pessimistic reading does not sufficiently distinguish between the principle of an abstract responsibility and the phenomenal or ontic reality of its enactment, when it is our conduct with regard to specific others that gives content to the principle; it is the only way it can be cashed out. On the other hand, it could be argued that I am called to this responsibility precisely because it is in the name of all others that I am held to be responsible. The principle of responsibility, and what underlies it, is prior to any act on my part, though it derives from a history of responsibility, that is to say, from the memory of an immemorial debt owed to all, but to victims in particular. There remains, nevertheless, a dilemma which only an idea of justice and the exercise of conscience can mediate in practice, so that in expressing responsibility for a particular other I am obliged to make an ethical judgement. It is in the absence of justice and conscience that I betray and kill. For example, I may forgive an oppressor for my own suffering, but I have no right to do so on behalf of another's suffering. Dostoevsky's instructive story 'Why does God permit evil?', from *The Brothers Karamazov*, illustrates the dilemmas involved in deciding what one may forgive and what it means to forgive, and on behalf of whom may we forgive. It incidentally shows the impossibility of overcoming some 'differends' when justice involves those who are no longer alive, unless one were to invoke some redemptive sacrifice like that of Christ. I have indicated, in Chapter 1, that the exercise of a conscience is the result of an apprenticeship and thus tied to historicity, that is to say, tied to the accumulated wisdom dispersed in the memory and 'texts' of a culture, and which one must learn through an hermeneutical praxis. If we were to consider historicity and conscience to be separated and conjoined by the spacing of *différance*, we could then think that it is precisely the caesura produced by the forgetting of that relation in the concept of transcendent origin(s), or in originary moments – for example, in the idea of original sin – that allows the idea of an absolute other to be insinuated.[3] The search for ontological security in the guarantee of transcendentals is paid for in terms of the sacrifice of the other, specifically the other who can be excluded on the basis of otherness or unbelonging, that is, those who are not recognized by the Other, or those who cannot be gathered into the sameness of an originary identity, for instance in the notion of race, the *ethne* or the faithful. Furthermore, within the narratives of being in the Abrahamite religions, the consciousness of temporality is tied to a sense of abandon-ment and lack or fallenness, provoking the repression of the trace of the becoming-conscious, and its incorporation or inscription in the interiority of the soul.

   The line which Derrida explores instead implies that the absolutely other – Other or God, and thus a transcendent principle demanding the sacrifice of a life, an infinite gift – is an idea that feeds sacrificial war, so that the place where death is given in the story of the sacrifice of Isaac is today a place of dissent and discord, 'fought over by all the monotheisms, by all the religions of the unique and transcendent God, of the absolute other' (1995b: 70). Derrida reminds us that this place is located on Mount Moriah at the place called the Dome of the Rock, in Jerusalem, near the Aska Mosque associated with the sacrifice of Ibrahim; it is where Solomon decided to build the House of the Lord, and where once stood the grand Mosque of Jerusalem; today, it stands above the Wailing Wall and close to the Way of the Cross. It is worth pointing out that in the discourse of Western philosophy, the hyphen linking Judaism and Christianity silently erases Islam from Semitic thought, casting the Islamic world into invisibility when it comes to a genealogy of modernity. Derrida, to his credit, has constantly addressed the Eurocentric assumptions of the discourse of modernity, for instance regarding the implication in Kant that the European hegemony was somehow a hidden design in nature, a 'teleological ruse of nature' that would have prescribed the privilege of Greco-Roman Europe in the foundation of history as the history of the emancipation of the whole of humanity (Derrida, 1997: 26–30). I shall have more to say about the question of monotheism and transcendence in Chapter 3, in my analysis of the repetitions of the same and the unique, that is, the plays of identity in the secularization of the narrative of emancipation, the stratagem which inaugurates modernity as a project that preserves and retains the desire for Oneness and the Same in the priority it grants to the idea of one history, one humanity, one subjectivity.

Another aspect to examine concerns the trembling of being when exposed to the complete unknowability of the future and to a power beyond comprehension. A vital difference appears here between Judaism and Christianity. In the eschatology of Judaism, the promise of emancipation, not guaranteed by an event like the sacrifice of Jesus, does not tell the Jew how to act in the present. The commandments do that, but there is an abundance of them, and they are open to interpretation. Conscience acquires a different meaning, therefore, as both obedience to the law (Halakah), that is, the discharge of a performative duty, and a decision regarding the good for which reflective judgement must rely on the enigma of wisdom. By contrast, in the case of Christianity, the promise of emancipation or redemption has clear implications about how one is to act in the world. In both cases, though, there is the injunction to constantly inspect one's conscience; indeed, to imagine that one has a conscience, whence also arises a paradox of responsibility that Derrida (1995b) points out, namely, that the logic of the assumption that one knows what one does opens up the possibility that a science, or an objective set of rules for decision-making on the basis of a science or of a knowledge, could absolve conscience of responsibility for decision or judgement. The history of modernity provides ample evidence of this temptation, within a secular narrative of becoming, to shift the burden of responsibility onto a positive science rather than face up to the fact that the subject of responsibility is a named person and that the responsible person is 'this exposing of the soul to the gaze of another person, of a person as transcendent other, as an other who looks at me, but who looks without the-subject-who-says-I being able to reach that other, see her, hold her within the reach of my gaze' (Derrida, 1995b: 25). The Levinasian conceptualization of the face relation and the absolute alterity of the other for whom I am nevertheless responsible is evident in this formulation.[4] So, on the one hand, we find the instrumentalization of responsibility and of judgement into a fixed set of rules to be followed, that is, we find the privileging of *logos* and, at its extreme, a performative rationality, whilst, on the other hand, there remains the burden of knowing that one only half-knows, that there are no guarantees, yet that one must act as if for the first time, re-enacting the diremptions inherent in the ethical.

Lyotard (1993) comes to this point in a rather different way that throws added light on the question of the specificity of modernity and its form of subjectivity. He argues that neither in the secular discourse of the West nor in the Christian discourse is there a clear answer to the question of what it means to be liberated, which is the goal of emancipation, that is, the liberation from temporal powers that constrain our liberty or inflict pain upon us, or the overcoming of an interior insufficiency, a weakness of the soul, whatever keeps us in the state of infancy or immaturity – to signal again Kant's definition of the Enlightenment. Lyotard points out that it comes down to maintaining the separation between the three orders which distinguish the different stakes of judgement, that is to say, truth, the good and the beautiful. However,

> the Western modern ideal of emancipation combines all the orders; to ensure for oneself complete possession [ownership] over knowledge, over the will and over feeling. *To give to oneself* the rule of knowledge, the law of the will [*vouloir*], and the control over affect. He will be emancipated who owes nothing to anyone but himself. Liberated from any debt owed to the other. (1993: 7, original emphasis)

The agent of responsibility

This auto-emancipation which is an auto-constitution pretends that it can liberate itself from the anguish which provokes the trembling of being and from the vulnerability of the relation to the other. Lyotard argues that when 'man' owes nothing to the other: 'He liberates himself from the other by exteriorizing the other, then by attacking/seizing the other [*en lui mettant la main dessus*]' (1993: 8). This is starkly illustrated in the history of the conquest of America, and countless brutal episodes in the course of colonization, linking the 'othering' of the other to the 'knowledge that kills' and to dispossession and domination, as I will show in the next chapter. Derrida, for his part, examines the implications of regarding the other as the absolute other, for instance in the idea of God as such an other, or in Levinas's insistence on the infinite alterity of the other, linking it to the assumption of the absolute singularity of the other.[5] To start with, it means the impossibility of distinguishing between the ethical and the religious, which renders incoherent the grounds for responsibility, for what principles, then, apart from the unconditional duty and the imperative to obey the law or follow the commandment because of its sacred – and thus secret, unfathomable – provenance, would ground responsibility in the immediacy of the face relation outside the disavowals inscribed in the imaginary of transcendental discourses? If the law is the only limit which circumscribes responsibility, and if it is not possible to separate out the realm of the religious from that of the legal and the political, how is one to assign responsibility when it is a matter of judging the societies which, for example, allow millions of children to die of hunger (so that the affluent may eat well), this 'sacrifice of others to avoid being sacrificed oneself' (Derrida, 1995b: 86), organized as an integral part of these societies' own good order and well-being? The law of secrecy in Christian teaching (Derrida discusses Matthew 6: particularly the passages chosen by Kierkegaard at the end of *Fear and Trembling*) comes to be interiorized in the soul or the heart, so that the light of the good no longer shows itself as an external visible good but proceeds from an interior invisible source, motivating sacrifice as gift, and as sign of goodness.

The elaboration of a notion of the origin and foundation of interiority as sacred and secret inaugurates religion, a *mise-en-discours* of being that diminishes the archaic dread by securing the individual to the closed space of a community, the closed space of its universe of meanings. The closure is removed from questioning by being established in the inaccessibility of a divine or transcendent will. Its erasure is exchanged for the promise of an eventual but transcendent fulfilment, a promise of Life. The only injunction is to have faith and to repeat the gestures of submission: believe and you will be saved, or, in the Althusserian model, submit and you will be recognized. Ready-made answers are provided there that repeat and confirm the intelligibility of the world in accord with transcendent foundations that remove individual will and intentions from the order of things: Thy will be done. Human destiny was literally in the lap of the gods, though responsibility for one's action in the world, especially in the Semitic religions – Christianity, Judaism and Islam – is returned to individual conscience. It is well to bear in mind that before modern times the question of what lies between the world of humans and that of the gods was the question that had but another question for answer; in other words, it was the the enigma hiding a forbidden knowledge that doomed the questioner in advance to the fate always-already decreed by the Sphinx. Therein lies another aspect of secrecy, namely, that the secret is precisely that which must not be known: origin of the taboo, and the secret of the Law (of the Father) – which Oedipus transgressed.

The trouble with the religions of the Book is the abyss which is created between the sacrificial love bound to the love of the absolute Other and the caring love bound to filiality, and to the desired other. The former is tied to the notion of an absolutely inaccessible secret compelling us to a incalculable duty, including the sacrifice of oneself and one's own; the latter is grounded in another economy: the 'law of the home, of the family and of the hearth' (Derrida, 1995b: 88), requiring a different kind of listening and feeling. What I wish to bring out in my analysis are the connections that appear between finitude, beingness-in-the-world and the economies of the gift and of sacrifice. In the background the question of emancipation remains, keeping visible the economy of desire which motivates it. The lesson I draw from the economy of sacrifice attached to monotheism and to a transcendent divine authority is its mutation in the secular discourse of modernity, particularly in its occidentalist form, whereby the disempowered and dispossessed 'other' is sacrificed, as an inevitable cost, in the name of the 'growth' and well-being of the modern social order as a whole. This notion of sacrifice, as I have noted, is expressed in the dictum of the civilizing mission of imperialism: we are your masters because we want to save you for a better future, by sacrificing your culture and way of life in exchange for the occidentalist gift. We find this idea of sacrifice in J.S. Mill's view of Indian civilization or in Balfour's 1910 declaration that Said (1978) interrogated.[6] From the nineteenth century, salvation and emancipation are transformed into the promise of 'development' and 'modernization' presented as ultimate goods, the gift or reward of 'civilization' that will be bestowed at the right time, provided the colonized 'other' renounces her 'otherness' and acknowledges the law of Europe. Kant's prescription of a 'universal cosmopolitical state', as Derrida has pointed out, advocates the political unification of the human species and all nations under the aegis of European hegemony, when Europe would 'one day give laws to all others' (Derrida, 1997: 22). For the 'developing' world, the moment of the right time is endlessly deferred, since it is ever in the position of the follower, catching up with the standards and norms of advancement always-already accomplished by the West.

The colonial space of modernity and identity

With modernity, or, rather, beginning with the secular narrative of being that started to emerge with it, there appeared a narrative that returned responsibility for destiny to human agency, specifically to the notion of the subject understood as origin of responsibility and free will, able to exercise an unconditioned freedom. Freedom amplified the existential angst at a time when the Europeans' discovery of what they called the New World was to change history for ever. Let me make two connections that will give an idea of the direction in which I want to pursue the interrogation of modernity and modern subjectivity, drawing on Derrida and Morrison. Two questions will indicate the general orientation of my analysis: How are we to interpret the birth of Europe and its metonymic relation with modernity? And does that conjuncture, that is, the birth and coupling of Europe and modernity, ground and limit the civilization enframed by occidentalism? Another consideration follows this line of inquiry – if, indeed, it does not precede it – raised by Derrida in his analysis of Jan Patocka's essay on the birth, expansion and future of Europe, which he had expressed in terms of an ailment which damns 'modern civilization' inasmuch as it is European, specifically, 'why does it suffer from ignorance of its history, from a failure to assume its responsibility, that is, the memory of its history *as* history of responsibility' (1995b: 3–4, original emphasis). Derrida goes on to point out that it is not a matter of insufficient knowledge, but that European historical knowledge 'occludes, confines, or saturates those questions, grounds, or abysses, naively presuming to totalize or naturalize them, or . . . losing themselves in the details' (1995b: 4). To avoid totalizing closure, or amnesia, the problem of history must remain open: 'History can be neither a decidable object nor a totality capable of being mastered, precisely because it is tied to responsibility, to faith, and to the gift' (1995b: 5).

My interest lies in the conditions that over-determined closure and forgetting, the trauma and violence that motivate erasure and repetition. For that reason, I would like to reterritorialize the question on the terrain of occidentalism, that is to say, within the conceptual space enunciated at the juncture of the becoming-West/ern of Europe and the becoming-modern of the world. It is affiliated with the idea of modernity as the history of humanity in the singular and the idea of 'History' as the becoming-Western of humanity. Occidentalism, therefore, is the space of the co-articulation of logocentric reason, technocratic rationality and imperialism by way of an egocentric ontology of being. It inscribes the privilege of the West as the superior locus of world-historical development, and the modern Western subject as the agent of that process. My intention is both to deconstruct this space and to break with the imaginary it supports. My analysis is therefore located within the conceptual space of 'postcoloniality' since, as I explained in Chapter 1, that space is constituted in the process of the deconstructive critique of occidentalism; it attempts to imagine the beyond of occidentalism.

Robert Young makes the important point that colonialism 'constitutes the dislocating term in the theory/history debate' (1990: vii), a thought which I would locate, on one side, in the shadow of the ending of one form of global domination in the form of the imperial world order, replaced by more complex forms of subjugation and power, and, on the other side, in the longer history of the subject that I am trying to reconstruct by examining the conceptual shifts and breaks that transmute the more archaic search for an emancipatory meaning to human existence into the project of modernity. Young notes that there has emerged a politics associated with what one can loosely call poststructuralism which, like in Cixous's work, 'weaves capitalist economic exploitation, racism, colonialism, sexism, together with, perhaps unexpectedly, "History" and the structure of the Hegelian dialectic' (Young, 1990: 1). This critique, whilst it targets the same oppressions as Marxism, operates a distance from it in its rejection of the classical Marxist view of history as the narrative of the unfolding of a rational system proceeding according to the logic of the (Hegelian) dialectic, driven by inherent contradictions. It is a world history, co-opting all other cultures into its universalizing stream. It is well to remember that it is the tendency within the logic of the dialectic to reduce the other to the same, through the concept of the *Aufhebung*, even when recognizing the other as the negation of the same, that produces the double bind of difference, namely, that difference is both necessary, as negation of the Same, yet it is transmuted–absorbed into the Same, or the One, through supersession. The uncanny resemblance with the logic of the logocentric subject means that the notion of a universalizing and totalizing History repeats what Cixous called the 'masculine Empire of the Selfsame' (cited in Young, 1990: 3). At one level, therefore, the appropriation of poststructuralism within feminist and postcolonial (post-Black, post-Bandung, post-'Third World') politics joins with the dissident politics of opposition to phallogo-Eurocentrism, a politics, therefore, of the future as possibility, specifically the future as the becoming-responsible and becoming-ethical of humanity.[7]

Let me add another voice to emphasize this standpoint. In her powerful critique of American literary imagination, Toni Morrison (1992) makes a telling connection between the conditions that shaped people's lives at the time of colonization and slavery, and the writing that expressed European experience at the dawn of modern times. For the early Americans, this writing explores the encounter with the new forces and contradictions, translating the old fears and insecurities, tied to a memory of Europe, to the context of the new possibilities and risks that awaited in the New World. The literary imagination transferred the historical, moral, metaphysical and environmental fears inscribed in European culture onto the bound and violently silenced black bodies of a 'slave population that was understood to have offered itself up for a meditation on human freedom in terms other than the abstractions of human potential and the rights of man' (1992: 38). Indeed, 'Nothing highlighted freedom – if it did not in fact create it – like slavery' (1992: 38). The conjunction of blackness and enslavement enabled the 'not-free' to be tied in the modern imaginary with the 'not-me', producing 'a brew of darkness, otherness, alarm and desire that is uniquely American' (1992: 38). The point she makes about how in American literature the concerns of 'autonomy, authority, newness and difference, absolute power [became] shaped by, activated by a complex awareness and employment of a constituted Africanism' (1992: 44) can be extended to apply to the relationship between modernity and colonialism generally. I draw attention to this connection in order to make clear that the refiguring of modernity is not a matter simply for the 'West'. Colonial enterprise introduced a new scale, an excessive scale – vast expanse of brute nature, unknown cultures, uncharted territories – against which the emergent modern subject could measure its (in)significance and its potential grandeur. The becoming-modern of the world which colonialism and imperialism accomplished over the centuries makes the question of what, and who, comes after modernity and after occidentalism a question that concerns everyone.

We need, however, to rework the terms and the terrain of the debate. The two most familiar targets concern the notion of reason privileged in a particular Enlightenment discourse and the notion of subject inscribed in the 'philosophy of the subject'. The work of critical theory, especially in Adorno, Horkheimer, Benjamin and Habermas, has already demonstrated how a totalizing reason allied to a universalizing History tends towards domination and totalitarian and terroristic forms of governance. But the question is not so much what has gone wrong; rather, it is the recognition that these tendencies were intrinsic to the worlding of the world that colonialism and modernist imperialism instituted. The case of Nazi fascism and the Holocaust will allow me to indicate the displacement in the analytical gaze which the postcolonial standpoint operates. Already, Fanon, quite some time ago, had drawn attention to the view that fascism can be seen as the returning home to Europe of the despotic impulse of totalizing reason. Indeed, it could be argued that the fact that Germany did not participate, initially, in the imperial enterprise, that is to say, the fact that it did not bind the notion of the nation and measure its greatness and validate its progress by reference to a global project, that is, by reference to an exteriorization of the nation's will and agency projected onto a universal scene, meant that it had to find within itself the proof of its maturity and advancement. For European nation-states like France, England, Spain, imperial success and the exercise of a subjugating power acted to confirm the tropes of progress and greatness. Germany, in spite of becoming a great power in the nineteenth century, had instead to find within itself the signs of progress, it had to turn to its own 'essence' to discover the qualities that would exemplify the superiority and authenticity of the race. The proof of these qualities could only come from acts and achievements that, in taking Germany itself to be the object of its project of emancipation and aggrandisement, brought about the instrumental becoming of the nation as the authentic race, the promised race. The totalizing and narcissistic nationalism which the absence of an external empire provoked in the period of fascism has affinities with and kindled deep-seated feelings, nurtured in the course of German history, that for a long time tied Germans to the soil and to community, to a sense of home (*Heimat*). The fact that Germany as nation-state was of recent, Bismarckian, foundation only amplified the investment in mythical origin and in the fantasmic character of the authentic, pure race. We know the extent to which the unity and authenticity of the race was performatively staged and embodied in the mass demonstrations of the spectacular folding of the community upon itself in its specular (mis)recognition. The public square became the cathedral sacralizing the authenticity of the race, thrust together by the force of the lack which drove it there. There, in the sight of its icons, the communal host pledged itself to its historical destiny. In the previous chapter I pointed out the logic which bound this excessive desire with the violence of the Holocaust. An economy of sacrifice is at work there too. Fundamentalism today has often repeated these gestures and stratagems. My analysis shows that postcolonial deterritorializations can open up a space from which to rewrite the history of Europe, and to question the categories and epistemologies that have authorized the occidentalist narrative of modernity as a project of the becoming of humanity as universal History. The same displacement opens up the history of the present to a renewed reflection on the relation linking responsibility to historicity.

The question of the subject is less clear, for although the critique of logocentrism points to its complicities with a totalizing reason, that critique by itself does not provide ways of refiguring the question of the 'who' of action and the problem of agency. In particular, from the point of view of a politics of difference, that is, a politics that does not wish to subsume the interests and difference of the other into universal categories, problems emerge that concern the grounds of a different discourse of being that would eschew ontological and epistemological violence. The work of Levinas, as well as philosophies that draw critically from the phenomenological tradition generally, has appeared to provide a new point of departure. It is the terrain that my own exploration will develop in search of a position that refuses the supplementarity of the 'other' – woman, the non-European and non-white – in the elaboration of a narrative of emancipation. The question is how to respect the alterity of the other without essentializing difference and without grounding ethical principles in the terrain of the philosophy of the Same and an economy of sacrifice.[8]

On subjectivity

Let me, for the sake of argument, start with the idea of the 'I' as a (non-Husserlian) *epoché*, that is to say, the idea which develops the view that the constitution of the 'I', as a point of subjective reference, describes the emergence of a position in language and in speech which gathers to itself and is itself the resultant of an historical process of formation whereby an originary intentionality and consciousness are 'made real': as the place from which speech issues and as the location of agency. The 'I' would be the place-marker for presence, in practice the presence of a particular self, or the place from which a named person enunciates itself as the one who is called to responsibility: I, Abraham.[9]

The point of using a term like *epoché* is that it enables me to inscribe the spatial and temporal dimension of subjectivity in a theorization that respects the historicity of being. What it does not do is signal a break with the problematic of the 'I' as origin or final destination of the process of constitution, as *arche* or *telos*, that is to say, the problematic of presence. The move away from this way of conceptualizing subjectivity makes us recall that Derrida invented the term *différance* to point to temporization and spacing and their conjointness in the process of signification. The question of the 'who' is implicated as soon as we speak of signification. However, we would remain on the terrain of the 'I' as unitary singularity if we were to prioritize the question of the 'who' before immediately examining what the implications of *différance*, and temporalization and spatialization were, from the point of view of the other, that is, if we thought that the question of subjectivity could be answered prior to the theorization of the relation to the other.[10]

For that reason, I will propose that 'I' and my other belong to the same *epoché*: an I by itself does not exist. This is the basic proposition of heteronomy; it implies that there is a double differentiation and a double inscription in the process of institution of an 'I'. I shall examine this proposition below. First, I want to point to what I am leaving behind in this approach. To begin with, I am breaking with the metaphysics of presence, that is, the idea of the 'I' emerging as the result of a process of the doubling or folding of the 'I' upon itself to constitute an absolute interiority, an interiority that requires reference to no other except itself, its own process of cogitation: the I who is the seat of the *cogito*: I think, therefore I am.

Second, I am breaking with Lacan's version of the emergence of the 'I'. For Lacan (1966a), the mirror stage is a three-term series or process involving the 'real', the imaginary and the symbolic, out of which the 'I' emerges. Lacan does posit the relation to the other as vital, for it is in the moment of splitting from the other that a being accedes to subjectivity, as a singularity, carrying the burden of an irrevocable loss (of the other, and of the object). With the Lacanian problematic, the 'I' imagines itself to be as it fantasizes the other to have constituted it. In other words it is an 'as if' recognition, shaped by the wish and by desire and thus condemned to misrecognition. In the process the real too becomes embroiled in the same distorting mechanisms of the mirror stage, caught in the endless shunting between the imaginary and the symbolic, yet functioning as the necessary third term that binds all three moments of subjectivity. The assumption of an inevitable misrecognition supports a pessimistic thematic of being, blind to the joyful aspects of the process of emergence of the 'I' into selfhood, prioritizing instead the traumatic elements of the experience. In this economy of subjectivity, the trauma of the (conjectured) Oedipal drama leaves traces that cannot be erased, and which must bind me to the Law and to a particular libidinal economy. I am, of course, bracketing the Freudian account which reduces the economy of desire to that of sexuality and to the space of the libidinal scene and its psychic consequences. To the ontological poverty of this reduction must be added the well-established phallocentrism of Freudianism's account of female sexuality and the implications for gender difference (Deleuze and Guattari, 1985; Irigaray, 1984). Apart from the privilege of sexuality – is this Judeo-Christian too? – the problematic of representation in non-Lacanian, non-feminist psychoanalytic theory, although subversive of the *cogito* and clearly not realist, does not break with egocentric assumptions. What follows is an attempt to construct a conceptual space which secures such a break.

Folding

Within the social sciences, the elaboration of the mechanisms that operate to constitute the 'who' of subjectivity follows some fairly well-trodden paths, which take for granted a self-centred subject, and which aim to explain 'behaviour' by reference to a science and what this assumes about the object of knowledge. The basic approach is framed by the model of a social outside that gets inside the subject through processes of 'socialization' or by means of a psychologization of the individual. I shall not engage with this model, having done so elsewhere (Henriques et al., 1998 [1984]). One approach which appears to undermine subject-centredness follows Foucault in accounting for the subject in terms of effects produced by apparatuses of formation, disciplining, normalization and regulation of the social and of the subject. We would of course have to add to this account the explanation of how the sense of a 'who' as an interiority comes to be constituted, either as part of this process of formation or as something requiring, in addition, a 'regime of the self', instituted in techniques of self-inspection and in 'self-steering mechanisms', informed by particular discourses and codes that provide each person with the discursive and practical tools for judging her/himself. For example, what does it mean to be a good parent? How do I know that I am doing the right thing as a parent? What authorizes the practices that I am supposed to follow? Within a Foucauldian analytic, a genealogy of the discourses and the practices of parenting from the nineteenth century would establish the range of technologies and normative discourses and their mutations that, since the emergence of the sciences of the social, have operated in the process of formation of the subject as the good parent.

This range of technologies of the social is nicely detailed by Nikolas Rose (1996), who adds several remarks that locate the problematic of subjectification beyond the models of socialization or psychologization of the individual. Rose recognizes the reference to an interiority in histories of the self, but proposes the view that interiority is the result of the 'infolding of an "exterior"' to constitute an 'inside' or soul (1996: 142). Furthermore, the infoldings are 'stabilized' in two ways: first, the functioning of a biography which articulates the relation we have to ourselves in the form of a narrative or memorization of how we think we have come to be the person we are; and, second, by reference to the relation we have with the spatial dimension of being. Human beings, he says, are 'emplaced, enacted through a regime of devices, gazes, techniques which extend beyond the limits of the flesh into spaces and assemblies' (1996: 143). The spatialization of being and the narrativization of being are conjoined processes, producing the human being as 'a hybrid of flesh, knowledge, passion and technique' (1996: 144).

Let us see how this position might direct our gaze when we look into the case of the constitution of the good parent. We could then examine what is left unaccounted for. We recognize, to begin with, that the human technologies, both disciplinary and pastoral, that participate in the process of formation have a genealogy that we can reconstruct as a history of strategies, purposes, normative orientations, and so on, that have become codified, instrumentalized, institutionalized and routinized, inscribed in the spatial and temporal lifeworld, distributed as know-how and expertise amongst agents and agencies that function to bring about desired ends. The parent is located within these already constituted 'hybrid assemblages' (that are open to variation and change over time); s/he becomes apprenticed to a stage of formation. S/he encounters advisers and experts, like doctors, nurses, health visitors, in a variety of sites like clinics and hospitals, nursery schools and crèches which have been disposed in such a way as to structure the relations of power and authority and the encounters that can take place. We go to such places with the 'right' attitudes and with particular expectations, including the willingness to accept the authority of those vested with the power to advise and guide or judge. The system of authority is supported by texts and child-care manuals and magazines that prepare us for the 'role' of parenting. There exist too a whole range of equipments and objects, books and toys that provide the material support for the practice of bringing up a child, without which it would be impossible to translate codes, rules and know-how into a routine of tasks and behaviours and communicative action. Every parent constantly scrutinizes her/himself, not only checking out whether s/he is following the proper procedures and methods, but also judging her/his level of commitment and effort, her/his willingness to learn and improve, inspecting secret desires and guilts. In this way, each of us constructs ourself as a parent and reconstructs the relation we have to ourself.

Rose's analysis of the modern process of subjectification ends with a number of remarks about the rationalities of the new machinery of the governance of oneself and of the social which is now appearing. He points to 'new ethical vocabularies', valorizing notions of autonomy, choice, enterprise, lifestyle, that may well be establishing new 'dividing practices', 'new modalities of folding authority into the soul' (1996: 145) and new forms of self-government grounded in 'rationalities of contracts, consumers and competition' (1996: 146). For Rose, it is possible to gain a critical purchase on these mechanisms by way of historical explorations that can 'unsettle' established forms of subjectification. This development is relatively familiar territory for those who are trying to rethink our presentness in the light of the work of Foucault.

Yet I cannot help thinking that there are other key elements of beingness that exceed the apparatus of formation and self-formation that I have sketched. I am going to try to discuss them by reference to the groundedness and the 'groundlessness' or, rather, ungroundedness of our being in the world. To begin with, it seems to me that we need to be able to account for the fact that a new experience like parenting – or, indeed, living with a partner, or settling in a different country, and so on – significantly reshapes our biography, occasioning the revaluation of previous relations, for instance with parents, partners, friends. Such events result in engagement in a whole new range of activities tied to new locations like schools, communities, and organizations like child-care groups, with the result that our orientations and concerns, our expectations of ourselves and our life-projects become altered. An additional source of knowledge and value derives from friends and relatives with whom we compare and exchange experiences and stories and reflect upon our conduct both as a parent and in relation to a biography that includes the reactions (for instance of approval or disapproval) and the expectations and demands of others. Thus, the process of formation and change of particular 'identities' involves, in addition, interactions that, although regulated by *ad hoc* steering mechanisms, are relatively unstructured and open to negotiations based on friendship and trust. At the end of this process of refiguration we have different and new kinds of stories to tell about ourselves; we are in a sense no longer who we were before.

All of this change has to do with the grounded character of selves and with something else that in part relates to the question of an 'ethics of the self', that is to say, the (culturally and historically specific) relation to oneself that we develop in relation to particular corporeal, intellectual and hermeneutic or self-reflective regimes which guide us in the ways we are supposed to walk, talk, eat, dress, make love, think, plan, reflect upon our actions and motives, and so on, as part of coming to understand ourself as a particular individual. I say in part because the extensive recent literature on the fashioning of the self has not sufficiently broken with the perspective of the singularity of the self. I want instead to point to the view that 'self-steering' and 'self-fashioning' devices are not merely heuristic devices; the way they work involves more than the infolding of an exteriority to constitute an interiority, more than a particular form of learning to be the person we become. In the example of parenting, it is significant that the technologies of subjectification are given a practical realization as part of relations between persons, minimally between the child and a parent, more routinely as information, knowledges, opinions, anecdotes, reflections and questions that are exchanged in episodes of communicative action involving children, friends, relations and authorized advisers and agents, often occurring in sites that are relatively open spaces like the schoolyard and the neighbourhood or the café and the pub. In this way, general, abstract rules and knowledges and ways of doing are translated into a social reality involving the face-to-face interaction of associative communities. The process describes the social institution of the lifeworld. A domain of inter-subjectivity mediates the application or functioning of the devices and apparatuses of subjectification, inflecting the meanings and values we come to attach to particular experiences and thoughts; for instance, we trust the opinion of a particular doctor or expert more than that of another. Ideally, the process of subjectification works best when it appears to be the result of unforced choices and wills. In any case, visible power or power lived as imposition sets up resistances and tactics of evasion that undermine normalization and challenge normative principles.

Bonding

The processes of self-formation must be seen also as ways of bonding with particular others, ways of building trust and solidarity, that is, ways of establishing one's 'self' in terms of particular durable relations to specific others, at the same time as in terms of the relation one has with oneself. The one implicates the other in the form of a double inscription. For example, we can say that the work we do upon ourselves to become a parent is integral to the work we do in constituting an infant as a particular subjectivity; the two subjectivities grow together. Let us think of it as a choreography, a process of learning to be one with the other, with the complex baggage of narcissism, seduction, identification, pleasure, separation and pain which accompanies this complex elaboration of individual identities. The grounded dimension of being, then, refers to the range of mechanisms, devices, discourses and sites involved in these processes, as well as the embodied interactions in relational encounters that together enact the practice of everyday life and constitute the materiality and the inter-subjective reality of the lifeworld.

Let me add another dimension to the question of subjectification which emerges when we recognize its enigmatic character, and which obliges us to relate the groundedness of being to a transcendent or liminal domain. This presencing of something unpresentable in the space of the 'happening' of being harbours a seemingly timeless dimension, irreducible to ground, and so to technologies, yet paradoxically finding its support there. A thought of Levinas (1969) will allow me to present one aspect of the kind of questioning that I have in mind. It is the distinction which he makes between the saying and the said. In the relation to the other, the saying concerns the 'face relation', that is to say, it occurs in a situation that places us in a position of absolute responsibility for the other, open to the silent demand of the other, thrown into a relationship beyond the rules of contractual arrangements or reciprocal obligations. Intimations of an infinite measure surface here to point to a reflection about foundational principles to which I will return.

I would like to indicate this other dimension by turning to a number of texts where we discover a different kind of discourse, a different relation to oneself which events like becoming a parent produce. It is a relation that cannot easily be brought within the compass of the framework of governance or of the idea of the emergence of an interiority by reference to the infolding of a describable outside. Listen, for example, to Kristeva (1983), who in the essay 'Stabat Mater' pursues and links several themes concerning the maternal body and the fleshy and 'spiritual' lived relation to the foetus and the infant. In this instance, she uses this relation as a basis for a meditation on the place of the different figures of Mary in the Christian discourse of emancipation from finitude and from death. She proposes the idea of the 'humanization of Christianity' from the fifteenth century through the (older) cult of Mary, thereby linking the theological arguments about humanism to changing representations of the feminine in the West and to the theme of love and ethics. She argues that none of these strategies of language can exhaust the 'unsaid' and the unsayable about the maternal body:

> [N]o signifier can exhaust it without remainder. . . . As much as it is concerned with each woman's body, this heterogeneity which cannot be subsumed by the signifier is nevertheless violently fractured by pregnancy (basis of culture and nature) and with the arrival of the child (which brings a woman out of her unitariness and gives her the chance – but not a certainty – of access to the other, to ethics). These particularities of the maternal body make of a woman a being made up of folds, a catastrophe of being that the dialectic of the trinity and its supplements cannot subsume. (1983: 245)

The phenomenology of the invisible relation of the foetus/ infant with the mother, which Kristeva transcribes in the marginal text of 'Stabat Mater', as its supplement, bears interesting comparison with Irigaray's account of the mother/child dyad specified in her work *And the One Does Not Move without the Other*. The title functions as the index of a double economy of identity whereby the one comes to define itself by reference to the other, so that the subject is more than one but less than two, exceeding singularity yet not abolished in the process of identification. The relation of the subject to its other is analogous to the relation of the visible to its invisible side. Consider, for instance, this passage: 'If I leave, you no longer find yourself. Was I not the deposit that secures against your disappearance? The place-holder for your absence?' (1979: 16). Or this: 'And why should some other wound have been imposed upon me? Did I not already have my/your lips? And this body open to the gift that never could we have finished giving each other. To speak each other' (1979: 21). The intimacy of the writing here and in the rest of the text should be set against Irigaray's (1984) reflections about the ethics of sexual difference. What then comes to light is the attempt to relate the economy of selfhood or 'identity' to the economy of the body – beyond sexuality and gender, but not excluding them, taking its cue from Merleau-Ponty's *The Visible and the Invisible* (1968) – and the economy of the gift. It is when we proceed in this way that the invisibility of what lies in the shadows of technologies and machineries of subjectification alerts us to the other dimension which I have signalled. I shall develop this connection below.

Desiring

For now I want to add other texts and authors to make visible the kind of reflection about our beingness in the world, our groundedness in the here and now, that, starting with some defining moments like engendering another being or caring for an other or loving and giving, provides the occasion for a meditation on the ontological, ethical, epistemological and existential questions that an examination of the machinery of subjectifica-tion does not in itself yield. They are not, for all that, questions that we can

simply relegate to specialisms or ignore on the grounds of arcane philosophical interest. There are many and different paths one could follow to
pursue the exploration which I am proposing. One approach is to limit its
interrogation to the performative character of the technologies that, in the
modern form of sociality, constitute a subject as subject of particular
regimes of behaviours and reflections. Another recognizes the limitations
and insufficiency of discourse, and of the letter of the law, to voice the
unsayable, or to provide ready-made answers to the experience of the abyss:
lack, finitude, loss of the other or the object, temporality and historicity of
being. There has existed for a long time a third way, buried in the history of
being, namely, the stratagem of deferring or banishing the anguish and
terror of the indefinite and indeterminate by fixing the discursive grounds of
such questioning to unquestionable principles or dogmas functioning as
transcendental guarantees, putting them beyond what is open to question
and doubt. Many people find this route in religion, and, increasingly,
through the securities and totalizations of fundamentalism.

One set of considerations that I want to put on the agenda concerns the
positivity of desire, the pleasures of the body, the search for plenitude and
the promise of joy, something fundamental to being that the social sciences
and rational reconstructions of historical periods and the formation of
subjectivities do not fathom. I should include amongst the latter the
Hegelian analysis of the relation to the other in the emergence of consciousness or the emergence of the self as a differentiated self; the master–
slave thematic, in particular, proposes a model in which the recognition of
the other is instrumentalized into the tactic of the objectification of the
other for the subject's own ends. I side-step the Hegelian problematic
because I want to focus on a line of thought that implicates a longer
genealogy of the subject of which the subject of modernity is but a segment.
It aims to join ontology and phenomenology, seeking something of lasting
value in the passing moment, to paraphrase Baudelaire.

A good deal of important work on the embodied character of subjectivity
has been done within feminist theory, for example in the work of Irigaray or
Cixous generally, and specifically in Grosz (1994), Braidotti (1994), Gatens
(1996), Butler (1990, 1993). The lessons from this corpus concern the
subversion of the tired dualities in Western thought between mind and body
in which mind is privileged, and the consequent neglect of the 'unruly',
'disruptive' body that must be tamed by masculine reason. One consequence
of dualism has been the removal of consciousness 'from direct contact with
other minds and a sociocultural community' (Grosz, 1994: 7). The project of
'contesting the domination of the body by biology' obliges us to 'rethink the
opposition between the inside and the outside, the private and the public,
the self and the other' beyond forms of essentialism and originary centrings
(Grosz, 1994: 20). Grosz thinks the relationship between nature and culture
in terms of 'interimplication', marked by difference and the logic of
reciprocal supplementarity. The rejection of dualism, historically reduced to
oppositions, draws attention instead to the point of view of an embodied

subjectivity and 'psychical corporeality'. The body is constituted as both material and psychic space incorporated within the lifeworld. Grosz suggests a concept of human materiality that implies continuity between it and organic and inorganic materiality; it is a materialism beyond physicalism. An implication is that 'corporeality must no longer be associated with one sex (or race)' (1994: 22). One would need to imagine 'a plural and multiple field of possible body "types"' (1994: 22), such that that the body functions as a threshold concept between binary pairs – male, female, say – problematizing them (1994: 22). Thus, the body 'is neither – while also being both – the private or the public, self or other, natural or cultural, psychical or social, instinctive or learned, genetically or environmentally determined' (1994: 23). Later, in Chapter 5, I will establish that the body is the 'primordial ground' of being (Merleau-Ponty, 1968), and that it exists as monument in the sense of memory embodied, spatialized and temporalized in the world of objects.

The fundamental problematization of embodiment and subjectivity is differently pursued in the work of Butler, where she grounds the discussion in issues of gender and sexuality as sites for troubling phallogocentrism and challenging the limitations of positions (for instance, Foucault, constructivism) that, whilst radical and subversive, have started to reveal lines of fracture in the light of more recent subversions. The problem has been the question of allocating the share of cultural determination against the claims of critical agency without which one cannot imagine counter-hegemonic acts of dissidence or opposition. Perhaps it is a matter of rethinking the concept of constitutive construction, so that it is understood as a constraint limiting the process of normalization and stabilization of subjectivities. Then we could think that bodies 'only appear, only endure, only live within the productive constraints of certain highly gendered regulatory groups' (Butler, 1993: xi). The constitutive process involves both material and discursive practices. The two are articulated in the performative instantiation of a norm in a practice, provided one understands performativity as 'the reiterative and citational practice by which discourse produces the effects that it names' (Butler, 1993: 2). As an illustration, one could think of the acts and signifying practices through which a subject recites itself as racist or heterosexual, that is to say, repeats through gestures and speech the regulatory norms which materialize a particular 'identity' in a body. The body, in Butler's theorization, is always-already materialized, it is not the blank slate upon which discourse writes the subject; rather, it is always in process of formation and re-formation as effects of relations of power. The question of identification, whereby a particular subjectivity emerges, is tied up with the performative character of regimes of instituting particular normative and normalized ways of being. Power operates in these mechanisms at both the material and discursive levels, so that, concerning specific dimensions like sexuality and gender, 'the symbolic ought to be rethought as a series of normativizing injunctions that secure the borders of sex through the threat of psychosis, abjection, psychic unlivability' (Butler,

1993: 14–15). The symbolic thus appears to have the force of 'law', though what is 'forced' 'is a citation of its law that reiterates and consolidates the ruse of its own force' (1993: 15). This designates also, presumably, the coefficient of its effectivity, when we remember that Foucault thought that power was the more effective the more it could conceal its operation as power. Butler identifies the agency inside the process of citation of power, so that transgressive subjectivity would be constituted inside the relations of power and not outside them. One can see how the risk of invoking a voluntarist agent when it is a matter of resistance motivates a theorization of constitution that tries to locate both the normative and the transgressive inside the field of operation of power, though one then has to differentiate power – so that it is not the same power or the same mode of operation of power or the same target that is involved – and heterogenize the domain of the symbolic, as agonistic sites producing mobile, polyvalent subjective positions. Or one could locate such sites when considering cases like the implantation of Western culture in the colonies through the apparatus of schooling. Bhabha's (1994) analysis of mimicry in India or Trinh Minh-ha's (1989) exploration of uncolonized spaces in subjugated cultures in South-East Asia, and Appiah's (1992) uncovering of the practices of resistance to British rule in Nigeria show that resistance and transgression are conditioned by prior diffractions of power, so that power itself must be pluralized, here between colonialist subjugative power and indigenous authorizing narratives and narratives of identity inscribed in subaltern forms of sociality and memory. So, when examining the performative effects of subjectifying power, one would still have to posit relatively uncolonized arenas in the process of formation, for instance in Foucault, 'bodies and pleasures'. This point is taken up by Butler (1999) when she examines the break away from 'sex-desire' to 'bodies and pleasures' in Foucault's problematic of sexuality, where the latter is made to counter the force of subjugating power in prescribing a normative sexuality, thus normative gender relations, and the consequences of that shift from the point of view of social regulation. A difficulty is that the tactical reversal of regulative sexuality through the agency of bodies and pleasures implicates a different register for thinking agency, one that is not clear in Foucault, for how can there be uninvested spaces, or spaces that are not immediately co-opted, or spaces that exist in a new time yet to appear? Foucault's thinking about this, and the element that Butler exposes, is that desire demands a separate history, tied to a genealogy of the subject which addresses the question of how and why the subject has come to understand itself by reference to the notion of a desiring subject. As Butler points out: 'To deny the sphere of desire, or call for its replacement, is precisely to eradicate the phenomenological ground of sexuality itself' (1999: 19). The way out of the quandary is to turn to the question of historicity and the problematic of narrative identity, which I will introduce below.

There is another set of considerations, still in answer to the question of our 'presentness', that opens up the question of 'identity' and subjectifica-

tion in some unexpected ways. I am thinking of the problematic of resistance to colonial forms of subjection/subjectification and of the disjunctions
that operate to fracture subjectivity in that field, and that reveal the imbri-
cations of power in the process in a different light. They add to the
problems that emerge when we try to think through the historically contingent features of the constitution of subjects with respect to the institution
of particular forms of the social world, problems which relate to the complexity of the process of constitution and its underdetermined character.
My approach is to consider the constitution of subjects in and for modern
imperial power and its form of governmentality. There are two lines of
argument which motivate such an approach. As I argued in Chapter 1, the
legacy of this history still operates in the social and cultural spaces terri-
torialized by colonialism and imperialism, particularly in the technologies
and apparatuses – for instance, the educational system – of the constitution
of forms of sociality and of the regulation and administration of populations. The consequences, though diverse and ambivalent, have often been
disastrous from the point of view of resistance to the occidentalized and
capitalist models of modernization and by reference to the failures of these
models which today increasingly provoke a turn to fundamentalism.

The other reason brings up one of the basic propositions that I am
developing in the book. It concerns the claim that a way of locating the
specificity of the modern discourse of the subject is to regard Europe's
discovery and subjugation of the New World and its peoples and cultures,
and the colonizing project as a whole, to have been one of the vital conditions which shaped that discourse. I shall develop this view in the next
chapter, where I will examine the displacements and the transformations
that stage the birth of modernity and its subject. The historicity of our
presentness is made up of the intertwined genealogies of modernity, subjectivity and colonialism. Capitalism binds them at strategic points, acting
as a chain, although the history of capitalism is not itself independent of the
other histories.

Let me use the work of Fanon as a point of entry into the range of
problems that I want to explore. There is a classic incident recalled in *Black
Skin White Masks* in which a little white boy, upon seeing Fanon in France,
points him out to his mother and exclaims 'Look, a Negro!'; and again
'Mother, see the Negro! I'm frightened!' (1970: 79). Fanon uses this incident
to develop a meditation on blackness and to reveal the crisis of identity, an
already fragile identity, which the gaze of the other precipitates when the
gaze is structured not by the face relation but by the dread of the stranger
as the racialized other. He at first reflects on how his carefully nurtured
cosmopolitan persona, nourished by all that 'civilization' has to offer, is
annihilated in the moment of being identified as the bogey-man of racist
myths and stereotypes. The reiteration of naming: 'Negro', the pointing
which interpellates Fanon, at first not quite believing he is the subject of the
citation in the position of the frightening 'other', the boy's bodily gestures,
expressing fear, distance and exclusion, all these mechanisms, at once

discursive and embodied, performatively lock him into an identity he thought his formation as intellectual had cancelled.[11] In that moment, Fanon discovers that his body had been given back to him 'sprawled out, distorted, recoloured, clad in mourning' (1970: 80). Skin is the intransigent barrier, the marker of a 'racial epidermal schema', laden with what he interestingly calls 'historicity' (1970: 79), and carrying the inheritance of narratives of native excess and violence. He feels unable to escape the fact that he is held responsible for his body, his race and his ancestry. The black body is already inscribed in a chain of signifiers locking the 'black' subject into a discursive field in which the metonymies of savagery and inferiority are repeated along the colonizer's historical narrative of race and colonial subjugation. It is a narrative that Fanon recites in his trawl through the occidentalist discourse about black people. Fixed into position by a history outside his control, Fanon wants to know how one could come to terms with the dislocations and the splittings inscribed in the black body, and still be a man.

Anonymity and invisibility do not help, they do not dispel the terror of being overdetermined and fixed in an unlivable identity. The strategy of a search for the recovery of a different self, not amputated and objectified, at first takes Fanon back to the narratives of blackness, refigured in the discourse of Negritude, celebrating a 'primitive mentality', the rhythms of which the tom-toms of memory beat into the body of the black man. He remembers too the narratives of the achievements and triumphs of Africa that colonialism had erased and its irreducibility to the debilitating abstractions of Western philosophy: 'From the opposite end of the white world a magical Negro culture was hailing me' (1970: 87). One is reminded of Benjamin's perceptive remark about history when the danger of subjection to the 'ruling class' is revealed: 'To articulate the past historically does not mean to recognize it "the way it really was"' (Ranke). 'It means to seize hold of a memory as it flashes up at a moment of danger' (1973: 257). The strength to continue to resist, the resilience of the spirit that the black man needs to combat the accumulated burden of subjection, has to draw from something less totalizing than Western theory, from 'an almost substantive absoluteness' (Fanon, 1970: 94). So Fanon turns to the poetry of Negritude to find the vocabulary and the voice in which to articulate the mixture of pain, rage and hope that assails and drives him. This is because writers like Senghor, Césaire, Roumain, Wright, Diop, whose texts he cites, point to the polyvalence of 'Blackness', dissolving the white, univocal category of 'otherness', and strive to make visible the memory of Africa 'like a splinter in the wound'. They share with Fanon the desire to transmute the suffering of abjection into a world-transforming project. Their poetics is steeped in a barely legible past and in the body as the irreducible experiential core of being, attempting to make present or to bring to presence a future whose becoming would abolish the horror of the present.

Fanon's text, like those of Irigaray and Kristeva, but for different reasons, refers to a *poiesis* in the effort to apprehend the unpresentable dimension which no rationalized account can deliver to consciousness. It also brings to the fore the issue of the effects of power in the constitution of subjects, particularly the way antagonistic narratives provoke dislocations in the temporal and spatial dimensions of the 'lived' that are experienced as splittings, double-consciousness or even schizophrenia. Indeed, several themes can be picked out from the texts of these authors that I will explore through the concept of narrative identity. They concern the theorization of the body, the place of memory and of historicity in the formation and transformation of subjectivities and their stability or instability, the economy of desire, the problem of the narratives that constitute the 'reality' of the lifeworld.

On the narrative character of identity

I will start with the arguments that consider temporality to be the defining characteristic of human beings. In a very fundamental way, time determines the horizon for any understanding of being. As soon as we think of our-selves as conscious beings, we think time, and we cannot think time without bringing up the question of consciousness, specifically, the consciousness that we exist in time, stretched out between a remembered past, an evane-scent present and the anticipation of a future. We know ouselves to be fateful and fatal beings, judging our presentness by reference to the spacing and trace of time. Like Heidegger, Ricoeur considers the having-been, the making-present and the coming-towards to be the three moments, indeed, the co-articulated moments, of the temporality of being; they mark the space in which we question ourselves as to our way of being.

Yet a basic aporia of time is its inscrutability. This may well be because we are encompassed by time. The avenue that Ricoeur follows is to explore the possibility that narrative is the form in which we can overcome the unrepresentability of time (when we think of it in the singular), and the device by which we express the lived aspect of temporality. The underlying idea is that the act of telling a story 'can transmute natural time into a specifically human time' (Ricoeur, 1984: 17). In Ricoeur's approach, the term 'narrative identity' seems to join up two problematics: one which is about subjective identity and the other concerning the relation of history and fiction in the process of the figuration of temporality. It does so by establishing that time, and the way it is lived, provides the common ground for their co-articulation. Ricoeur draws a distinction between identity as sameness (*idem*) and identity as selfhood (*ipse*), that is to say, on the one hand, identity as something that remains identical to itself over time and, on the other hand, an entity that considers itself to remain the same being in spite of changes over time, for example in a person's biographical history. Identity is not the sameness of a permanent, continuous, immut-able, fixed entity; it is instead the mode of relating to being that can be characterized as selfhood. Self is not a fact or an event, it is not reducible to the facticity of things-in-themselves (or Heidegger's ready-to-hand). The identity of a person, or a group or a people, takes the form of stories told.

Narrative identity, however, should not be understood as another name for biography or as a way of talking about the interiorization of the stories of a life to constitute personal identity. Indeed, Ricoeur's analysis is primarily located not on the terrain of a psychology but on that of ontology. Narrative identity appears in his discourse of being as the concept that enables us to think of the mediation between the phenomenological and the cosmological apprehension of time. Narrative is thus the way of joining up the 'time of the soul' with the time of the world. In a sense the 'self' as a meaningful and meaning-making entity appears at the point of intersection of two kinds of reflection on our beingness or existence. On the one hand, we find the stories and memories that express the time of being-in-the-world and of being-with, the duration of events and experiences in the everyday: the time it takes to do countless mundane things at home or at work, and the time it takes for our children to grow into adults, the time of birthdays, commemorations, the scansion of temporal flow in every life. The cultural specificity of this experience of phenomenal temporality is a matter that is too often neglected in Eurocentric theorizations of time.[12]

On the other hand, bound up with phenomenal time are the questions which surface about time in the singular, thus about finitude, and about what gives meaning to life at the general, cosmological level. It is a matter of evaluation, guided by a history of reflection about what is liminally present in the significant events of our existence, yet transcends biography, concerning the apprehension of a sublime dimension to human existence, an experience of the ecstasy and epiphany of being. So, at one level, temporality encompasses the historical and cultural space of the emergence of the who of action and meaning, and at another level, it opens onto a critical hermeneutics and to a reflection which points to the apprehension that a self 'does not belong to the category of events and facts' (Ricoeur, 1991: 193). We shall see how the implications for the formation of subjectivities and issues of refiguration and transfiguration link up with Ricoeur's approach in a way which avoids the collapse into species of psychologism, determinism and essentialism.

Narrative, Ricoeur tells us, 'constructs the durable properties of a character' (1991: 195). It does so by emplotting the events of a life according to the rules of storytelling, relying upon the modalities of plot already existing in a culture. We make sense of our actions and the events in our lives by inventing fictions that figure them in the domain of the imagination. The sense of narrative identity that Ricoeur develops stresses the view that every identity is 'mingled with that of others in such a way as to engender second-order stories which are themselves intersections between numerous stories. . . . We are literally "entangled in stories"' (Ricoeur, 1996: 6).

In order to understand the mechanisms at work in subjective formation and change, we need to examine the three mimetic functions of narrative described by Ricoeur. Mimesis 1 refers to the prenarrative features that express basic human desire; it describes a 'semantics of desire' (Ricoeur, 1988: 248); this formulation suggests perhaps the thetic function or phase of the signifying process as understood by Kristeva. I draw attention to Kristeva's (1974) analysis of *signifiance* because she makes a systematic connection between the process of identification and the process of signification by way of the functioning of the economy of desire, so that the complicity between sign and propositionality is underpinned by the relation between the semiotic and the semantic fields, in which the thetic functions as, at the same time, rupture and frontier, and thus as relay (Kristeva, 1974: 41–2). My juxtaposition of Kristeva is meant to keep visible the psychic level of the process of figuration and refiguration, a level which is not so clear in Ricoeur, but which my discussion of Fanon brings to the fore. Mimesis 2 arises from the creative process of the configuration of experience, whilst Mimesis 3 refers to the narrative identity which results from repeated rectifications of Mimesis 2 in the course of reflection and rememoration. Thus, the third mimetic relation relates back to the first by way of a transformative praxis applied to the second (Ricoeur, 1988: 248). Every narrative identity is a refigured identity, involving the action of a *poiesis* which accomplishes the weaving of the phenomenological and cosmological dimensions of being, working the fictional into the historical narrative to constitute a 'third-time' (1988: 245). The consequence is that the 'fragile offshoot from the union of history and fiction is the assignment to an individual or a community of a specific identity that we can call their narrative identity' (1988: 246). It is this identity which is refigured through the application of particular types of narratives existing in a culture which, through self-reflection, performs a hermeneutic and critical function. The constant refiguration of identity, or its possibility, brings up the question of the kind of narrative promoting such a process, so that narrative becomes the 'name of a problem' (1988: 249).

The point is that although '(l)ife is woven of stories told' (Ricoeur, 1988: 246), these stories are not purely imaginary or fictional, for they make reference to a domain of reality that can be verified through attestation or testimony. On the one hand, the stories we tell about ourselves are segments of other people's stories about themselves and us, so that a self 'happens' at the point of intersection of many real lives. On the other hand, some of these narratives tell of events involving a whole community or period of time, that is, they inscribe a history, so that every self occurs 'at a point of intersection between fictive and historical narratives' (Ricoeur, 1991: 186). Although history takes the form of a narration, it is important to avoid reducing history to a species of fiction,[13] and thus abolish the question of truth, for instance regarding the Holocaust or colonial oppression. Ricoeur insists on maintaining the polarity between the two, using the notion of debt to make visible the responsibility which history owes to those who have been, namely, the responsibility to ensure that historical narrative does not fictionalize the dead, thus killing them twice over, but must 'return their "having-been" to them' (Ricoeur, 1991: 186). The narrativity of identity does not abolish the 'reality' of the who, but shifts the question of the truth of subjectivity onto the ground of inter-subjectivity. The shared character of identity, the way in which we can think of ourself as a particular self only by reference to being-with-the-other, means that identity is always-already cultural. Indeed, self-reflection is the process whereby we apply to ourself historical and fictional narratives sedimented in our culture, so that 'self-constancy refers to a self instructed by the works of a culture that it has applied to itself' (Ricoeur, 1988: 247). The example of becoming a parent that I noted earlier demonstrates how the process of figuration and refiguration brings into play the scripts and plots existing in a culture; they fill with content the vocabulary of selfhood that gives meaning to the events of a life and validates the sense of who we are.[14]

From what Ricoeur says, we could consider the refiguration of particular selves to occur, for example, as the result of 'working-through' in psycho-analytic practice or as the result of a process of rememoration when the biographical content of narrative identity encounters the historical refigurations and rectifications performed by historians. This is demonstrated in the way that feminist and 'Black' history have participated in the reconstruction of identity by giving people a different past and a different temporal framework for anticipating possible subjective projects. In the everyday, it is important to recognize that the most common narratives and narrations that function as models or scripts for 'identities' are now to be found in novels, films, plays, poetry, traditional tales, parables, and so on, in which lives are emplotted and secrets of 'living well' are revealed or communicated in the form of lessons. The practice of everyday life is suffused with knowledges of all kinds, sometimes drawn from or authorized by theoretical accounts, for example about the function of sexuality in the formation of the psyche, which become part of the stock of narratives people apply to themselves. In that sense, the three mimetic functions as described by Ricoeur should be read as shorthand for the complex process of the rectification of selves, a process irreducible to a simple linguistic event. The refiguration of identity depends on the conjunction of particular phenomena, involving action with others, and the retelling or re-emplotment of the biographical elements of a previous identity: it is a labour. It depends too on the quality and provenance of the narration, that is, its density, richness, depth, insight, emotional weight, voice, point of view or, more generally, everything that makes it an inexhaustible source for the hermeneutic task and that operates to disrupt normalizing closure.[15]

The process of subjective change has a diachronic dimension which Ricoeur indicates when he refers to the inscription of a notion of 'traditionality' located in the conceptual space bounded by the three-fold relation of mimesis. The term is used to try to account for the effectivity of history upon us, the way in which the past affects us independently of our will and the way we respond to the effect of history through an articulation of the past and the present. In that sense, traditionality can be understood as the term referring to the interweaving of two 'temporalizations of history' (Ricoeur, 1988: 219) that cross each other, constituting particular identities at the points of intersection. A 'who' appears at that point of intersection where the history of a culture, sedimented and transmitted in its stock of knowledge, its narrations and 'texts', crosses the history of a named subject, constituting a particular consciousness. This is the mechanism by which we are so to speak sutured in history. Perhaps we could also try to imagine this process according to the analogy of the envelope, in the mathematical sense, rather than think of the crossing in terms of the point, since the latter tends to invoke a static moment rather than a continuous line or curvature. There is always the temptation to limit the indefinite character of the process of articulation, and thus the anxiety of uncertainty it provokes, by attempting a 'fusion of the horizons' (Ricoeur, 1988: 221) of the space of experience and the horizon of expectation, forcing their coincidence or correspondence, usually effected by ideological functioning of a totalizing doctrine or discourse or a metaphysics of transcendence.

Ricoeur's understanding of traditionality, besides, precludes the for-getting of the past, whether it is an active forgetting (as advocated by Nietzsche), or the result of repression or disavowal, or whether it is achieved by means of the obliteration of the past through a brutal break with it, for example in ethnic cleansing and some forms of fundamentalism. The narrative of the present must remain open to the recognition of a heritage, or roots (Gilroy, 1993a), with which one must come to terms. The problem concerns the way in which this dialogue with the past can be both dialogical and dynamic, that is, how the refigurations of the past and the present mutually condition each other whilst relating to the future as possibility and as difference, implying the effects of different 'routes' (Gilroy, 1993a). Modernity as a period attests to the recognition of the tension between the two and the variability of the relationship between them. Any strategy which seeks to collapse the two is an attempt to refuse the possibility of a judgement of our presentness by reference to the differ-ence between an imagined past and a projected future, and its legitimation in terms of some value like emancipation.

It is important to bear in mind that the issues of debt and of respon-sibility are implicated in this notion of a judgement of history, and, by the same token, the point of view of an ethics in the temporalization of history. In other words, the way we narrate history – whether as difference, repe-tition, as logical necessity, and so on – carries with it normative or pre-scriptive values since, in constructing the world in a particular way, every narration attempts to persuade or direct the reader or listener to act in a certain way. For example, an account of someone's action that relies on explanations in terms of genetic determination or essential tendencies – the debate about gender or ethnic differences is burdened by a surfeit of such claims – removes that action from the possibility of transformative practices, and thus from the openness to change on the basis of ethical considerations. But, as Ricoeur has pointed out, 'narrative already belongs to the ethical field in virtue of its claim – inseparable from its narration – to ethical justice' (Ricoeur, 1988: 249).

Some lessons for (dis)identification

Let me pick out a number of themes as a way of summarizing the points that I want to signal in relation to the question of subjective transformation generally, and the question of postcolonial identity and its refiguration as a special case. At the level of the general protocols of analysis and critique, I would point out again the inter-subjective and cultural dimension of identity, against notions of the autonomous singularity of the self and the conceptualization of a self-present 'I' acting as the originary point of agency. This heteronomous dimension is tied to the priority granted to temporality in the understanding of being and the implications for the theorization of identity and subjectiviy, particularly the emphasis on the inter-connectedness or 'articulated unity' (Ricoeur, 1988: 70) of the three ecstasies of time: the having-been, the making-present, the coming-towards. Central to connectedness is the functioning of the indirect discourse of narration as a way of giving reality to, or making phenomenal, the onto-logical standpoint.[16] Narrative, as I said, mingles our individual history and our identity with that of others and their stories, so that I am always multiply dispersed into a series of stories and acts involving others and their stories. This aspect of being-with is repeated in the connection of tem-porality and historicity through narration which I have examined by reference to the cultural and inter-subjective location and nature of the mechanisms for the (re-)formation of subjectivity. This location is far from being discursive alone, for we exist as embodied entities coupled to the material world. The standpoint of embodiment brings into focus the place of affect in these mechanisms. The sense of historicity that I have been developing considers both temporality and spatiality to be its constitutive dimensions, so that the world to which the subject is coupled is at once archive and monument, the space of a memorialization and of dwelling for being, and the space for an apprenticeship into ways of living that necessarily inscribe the ethical dimension.

It is important to highlight a number of problems relating to the effects of power for which we do not find clear indications in Ricoeur, in spite of the recognition of the agonistic terrain of the production of historical narratives. In particular, we need to address the question of the effects of power at two inter-related levels, the historical and the biographical. At the general level, there are the effects that operate in the making and telling of the particular history of communities and periods, so that every history is a particular temporalization, configured in the metanarratives which provide the broader canvas in relation to which individuals in any society locate their own minor or 'little' narratives. For instance, Fanon's counter-narratives of Africa, set against the occidentalist version and its narration of modernity, reveal the economic and racist interests that have shaped the latter version. At the other level, which refers to the domain of the experiential, we know that it is impossible to make sense of individual lives outside considerations of gender or race, class or caste, and so on, and the power relations invested in them. So, in trying to transform subjectivities, one cannot avoid interrogating the power relations inscribed in everything that fills identities with content, namely, the cultural imaginary and memory constituted out of the authorizing great ideas, the beliefs, the myths, the sayings, the models and examplars, the stories of deeds done, as well as everything that has been sedimented in the artistic output of a culture. It is for this reason that the remaking of postcolonial identities implicates the revision of the history of modernity. The politics of difference attached to feminist, postcolonial and other struggles provide ample evidence that this connection is inevitable. In keeping visible the 'big picture', I want to signal that such a revision engages with a utopian anticipation of the future, that is to say, it calls up visions of alternative 'big pictures', thus alternative grand narratives.

To illustrate this, we can return to the text of Fanon, to the place where we find him describing how he feels entrapped in the narratives of colonial discourse about Europe's 'others' and constrained by the specific 'traditionality' in the narration of modernity. The past as told from the point of view of Europe and the colonizers is precisely what burdens him. It is a past that he cannot refigure whilst he remains within a particular '*mise-en-discours*' and temporalization of history that appear to provide him with the instruments for the refiguration of identity, yet prove to be inadequate because the metanarratives of progress, rationality and emancipation, and liberty, that frame the conceptual and tropic space of this narration happen to be, at the same time, the shackles that bind him even more firmly the more he struggles with and against them. The force of these discursive shackles derives from the fact that they conceptually organize and encase the world and the imagination within the boundaries of narrativizations of experience that already inscribe the 'other' within an idea of 'otherness' that they have themselves specified. The embodied character of subjectivity intensifies the sense of being entrapped.

Something else is called for which Fanon finds in a different voice, interestingly in the poetic recovery of the memory of blackness and subjugation/subjectification, a memory denied in the discourse of the 'master', disavowed by the (liberal) cosmopolitan intellectual, yet lived as the trace of trauma, ready to erupt in violence. The injury of colonialism, multiply inscribed – in the body, in the psyche, in culture, in history and in the lifeworld – is refigured through the recognition of shared suffering transmuted in writing and 'art', and, just as centrally, through the transformative work of a critical hermeneutics. The argument here claims that there exists an artistic practice, mimetic or otherwise,[17] that reveals the concealed or unpresentable features of experience and thought, working at the level of the intuitive and of the imaginary, bringing to presence a sublime and liminal dimension. The implication in both Ricoeur (1992) and Fanon (1970) is that without the work that art performs, that is, without *poiesis*, and the work of refiguration that it enables us to perform with respect to the 'who' of identity, life would be incoherent. From the point of view of resistance or counter-hegemony, the chemistry of disidentification works by alchemy, requiring a brew of a critical narration and incantations of an auratic power distilled in the alembic of poetic transfiguration. I will examine this in detail in Chapter 4, by reference to the idea of an ethics and an aesthetics of the self and in my discussion of the sublime. I will use Toni Morrison's *Beloved* as a case.

It is important, equally, to theorize the process of changing the subject by reference to ways of dealing with loss and trauma, that is, fully recognizing the centrality of affect for the process. Fanon's account of the sense of annihilation he experienced, and the Negritude writings to which he turned in search of another speech, express a multiplicity of losses: of identity and self-esteem, of history and rootedness, of face and agency. They pour into the abyss of an anterior and primary – that is, ontological – loss and lack, adding to the weight of anguish that pulls the abject 'other' into the cycles of psychic suffering. Fanon discussed the range of possible responses, such as self-hate, despondency, melancholia, violence. Clearly his own response, like that of Césaire, for example, has been to invent ways of mourning and ways of overcoming these pains or ways of transmuting the memory of subjection into a transcendent dimension, drawing from the language of myth and the rhythms of another, fantasmatic and immemorial, way of being. At the end of *Black Skin White Masks* Fanon invokes a utopian dimension – a relocated, non-Eurocentric humanism in this case – in his search for the legitimating principles of resistance and the basis of self-transformation. So hope and the promise of joy, along with historicity and responsibility, are also part of the equation.

The theme of an emancipation and of a liberation returns. It requires rephrasing in a new secular idiom. This new discourse of the desired future and of an acceptable present is inevitably inflected by the history of modernity, and the language that had developed with modernity to speak of emancipation and enlightenment. But it cannot be written except in the course of a rewriting of the history of modernity and the philosophical discourse which has nourished it, that is to say, in the course of a critical engagement with how the experience of modernity has been temporalized and monumentalized, and what it has signified. This is where the post-colonial (and feminist) question(ing) occupies a decisive place from the point of view of critique, for it is a questioning from the underside of modernity, its unspoken or hidden history, cast out as a poor relation, yet which carries within it the trace of the supplement that will undo the triumphalist narrative of emancipation. It opens up to a different reflection the 'hermeneutics of desire', the economy of sacrifice and the economy of the gift and their relation to the question of ethical responsibility and the temporality of being.

Notes

1 The elaboration of this task takes Levin through a reading of Heidegger and Merleau-Ponty juxtaposed with an interpretation of Freud and Jung, a road I have not pursued here.

2 Bunyan's *Pilgrim's Progress* is an early example of the resilience of the theme of *Homo viator* in the modern era.

3 Is the gap also the space which metaphysics is made to fill?

4 I should emphasize that alterity is not otherness. Alterity does not implicate alienness but separation from myself, as an other, but an other who remains inaccessible. Not only must I respect the singularity of the other, I cannot take the place of the other. The test of alterity, it could be argued, is that I cannot take upon myself the suffering of the other – my child, a lover – in order that she may not suffer, however much I may wish to.

5 See also the discussion of violence and metaphysics in Derrida (1967).

6 We find its pathological expression in the US military strategy in Vietnam, in the decision in favour of the saturation bombing of the land on the grounds that 'we had to destroy it in order to save it'.

7 My choice of language evokes a resonance with the goals of Enlightenment philosophy, which might be thought surprising. What I have said so far should indicate, however, that the interrogation of the concept of 'History' and of the discourse of the Enlightenment is far from being peripheral to postcolonial critique; they are indeed central to it.

8 It follows from what I have said that this economy covers both self-sacrifice, as in Puritanism, and the sacrifice of the 'other' for the sake of bringing about a universal cosmopolitan identity.

9 My understanding of the concept is clearly different from Husserl's (1970), although informed by that problematic and subsequent discussion, for example in Ricoeur's (1992) inflection of the concept towards the 'who' rather than the 'what' or the 'why' of action.

10 Psychology, and the social sciences generally, do this; it is an assumption which is in keeping with the manner of the birth of the modern subject, as I will explain in Chapter 3.

11 As I pointed out above, Butler understands preformativity thus: '[p]erformativity must be understood not as a singular or deliberate "act", but, rather, as the reiterative and citational practice by which discourse produces the effects that it names . . . [it is] that power of discourse to produce the phenomena that it regulates and constrains' (1993: 2). This privilege of discourse, it must be said, is affiliated to the problematic of representation, which conceals a nostalgia for another privilege: that of the logocentric subject . . .

12 Temporality as lived is culturally and historically variable, as a good deal of ethnographic analyses have established. See also Fabian (1983), Osborne (1995).

13 The discussion of history around the work of Hayden White is instructive in this context (see White, 1978).

14 I would like to signal the element of refiguration which involves the anamnesis of what has been disavowed and buried in the course of previous figurations of subjectivity. The process of changing the subject is therefore a very complex one, working at the psychic level as well as at the cognitive, the ethical and the aesthetic levels.

15 Grand narratives have functioned in this way, for instance in the guise of Marxism or feminist and colonial narratives of liberation.

16 Note Ricoeur's differences from Heidegger, for instance in his critique of Being-towards-death. Furthermore, his understanding of historicality binds it to the notion of being-with and the 'they' or communitarian side of being-in-the-world (see Ricoeur, 1988: 71ff.). Ricoeur has reservations about Heidegger's emphasis on the singularity, or aloneness, of the self, for example in Heidegger's remark that we all die alone, and in his failure to prioritize being-with and the 'they'.

17 I use mimesis in the light of Taussig's analysis of 'active yielding' (1993: 46) to what is presented in certain kinds of representative or mimetic practices, indicating a functioning which reaches beyond mere repetition or mechanical imitation. Clearly the domain of the aesthetic is implicated as soon as we speak of a mimetic function.

3

ON THE EMERGENCE OF MODERNITY
AND THE BIRTH OF THE SUBJECT

Auspicious beginnings

Three episodes set up the scene for what I will elaborate in this chapter. The first episode concerns Descartes's gesture that expresses the principle of *tabula rasa*, the symbolic brushing aside of all previously existing claims to know, the performative instantiation of the systematic doubt to which all knowledge must be subjected as a starting point for the production of truth. What does this principle achieve? Bear in mind that knowledge, until modernity, was a matter of the proper reading or application of the truths inscribed in the authoritative texts handed down through the ages. The more ancient the text, the more it was supposed to be primary and decisive, commanding respect in disputes. Descartes's gesture at once erases this whole tradition, breaking with the deference to the past, announcing the futurity of truth: knowledge is the yet unknown or uncertified truth awaiting proof and confirmation in the future. This is supposed to be achieved by means of a general method, based on the rational examination of the empirical evidence and the arguments, without respect for any authority save that of Reason and the objectivity of the process. Opinion, from whatever authority, counted for nothing by itself. The knowing subject had to rely on 'his' own intellectual work.[1]

Tabula rasa, in making invisible the effectivity of the intellectual community in the process of production of knowledge, effaces the relation to alterity at the same time as it annuls the historicity of discourse, privileging the individual's solitary mental activity: 'I found myself constrained, as it were, to undertake my own guidance' (Descartes, 1968 [1637]: 39). The relation to the other is dissimulated in Descartes's thought in the doubling or folding of the 'I' over or into itself expressed in the 'first principle of the philosophy I was seeking' (1968 [1637]: 54), namely, I think (therefore) I am. In this way Descartes installs the subject as self-present, that is, as present to itself in consciousness; it is a presence that requires no validation from outside or from other human beings. The notion of self-presence and the vicissitudes of the relation to the other in the emergence of modernity is one of the central themes that I want to explore in this chapter.

The second episode records the extraordinary change which marked the space between the modern era and the period that preceded it. Easlea summarizes it thus:

> In 1500 educated people in western Europe believed themselves living at the
> centre of a finite cosmos, at the mercy of (supernatural) forces beyond their
> control, and certainly continually menaced by Satan and his allies. By 1700
> educated people in western Europe for the most part believed themselves living in
> an infinite universe on a tiny planet in (elliptical) orbit about the sun, no longer
> menaced by Satan, and confident that power over the natural world lay within
> their grasp. (1980: 1)

Easlea's analysis charts the transformations in the perception of the
natural world and in the emergence of an astonishing confidence in
the capacity of human beings to determine their existence, expressed in the
daring ambition of exercising a sovereign power over the forces of nature,
and the determination to bend nature to human will and intentions. His
account of the birth of mechanical philosophy and of modern science brings
out the alliance between a masculinist epistemology and the desacralization
and disenchantment of nature, emptying it of magic and spiritual content, a
step made necessary if nature were to be available for ownership and control
and for experimentation directed by human will and interest. What we
apprehend from Easlea's reconstruction of this key moment of the emergence
of modernity is the impersonal, abstract, cold, instrumental rationality which
comes to replace the substantive reason and spirituality of a Paracelsus, and
the increasing instrumental linkages between knowledge and secular power.
Equally, one could detect in the zeal of the witch-hunts in the sixteenth and
seventeenth centuries and the ruthless excess of the Inquisition the secret
anxieties which the fundamentalism of the time tried to disavow and project
onto the practices and groups – women, unbelievers, heretics – constituted as
the signs of danger.

Easlea, astonishingly, makes no reference to the effects of the New World
on these momentous changes, so that it appears as a distant, non-effective,
context. Which brings me to the third episode. The first act of the Spanish
conquistadors upon landing at Guanahani in the Caribbean was to plant
the royal standard and to take possession of the land in the name of the
King and Queen of Spain and for Christianity (Columbus, 1988 [1492]: 53).
The account which Columbus gives in his journals would like us to believe
that first contact already yielded significant information about the natives'
beliefs and responses to the strangers, enough to lead him to conclude that

> They should be good servants and very intelligent, for I have observed that they
> soon repeat anything that is said to them, and I believe that they would easily
> be made Christians, for they appeared to me to have no religion. . . . I will bring
> half a dozen of them back to their Majesties, so that they can learn to speak.
> (1988 [1492]: 56)[2]

He soon noticed too that they appeared healthy and strong, wore gold
jewellery but had no weapons, and, not surprisingly, decided his men could
'subjugate them all and make them do whatever we wish' (1988 [1492]: 59).
In the conquistadors' minds, the aim of ownership and the project of conversion were instituted from the very beginning. Knowledge was to follow
swiftly, although at first none of the colonizers spoke any of the native

languages. The conquest of America inaugurates a history of the West whereby knowledge, ownership, subjectification and subjection became intertwined, locked together by incredible violence.

The first two episodes register, at the level of history and of signification, the distance separating the modern age from what preceded it. The problem which arises concerns how we are to understand this caesura and this transition, so often examined, in countless texts about the specificity and conditions of the emergence of modernity, dealing with the emergence of modern science and the heliocentric view of the world, the birth of rational capitalism, the Reformation, the development of the modern state and its apparatuses, principally the law, and the discursive constitution of a new, phallogo-Eurocentric subject. My analysis of the transition is constructed in the margins of this literature, in answer to the question of the part colonialism and the European encounter with the New World played in the unique conjuncture which has conditioned our world. Until recently, in spite of Hegel's (1995) analysis of the epochal threshold of modernity, this question had been much neglected in Western discourse concerning the birth of the modern world and its destiny or destination so far. To find the recognition of the centrality of America and colonialism in the emergence of modernity, we have to wait for a series of revisionary studies such as Todorov's (1992 [1982]) account of the conquest of America or Pagden's (1993) analysis of Europe's encounter with the New World, and the earlier work of Lévi-Strauss (1952).[3] A number of accounts from the 'Third World', and elsewhere, heralded this recognition, for example in O'Gorman's (1961) work. Equally the analyses correlating slavery and capitalism implicate the connection with modernity, as in Eric Williams's (1964) study of capitalism and slavery and C.L.R. James's (1938) exploration of the uprisings in San Domingo and Haiti.

What is surprising is that even profoundly challenging and instructive analyses have been guilty of this neglect, exemplified in the tendency to look to events in Europe itself as sufficient basis for understanding the transformations. For instance, Foucault's *The Order of Things* (1970), a work which has transformed the way we now perceive modernity as an era and the way we understand the shifts that make sense of it, makes little reference to the importance of the New World for the discursive and epistemic transformations he analyses. Cascardi's *The Subject of Modernity* (1992), takes as an organizing principle Weber's thesis that the disenchantment of the world is intrinsic to the process of rationalization characterizing modernity; yet his exploration of the displacements that result in the overcoming of historical explanations by philosophy and by science finds no place for the effects of colonialism. Charles Taylor's (1989) important and thorough analysis of the making of the modern concept of the self discusses the anxieties which lead to the Lutheran *regiornamento* without reference to what was happening outside Europe, although he takes account of the critical interventions of anti-colonialists like Diderot and Herder in the eighteenth century.

With a few notable exceptions, for example J.H. Elliott (1970), historians fare little better. For example, G.R. Elton's classic study of reformation Europe mentions the expansion of Europe only to say that 'Cortéz and Pizarro added empires to Spain' (1963: 319) and to note the sixteenth century's boom arising from the expansion in trade and the increase in wealth, showing the importance of the Atlantic seaboard for establishing 'European hegemony on Earth' (1963: 324). In these works, and others too many to mention, there is a remarkable absence of the realization that the encounter with the New World and its peoples fundamentally challenged the European imagination and freed a space for the eruption of newness. It is one of my principal aims in this chapter to establish the 'supplementarity' (Derrida, 1982) of this tale in relation to the occidentalist narrative of modernity and in the analysis of the logocentric subject, that is to say, to disclose the constitutive function of colonialism that the conventional accounts must leave in the shadow in order for Europe to appear as the self-constituting centre of the world, owing nothing to those it positions as its 'others'.[4]

I have another reason for raking over the grounds upon which modernity was born. Postmodern critiques of what is wrong with modernity claim to have eliminated the concepts of Reason, the Subject and History as the master tropes that organize our understanding of the present. A good deal more has been evacuated with these deconstructions, provoking problems for the questions of agency and of the foundations for a different vision of emancipation, aspects of which I will examine in the final chapter. It seems to me that many of these critiques, and the implications that have been drawn from them, for example for feminist and 'Black' politics, stick too closely to the philosophical terrain they are trying to avoid in attempting to reformulate the problem of possible emancipation.[5] There is therefore a tendency to singularize notions of reason, subjectivity and history and thus to miss out on the deeply fractured character of these master tropes and the ambivalences and rifts inside the discourses that sustain them. A sensitivity to the tensions goes together with an awareness of the constant play of power in their production, showing up, precisely, in the ambivalences and splits. For instance, the fiat of *tabula rasa* might silence the historicity and collaborative nature of the production of knowledge, appearing to privilege the role of individual genius in the history of the sciences, but it cannot obliterate it entirely. The collaborative, communicative and inter-discursive reality of the production of knowledge remains as trace in the discourse and cannot be avoided in the lived relations of production.[6] It is possible to read between the lines, and thereby make power visible wherever it operates to establish closures or to silence antagonistic positions. In other words, it is possible, through appropriate deconstructive tactics, to recover an idea of the stakes in the discursive stratagems that aim to suppress them. With regard to the period of emergence of the discourses of modernity, what I would be trying to establish is that the telling of the suppressed tales of the institution of modernity is an act that itself opens up spaces, or breaks with habits of thought, and thus enables us to think of the postmodern in the positive terms of its futurity, the newness to come, rather than in the negative terms of the rejection of the modern.

Knowing the other, possessing, killing

Now, the limit of the old is not automatically or necessarily the threshold of the new. Between the limit of the old and the beginning of the new is the violence of every beginning, the originary tear which marks the place where the new appears. Such is 1492. The date designates the violence of the birth of the West, the New World paying for its newness, and that of 'Europe', with the annihilation of its previous existence. Equally, 1492 replays the myth of origin, in that it is only retroactively that we are able to name it as the founding moment and mark it with its birth-mark. This naming is thus symbolic to some extent, for it is clear today that modernity is a unique phenomenon in human history, and that the conjuncture that produced it was equally unique.

The changes and events which figure in the conventional accounts of the discourses of modernity are familiar enough. But what, from the point of view of a genealogy of the present, are the lessons here for us in their refiguration in the light of postmodern and postcolonial theory? My orientation is towards the reconstruction of the conceptual shifts which, through a process of filiations and affiliations, discursively constituted the modern imaginary. Foucault, in *The Order of Things* (1970), attended to some features of this genealogy of modernity. What concerns me here is to locate this imaginary in relation to the longer history of the discourse of being that I am developing throughout the book. The immediate problem hinges on the co-articulation of the conditions and elements which have enabled the discursive formation of modernity to emerge in the course of the 'long sixteenth century', and which have ensured the triumph of the rationalized, individualized, desacralized, racialized imaginary of occidentalism.

When we turn to Todorov's (1992 [1982]) or Pagden's (1993) account of the institution of modernity, patterns and developments central to the discourse articulating modernity's self-understanding appear right from the time of European encounter with the 'New World', including the contradictions and aporias repeated in the legitimizing discourses produced to justify the project of European Western hegemony. Interestingly, Todorov (1992 [1982]) writes the account of the conquest of America as a meditation on the discovery that self makes of the other, especially of the other whose strangeness brings the self to crisis. It is a story of the present, that is to say, a genealogy in the way Foucault understands this term, narrated for 'its tropological or ethical meaning' (Todorov, 1992: 4). It is, in that sense, a lesson, the first lesson of modernity, 'for it is the conquest of America that establishes our present identity; [it marks] the beginning of the modern era' (1992: 5). The othering of the other is accomplished in an unending production of discourse about the inhabitants of the lands of which the colonizers were busy taking possession. It was intrinsic to conquest and subjugation. From the start, knowing the other, taking possession and exercising power over the objects of knowledge are interwoven in the story of the conquest and subjugation of the New World. Already we can discern the break with the Augustinian principle of the trinity of mind, knowledge and love,[7] a principle which dictates that knowing and loving are bound together. Instead what seems to be at work here is the modern, occidentalist and instrumentalist principle which binds knowledge to domination, clearly articulated later in mechanism, which I will discuss below, developing into the dominating impulse in instrumental rationality, as Adorno and Habermas have extensively argued.

When we read the contemporary European accounts of the 'discovery' of America, we do not immediately detect signs of modern thinking. For instance, Todorov's (1992 [1982]) analysis notes the extent to which Columbus in his journals gives credit to God for every discovery and every acquisition of wealth. For one thing, Columbus, like his patrons, Isabella and Ferdinand of Spain, was apparently obsessed with the project of a new crusade to convert the non-believers and seemed to have been utterly convinced that divine design determined every happening in the world, and that all the events of the 'discovery' and of the colonization of the Indies were outside man's control. It may appear paradoxical that such archaic beliefs and passions and anxieties should usher in the new age. Yet the history of colonization demonstrates that they remain encrypted within the acts which prepare modernity, and are repeated throughout its history. We need to contextualize Columbus's declarations of intent by noting his obsession with finding gold, as Todorov is keen to point out. For instance, barely a day after landing, 13 October, 1492, his single-minded concern appears to have focused on obtaining sufficient information in order to locate gold. The reality of colonization, as we know today from many sources, was that pillage was its central purpose or result; the wealth stolen provided Europe with the capital that contributed to the birth of modern, rational capitalism and the lift-off for industrialization.[8]

The cohabitation of the medieval and the modern should not surprise us: did not Newton support alchemy and the belief in occult forces whilst helping to consolidate the mathematization of nature? And do we not find elements of archaic anxieties and disavowals, expressed at their extreme in all forms of fundamentalisms, recurring at times of crisis throughout modernity? It is only slowly that have emerged the conceptual framework and the particular narratives we have come to associate with confident and triumphant modernity, cobbled together in the course of historical developments that at the time were indeterminate, and not the result of some grand plan or the inevitable consequences of some logic of development. Retrospectively, we imagine an underlying purposive rationality to the thoughts and to the sequence of events, but it is only retroactively that we are able to attribute historical coherence to them. Indeed, It is the discourse of modernity itself which prescribes and reconstructs for itself, as one of its significant or defining characteristics, the coherence we wish to find in the events of the beginning, as well as its opposition to what it calls the traditional.[9]

That is not to say, of course, that this beginning was not marked by the violence of *différance*. The eruption of the historical event was registered in the real violence of genocide and the shattering disruptions in beliefs about the world. From the earliest contact, the conquerors experienced the New World, this arena reached after the greatest uncertainties and risks, as a space of the dissolution of certainties, a space that had to be renamed and appropriated in the guise of the old, the Old World renewing itself on this alien soil: *Neuva España*, New England, *Nouvelle France*. In this naming, newness is tamed with the marks of familiarity, so that its fantasized identity with the old can hold out the promise of new birth. The fact that Europe – Spain and Southern Europe in particular – had recently put an end to hundreds of years of Arab and Turkish domination and needed to reconstitute itself, and give itself a new identity, is not irrelevant to the whole colonial project from the beginning. The year 1492 is the date when the Moors are finally expelled from Spain, as Columbus himself notes in the first paragraph of his log-book,[10] it is also the year in which the Jews are brutally deported to North Africa. 'Ethnic cleansing', and, with Columbus and his backers, the fantasy of Christianizing the world whilst amassing untold riches – an irresistible combination – forms the backdrop to New World colonialism and the othering of the other. This splitting of the people is repeated in the history of the becoming of the West; its iteration can be detected in the tropes of East and West, civilized and (new) barbarians, humans and non- or sub-humans, them and us, subjects and non-subjects.

Let us look at this in some detail, for the story is more complex than the one we might be tempted to tell, and more instructive for it. It is clear from the reports made at the time that the world the Spaniards destroyed was not a savage one, but one which the early chroniclers had claimed to be as 'civilized' as Spain, if not superior. Cortés, the conqueror of the Aztecs, described their artefacts with admiration, marvelling at the workmanship in the buildings and in the jewellery, the order, beauty and grandeur of the cities, the fineries of the nobility. Yet within a short space of time this paradise had been destroyed. As Todorov puts it: 'not only did the Spaniards understand the Aztecs quite well, they admired them – and yet they annihilated them; why?' (1992: 129).

It must be recognized that from 1492 the majority of the conquerors – a motley crew of adventurers, criminals, obsessives, soldiers, sailors, priests and dreamers – were quick to regard the natives as sub-human, certainly savage, possibly begotten by the Devil and beyond redemption.[11] The violence inflicted on them – a very medieval violence when we remember some of the events and practices in Europe – the widespread use of torture, say – was often viewed as 'just punishment' for the Indians' 'innate wickedness'. After all, was the way of life, the beliefs and the practices – like human sacrifice and cannibalism – of these 'alien' peoples not an offence to the (Graeco-Christian) idea of the integrity of the human race? It is a point Pagden (1993) makes in stressing the extent to which the encounter with America and its peoples struck at the founding concepts of European thought about itself and about the world. For Europe, the response to the shock of the new was to devise the means for taming or assimilating the 'savages' or, failing that, extermination.

The kinds of massacres that occurred cannot be explained by reference to simple greed. The extent of the extermination can be judged from the population figures accepted today as reliable, namely, a decline in the population from eighty million in 1500 to ten million fifty years later. In Mexico alone the decline was from twenty-five million to one million by 1600 (Todorov, 1992: 133). These figures gain an added dimension when we turn to the tales of cruelty which tell of how the Spaniards regularly burned their victims alive, or severed limbs, cut out tongues and sliced off noses, penises and breasts; children and babies were often thrown to the dogs, to be eaten alive while their mothers were forced to watch. The inventory of cruelty is chilling. The horror of extermination is symbolized in the contemporary fable of the ten plagues sent to punish the people of Mexico (Todorov, 1992: 135, citing Motolinia's *Historia*).

Todorov's explanation is that the Indians were not regarded as properly human; the Spaniards 'do not speak *to* the Indians' (1992: 132, original emphasis). The failure to acknowledge the other subordinates knowledge to power. The step from possession to destruction, for Todorov, is brought about by two factors. On the one hand, the thirst for riches (which Las Casas also stressed), but in the context in which all other values had become subordinated to the value of money, including the possibility of acquiring spiritual values: 'This homogenization of values by money is a new phenomenon and it heralds the modern mentality, egalitarian and economic' (1992: 143).

Todorov's second line of explanation points to the weakening of the social fabric and of moral principles in the metropolitan countries during the period of crisis in hegemony which coincides with the voyages to the New World. The result was a proportional reduction in the authority of the law, so that the combination of distance and the categorization of the colonized as sub-human aliens cancelled the law and revealed 'a modern being . . . restrained by no morality and inflicting death because and when he pleases '(1992: 145), doing it for pleasure and as a way of demonstrating the ultimate power of inflicting death at will.[12]

So are money and a modern will both effect and condition in the emergence of modernity? And what ethical meaning does the history of the conquest make us consider when we reconstruct it as a history of the present? It is impossible to read the catalogue of massacres, of inhuman tortures and mutilations which Todorov relates without being compelled to ask what manner of civilization could perpetrate these acts, what shadow this history casts on our own history. For instance, do not the Holocaust of the Jews and the routine tortures of opponents and radical activists in all parts of the world today alert us to the continuity of ways of thinking about self and other, or the continuity of forms of power and of archaic fears and obsessions which even now oblige us to use this rememorization of modernity's beginning as an occasion for working through our own presentness, that is, for reflection on who 'we' are in the present?

The dispute between Las Casas and Sepulveda, culminating in the debate at Valladolid in 1550, is revealing from the point of view of the attempt to conceptualize the other within the existing European epistemological order, and the ontological ambivalences that surfaced from 1492, and have continued in the discourse of 'otherness' throughout the modern period. The specific point at issue in the debate concerns whether the enslavement of the Indians was compatible with Christian doctrine. Sepulveda's position is an odd combination of Aristotelian principles and a harsh Christianity. He believes that the natural state of affairs for human society is one in which hierarchy, not equality, is the norm, determined on the basis of naturally occurring superiority and inferiority. All hierarchies are based on the 'domination of perfection over imperfection, of force over weakness, of eminent virtue over vice' (in *Democrates Alter*, cited in Todorov, 1992: 152). Thus, the body must be subject to the soul, slaves to their masters, women to their men. This is all very Aristotelian. A simple metonymic chain of equivalences connects the binary oppositions set up according to the model whereby the Spaniards occupy the superior pole. The same chain dictates that Native Americans can be placed in a relationship of contiguity with women and the bestial and with evil. The war with the indigenous populations of America can then be justified on the basis of arguments about their bestiality, apparently evidenced in the claims about their cannibalism and the practice of human sacrifice. For Sepulveda, war against them is a just war because the aim is to save souls damned because of the worship of 'false gods', and every soul saved was worth the countless lives lost. Sepulveda conceptualizes difference as pathology or as a sinful departure from the Christian and European norm.

Las Casas, on the other hand, starts with the principle that all human beings are equal and that the Christian commandment to love one's neighbour as oneself cannot admit the Aristotelian belief of natural inferiority. Everyone can become a Christian, and thus an equal. This view is also the official position, expressed by the Spanish monarchy in the early sixteenth century when it forbade slavery. The official aim of the conquest remained that of evangelization. All men were the same and could be touched by God's grace and relinquish barbarity. From his own extensive observations, Las Casas argued that the Indians had shown the qualities – of gentleness, decency, obedience, peacefulness – which made them ideal candidates for conversion. Todorov argues that the assumptions about the indigenous people's simplicity, generosity, and so on – attributes of the stereotype of the 'noble savage' – meant that the differences between cultures were erased, so that one learned little about the colonized themselves. Las Casas, it seems, was primarily interested not in understanding the Indians, but in establishing whether they were ready to receive the teachings of the Church and thus escape their condition, conceptualized as 'arrested development'. Las Casas intended to proceed by the peaceful means of persuasion. Not that this view in practice diminished the inhuman cruelty with which the Spaniards routinely treated the colonized. They did not see the irony in baptising their captives, then doing them the favour of hanging them, because they were then Christian, rather than burning them, which would otherwise have been their fate. The early descriptions of Las Casas feminized the New World, with the implication that, properly managed, the inhabitants would become docile labourers and produce great wealth for Spain. As he got to know the indigenous cultures more, his views became more liberal; his extensive documentation of the daily lives and cultures of the colonized provides us today with the evidence that is used on the side of the prosecution in the trial of colonialism. Las Casas ends up as a defender of the rights of the Indians, but the reality is that although he won the argument at Vallodolid, slavery and genocide became the acceptable norm.

Given the context of the conquest of America, to which we must add the crisis in hegemony consequent upon the loss in authority and leadership of the Church, which I discuss below, the process of othering and subjugation involved disavowals of interests and desires, and projections of ambi-valences and fears which shaped the discourse legitimizing what was being done to the natives. The explanations for the brutality of conquest should be seen as the performative institution of a world in which European brutality, by a specular doubling in the imaginary, confirmed the construed savagery of the natives. The latter were discursively constituted into alien creatures beyond understanding, refractory to being 'civilized'; they were stereotyped as people who could be tamed only through the application of a constant and vigilant violence. Violence was not disavowed, but seen as necessary, the proof that it was the 'only language' that the 'savage' understood. Violent subjugation became an inevitable duty, dictated by reason, instrumentalized, thus also rationalized, and not the sign of inhumanity. The history of colonialism shows the extent to which this attitude is repeated in other parts of the world and acquires the status of common sense, though not without provoking a good deal of soul searching for the more humanitarian of Western liberal thinkers. When viewed against the lofty ideals of the Enlightenment project, or the claims of the 'civilizing mission', the history of the systematic terrorism of Euro-pean colonialism has driven people like Fanon (1967) and Sartre (1967) to condemn the whole enterprise as intrinsically murderous and inhuman, a challenge to the grand narratives well before the disruptions of the postmodern. For now it is worth examining the effects of colonialism for the effort within the discourse of Western self-understanding to reconcile the humanist and universalist elements in the project of modernity with the fact of systematic oppression and exploitation.

Othering the other and the project of subjugation

The task of subjugation involved the systematic production of knowledge about the conquered peoples and their lands. It is difficult to overestimate the effects of this production for early ethnography, for cartography, natural philosophy, cosmology, the knowledge of languages and of new foods and drugs.[13] Two conclusions are central to my re-evaluation of modernity and the modern subject. First, the new discoveries force a break with the tradition of interpreting everything by reference to the principles and concepts established in the ancient European texts, for not only did the latter have nothing to say about them, but the descriptions and claims which existed in these authoritative sources were contradicted by the evidence from America. As Pagden (1993) has argued, this came about at a time when the authority of the ancients was being severely challenged anyway. Second, the negative evaluation of the other led to 'the understanding that kills', driven by the logic whereby 'grasping leads to taking and taking to destruction' (Todorov, 1992: 127).

A profound ambivalence splits the relation to the other – on the one hand, we find the claim to know, already evident in the thought of Las Casas and many other commentators, and, on the other hand, we encounter the urge to shut the other out into the opacity of the unknowable alien, to be excluded or reduced to the status of a beast of burden and treated accordingly. Both views fit within the intelligibility of the early modern imaginary. The Christian conceptualization of the human being dictates that all humans are God's children and are thus essentially the same and knowable. The corollary of this is that the stranger can be regarded as the dangerous progeny of Satan who must be destroyed to protect the believer from evil, or else categorized as a sub-human group, fit only for slavery. Foucault notes that in his study of madness he had tried to establish the history of the other as a history of something which is at once interior and exterior, thus to be excluded because of the threat to the integrity of identity: 'The history of the order of things would be a history of the same – whatever in a culture is both dispersed and related, thus to be distinguished by marks and to be gathered according to identities' (1966: 15). The Native Americans were sufficiently different and distant to allow for an easy slippage from the category of human to that of the non-human, especially considering that the system of classification and of representation in what Foucault calls the 'classical period' was still structured in terms of series of binaries and in terms of correspondences. Human beings split neatly into good and bad according to a line dividing the faithful from the infidel, the God-fearing from the satanic and beastly. The medieval bestiary, after all, accommodated the most irrational of fantasies.

The ambivalences in the conceptualization of the other during the Renaissance appear in a different light in Michel de Montaigne's (1958 [1580]) discourse on the cannibals, split as it is by a basic dilemma about whether the Native Americans are like the Europeans and belong to humanity or whether they are so fundamentally different that the laws, the rules of morality, and so on, that apply in Christian Europe cannot be extended to the New World. He seems genuinely to believe that they are human, but his 'noble savage' version locates them at an early, more natural stage of development, and thus, for him anyway, a better stage than the civilized, unnatural, thus corrupt, stage of his own society. More's *Utopia* classically refigures America within the out-of-timeness of a fantasized land of perfection (as he imagined it), inscribing the Native Americans as 'figurants' into an ahistorical space in which Europe can play out its drama of becoming.

The trope of the noble savage is revealing when we consider the para-doxes it conceals. On the one hand, someone like Montaigne or Las Casas can use it to point to metonymic connotations of innocence and honesty, as did Rousseau later. On the other hand, the idea of noble savage fixed the 'other' to an archaic temporality, that is to say, to the time of humanity's primitive state, when it was still outside civilization and outside morality and good order. The noble savage was living proof of the advancement of Europe beyond that archaic stage, a validation of its moral and cultural superiority. The trope expels the colonized out of history whilst inventing a history for the colonizers, namely, the history of a civilizing mission, at first understood as a Christianizing mission, before mutating in the nineteenth century into the project of a planned re-formation of the 'natives' every-where. The dilemma remains deeply inscribed in the debates and the critiques of society and of existing values in the eighteenth century out of which Enlightenment emerged split between, on the one hand, the rational instrumentality of a 'positive' science bent on achieving complete control over the natural and the social world to create its vision of the ordered society, and, on the other, a vision of emancipation and liberation which regards the 'promise of joy' to refer principally to the spiritual or liminal dimensions of human desire, a dimension refractory to instrumental control. The tension surfaces in ethnography and anthropology (the older moral philosophy), repeating the earlier divide between a subjugating/subjectifying knowledge – the knowledge that kills – and a knowledge which, in principle at least, is supposed to promote dialogical communicative understanding.

Pagden's (1993) detailed examination of the ramifications of the con-ceptualizations of the other provoked by the collision of Europe with the cultures of the colonies brings out the diversity of responses and helps us reconstruct the stakes in these constructions of otherness. The catalogue of views and stories about the New World demonstrates that Europeans' interest lay not so much in a desire to understand the other as in the endeavour to make sense of its own understanding of itself and of the world once the disruptive newness of what Europeans had discovered had shattered the pre-modern worldview. By the eighteenth century, a vast archive of knowledge about the other had been produced, describing different traditions, belief systems, religions, customs, values, languages, the great variety of species and climates, geological and geographical characteristics, data of all kinds: enough to encourage Europeans to envisage a 'general science of man' and, like in Humboldt's *Kosmos* (1846), to dream of 'a new kind of planetary consciousness' (Pratt, 1992: 119–20). Many of the thinkers who tried to theorize and systematize the accumulated new knowledge about the world thought they could refigure the world around the figure of 'man', imagined in terms of a general, theoretical entity that could encompass the variety of cultures existing across the world. At least, radical Enlightenment thinkers like Voltaire, Humboldt, Herder, Diderot and Rousseau, who were deeply critical of their own cultures, expressed powerful anti-colonialist views.

Increasingly, from the eighteenth century, the question of how to explain differences becomes a central problem in the theorization of the other and of 'man'. All the explanations take the form of a general theory applying to all human 'races', for instance about the effects of climate and the environment or about a processs of civilization. One widely debated general theory in the eighteenth century proposes disjunctures in the moral and intellectual development of 'civilizations', graded in terms of increasing complexity. According to this problematic of culture, the Americas would be located at the beginning of the process, its 'arrested development' shown in the familiar claim about the 'immaturity' of indigenous languages. For Herder (1997 [1800]) and Montesquieu (1977 [1721]), the environment determined culture, disagreeing in this with the more complex views of Diderot (1995 [1773]) about the effects of 'climate' – which for him included the land and attitudes to land – and of Hume (1882, in Pagden, 1993), who could not see how differences in climate could account for differences in manners. Herder drew from his interpretation the conclusion that the possibility of the rational planning of universal enlightenment was a delusion, and that cultures were incommensurable, supporting his view that Europe should leave other cultures alone. Herder's position is a strange mixture of the orthodox and the radical, going against the universalism of many other Enlightenment thinkers. Yet his position is in the end, I think, conventional in outlook, for apart from condemning the colonial project of a civilizing mission – on the basis that all cultures are equal since there can be no independent criteria for judging their relative merits – he proposes no vision of how any improvement in society could be achieved by reference to an ideal construct. Pagden (1993) makes the important point that Herder's argument in favour of cultural pluralism, when coupled with the claim of incommensurability, leaves no place for an ethical response to the suffering of the other when that other belongs to a different culture. Diderot (1955), at least, while condemning the violence and disastrous consequences of colonial expansion for the colonized – for instance, the spread of a cosmopolitan culture abolishing cultural diversity – hoped that one of the effects of forced assimilation could be reciprocal understanding and the exchange of values.

In spite of the different assessments of the consequences of colonization for the colonized, and the different views of the basis for the universal project of the improvement of humanity – rational planning versus moral and aesthetic development as in Schiller and Goethe – what is striking is the recognition that the colonial process had opened the way for thinking globally and in terms of universal principles applying to societies. A long history from the birth of modern science and that of the modern epistemic subject, together with the application of a principle of mathematization to explain the formal properties of all natural phenomena – a *mathesis universalis*, explored by Foucault (1966) – leads to the point at which Enlightenment thought can take this recognition almost for granted. For instance, Humboldt (in Pagden, 1993: 166–7) described the discovery of America as a unique event, announcing a new age in which one is able, for the first time, to contemplate the interconnectedness of all things according to a 'great chain of being'. This leads him to imagine the possibility of the unity of a scientific understanding of the world, to see it whole and to understand for the first time the relations between the parts. The new knowledge would be the achievement of a patient, scientific, cooperative and progressive effort to understand the world on the basis of data obtained from across the continents; this knowledge would be for the benefit of everyone. Humboldt's view of the scientific approach to knowledge is typical of the optimistic attitude of the confident Enlightenment intellectual for whom the plight of the colonized was either the inevitable consequence of the progressive march of history or a temporary price to pay for future integration into a better form of society. Even the misgivings of Diderot are tempered by the argument that commerce could reduce cultural differences and encourage peaceful encounters, replacing the destructive clash that had so far been the pattern within colonialism (in Raynal, 1770, cited in Pagden, 1993: 169–72).

Generally, during the crucial period of the consolidation of the colonies, elements of modernity and of traditional thought co-exist within the conceptual framework and the imaginary of European culture, allowing for great ideological flexibility to suit every interest. The co-existence of the modern and the traditional is a feature which never really disappears, even when the discursive apparatus of modernity becomes more coherent and autonomous in the sense that its different conceptual elements come to refer to and support each other within the perimeter of well-regulated discursive formations, for example in the problematic of subjectivity in the social sciences from the nineteenth century. I leave aside the dissident scepticism of Vico (1730), who fashions his discourse according to geometry, or so he declares (1982: 269), to invest it with scientificity, yet relies on an apparatus drawn from classical Greek, Latin and Renaissance texts to establish his general principles applying to a universal idea of humanity (without any reference to the colonies).

From the point of view of archaeology, what we need to piece together are the effects of rational capitalism, and the juridico-administrative system of disciplining and regulation which begins to appear from the sixteenth century, at first in the colonies through the work of the missions and the vehicle of language and religion, the law and the economy. A form of governance emerges which is remarkable for the similarities with the form of imperial governmentality which is initiated in India in the nineteenth century, then in Africa, though it is not as systematized. The role of language and knowledge in the process of subjugation and subjectification and the role that rituals of power were thought to play in establishing the authority of the 'masters', already promoted by Cortés, are common characteristics in structuring and staging colonial strategies of power. The long history of colonial governance forms part of the genealogy of modernity in showing the centrality of colonialism in the development of the apparatuses of modern governmentality.

Transitions and displacements

Foucault (1966) famously begins his analysis of our era by deconstructing the painting *Las Meninas* by Velázquez (1656) in order to uncover the play of visibility and invisibility in the representation whereby power structures the gaze and establishes the points of authority. His analysis reconstructs the point in the genealogy of the problematic of representation at which the sovereign gaze – doubling into the gaze of the sovereign – symbolically comes to locate the intersection of the standpoint of the spectator, the painter and the model who is being painted. The point at which these three ways of looking converge is external to what is represented in the painting, thus invisible, yet projected inside the picture through the artifice of the three figures who structure Velázquez's painting: the painter, the spectator/ visitor and the king and queen. But the perspective of the ideal gaze – that of the epistemic and sovereign subject – is undermined in the act of seeing since it makes visible inside the picture what belongs outside it, creating the sense of a gap or an absence which reveals that 'the deep invisibility of what one sees is in solidarity with the invisibility of the one who sees' (1966: 31). Foucault suggests that this attempt at making of representation a total representation – the ideal of classical representation – betrays an emptiness concealed in the deep-structure of the classical *episteme*: 'But there, in that dispersion which it at once gathers and distributes, an essential emptiness is imperiously indicated from all sides: the necessary disappearance of what founds it, – of the one to whom it resembles and of the one in whose eyes it is nothing but resemblance' (1966: 31).

At stake in all this is the question of presence and self-presence: is the subject to be centred upon itself, requiring no other perspective or foundation or guarantee, or does the subject always dwell in lack, missing the plenitude of a radically interior consciousness, falling short of the place from whence it claims sovereign authority over what it knows and sees and over what it proposes? Foucault's line of inquiry traces the shift towards a properly modern problematic of representation from the previous model in which the correspondence between representation and what is represented is guaranteed by a system of similitudes and analogies which translates the conviction that the coherence of the world derives from divine design and can be read in the signs marking every object of the world with the mark proper to it. They are the marks which those attuned to the immanence of this coherence can decipher. Knowledge was a matter of an interpretation of the signatures deposited in things which those blessed with grace could reveal through a hermeneutic practice, validating the proposition – central in the sixteenth century and in the medieval imaginary – of a fundamental resemblance between the microcosm and the macrocosm, binding ordinary life to the divine order in a great chain. This is clear in the work of the 'natural magicians' like Paracelsus, Campanella and Porta, discussed by Foucault (1966: 33–49).

If the question is how the shock of the New World was registered on the terrain of both epistemology and ontology, we should expect that well before Descartes's re-centring of the subject and the epistemological break signalling how 'things and words declare their separation' (Foucault, 1966: 58), important shifts would have begun to surface to undermine the conceptual framework of the time and indicate the increasing incredulity towards the grand narratives founding the intelligibility of the pre-modern world. My interest in the *episteme* of this period as described by Foucault relates to the fact that his archaeology uncovers in the reorganization of knowledge before Cartesianism the emergence of an ambivalent and hesitant centredness, which figures like Cervantes, Montaigne, Agrippa, in their different ways, enable us to apprehend. We find elements of this new attitude to the self expressed in a great deal of Renaissance art and writing and in key figures in the struggle between natural magic and mechanical philosophy, even when such explorations of the interiority of the self are tempered by a suspicion of the 'moderns', as in Montaigne.

This secular discourse of modernity breaks with the signifying system of the old order, dispersing and secularizing the sites of knowledge, of morality, and of aesthetics. It does not do so all at once or according to a predictable pattern; the sense of an immanent coherence is discursively reconstructed much later, in the concept of History, and in the idea of an historical project which once again promises the possibility of plenitude (or joy), that is, with the philosophers of the Enlightenment like Kant and Hegel. The postmodern abandons this tradition altogether, that is to say, it abandons the idea of a necessity in the world, discoverable by the scientist or the intellectual who would be in a position to legislate on the basis of the universal truths thus discovered. Postmodern scepticism brings into visibility the older *episteme* which modernity had erased. The problem is that the postmodern, in promoting pluralism and in accepting the contingency and indeterminacy of social phenomena and of human history, relinquishes the possibility of reconciling the different spheres and the anticipation of an ultimate coherence and unity. As I discussed in Chapter 1, this position is not without its problems from the point of view of ethics, and from the point of view of what is to be done, given that exploitations and oppressions of one kind or another have become almost naturalized everywhere.

Faith and reason

If we try to imagine the world and society before the long emergence of modernity, we find mainly feudal and tribal systems, based on clear stable hierarchies regulated by blood-lines and custom. The question is: On the basis of what did people make sense of their lives in these circumstances? What foundations guided how people should act towards others, partners, children, friends, subalterns, masters, the stranger? What structured the distribution of duties, responsibilities, obligations, and liberties? What were the grounds for the protocols, and what general principles informed judgement? In other words, what functioned in the place of the 'grand narratives'? The discourse of modernity would say that it was not a question of grand narratives as we understand them today, but of forms of governance that determined the duties, obligations, responsibilities as well as the identities and subjective positions, and the values which should have normative force. The norms of the normative were grounded in custom or tradition, authorized by reference to a religion rather than by secular principles; in this way, the discourse of modernity marks and invents the difference between itself and what preceded it, at the same time providing itself with the measure for passing judgement on the kind of society which it supplanted. In Europe as much as elsewhere, complex communities, at the structural and foundational level, were cemented by way of a shared religious belief system. This means that a domain of the sacred, transcending particularities of cultural differences, operated to establish the commonality of goods and to authorize customary practices in the last instance. Still today, for most people, religion, or a proto-religious discourse, remains the discourse which orders the world and gives voice to the deep-seated anguish produced by human forebodings of finitude, of extinction and loss. The transcendence of God or gods and their permanence provides the space for the projection into an infinite domain of all the central ontological questions that all cultures have had to confront.

I have pointed out in the previous chapter that the interesting shared characteristic of the Semitic religions is their monotheism, the notion of one, unique God, conceptualized as the centred, unitary expression of a transcendent Will. Additionally, in Christianity, God is humanized and anthropomorphized. He has a son, whom he loves yet is prepared to sacrifice to redeem human beings. Love and sacrifice, gift and debt become bound to each other in the Christian imaginary, beginning a long and tortuous history which still enfolds today. From the point of view of the displacements that modern thought establishes, it is interesting that Christian doctrine binds conscience and intellect, the good and truth, ethics and epistemology, whilst modernity separates them, then attempts to reconcile them by way of the functioning of aesthetics in relation to subjectivity. This is an issue that I shall examine in the next chapter. What I want to signal at this point is the fact that the Cartesian re-centring of unitariness and presence in the (logocentric) subject by the same token re-centres will and responsibility within the subject, so that in the secular discourse of subjectivity the subject must be both conscience and consciousness/intellect; 'he' must take responsibility for both the good and truth. The good is made subordinate to truth, through the agency of reason, burdening philosophy with the conflicts and diremptions, for instance between law and ethics, which Kant tried to work through in the different problematics in the three Critiques. Gillian Rose (1992) provides an insightful analysis, refusing either the reduction of law to ethics or the subsumption of ethics under the law. Her analysis attempts to leave a space for responsibility and judgement to operate, implicating that this space must engage with the question of the 'who' of agency and of the relation to the other, a position for which I have been arguing in the previous chapter, and which I will address again in the final chapter.

Before I pay more detailed attention to the fault-lines in the Renaissance imaginary which the discovery of America cracked open, I wonder whether it is not possible to get an insight into the intelligibility and *Weltanschauung* of the old order by seeing the cathedral as the material and symbolic expression of that order. The cathedral gathers within its space the purified signs of everything that the Christian community holds to be the most sacred. It is the repository of the history of the community and of the Church itself. It is a monument to the oneness of community and it is its memorial, metaphorically and physically containing and holding within its sanctuary, the security and sanctity of the community, making it whole and holy, and secure against attack. The essential and most intense moments of the story of Christ and of redemption are told there, in the depictions of the Stations of the Cross, in the stained-glass windows, the statues, the paintings, the frescos, the relics, that is to say, in the language of the greatest art of the time for all to experience again. The allegories of the human condition and destiny have become sedimented in the narratives of the history and foundation of the Church. The formation of the community is refigured in terms of something that transcends it yet restitutes it as a never-ending story of the redemption of everyman. It is transmuted and made present in the biblical tales and the story of evangelization represented in the artwork. Its heroes are celebrated in the statues and the relics, the tombs and plaques. The history is symbolically re-enacted in the rites, reaching across the span of time to touch the originary sacred moments, as for instance in the liturgy of the (Catholic) Mass and the invocation of Christ's thaumaturgical presence in the Eucharist. The readings from the sacred texts repeat the articles of faith and the principles binding the community in obligations and values and beliefs.

The construction of a cathedral, like the one in Strasburg or Chartres, is a uniquely complex and long project involving generations of planners, paymasters, artisans, engineers and artists of every description, putting to work the most highly developed skills and the most advanced technology available to create this site which contains the whole community, distributed inside its space according to the ranks and stations outside its perimeter, a site where the whole community unites in the sight of the divine gaze which gives it its coherence and unity. It is a gaze which recognizes and individualizes every member, calls each Christian by name, the name given at baptism, and holds out the same promise of redemption and eternal life for each. The cathedral is the metonymy of divine order on earth, a microcosm reflecting perfectly the macrocosm. The place is so constructed and decorated that the believer must lift up her gaze to see and wonder and submit in the act of beholding, becoming subject to the Subject, accepting in awe her place in the scheme of things. Every Christian is enchained within a divinely ordained system through the disposition of the signifiers within the spatiality of the cathedral, connecting the transient and fragile to the immortal and infinite: validating the meaning of the sacred in its existential dimension. Art and music play a central role in the constitution of this space to ensure that the auratic and the authentic combine to liminally produce the Presence of the One in whose mind everything is as it is in its rightful place. Within the space of the cathedral, music in particular enables the believer to empty the self whilst filling the soul, an ecstatic experience.[14] The performative function of the iconography in the cathedral – and, in a less complete and overwhelming manner, in all churches – is striking, and all the more subjugating for relying on a self-referential frame of understanding. The cathedral, then, is the space where the harmony of faith and reason is reflected in every aspect, repeating the harmony of the divine order. It is the Christian materialization of the cognitive, ethical and aesthetic dimensions of human existence. It implicitly recognizes that the experience of the sacred and that of the aesthetic share the capacity to transport the subject out of herself through an experience of the sublime, that is to say, through the intimations of something that transcends ordinary representation and feeling, something which is basically un(re)presentable yet can be intuitively and liminally grasped, and is a pure joy.[15] Beauty, goodness and truth call to each other there, sheltering the fragility of human existence within the spiritual comfort and security of a transcendent dimension.

Ordinary life, of course, was far removed from the sublime spatiality of cathedrals and other sacred places. In the period which forms the background against which I would like to locate the event of the colonization of America, feudal Europe experienced a series of disruptions and crises which are often cited as sufficient conditions for the abandonment of the old stytem of intelligibility and authority, even before the 'world turned upside down' in seventeenth-century England (see Hill, 1975). The main events, whilst analytically distinguishable, are difficult to disentangle at the level of history and of discourse, since they are woven into each other in their phenomenal reality. One broad theme is that of the intellectual and moral decadence of the Church and the breakdown of its pastoral function because of neglect and corruption, often to do with the contradiction between the increasingly secular interests of the Church as an organization and its spiritual role.[16] One response to the turmoil has been the emergence of dissident Christian movements (Wycliffe, Hus, Luther, Calvin and, of course, the terrorism of the Inquisition) and Renaissance Humanism. The latter is itself conditioned by a number of developments which include the effects of new translations of ancient Greek and Arab texts from the thirteenth century,[17] and the spread of a print culture after the technological innovations in printing following Gutenberg, Caxton and others. I suppose the most profound effects have been felt in the transformations in people's understanding of natural and cosmological phenomena, though it is difficult to separate the scientific arguments and stakes from the religious and political, or to do so as easily as we have come to assume we can do about science today.[18] One would need to add to this list the material and institutional changes such as the Black Death (1347–52), the emergence of city-states and the break-up of the Holy Roman Empire, the defeat of the Arabs in Europe in the fifteeth century, changes in weather (little ice age in the fourteenth century), and the consequences of wars, especially the disruptive Hundred Years War (1337–1453).[19] However, my focus concerns the shattering of the discursive edifice constructing the intelligibility of the order of things before modernity. To that extent my attention is directed at the arguments within Humanism and within science, that is, the epistemological, ontological and theological arguments which chart the discursive shifts.

There are two major sites of struggle to consider: that of the epistemological conflict dividing natural magic from mechanical philosophy, and the terrain of the theological rebellion initiated by the Reformation. The outcome conditioned Cartesianism and the spirit of rational capitalism (though the inter-dependencies amongst the relevant factors suggest not a relation of determination but the co-articulation of structured–structurizing mechanisms).

The place to start is the success of Aquinas in the second part of the thirteenth century in resolving the tensions between the demands of faith and those of reason by redefining the distinction and the relationship between the two, founding the former in the revelation of the Scriptures and allowing reason, as natural reason, to draw from experience and common practice whilst respecting the teachings of the ancients, especially the Greeks. Aquinas placed 'sacred doctrine' or 'sacred science', by which divine revelation makes known to 'man' the 'truths which exceed human reason' (1945 [1259–73] Summa, Part One, First Article), above the philosophical sciences, which investigated bodies of knowledge derived by way of the senses. This is because '(s)acred doctrine derives its principles, not from any human knowledge, but from the divine knowledge, by which, as by the highest wisdom, all our knowledge is ordered' (Summa, Part One, Sixth Article). This also implied that the philosophical sciences, relying on natural reason, could not contradict whatever is revealed in the Scriptures (Summa, Part One, Sixth Article). Aquinas managed to Christianize Aristotelian physics and cosmology, removing the Church's objection to the Ptolemaic astronomical system, and so, ironically, preparing the ground for the work of Copernicus. The reconciliation of the claims of the Scriptures with the learning of the ancients secured the authority of the Church. This, however, depended on the competence and credibility of those authorized to interpret the sacred texts. An important point to make in this context is that the privilege of writing in the Semitic religions, deriving from the privilege of an originary truth revealed by God at a specific time and preserved in the authenticity of the written word in sacred texts – the Talmud, the Bible or the Qur'an – places a burden on interpretation, and thus on an hermeneutics, and on the interpreters, namely, the priesthood, the theologians and scholars. It is interesting that it is said in the Haddith that when a scholar dies Islam is breached. When the Christian Church and its officers could no longer command respect and authority (because of widespread corruption and the increasing venality of the priesthood in the period leading up to the Reformation), the way was open for attempts to re-examine the meaning of the Scriptures (philology making matters worse by showing up discrepant translations and versions), as well as to pay closer attention to the heritage of the ancients, some of it newly available through translations from the Arabic and the Greek in the twelfth and thirteenth centuries, as Crombie (1961) points out.

The problems confronting the intellectual before the Cartesian inauguration of the subject-centred epistemology are played out in Montaigne, an exemplary figure of Renaissance Humanism. In his thoughts we find the unstable combination of respect for the authority of the ancients and the emergence of a critical independent discourse at odds with existing power relations and the language of legitimation. A look at his attempt to make sense of the tensions in the conceptual framework of early modern Europe will bring to light the disjunctions that Cartesianism comes to resolve. Montaigne's *Essays* is at once a symptomatic and enigmatic text. Published in 1580, it occupies a point in the sixteenth century coinciding with the disruptions of the Copernican revolution and the discoveries and the new apparatuses that led to Galileo's work; it appears on the eve of the consolidation of the colonial expansion of Europe and the accumulation of wealth from the colonies. The background includes the Lutheran and Protestant challenge to Catholic orthodoxy in Western Europe, the dissident movements of natural magic and Hermeticism, the emergence of state power after Machiavelli, adding to the discoveries and technological transformations – printing and the transformations it brought about; the invention of perspective by Brunellesci; the beginnings of calculus; the new theory of the body – which belong to the context of Renaissance Humanism. The departure in Montaigne is not so much the inspection of one's interiority in an autobiographical form, since Augustine made that break a good deal earlier, although for the latter it was a matter of a turning inwards in the search for God since, for him, it is God who directs our power of understanding and reveals His truth in us directly; we find God in us more than in His works, which we cannot fully comprehend anyway.[20] Montaigne's (1958 [1580]) reflections are nourished not so much by the

Church's teachings as by the classics; there is hardly any mention of the biblical texts, but constant reference to the ancients, though this protocol was fairly normative in intellectual debates at the time; even Bacon's texts, driven by his desire to break free from the binds of the 'idolas' and inaugurate a new science distinct from classical knowledge, abound with references to the Greek and Latin masters. It is not that Montaigne is a dissident from the point of view of theology, far from it. Indeed, in his essay on truth and error, where he argues for the recognition of limits to what human minds are able to understand, he is content to accept the authority of the Church, criticizing others for not realizing that 'we must either submit to the authority of our ecclesiastical government, or we must dispense with it altogether' (1958 [1580]: 90). Interestingly, later on, after the episode with the 'cannibals', and in the essay on experience, for example, he distances himself from those who would refer to the 'actual words of the Bible' in support of their views.

Montaigne's self-introspection is not a precursor for the Cartesian model, nor does it share the anxious and lonely search for signs of salvation which besets the Protestant. He is guided by the views of the classics, favouring Plutarch, Seneca and Cicero, with occasional references to Horace, Virgil, Plato. He finds the 'moderns' worthy, like Boccaccio (the *Decameron*) and Rabelais, but he frankly prefers the ancients, whom he considers 'fuller and more virile' (1958 [1580]: 161). In his early essays, he defends the view that one should defer to the authority of the ancients on the grounds that it is 'foolish to oppose the authority of so many other famous minds of antiquity' (1958 [1580]: 162). No hint of *tabula rasa* here. Unlike Descartes (1968 [1637]), for whom the ability to decide between true and false knowledge was absolutely central (*Discourse* 2), he seems content to live with a degree of uncertainty, recognizing the limits of what we are able to know, for we cannot 'claim that our brains have the privilege of knowing the bounds and limits of God's will, and of our mother nature's power' (1958 [1580]: 87). He subscribes to a 'natural theology' which reconciled observations about nature with revealed truth, arguing that 'man', when enlightened by God's grace, can read the Book of Nature properly (Montaigne, 1987 [1580]). He could not have been popular with those advocating the uncovering of the truths of nature as a way of exercising dominion over her, like Bacon and supporters of mechanical philosophy. He thought we should come to understanding through careful reading and self-critical reflection upon the great texts, for they awaken our reasoning powers and put judgement to work.[21] He argues that the main point of a good education should be the acquisition of virtue, claiming that it is virtue and not intellectual dexterity which is the highest achievement; virtue commands valour, moderation, righteousness, self-discipline, and leads us to want a natural order (1958 [1580]: 68–9). These suitably aristocratic, yet also very Greek, sentiments are not uncommon during this period, though they differ sharply from the discourse of the self of the anxious Christian, worried about salvation and contemplating the sacrifices, mainly of the pleasures of the flesh, that have to be made to make oneself worthy of it. Virtue, however, is not tied to the purity of reason, or indeed the purity of the soul. Montaigne is neither Cartesian nor classical, but in-between, placing value in critical thinking and a dose of scepticism as well as partaking in the concern for the self which the sixteenth century explored in so many different forms in the works of the Renaissance (see Greenblatt, 1980).

Montaigne's unorthodox humanism is strikingly revealed in his essay on the cannibals. There is no mention here of the theological issues, but an attempt to understand the New World by searching for clues in the 'testimony from antiquity' whilst retaining a degree of scepticism about the so-called 'experts'. He does not believe that 'there is anything barbarous or savage about [the cannibals], except that we call barbarous anything that is contrary to our own habits' (1958 [1580]: 108), for, he points out, we tend to regard our religion and political system as perfect. This remarkable independence of thought appears to be undermined by his view that the nations of the New World are 'close to their original simplicity . . . governed by natural laws and . . . are in a state of purity' (1958 [1580]: 109). The familiar invocations of the simplicity and innocence of the 'noble savage', repeated by some of the conquistadors, metonymically recall European visions of a golden age in a variety of writings going back to Plato. Montaigne writes that, in this society

> there is no kind of commerce, no knowledge of letters, no science of numbers, no title of magistrate or of political superior, no habit of service, riches or poverty, no contracts, no inheritance, no divisions of property, only leisurely occupations, no respect for any kingship but the common ties, no clothes, no agriculture, no metals, no use of corn or wine. The very words denoting lying, treason, deceit, greed, envy, slander, and forgiveness have never been heard. (1958 [1580]: 110)

This idyllic and fanciful description echoes other projections of the fantasies of the 'civilized' upon the pacified other; it says much more about the colonizers than about the colonized. The myth of the noble savage, as we know, is repeated across the centuries in support of the critiques of existing European culture, as in Rousseau, or in nostalgic hallucination of a lost plenitude. At least in Montaigne it is used as a tactic for criticizing his own culture. He makes a number of claims about the way of life and beliefs of the Native Americans he met to establish their sociability and unity as a community, adding that they believe in the immortality of the soul, presumably to clinch the argument that these so-called 'primitives' are far from the evil beings depicted in much of the literature; they qualify in every respect as human beings. In many ways, Montaigne is using his account of the Native Americans he met to operate a distantiation from French culture, enabling him to make the point that the barbarity of torture in Europe surpasses that of cannibalism, arguing that it is more barbarous 'to tear by rack and torture a body still full of feeling, to roast it by degrees, and then give it to be trampled and eaten by dogs and swine . . . than to roast and eat a man after he is dead' (1958 [1580]: 113). The critique of his contemporaries is basically a moral one, comparing their deceitfulness, cowardice, dishonesty, zealous intolerance and love of riches with the lack of such defects in the Native Americans. The most significant claims, from the point of view of the discourse of modernity and the notion of the subject it inscribes, come when he tells us the natives told him they consider men as 'halves of one another' and could not understand how the French could tolerate such great inequality in wealth that some people seem to have nothing and are forced to beg, whilst others have an abundance of everything. Clearly, Montaigne wanted to signal that such poverty and inequity was unethical on the grounds that the other is in some way a part of myself and that I owe a fundamental responsibility for her or his well-being. Once again, we can surmise that Montaigne, in privileging the primacy of the relation to the other, would have radically opposed the notion of a self-centred, unitary, solipsistic subject which later becomes normative with Cartesianism and modern political philosophy.

Renaissance Humanism basically attempted to construct a space between reason and faith, defending reason yet recognizing the place of faith, typically in Erasmus's principle of *via media* between doctrinal truth and spiritual peace whereby one can 'affirm without deciding' (Lortz, 1968, cited in Ozment, 1971: 7). The problem is the extent to which the recon-ciliation of faith and reason achieved by Aquinas came under pressure, with reason disputing faith as a consequence of the new knowledges re-emerging in Europe in the fourteenth and fifteenth centuries, whilst faith, at least the faith of the people in the Church rather than faith in God, no longer commanded unquestioned authority. The background includes the moral and intellectual decline of the Church establishment in the Middle Ages, as well as theological shifts which themselves led to the questioning and exploration of doctrine. If we bear in mind that until recent times in Europe, daily life was constantly beset by disasters of one kind or another – wars, pestilence, illnesses, famine, catastrophes of nature – the need for clear and simple beliefs and for total faith in the sacraments and in prayer or in magical powers was equally constant and total.[22] Apart from the religious movements, dissent took many forms, from support for the auto-nomy of states against medieval papacy (as did Ockham), to the advocacy of individualism in the notion of the free will of each person.[23] It is the work of Luther – significantly appearing after the event '1492' – which has historically proved to be decisive for initiating the kinds of discursive displacements that I am looking for to account for the reconstruction of an imaginary announcing the modern mind.[24]

The central departure in Lutheranism was the separation of faith and reason, Luther claiming that faith alone was necessary for salvation (*sola fide*). This proposition is tied up with the privilege that Luther accords to the love for God: Thesis 95 says: 'it is a subtle evil to say that the love of God is, even in intensity, the same kind of love as that for creatures', rejecting the opinion (specifically, that of Biel) that one could love God and God's creatures in the same act. The proposition which is thus rejected by

Luther is that the love for God and the love for other beings and creatures implied each other, that is to say, an act of love for one's fellows, as in friendship, partakes of the love for God, even if it is not of the same intensity. Luther's Thesis 94 adds the following view to the grounds for rejecting the connection between the love for other beings and the love for God: 'It is a subtle evil to say that the same act is both enjoyable and useful', thus introducing a distinction between the pleasure one finds in mundane love, and the feeling one has for God, supported by the injunction that one should, for Luther, place the love of God in a different category. Gone is the view (of Biel) that in loving God one should also love God's creatures, including non-believers, as a token of this same love and as the basis for charity. The break of this link between love for the other and love for God is total: 'To love God is to hate oneself and to know nothing beyond God' (Thesis 96). To get a fuller picture we need to bring into the equation the connections between grace and charity and will. Here the main shift refigures the relation between charity and grace and the love for God. Charity is reserved for the relation to God, whilst grace becomes a univocal gift bestowed by God on proof of merit: Thesis 57 says 'God cannot accept a man who does not have His justifying grace', whilst Thesis 94 claims that charity means to know nothing but God (see Vignaux, 1971, for a detailed analysis).

This (far too brief) excursion into the misty territory of theological disputes and historical conditions is intended to reconstruct the genealogy of the Cartesian subject, working backwards to point to the necessary steps like the detachment of reason from faith which allows reason to find its way without having to assume the intervention of God's grace in its journey of discovery – a new twist to the notion of *Homo viator* inaugurating its modern trajectory. Furthermore, the Lutheran relocation of the agency of grace and the meaning of charity in the act of loving God for Himself draws the Christian subject further into the solipsistic knot of individualism, for, with the Reformation, the other recedes from the acts of charity which the Christian was meant to perform as an expression of the love for God. Protestantism loosens the responsibility the subject might have felt for the other, disaggregating humanity into singular individuals who must look to themselves and their individual consciences for their salvation. The *viator* principle in Christianity, basically an expression of the temporality of being suspended between a known past, an indecisive present and an unknown future, is reformulated into a personal journey of redemption involving oneself and an unknowable God. Protestantism, in reconstituting the relationship between faith and reason, seems to want faith to be the outcome of rational consideration, whilst wishing to ensure salvation by anchoring faith to a regime dictated by the application of reason.

The relative autonomy of reason and faith has important consequences from the point of view of the discursive displacements which enable the Cartesian identity of subject and mind to found the subject in the epistemic space formerly occupied by God, the ideally present Being. God, as in Descartes, can then function as guarantor of Reason, but, unlike in pre-modern epistemology, it is no longer necessary for Him to take a direct part, as final arbiter, in the process of knowledge.

The mirror cracked

Before the seventeenth century, however, neither Humanism nor the Reformation by itself was sufficient to displace the intelligibility of the world founded on the notion of a divine order replicated on earth. The greatest challenges came from theology but were provoked by the disruptions in the epistemological foundation arising from the developments in science and in the new knowledge of the world derived from the discovery of America by Europe, that is to say, disruptions of the discursive apparatus that authorized the system of (feudal, pre-capitalist) power and that legitimated customary practices and relations. I shall argue that the decisive terrain on which this was fought out was that of subjectivity, reaching a point of reorganization or relay with the re-centrings associated with Cartesianism.

Foucault (1966), in proposing an archaeology of the *savoir* which is inscribed in and constructs the coherence, during what he calls the 'classical age' – the seventeenth and eighteenth centuries – between the theory of representation and theories of language, looks at the functioning of the system of similitudes describing the network of resemblances and differences which form the conceptual framework for the 'prose of the world'. He identifies four such systems: those of conventionality, emulation, analogy and sympathies. These set out the manner in which the world is conceptualized in terms of a model of reflection, mirroring what it is in its essence, and thus of how it has always been. One reads this prose using the signatures or marks that have been etched on the surface of things, that make visible or serve as indices for the hidden qualities inherent in the objects of the world. This concept of signature reveals the essential properties of what exist on earth and their inseparable relation to the heavens. The natural magicians, in particular, had systematized this conceptual framework most clearly. Porta (1650) speaks of a continuous chain of reciprocal relations between plants and animals, and animals and 'man' which establish a unity between God and the material world. Similarly, Crollius (1624) rhetorically asks: 'Is it not true that all the weeds, plants, trees and other things that come out of the gut of the earth are so many books and magical signs?' (in Foucault, 1966: 42). Paracelsus, the restless spirit, living to the full the risky excitement of the times, is convinced that life and nature reflect each other to form a dyad: 'life–nature', so that nature would be life-giving, and everything in nature, the stones and metals and the stars, would be animated by a life-giving force. This living nature is itself the 'signature' of the Creator, and everything carries a signature of its specific essence in its being. There was nothing to fear in nature, provided one approached the world with reverence and faith and purified oneself in the search for truth (see Koyré, 1971).

Alongside this system of sympathies and similitudes is the Aristotelian–Thomist cosmology. Its main components consist of the following propositions: the Earth is the centre of the universe; heavenly bodies are perfect spheres and move about the Earth in perfect circles (except the 'wandering stars'); the cosmos is finite; all motion is in straight lines towards the centre of the Earth or the centre of the cosmos. In addition, the explanatory and conceptual framework is framed by a number of principles consistent with the cosmology. Basically this asserts that earthly and celestial forces and 'faculties' are related according to a series of oppositions and dualities which determine that the Earth is barren and inferior and terrestrial nature is female and inferior; they specify a number of couples associated with inferiority and superiority, namely, imperfect/perfect, base/noble, passive or inert/active or life-giving, discord/harmony. Other propositions which complete the system claim that everything is made up of four elements – earth, water, fire, air (plus ether) – which can be hot or cold, dry or wet, heavy or light. Additionally, special forces like *vis viva, vis imaginativa, vis attractiva* – the so-called 'occult' qualities – add to the system of sympathies and antipathies to explain the behaviour of all objects, for example the sympathy between the Moon and Earth's waters accounting for the tides. Life itself was distinguished according to the hierarchy of three souls: vegetable, animal and the rational soul; the last was possessed by male human beings, so that man 'stood at the apex of the scale of material things and at the base of the scale of spiritual beings' (Crombie, 1961: 172).

There were elements of the medieval conceptual framework which did not quite fit neatly within the Aristotelian–Thomist system, such as Galen's medicine, Arabic alchemy and chemistry, Greek mathematics, and craft knowledges of one kind or another. Daily life was suffused with customary practices that included women's lore and knowledge of bodies and medicine, and all the beliefs and practices that a triumphant modern science would subsequently call superstition. They were sometimes sources of resistance and served to feed the accusations of witchcraft during the moral panic, in the course of the 'iron century' of 1550–1650, which targeted women as the enemy within, on the grounds that women, considered as the 'weaker vessel', succumbed to the power and seductions of Satan (see Kamen, 1976). The framework nevertheless was central in legitimating the aristocratic feudal order and so functioned as the dogma of the time, with ideological consequences and effects for the 'regime of truth'. It is this deep system of sympathies and similitudes, and the dualist cognitive frame of knowledge, which becomes suspect and begins to crack.

I have noted some of the reasons given for this crisis, to do with problems internal to Europe, serious enough to require the setting up of a theological police in the shape of the Inquisition from 1230 to enforce doctrinal conformity. But it is not until the turn of the sixteenth century that the crisis in hegemony reaches a turning point. In other words, it is after the beginning of the encounter with the New World and colonization that the situation reaches a point of transition. I would not like to give the impression that the shift to modernity was a reactive one, a solution to the break-up of the old order. Rather, the new discoveries and technologies, together with the new wealth and opportunities that America delivered to Europe and shifts already taking place in the relations of power between European states and with the Roman Church, contributed to the birth of a positive and confident, if spiritually anxious, attitude.

The first phase in the disruption of the European medieval regime of truth took the form of the confrontation between natural magic and the Thomist explanatory framework. At stake was the authority of Christian grand narratives challenged by Jewish and Islamic scholarship (the Cabbala, Rosicrucianism, Hermeticism and the many variations), and the fact that the ambivalent relationships separating and connecting them inscribed all the fury of doctrinal disputes and the violence of power and its underlying interests. One of the early issues to divide natural magicians from the scholastic tradition, and, for different reasons, from the advocates of mechanism, was the concept of life and nature. The former were closer to the ordinary people, learning from them about the life-giving and life-sustaining properties of the earth, as, for example, Paracelsus, who claimed he learned much from women and from common lore (Koyré, 1971: 188). The idea of the barrenness of nature, asserted by the theologians and bookish philosophers, was incompatible with their beliefs. Cornelius Agrippa, in the *Corpus Hermeticum*, declares that 'this great body of the world is a soul, full of intellect and of God . . . see that it is alive, and that all matter is full of life' (in Yates, 1964: 31, 34). Paracelsus, as we saw, thought of the whole of nature as a living entity, animated by magical properties, but a basically divine magic, that can be put to good use (Koyré, 1971).

Interestingly, most of the natural magicians supported the peasants and the poor against the rich 'parasites', as Paracelsus called them (Easlea 1980: 108), and some, like Campanella in his utopian work *City of the Sun* (1623), imagined a world without private property, where everyone laboured equally and shared in the 'common wealth'.[25] The ambivalent attitude towards women is another interesting feature at a time when both the older Thomist position and mechanism were resolutely patriarchal and against the participation of women in the process of production of knowledge. The development of mechanical philosophy and its rejection of occult forces, its epistemological exclusion of emotions and everything that could be associated with unreason, must be seen as a response in opposition to Aristotelian metaphysics, natural magicians, the suspicion and power of women, and against all those who searched for ways to use the forces of nature in harmony with it.

The views of Francis Bacon, England's Lord Chancellor in 1618, express very clearly the key principles which guided mechanism. He distinguishes his support for 'experimental philosophy' from the natural magicians' practice of experimentation by a clear rejection of all occult forces, distancing mechanism from any hint of flirtation with the forces of evil. Instead he proposes a simple methodical process of uncovering the 'secrets still locked in nature's bosom', an experimental method that will 'extend the bounds of human empire, establish the dominion of man over the universe' and inaugurate the 'masculine birth of time' (Bacon, 1859 [1620], Vol. 4: 42; Farrington, 1970: 59, 92, 96).

Mechanism, then, is a polemic against Aristotelianism and natural magic. Against the former's scholasticism it advocated the experimental science which had been growing in confidence alongside mercantile capitalism – in optics, civil engineering, architecture, navigation, mechanics, military technology, metallurgy, chemistry before Boyle, and in the development of and fascination with instruments. It fought against any appeal to 'occult' forces and rejected the idea of a symbiotic relation to nature which natural magicians and Hermetic philosophers alike accepted. The knowledges inherited from the ancients were inadequate, as the discovery of the Americas had shown. Mechanism stood for the search for mechanical causes alone: discoverable, ascertainable through observation, and quantifiable. The new science would proceed by way of a system of checks, rejecting received ideas – Bacon's 'idolas', associated with rhetoric and conjectures, seeking the orderly growth of 'man's power . . . over the universe' (Bacon, 1975 [1620]: 11). Its principle is that all matter is lifeless and inert, subject to mechanical causes; everything is to be conceptualized in terms of motion or the effects of motion: size, shape, velocity, rest and position. Interestingly, Bacon's scientific achievement 'was completely negligible' (Koyré, 1978: 1), a fact which reveals the political stakes in the disputes.

Bacon's *Novum Organum*, a manisfesto in favour of the ideology of the emerging modern science and of the scientific mind as the basis for social reform, became a second Bible for many radical Puritans in the English Civil War: 'Baconianism was almost as influential as Puritanism itself in providing a fighting ideology for the Parliamentary cause' (Dickson, 1979: 10). The Cromwellian army was modelled on the rigid discipline it prescribed; the beginning of social statistics in William Petty's *Political Arithmetic* (1682) and social planning was guided by its prescriptions; the Royal Society initiated by Baconians (1662) was built on the model of rational debate that Bacon enshrined in the House of Solomon. Dickson has argued that the attraction of Baconian philosophy

> lay not merely in the fact that it offered a method for achieving useful knowledge, but that this method was a blueprint of the capitalist labour process, both in the way that he suggested that science as a social activity should be carried out, and in the particular forms in which it presented both things and people. (1979: 11)

The important affiliations between mechanical philosophy and the emerging labour process and social relations grounded in commodity exchange were cemented in the idea of a disenchanted nature, available for 'man's' purposes, and mechanical philosophy's support for the rationality of domination.[26]

Mechanical philosophy gained support amongst a growing community of scientists, artists, craftsmen, philosophers, who exchanged information and ideas. Its supporters were often politically radical, which might seem paradoxical until we remember that its ideological effect was to legitimize the rejection of the older social order and construct positions for new identities, specifically, the masculine rational subject. Mechanism rejected the restraints of feudal relations and worked for the new form of centralized state power appearing in seventeenth-century England.[27] The crucial element from the point of view of the inter-discursive effects and relationships I am trying to reconstruct is the way in which a particular notion of rationality begins to be constructed from the sixteenth century and functions as a relay point in the mutation of the older conceptual framework.

Mathesis and rational necessity: the new order emerges

Mechanism, however, did not establish a new principle of order sufficiently universal and compelling to replace the feudal order. For instance, although Bacon's prescriptions functioned to legitimate the orientation of the moderns in their rejection of the ancients, his understanding of the scientific arguments was rather hazy, and he continued to look to the Greeks for inspiration in the development of his thoughts. It is the principle of a *mathesis* that managed this shift. The function which mathematics played in the emergence of the new order is foundational and not simply the result of the mathematization of the world in the sixteenth and seventeeth centuries as part of the effort to frame the understanding of nature within mechanical and measurable parameters.[28] What I am arguing, following Foucault (1966), is that mathematics entertained a special relation with the whole of the '*savoir*' of the seventeenth century. It became a universal method of analysis, a method whereby things were conceived in relation to an ideal of order in the same way that previously it was the relation to interpretation – signatures, sacred texts, traditional sources of authority and of truth – which structured the imaginary.

For Foucault, the important feature of *mathesis* – that 'universal science of measurement and of order' (1966: 70) – is not 'the success or failure of mechanism, or the correctness or impossibility of mathematizing nature, but precisely a relation to *mathesis* which until the end of the eighteenth century remains constant and unchanged' (1966: 71). This relation has two main aspects. First, there are relations between things that can appropriately be thought in terms of order and measurement, with the possibility of the reduction of the problem of measurement to that of order. Second, there appear a number of empirical sciences – natural history, social statistics, general grammar and the analysis of wealth – which, although not constructed on the basis of mechanism or mathematization, 'are founded against a background of a possible science of order' (1966: 71).

It is clear that the paramount issue for Foucault centred on order and ordered relations, including the principles which ground them and which together constitute an *episteme*. The idea of a fundamental order and harmony in the world is of course not new, since harmony was a testimony to the presence of God. The ancient Greeks, like the Pythagoreans in the fifth century BC,[29] also shared this sentiment of an harmonious order in the world. The difference concerns the different conceptual frameworks grounding order. Aristotelianism is basically an organismic view. From the fifteenth century the idea that mathematics provided the principle for ordering the orderable became widespread in Europe amongst the neo-Platonists like Pico Della Mirandola (1463–94), though he placed greater store in faith than in reason. In the arts, Alberti (*Della Pittura*, 1436) urged all painters to study geometry; Da Vinci (1452–1519) had counselled non-mathematicians against reading his work; Palladio, the architect, in 1560, defined beauty in terms of the correspondence of the whole to the parts and the parts amongst themselves so that each element of an edifice would be necessary for the harmony of the whole. Mathematics also figured centrally in the utopian visions of Calvinist Geneva as the perfectly ordered society, in Campanella's *City of the Sun* and in Hobbes's *Leviathan*, the latter combining the assemblage of a machine with the proportions of geometrical regularity. So, for most scholars from the sixteenth century, mathematics expressed the harmony in God's work, a harmony one apprehended through a proper attention to the underlying truth in creation, not through the human striving for knowledge by the use of reason alone. Indeed, the figure of Dr Faustus[30] is a metaphor for the dangers and vanity of seeking power over nature and ever greater knowledge, rather than accepting inevitable limits to the scope of human understanding.

As I have pointed out already, the search for new foundations for order occurs at a time of disorder in Europe, marked by peasant and popular uprisings and the violence of the witch craze,[31] the disruptions of the Holy Roman Empire, the beginning of mercantile capitalism, which was given an enormous boost from the time of the discovery of America, and, as I have explained already, the extent to which the New World upset the assumptions about the world, its species and plants, and the diversity of people who live in it. The argument that knowledge of the New World was directly in conflict with the regime of truth based on the Scriptures and the ancients is demonstrated by the fact that America proved Ptolemy's geography completely wrong, which already reduced his credibility when it came to the debates about the Copernican heliocentric theory.

From the point of view of epistemology, one of the most significant breakthroughs came in cosmology, namely, through the Copernican revolution and the work of Galileo. The great transformations in European navigation, no longer confined to the Mediterranean and northern and western parts of Africa, placed enormous stress on the Ptolemaic system, which was cumbersome, involving lengthy calculations of epicycles and anomalies (like the retrogade movements of the planets). The Copernican suggestion of a heliocentric model made calculations easier in many ways and reduced the number of anomalies, but was contrary to the biblical account and Thomist cosmology. It is not until the work of Kepler (*Mysterium Cosmographicum*, 1596) and the telescopic discoveries of Galileo and his theoretical propositions (in the *Starry Messenger*, [1610], and *Dialogue Concerning the Two Chief World Systems*, 1962 [1632]) that the heliocentric view begins to look like a credible alternative. Even then enormous theoretical problems remained, for example about an adequate theory of inertia and about the Church's fundamental objections. The scientific arguments and evidences are complex; it is not necessary for me to repeat them to develop my analysis of its place in the emergence of modernity.[32] The points I want to emphasize centre on the place of reason in this emergence. To begin with, it was widely recognized that the Ptolemaic system was so inelegant and implied so many anomalies in the movements of the planets that it could not be reconciled with the idea of divine harmony, whilst the Copernican model restored harmony in the cosmos, and thus seemed more in keeping with the rationality of divine creation. The most important innovation, however, had to do with the shift in the basis for the explanation of natural phenomena from natural necessity to that of rational necessity. Clavelin's classic excavation of the Galilean saga comes to this conclusion:

> [T]hree contributions may be said to summarize Galileo's role in the formation of classical mechanics: the construction of a model of the universe that set cosmology on a new path; the translation into the language of mechanics of the traditional arguments against the earth's diurnal motion; and the creation of a geometrized science of the motion of heavenly bodies. . . . Galileo set himself the task of elaborating a conceptual system in which rational necessity took the place of physical causality; as the clearest expression of that necessity, geometry became the language of scientific research, it was transformed from a technical aid into the master key to the door of experience. (1974: 383)

We cannot find a better way of expressing the centrality of *mathesis* in the emergence of a new sense of what held the world together and the belief that human beings could uncover the properties and mechanisms which would explain how things worked. What I would emphasize is the mutual implication of rationality and mathematics; rational necessity not only takes the place of faith, it promises to deliver the secret of the harmony which faith previously underwrote. Rational necessity opens the way for the empire of Reason and for the (masculine and Eurocentric) privilege granted to the rational mind of the 'man of Reason'.[33] Rational necessity resolves the dilemma between faith and reason by securing faith in reason. Belief in the intrinsic rationality of natural phenomena is the principle which operates a break from the reliance on the ancient knowledge, that is, on the scholastic and theological regimes of truth. The theme of *Homo viator*, previously a central trope of the journey towards the virtuous life and the search for salvation, is transmuted into a different narrative of being in which 'man's' reason is freed for its own journey of discovery and its own empire of the truth. For this to be properly secured, however, required other developments, leading to the great re-centrings which placed the modern phallogocentric subject at the centre of the new *episteme*, starting with Descartes. My point, then, is that the symbolic act of a *tabula rasa* in the text of Descartes, together with the notion of a self-present subject which it secretes, appears with hindsight to have been one of the most significant inaugural gestures of modernity.

Cartesian thought and modernity

Let us look at the shifts and displacements which make up the modern imaginary of subjectivity. To begin with, as I noted earlier, the notion of a self-present being ideally applies to God, as pure or absolute Presence. God is the origin without *différance*, thus also without trace and without or outside history. In Christian theology, God is the origin without precedent, the cause of 'His' own existence (*causa causens*). The logocentric subject, in claiming self-presence, breaks with the Christian – and, more generally, Semitic – onto-theology that assigned to human beings the fixity of a place in the scheme of things by reference only to a divine creator, an infinite Being, who ultimately determined man's destiny and the limits of what one could understand. Of course, as we know, the Cartesian subject still required an ultimate guarantee, something that could not be questioned, that is, not texts, however sacred, but something transcendental in relation to human knowledge. For Descartes, this guarantor is still God, but the God of origins, a non-deceiving Being, beyond questioning, whom one could, indeed, must, trust completely, the Being who endowed 'man' with the intellectual power to discover the mysteries of nature. This endowment is a gift, given as a token of trust, requiring no other guarantee, for example of revealed knowledge written in sacred texts. Descartes, in his discussion of the functioning of God in his system – particularly in the Third and Fifth Meditations – makes no recourse to the Scriptures or to Christian doctrine. Cartesianism, in spite of the reliance on a divine guarantor, and the many appeals to God in the development of the arguments, disavows a religious foundation for knowledge, and so detaches epistemology from theology and from metaphysics, or, rather, slips theology and metaphysics into the 'oubliette' of the supplement, from whence it continued to haunt ontology, requiring to be driven out into the open by a 'hauntology' – to connect with Derrida's (1993) encounter with another 'forgetting', that of Marx. I will discuss later, in the next chapter, how the function of the sacred, in the discourse of modernity, becomes transmuted, especially in Enlightenment thought, into aesthetic experience and the experience of the (Kantian) sublime.

Within the onto-theological conceptual framework, the relation amongst beings, the relation I have to my other, to alterity, is specified according to the implication that each of us has the same ontological status by virtue of the same relation we entertain with the one God. Furthermore, each of us becomes bound by the same laws, the same values and responsibilities. Religious belonging was the main criterion delimiting the people as a category. It also works the other way round, that is, community is sanctified and cemented together by vesting its coherence and ethical force in a religion or in a mythical narrative of origin which retroactively authorizes it, acting as author and authority. The question is: what shifts does self-presence institute? The logocentric subject, according to the logic that I am pursuing, must evacuate the other, abolish the *différance* of the other, for the radical difference of the other undermines the metaphysics of presence by pluralizing being and relativizing presence.[34] The other, in Cartesian thought, is either reduced to the same by means of the category of mind – the universality of Reason, its unitariness and coherence – or cast out of humanity. Colonialism provides the exemplary scene where this is worked out, both in the reality of power relations and in the imaginary of colonial discourse.

The shift from theological foundation to rational foundation in the birth of modernity and the modern subject refigures the thematic of the constitution of the interiority of the self, attaching it now to notions of autonomy and self-mastery.[35] Instead of a care and a practice of the self, cashed out in terms of a secular ethic and an aesthetic, as was the case in classical Greek society according to Foucault, the modern notion of subjective interiority combines religious asceticism with the instrumentalization of the body (see Barker, 1984: 41–52), bringing both within the sphere of rational calculation, particularly with Protestantism. The Protestant, typically, was an anxious being seeking redemption through a calling, disciplining himself (the ideal type is masculine) in an effort to take charge of his destiny in spite of the indeterminateness of the chosen. This involved a routinized and normalized self-abnegation, unredeemed by moments of ecstatic or excessive pleasures – as it was for sexual pleasure with the Greeks whom Foucault (1984a, 1984b) discussed, or for the ecstatic experiences of the Christian in medieval times and even later, for instance in some Black American congregations – whereby the passions and the body are taken in charge and brought within the compass of a planned and reasoned strategy for minimizing the risks of damnation and maximizing the chances of salvation. Magic, the thaumaturgical intercession of the divine in the world, is banished in the rationalization of faith. The liminality of spiritual experience, or the immanence of the sacred, is foreign to this way of thinking. The instrumentalization of the body, its conceptualization as a mere tool, so consistent in spirit with the attitude to the material world of mechanical philosophy, is far from the notion of the body as possibly a vessel of the divine, a container for the Holy Spirit which the earlier mystical or magical tradition supported. There is no place in the Protestant (Puritan) ascetic world for carnivals and feastings, no surrender to the apprehension of something beyond the ordered and the presentable and representable of which human beings partake, for they threaten the

ceaseless effort to protect reason from corporeal desires and purge the soul
of passional impulses. Although Descartes himself does not shun the
passional and bodily world, Cartesianism joins with the Protestant ethic in
their obsession with the purification of reason and mastery over the world
of objects. Truthful or rational representation loses its auratic status to
enter the domain of the impersonal and objective point of view of a centred
subject,[36] whilst everything else is relegated to the, by definition, impene-
trable and unrepresentable world of superstition and to the 'feminine' chaos
of untamed emotions. The privilege of the mental and the intellectual which
they share gradually shapes the rationalization of culture, society and
subjectivity which Max Weber famously theorized.

The way of thinking about subjectivity which Descartes inaugurates, in
prioritizing the question of the purification and fortification of the *cogito*,
prioritizes at the same time the problem of the nature and constitution of
the interiority of the self. The subject's anxieties about its ontological status
were intensified in the context of the disruptions and the discursive transformations which appear in Europe throughout the Renaissance. Already
Renaissance Humanism, as I noted earlier, had increasingly turned the
question of subjectivity towards the disciplined inspection of oneself: the
motives, beliefs and thoughts, the uncertainties and fears, hopes and
feelings which might account for one's actions and which could help in the
reformation of 'character' and the civilizing process as described by Elias
(1982).[37] The 'I' who thinks and the self begin to coincide in the constitution of the notion of the particular person, already appearing in the writings
of Montaigne; this coincidence later develops in the concept of the ego.
Interestingly, the Cartesian discourse, after an account of this kind of self-
inspection in the first and second Meditations, constitutes the interiority of
the subject by way of the folding into itself of consciousness, performed by
the silent copula linking 'I think' to 'I am' in the famous Cartesian dictum .
What is born in this gesture is the idea of an authentic self, the 'real' me,
hidden, but already there, waiting to come into its own and reveal itself in
acts and speech and discoveries, guided by reason.

The other connection I want to signal is the reconfiguration of the
temporality of being which relates to the shift which self-presence implies
for the notion of consciousness. Consciousness is ever a consciousness of
existing in time, of my being held at every moment within a continuum of
time linking the past and the future to how I am in the present. This
temporality is, as I examined in the second chapter, a narrated temporality,
so that my sense of my own temporality, my consciousness of myself as a
particular self, and the particular narrativization of my existence in time are
all interconnected and are grounded in the inter-subjectivity of communicative action. Every self, in any case, is woven into the cloth of language.
Self-presence, therefore, as a strategy, grants to consciousness merely the
illusion of control, especially when consciousness is anchored to the apparent unitariness and fixity of an 'I' who would be the autonomous and
intentional agent of its own thinking. We are far even from Augustine's

perception of time as the horizon within which we can make sense of what we are in the present. Recognizing the present as something that cannot have duration – since the instant 'passes so rapidly from the future to the past that its duration is without length' (1961 [398]: 266) – Augustine argues that the past and the future exist only by virtue of being present: 'it is only by being present that they *are*' (1961: 267, original emphasis). Indeed, he goes on to say that the passage of time can be apprehended only as a movement 'coming from the future, passing through the present, and going into the past' (1961: 269). It is only in the mind, which, in performing the functions of 'expectation, attention and memory' (1961: 277) ties up the future, the past and the present, that I can have access to the sense of my being in time. We all exist in a temporality in which being is 'divided between time gone by and time to come' (1961: 279). This feature of time is 'true of the whole history of mankind, of which each man's life is a part' (1961: 278). Only God exists in a present not bordered by the past and the future, He is the Presence outside time. The Cartesian principle of self-presence not only departs from Augustinian temporality; it 'forgets' the basic feature of the temporality of being which Augustine brings out so insightfully, namely, that we are held between time gone by and time to come which only a narrativization in relation to a memory and to the anticipation of the future can transcribe into conscious thought and produce a self, as effect.

Furthermore, the principle of self-presence has no place for an idea of an heteronomous consciousness constituted through the internalization of the other in its structuralism, as demonstrated in the work of Vygotsky, Luria and Volosinov. The other, therefore, is doubly absent, effaced from consciousness and set outside as that against which the 'I' measures its singularity. The metaphysics of presence, however, cannot avoid the fact that time remains the horizon within which one is able to understand being at all; that is to say, this strategy falls short of finding a replacement for the idea of a timeless and infinite God as origin and foundation of all meaning, since the self-centred and self-present 'I' is an 'I' who cannot overcome finitude and who is open at every moment to the indeterminacy and contingency of the future: it remains a fallen or abject 'I' (waiting for the delusions of the *Ubermensch*). The aporia between the ideal of the immanent presence of the 'authentic' subject and the reality – and consequent existential anguish – of the unfixity and insecurity of actual selves takes until the Enlightenment, and Kant and Hegel, to be resolved. A central part of this resolution is the reformulation of the temporality of being by reference to a being-for-itself whose destiny enfolds as an historical process of becoming directed by self-reflection. The notion of 'History' as linear development, 'progressing' from a known past towards an unknown but pre-figured future, bursting with the new, emerges out of this refiguration of being and of the subject; it has become taken for granted in the discourse of modernity. Whilst this resolution historicizes presence, it does not undermine it, for the notion of being as 'being-with' or 'being-in-the-world-with-others' is not allowed to radicalize ontology, as Heidegger points out in his critique of Cartesianism (1962: 206).[38] The view of history as linear is already implicit in Descartes, since his epistemology theorizes the gradual uncovering of the truth and the progressive maturation of reason. History is no longer the repetition of a cycle, or the return of patterns that are eternal and unchanging in their essential characteristics. The idea of the future as an openness to the new – new understanding, new knowledge, new world – is, of course, central to modernity. It is to the rational, unitary, autonomous, free subject that responsibility is given for making that history, the history of his becoming and of the becoming of humanity as a whole. But who is this subject?

A central argument in Heidegger's critique of Descartes is that Cartesianism takes the meaning of Being to be self-evident, so that Descartes thus fails to 'master the basic problem of Being' (1962: 127). The distinction between the ontic and the ontological dimensions of Being are also confused because of this failure properly to examine the foundation of Being, a problem which Heidegger ties up with the fudge in Descartes between extension (the world as *res extensa*) and the (inaccessible) substantiality of the world, that is, between, on one side, the 'ready-to-hand', 'present-at-hand' and, on the other side, *Dasein*, the being-thereness of Being. The starting point in Descartes means that the Cartesian method cannot provide us with ontological access to the phenomenal, to the being-in-the-worldness aspect of the entities associated with Being, with the consequence that:

> The only genuine access to them lies in knowing [*Erkennen*], *intellectio*, in the sense of the kind of knowledge [*Erkenntnis*] we get in mathematics and physics. Mathematical knowledge is regarded by Descartes as the one manner of apprehending entities which can always give assurance that their Being has been securely grasped. If anything measures up in its own kind of Being to the Being that is accessible in mathematical knowledge, then it *is* in the authentic sense. Such entities are those *which always are what they are*. Accordingly, that which can be shown to have the character of something that *constantly remains* . . . makes up the real Being of those entities of the world which get experienced. That which enduringly remains, really *is*. This is the sort of thing which mathematics knows. (1962: 128, emphasis in the original)

I have quoted this passage at length because it both supports the arguments about the functioning of a *mathesis* in the re-ordering of the order of the world, and because it adds another perspective to it, which Heidegger expresses thus: 'Why was the phenomenon of the world passed over at the beginning of the ontological tradition which has been decisive for us (explicitly in the case of Parmenides), and why has this passing-over kept constantly recurring?' (1962: 133).[39] I signal this point of view now because several issues are involved here. On the one hand, there is the older problem of the possibility of a critical phenomenology that could take account both of our being-in-the-world and of what exceeds the phenomenal, but without placing the two dimensions in opposition to each other or privileging one of them; I will examine this in the final chapter. On the other hand, it can be argued that once it is accepted that there is a divine order implicate in the world that we may try to uncover, and once that order is grounded in the mind and will of God, it is tempting to imagine such an order at the most abstract level, in terms of a formal system, thus in terms of a *mathesis*. Besides, it seems to me that one can only proceed to this position if we can regard other human beings as abstract entities, disembodied, devoid of their way of being in the world, that is to say, their way of being with others and located in terms of a spatiality and a temporality anchored and enacted in the social and physical materiality of the lifeworld. This distantiation is introduced in its clearest form with the Reformation, but is intrinsic to *mathesis*. It is amplified in rational capitalism and in a world in which the stranger is regarded as alien, reducible to mere objects to be bent to one's will, as was the case in relation to Native Americans. I should note that today, accounting practices have completed the process of divesting human beings of humanity; people have become units appropriate for management practices and economic calculations, even in educational and medical establishments.[40]

I will pick out another key point to add to my list of the affiliations and co-articulations which frame the modern imaginary, namely, the implication that the abnegation of the body, or its representation as the source of spiritually debilitating passions and desires, transfers value to mind or intellect alone. The body–mind dualism, which Descartes is far from inventing, since it is present in other forms in European and other cultures, and in Christianism, reworks that older theme in terms of the spirit of domination and control which is inscribed in the modernist notion of rationality. Charles Taylor has pointed out that Descartes actually does not wish to abolish our passions, since they are necessary for reason to validate its ultimate sovereignty: 'Reason rules the passions when it can hold them to their normal instrumental function. The hegemony of reason for Descartes is a matter of instrumental control' (1989: 150). The greater the passion, the greater the dispassionate hold that the strongest rational minds can demonstrate. Cartesian thought joins up instrumental control in the pursuit of one's aims with detachment from the outcome. For Taylor, this is tied up with a (bourgeois) moralization of behaviour which interiorizes the sense of self-worth of a person: 'If rational control is a matter of mind dominating a disenchanted world of matter, then the sense of the superiority of the good life, and the inspiration to attain it, must come from the agent's sense of his own dignity as a rational being' (1989: 152). The turning inwards of the intellect is not the Augustinian search for the divine spirit within human beings but the path towards self-sufficiency through the autonomous operation of mind. One no longer proceeds from faith to reason, or maintains a distinction between the two whilst privileging faith. Instead reason itself leads to the inference of God's existence and to the mind's autonomy, as Descartes's careful sequencing of the arguments in the Meditations amply illustrates.

Lines of descent: modernity, occidentalism and new economies of power

In the discourse of modernity and of subjectivity, the inter-dependence of autonomous reason and a critical faculty is well established; both are seen to be necessary for the progressive transformation of life, as Kant has argued in relation to the idea of the Enlightenment. But the conditions in which the modern mind emerges have favoured an individualistic, dominating form of subjectivity, privileging the cognitive over the emotional and the ethical. Descartes cannot imagine how the other beings and things of the world could be interiorized as an integral part of being, in the way that, much later, Merleau-Ponty could propose the idea that the body and the mind should be regarded as constitutive of each other. Something is lost in the folding of the 'I' over itself in logocentrism. It is a multiple loss, for it adds the loss of the other to that of the sense of being corporally coupled to the world and the loss arising from the anticipation of the ending of a present pleasure – simple pleasures as well as sublime feelings – because we know in advance that they do not endure. They accumulate in the lost object that haunts ontology; we find it in different guises, in Lacan's notion of lack for instance. It masks another loss, more ancient, more immanent to human existence, the loss or fading of the self in the night of the temporality of being: we fall headlong into an indefinite future, away from a past that always-already sinks into the mists of memory, a past that is either an initial plenitude that cannot be recovered, or the memory of a yearning for plenitude that is ever postponed. The Christian (and Semitic) God, of course, promises the possibility of a time of plenitude to come. Modern times delivered the possibility of a kind of plenitude, in the making of history, one's own and that of the community to which one belongs, by means of one's own effort and will, and the will of the people in the form of the general will.[41]

We must not allow ourselves to forget, though, that resistances of one kind or another to this emergent dominant, but not yet hegemonic, order occurred throughout Europe. Think, for instance, of the Diggers and the thought of someone like Winstanley in England at the time of the English Revolution, or the 'hereticism' of the Cathars, or else the long and complex struggle within the conceptualization of nature and of the place of 'man' in it, a struggle which, as we saw, split the supporters of natural magic from those of early mechanical philosophy. In relation to Cartesian thought and the philosophical reworking of the relation between epistemology, ethics and metaphysics, we need only recall Spinoza's monist proposition of mind and body as aspects of the one Substance, ultimately grounded in the infinite fecundity and essential oneness of God, or his idea of the impossibility of discovering the final cause of things (in the *Ethics*). The Metaphysical poets in England and those supporting Hermeticism added their dissenting voices. Within Christianity, the Counter-Reformation attempted to stem the tide, although, judging by the work of the missions in the

Americas, one can hardly describe its position as radical. The more radical voices are those from the other side of power, though, even then, ambivalences about the founding principles remain to illustrate the agonistic character of the discourses of modernity, for example about the principle of universal rights in the work of Wollstonecraft.[42]

I have tried to say that epistemology came to be privileged in the founding discourses of modernity in part as a result of the disruptions which the discovery of America provoked for the conceptual structure that had framed explanation and meaning from Judeo-Christian times to the dawn of the Renaissance. The shock-waves further weakened the apparatus of Christian religion at a vulnerable time, so that the foundation of truth and of the good could no longer be encompassed within the boundaries of European medieval imagination.[43] Even so, the site of the struggle remained that of religion and theology, as witnessed in the dispute about slavery between Las Casas and Sepulveda, and the efforts within the Church to reconstruct the doctrinal basis of belief, namely, through movements like Protestantism and the Counter-Reformation, or to re-establish authority by means of the terror of witch purges.

The refiguration of the archaeology of modernity in line with the orientation of my enquiry suggests two directions to follow. On the one hand, the reconstruction of the coherence which is gradually discursively established from the Enlightenment and which functioned as the conceptual grid circumscribing how intellectual opinion understood and made sense of events and existence. Its main elements find expression in the grand narratives of modernity; they become dominant and normative in establishing the modern order of things, giving direction and purpose to human history. Alongside this development, often at variance with it, traditional interpretations, grounded in religious or quasi-religious beliefs, answered questions about the more intractable aspects of human existence, for instance concerning morality and spiritual experience.[44] The domain of the sacred remained very much alive, losing little of its ideological force, providing comfort for those not in a position to direct the affairs of men, or, indeed, secretly anchoring the most secular of positions in the transmuted form of transcendental principles or assumptions.

On the other hand, we must see in the co-existence of the modern and the traditional, the secular and the religious, signs of dissidence and spaces for resistance. For instance, Romanticism in the nineteenth century, however ambiguously, holds on to the thought of a spiritual dimension which instrumental reason could not express or grasp and often denied and tried to destroy. There is in this attitude the desire to preserve the elements, the monuments – traditional crafts and practices and ways of life, the natural habitat – which seem to keep alive and present a different temporality of being, the past and its historicity, the way we are attached to an immemorial time, as a station in time, which promises a kind of continuity, and validates the (Arendtian) idea that ontological security is bound up with the endurance of the 'works' that human action creates. Modernity, with its face set towards the future, constantly threatens to annihilate that world. The idea of works, rephrased in Ricoeur's problematic of community in terms of traditionality, and which I have discussed in terms of historicity, indicates the space that has often nourished oppositional forces, providing a grounding for action and the principles legitimizing and authorizing dissidence and alternative visions of the future.

What the new modern thinking gradually produces is the birth of the West, understood not just in relation to the non-West, but as a self-referential system of thought, universalizing its position and discourse, claiming objectivity about human societies and cultures, on the same basis as the natural sciences, its knowledge of itself and of all that it surveys drawn from the inspection of data gathered from around the whole planet. Europeans ceased to regard ancient civilizations – the Greeks, and, for some, Egypt and China[45] – as the epitome of what can be achieved, but as models that can be appropriated – for example, the Greeks – or emulated – for example, Chinese administration. Europe becomes the West, and thought becomes Western. And in the course of this centred, technologized, universalized, ethnocentric, masculine form of hegemony which I am calling occidentalism, the difference of the other is silenced or pathologized, the recalcitrant are marginalized or suppressed, and the subjugated are assimilated. Occidentalism is the institution of a particular imaginary, established in specific representations and tropes, in images, metaphors, symbols and signs which construct the frame of intelligibility of the West. This imaginary, functioning according to a structured–structurizing process, is inscribed in and structures the signifying practices that describe, classify, annotate, analyse, represent, prescribe and order the cultural and material world in ways that have too often become naturalized. In becoming the West, Europe locates itself as the intellectual, spiritual, moral and economic centre of the world, understanding itself as the motive force and the light bringing the whole of humanity to its maturity, to recall the terms Kant used to define the Enlightenment in 1784. Occidentalism recruited or compelled Europe's 'others' to join in the long march towards 'civilization'. For instance, in North America in the nineteenth century the concept of manifest destiny is used to justify the appropriation of what remained of Native Americans' lands.[46] The difference of the other no longer appears as a threat; a hindrance maybe, and the source of resistance to be quelled, certainly a source of evidence and experiences for reflection upon the human condition and for forging the policies and the means for the transformation of the world. The nineteenth century could proceed to imperialism proper, on the basis of a new form of governmentality founded in the emergent sciences of the social, as I have shown.

Todorov spoke about the crucial importance of money in accounting for the shift in attitude about the values heralding modernity. I have argued that the wider transformation refers to a whole range of conditions, the effects of which for modernity are more complex than imagined from the point of view of determination or structured articulation. I have also stressed that some aspects to do with the subject of modernity and the conceptualizations of the other and of reason need to be relocated when we shift the focus to the analysis of colonial discourse. In the course of these changes a new economy of power has emerged, to do with the new systems of administration and the emergent mode of production, as much as with the new basis for political authority. The inter-relationship between this new economy of power and the new economy of the body is particularly significant, since it is bound up with the sexualization and feminization of, at first, America, and, more generally, the colonized 'other', with the result that the 'other' is multiply inscribed in these new economies. From the point of view of the institution of the logocentric subject, two signifying stratagems combine to suture logocentrism into phallocentrism and Euro-centrism: the phallocentric gaze reduces woman to the place of lack, lacking the 'phallus' and lacking in reason, whilst the Eurocentric gaze reduces the non-European to the not-yet-being of underdevelopment, lacking presence and agency. Both subterfuges are necessary for the beingness, the self-presence and virile agency of the male white European to appear self-evident, validated in the masculine and Eurocentric discourse about women and the colonized.[47] A phallocentric or patriarchal culture and Eurocentric hegemony confirm the self-presence of logocentrism. It is clear that the rewriting of modernity and the question of how we are to understand its 'Aufhebung' must deal with the articulation of power, sexuality and desire with the other shifts I have highlighted in the discourses and technologies involved in the constitution of the modern form of subjectivity and in the system of knowledge and authority appearing with modernity.

It must be admitted that, alongside the technologization of the apparatus of subjugation ensuring subjectification and subjection, there emerges a literature of empire which, at its best, betrays a deep anxiety and ambi-valence that, from Last of the Mohicans and Hucklebury Finn, to Heart of Darkness and A Passage to India, reveals the troubled soul of the West, uneasy or cynical about the role of the civilizing agent that it had attributed to itself.[48] This anxiety is by no means typical or widely recognized, for Western thought and culture is dominated by a triumphalist occidentalism which sustains Western nations' self-understanding and Western individuals' identities: what it means to be French or English, European and white. Even a relatively radical position, such as J.S. Mill's, which passionately advocates the enlargement of suffrage and the defence of liberty, excepts the colonized from participation in the civilizing and humanizing process, arguing that the colonies, like India, should remain under the tutelage of the West for their own benefit. It is a surprise to find that the work of someone like Camus, apparently at odds with mainstream literature, betrays occidentalist preju-dices when it comes to Algeria, as Said convincingly shows in Culture and Imperialism (1993). Nevertheless, it is interesting that a counter-discourse of domination, aligned with earlier humanitarian discourse and revolutionary politics, co-habits with occidentalism. Although largely overshadowed and besieged, a critical and self-critical voice within modernity continues to undermine the spirit of domination and totalization in this other modernity, taking historically variable and specific forms. The question is: are these sufficient grounds for salvaging something from the culture and discourse of modernity when considering the question of possible futures and the form of subjectivity to come?

I have highlighted the violence of beginnings precisely in order to keep in the forefront the idea that the questions of who 'we' are must take on the form of an ethical inquiry as well as a judgement about what, if anything, is worth preserving from the history and achievements of modernity. My analysis of the effects of modernization throughout the world tends towards supporting the argument that in spite of local differences and the centrality and specificity of location in the mechanism of formation of subjectivity, the institution of a cosmopolitan 'we' has been in process for some time now, and that the recasting of the project of modernity for postmodern conditions may well rest on imagining the emergence of a different 'we' at the level not so much, or not initially, of everyday practice as at the level of a refigured ontology. It would be a critical ontology in Foucault's general sense, but without appearing to prioritize an individualistic project of becoming. Instead it would open onto a notion of subjectivity grounded in a reconstituted ethics and in a critical ontology, thus, by reference to the embodied and locatedness of subjectivity, and by reference to the primacy of the relation to the other, a relation understood as one in which responsibility, care and gift play a constitutive role, as I shall explain further in the last two chapters.

The turn to ethics is a position that I have noted on a number of occasions. Its main challenge is directed at the privileging of epistemology in the calculation of issues of emancipation and liberation, issues which modernity had transmuted and placed within the orbit of the 'great march of History' accomplishing the project of the becoming-mature and -free of both self and humanity. We find this turn, ambivalently, in Habermas's redefinition of the project of modernity when he argues that without a commitment to the ethical ideals which motivated the philosophy of the Enlightenment there can be no reason for preferring one system rather than another, or for opposing continuing oppressions and injustices. The judgement of Lyotard (1988b) about the grand narratives also applies the yardstick of ethics in considering whether after Auschwitz we can still attach any credibility to their claims of guiding and legitimizing the rational improvement of humanity as a whole. Interestingly, Charles Taylor's (1989) genealogy of the self transfers the line of questioning from 'who are we?' to 'what it is good to be', indicating in this way that the most important value when considering 'who we are in the present' is not to be decided on the terrain of conventional morality or of epistemology, but on the terrain of what he calls 'moral ontology'. This is because the problem of selfhood and that of the good are intertwined and because the urgent issues today concern 'respect for the life, integrity, and well-being, even flourishing, of others' (1989: 4).

Before I am able to suggest different answers to these questions, I need to examine further the question of subjectivity following the systematization of the discourse of modernity after the Enlightenment and with the consolidation of empire. Modernity really takes off from the end of the eighteenth century, instituting the world we now inhabit as inheritance and as burden.

Notes

1 It was not a rejection of graphocentrism, for modernity inflated the culture of the book; books now became the public site for demonstrating truth, provided it did so according to the new rules.

2 The claim that the 'natives' had no proper language and must be taught to speak (a European language) functioned as proof of their lack of development whilst legitimizing the use of language as the instrument for subjugation. The same tactic was used in Ireland, dramatized by Friel (1981), and throughout the colonies, repeating an older manoeuvre in the process of colonization.

3 For instance, Lévi-Strauss's illuminating essays on race and history published in 1952 are surprisingly radical in stressing the heterogeneity of cultures and their coalition in establishing progress of any kind, and pointing out the cumulative advancement of American cultures before colonization in the essay: 'L'idée de progrès' (see Lévi-Strauss, 1987).

4 It is clear too that my approach and my overall aim is different from Said's (1978, 1993) analysis of the constitution of European and Western culture.

5 The most debilitating aspect of this tendency is that of simple inversion, for instance privileging female or 'black' against male or white, whilst keeping fundamental assumptions unchanged, for instance about notions of agency or ethics or power, or, indeed, capitalism. I explained some of the reasons for this in Chapter 1.

6 A text like *The Double Helix* (Watson, 1970) shows up all these tensions and contradictions when it both acknowledges the contributions from a variety of scientists across different disciplines whilst appearing to construct Crick and Watson as exceptional agents, guided to the discovery of the structure of the DNA by rational labour and extraordinary insight.

7 In *De Trinitate* IX, in Taylor (1989: 136ff.) the other trinity ties together intelligence, memory and will.

8 There exists an extensive literature, including Amin (1974, 1976), Frank (1969), Jalée (1965), Rodney (1972) and Williams (1961).

9 It must be admitted too that it is the critical historical and theoretical discourses which have appeared with modernity that enable me to detect in the process of subjugation and appropriation of America the early indications of the shifts that I am trying to convey.

10 In the digest reconstituted by Bartolomé de Las Casas from Columbus's log-book, which has disappeared.

11 All of this fitted well the classification and the iconography ordering the world of the living in medieval Europe. Sub-human beasts were part of the medieval imaginary determining the place of every creature within the hierarchy of the great chain of beings.

12 Todorov forgets other violences of the same kind before modernity, for example the Romans, who at least did not pretend that colonization was for the benefit of the colonized.

13 Apart from the knowledges that Europe itself produced, for example in mapping the world (a Eurocentric, yet very resilient representation, as José Rabasa [1985] has argued), we should pay more attention to the introduction of foodstuffs, medicines, materials, plants, which have transformed Europe to a greater extent than recognized. For example, amongst a long list, Lévi-Strauss mentions 'potato, rubber, tobacco, and coca (basis of modern anaesthetics) which in many ways of course, constitute four pillars of Western culture' (1987: 40).

14 This is the case with other devotional music too, so that this functioning of music applies to Mozart's *Requiem* Mass and Monteverdi's *Vespers* as much as to the Quwwalli singing of Nusrat Fateh Ali Khan.

15 The proscription on the representation of God in Islamic religion intimates this idea of a transcendent realm. The divine is made present instead in other ways, through the Qur'an and the architecture and the geometrical beauty of the decorations, in the tiles, and so on, in mosques, that is, in places of worship and from which authority issues.

16 For example, the intellectual interests developing at the University of Paris from the end of the fifteenth century, which move beyond theological elaboration. An attempt to reconstitute this world and make more palpable the tensions and the stakes, as well as to translate the 'lived' aspect of the period and its turmoil, can be found in Umberto Eco's *The Name of the Rose* (1983).

17 See Crombie (1961) for the historical details, and the work of Étienne Gilson (1930) for an insightful analysis.

18 The view of science as an autonomous process that has emerged with the institutionalization of scientific practice from the Enlightenment has given credit to questionable ideological assumptions about the relationship of scientific knowledge to the domain of the social which neglect the effects of power, as well as, more pertinently, the extent to which the wider cultural context has effects within the process of formation of concepts. A great deal of work, starting with the shifts operated by people like Bachelard and Canguilhem to those like Latour, Woolgar, Mulkay, Knorr-Cetina, and so on, has demonstrated the social and cultural dimensions of the process of production of knowledge, without reducing science to some other level, or collapsing the difference between science and ideology. I explored the relevant issues in Venn (1982).

19 Braudel's *Capitalism and Material Life, 1400–1800* (1974), or Emmanuel Le Roy Ladurie's excavation of life in medieval times in *Montaillou* (1978), or indeed Barbara Tuchman's *A Distant Mirror* (1979) – this latter being a more dramatic version of the events leading up to the early modern period – gives some idea of the distance that separates the present from that period while making it possible to get a feel for the lifeworld and for imagining the everyday reality of pre-modern times.

20 On free will, see the work of Gilson (1930).

21 He disdains the practice of rote learning because for him, in this kind of exercise, memory repeats without understanding. See the essay 'On the education of children' in Montaigne (1958 [1580]).

22 See Emmanuel Le Roy Ladurie's (1978) description of the reliance of the ordinary folk on the active presence of the divine in daily affairs in *Montaillou*, or Frantisek Graus's (1971) view of the conditions which produced the crisis in hegemony that drove people to seek an answer in versions of the idealized imagined Christian communities of the past, as with the Hussite movement.

23 The disputes that raged from the thirteenth century are quite fascinating for their details, for example the movements founded in the Cabbala and in Hermeticism, that is, the attempt to join Egyptian and Jewish gnostic beliefs with elements of Christianity and of Greek philosophy – mainly Aristotle and Plato. They all risked provoking the wrath of the Church, and often did. See Yates (1983) or Easlea (1980) for a summary.

24 Some historians, like Lortz (1968), claim that the shift operated by Renaissance Humanism was the '*conditio sine qua non* of the Reformation' (in Ozment, 1971: 5).

25 In the seventeenth century, Valentin Andreae's *Christianapolis* (1619) and the Fama Fraternitatis also prohibit private property and urge the study of nature for the benefit of all, joining in this the position of the Diggers and the Levellers.

26 See Dickson (1979) and Easlea (1980) for details concerning the political interests and the question of gender, that is, the effects of power in determining the relevant discursive formations and their mutations during the early modern period.

27 It is well to remember that Hugh Peters, Hobbes and, later, Voltaire, Condillac, Condorcet, Jefferson and Locke, that is to say, people whose position relative to the dominant power of the time was subversive and radical, were all supporters of mechanical philosophy.

28 Galileo, Hobbes, Descartes and Newton, for example, were all convinced that the laws of nature were written in the language of mathematics, and that God must be a mathematician.

29 I prefer BC to CE, since the latter erases the fact that the convention in the periodization and naming of our era is European and Christian. I prefer to remember the historicity of these conventions.

30 In the German dated 1587; Marlowe's *Dr Faustus* is dated 1604.

31 See Thomas (1971) and Easlea (1980), and a good deal of feminist interrogations of the period.

32 See Easlea (1980) for a detailed and fascinating account of the disputes and, especially, a view of what was at stake. For an understanding on the scientific arguments, the work of Koyré (1978) and Clavelin (1974) is essential. The latter is one of the most insightful analysis of the epistemological shifts ushering modern times.

33 See Genevieve Lloyd's interesting argument about patriarchal reason in *The Man of Reason* (1984).

34 I have elaborated this argument elsewhere (Venn, 1993, 1996).

35 Recalling Foucault's analysis in *History of Sexuality*, Vols 2 and 3 (1984a, 1984b).

36 I would draw attention to my earlier analysis of the repositioning of the subject by reference to the invention of perspective – examined by Foucault (1966) in his interrogation of *Las Meninas* of Velázquez – as an example of the transitional moment in the displacement of the gaze and position of the knower.

37 Elias (1982) links the civilizing process with the process of pacification of the polity and the monopolization of legitimate violence by the state. Also see Greenblatt (1980), already mentioned.

38 See Hegel's phenomenology, and Heidegger's discussion of it in *Being and Time* (1962: 480ff.). Also Honneth (1995), for a contrasting analysis.

39 As noted by the editor of *Being and Time*, the discussion of this question promised by Heidegger has not been published (Heidegger, 1962: 133).

40 The critique of the foundational presuppositions in this way of thinking is long overdue; they hide other transcendentals and another metaphysics.

41 See Riley (1986) on the general will, the genealogy of which is central in the analysis of the process of legitimation and the agent who authorizes political action.

42 I don't think it is possible to escape the fact that we are all obliged to appropriate whatever tools we can from adversaries; we cannot entirely detach ourselves from their hold. We find it again in the thought of Marx in relation to Hegel, or in de Beauvoir about gender difference examined in the shadow of the Sartrian notion of (authentic) being, or today in the borrowings from poststructuralist and postmodern theory which much postcolonial theory cannot avoid. It is not possible to find unadulterated ground guaranteeing the authenticity and purity of the opposition to existing systems of power and authority.

43 Kearney's (1988) study of the shifts in the philosophical imagination circumscribing ways of being in the different periods of European history covering the *longue durée* that I have been reconstructing is a fruitful contrast to the kinds of accounts we have in, say, Weber or most histories.

44 For instance, in England canonical laws continued to regulate family matters for a surprisingly long time, right into the nineteenth century.

45 Bernal's (1987) study of the neglected African contribution to European culture provides food for thought in reassessing the genealogy of occidentalism, although he does bend the stick too far.

46 Typical is President Andrew Jackson's justification of appropriation: 'Humanity has often wept over the fate of the aborigines in this country . . . [but] what good man would prefer a country covered with forests and ranged by a few thousand savages to our extensive Republic?', cited in Searle (1992), p. 72.

47 See, amongst an extensive literature, McClintock (1995).

48 I have dealt with this in greater detail in Venn (1993) and (1996).

4

ENLIGHTENMENT AND AFTER

The critique of the present

Modernity is the permanent critique of that to which we belong. It is in his return to the theme of the Enlightenment that Foucault (1984c) summarizes in this cryptic way the ambivalence at the heart of the critical conscience of modernity, caught between, on the one hand, the demand for the constant interrogation of ourself and of the historical conditions of the period in which we exist, and, on the other hand, the recognition of the limitations which our belongingness to a culture imposes. The point of this questioning, he tells us, is to enable us to 'separate out, from the contingency that made us what we are, the possibility of no longer being, doing, or thinking what we are, do, or think', to give new vitality 'to the undefined work of freedom' (Foucault, 1984c: 46). This critical attitude is rooted in the Enlightenment, inciting us to problematize both our assumptions of autonomy and our way of being in the world; it harbours the 'permanent reactivation . . . of a philosophical ethos' (1984c: 42). For Foucault, after the intimations of a postmodernity and the critique of totalizing and instrumental reason, it is this ethos itself which we must salvage from modernity; it continues to inform the 'critical ontology of ourselves as the historico-practical test of the limits that we may go beyond, and thus as work carried out by ourselves upon ourselves as free beings' (1984c: 47).

Throughout the essay, Foucault returns to the question of limits and limitations, a caution against the excessive ambitions of universalizing projects with their legacy of violence and terror. He constantly defends the good of liberty and freedom, not in favour of the unbridled autonomy of the subject but in support of a self-questioning which refuses to erase the connections with the analysis of power and of knowledge and which now ambiguously gestures in the direction of an ethics and an aesthetics of the self.

My interest in a return to the Enlightenment connects with different departures signalled in Foucault's own refiguration, including the intriguing element of a renewed attention to the question of the who – who are we in the present? – an issue that has become central in the diversity of attempts to 'settle accounts' with modernity and imagine different projects and different politics appropriate for new subjectivities. Equally, Foucault's unexpected detour via Kant prompts us to wonder to what extent Enlightenment thought draws the conceptual loop beyond which we have yet to step, that is to say, how far are we 'beings who are historically determined, to a certain extent, by the Enlightenment'? (1984c: 43). Both issues underlie 'postcolonial' and feminist critiques of modernity and of the West, critiques which seek a space beyond it whilst recognizing that we still belong to the modern imaginary in ways that are often invisible and that therefore need to be unconcealed. The period of the Enlightenment was also a period of fundamental transitions in culture and in the theorization of human beings' place and meaning in the scheme of things. The range of questions raised within the cosmopolitan culture of the time, for instance about difference and rights, or about a purposive direction in human affairs, are echoed today in the context of a new cosmopolitanism. But what now could function in the place of the project of the Enlightenment which enframed such fundamental questions?

I think we would miss out on some fundamental features of modernity if we were to consider the renewal of interest in the question of subjectivity – around issues of hybridity, pluralism or reconstructed 'identities', and, more generally, problems relating to the 'who' – to be nothing more than the symptom of the resurrection of the subject thought defunct after structuralism. The question of the who is a profoundly ethical one. I have indicated that it has less to do with epistemological guarantees than with answering the question of what it is good to be. It calls for the elaboration of the principle of responsibility for my other beyond the security of attachment to doctrines of one kind or another. It is thus no longer a matter to be thought on the terrain of humanism in its various guises: Marxism, existentialism, liberalism, subject-centred or solipsistic projects of becoming which inscribe the 'philosophy of the subject'. It is clear too that something has remained of that great mythical and romantic figure released by modernity, the lonely *flâneur* who could be found wandering through the urban labyrinths, amidst the bright lights and the shadows, obsessed with the desire to see and grasp every fleeting thing before it disappears into the vanishing swirl of yesterday's fashion. The conditions that appeared with modernity together with secular narratives of being have intensified the tragic fragility of human existence, replayed throughout Western thought, theorized in the notion of being-towards-death, and which echoes in the background of Foucault's essay, through the evocations of Baudelaire's reflections on modernity. This figure, heroic or tragi-comic, searching still for the lost obscure object of desire, is now as likely to be scanning the hyper-real landscape of cyberspace as dreaming of its fifteen minutes of fame. Its resilience and mutations in conditions of postmodernity and postcoloniality, and the resilience of the conditions that sustain it, guide my exploration of the discursive horizon of modernity, particularly by reference to the hold the latter has on us.

The underlying issue I want to explore is this: if the project of a possible emancipation of the subject, as refigured by the discourse of modernity in terms of the projected plenitude of the rational subject, has proved to be a burden and an illusion, what forms of subjectivity is it worth fighting for now? Through what kind of interrogation would this newness come into the world? What new narratives authorize these new subjective projects? Foucault's reflections on the Enlightenment provide a point of entry into these questions and remind us of the dangers which attend all forms of becoming, and of the specific dangers, of totalitarianisms and ontological violence, which the history of modernity has demonstrated. The critique of the present engages with the wider ambition of Foucault's work as a whole to the extent that it has been his aim 'to create a history of the different modes by which, in our culture, human beings are made subjects' (1982: 208). As we know, he has pursued this agenda through interrogations of the objectifying and normative discourses that set out to determine the modes of being of 'man': that 'curious invention', as he puts it, at the heart of modernity's self-understanding. He has finally focused on 'the way a human being turns him- or herself into a subject' (1982: 208), enframed by an ethics and an aesthetics of the self, the broad lines of which are sketched in the essay on the Enlightenment.

I will use Foucault's engagement with the Enlightenment to draw out a number of lessons and to develop my arguments in the direction of the question of ethics and of aesthetics, and the reconciling function which they have been allocated within the problematic of modernity. I will then problematize the conceptual apparatus by reference to the critique of colonial discourse.

Foucault summarizes his approach in the concept of a 'critical ontology' that inscribes a being for whom autonomy and freedom are the conditions for the 'complex and difficult elaboration' through which it transforms itself into a 'work of art' (1984c: 41). The subject he envisions, who has returned with an 'attitude', is not to be confused with the self-present, imperial subject of logocentric Reason, for it is now an anxious figure haunted by the idea of its finitude, compelled by the task of 'inventing itself' but within 'the limits that are imposed' on it (Foucault, 1984c: 42). It is a Dionysian being whose will to power seeks not dominion over others but a form of plenitude – epiphanic perhaps – through the ecstatic and sublime experience of the artistic, inventive transfiguration of oneself. But does this redrawn project of self-actualization imagine a new form of subjectivity that requires conditions of possibility that break with those that prevailed in modernity? As I will show, it is not clear how far Foucault departs from the problematic of subjective 'self-fashioning' that has become a central theme since the Renaissance. If what he advocates is meant to have universal application, we would need to know what conditions free every person for the 'practice of liberty that simultaneously respects this reality [of modernity] and violates it' (Foucault, 1984c: 41). In particular, how do we reconcile the requirements of autonomy and freedom with the (Levinasian) ethical imperative of responsibility for the being of the other? Does this principle not implicate the necessity of a justice that must be rendered and must guide action, as Ricoeur (1988, 1992) has argued?

Before examining the arguments of Foucault in some detail, I would like to signal another set of problematizations of modernity that contribute to the task I have set myself. It could be argued that the interrogations of modernity lodged in the disjunctions signalled by the 'post' of 'post-colonialism' and 'postmodernity' have sought, as much as Foucault's work, to disrupt what Homi Bhabha has described as the vision of 'man as the signifying, subjectifying category of Western culture, as a unifying reference of ethical value' (1994: 237). The history of modernity has been pluralized by these disruptions, recounted in the register of a counter-modernity where different memories are reconstituted, telling the stories of the silenced or the marginalized whose experience of modernity has been, and continues to be, more profoundly ambivalent, at once holding the promise of possible freedom and joy, yet subjected to the violences – epistemic, ontological, psychic, physical – that have been intrinsic to its totalizing ambition.

An example of the fractal histories of modernity I have in mind is that of Paul Gilroy (1993a), who reveals the evidence of a counter-modernity developing alongside the Eurocentric narrative of a triumphant modernity, triumphant because it has attributed its victory over the subjugated to the universality and unitariness of the modern consciousness, which has thus become the signifier of its superiority. He follows Frantz Fanon, W.E.B. Du Bois and others in highlighting the doubleness of the consciousness of Europe's 'others', at once modern yet anchored in the soil of the vernacular cultures that modernity threatens to annihilate or reduce to subservience, finding in that space the ontological security and the subjective value that Eurocentrism and occidentalism deny non-white Western human beings. 'Otherness', in its occidentalist construction, remains split between the different narratives and temporalities of race, nation, universal projects; what that discourse undertands as the 'other' cannot be reconciled with the fictions of unitariness or essential natures.

Another important intervention has been Edward Said's project of demonstrating the reality of imperialism for the production and under-standing of modern culture in the 'West' and elsewhere. In *Culture and Imperialism* (1993), he reminds us that cultures are heterogeneous and hybrid ensembles; he shows that contemporary identities are complex and mobile, open to the effects of the 'contrapuntal' relations that shaped cultures in the period dominated by colonialism and imperialism. Earlier, in *Orientalism* (1978), he brought to light the processes and strategies whereby an 'otherness' had been constituted within colonial and imperial discourse, functioning as the counterpart, or supplement, as Derrida might put it, conditioning the intelligibility of the narratives of European superiority and the myths of Western autonomy. Said's work is aligned with the rewritings of modernity that refuse the forgetting of the violences and oppressions that have accompanied it. It is worth recalling Lyotard's (1988a) point that a certain 'forgetting' is intrinsic to the particular narrative of modernity as linear development that must periodically repeat the gesture of beginning from time zero, a gesture which consigns the past to the invisibility of the repressed. One effect of this repetition of immaculate or wilful beginning is that the 'post' of the postmodern stands for the signifier of the repression and erasure of the memory of modernity which a triumphalist narrative of the modern period would rather not confront. Lyotard suggests a rewriting of modernity which instead would perform a work similar to what happens in the process of 'working through' (*Durcharbeitung*) in the analytic experience, that is, the recovery of repressed knowledge, a point to which I will return.

Examples of this kind of 'rememoration', similar to the process of 'working through', are produced by those postcolonial artists and intellectuals who regard their work as a responsibility owed to those who have been forced into invisibility or silence by forms of oppressive power, as Toni Morrison (in Gilroy, 1993b) has noted. The narration of the past in the present, its refiguration in the sense Ricoeur (1991) understands it, that is to say, as at once a 'revelatory' and 'transformative' renarrativization of life, is allied to critique and to the process of emancipation. The functioning of art and the domain of the aesthetic, of *poiesis*, in refiguration and in subjective transformation is a theme I will develop in relation to Foucault's project of a critical ontology. In that respect, Morrison's perceptive remark about the centrality of the 'historical connection between the Enlightenment and the institution of slavery – the rights of man and his enslavement' (1992: 42) – begins to point to a different genealogy of notions of subjective autonomy and freedom in relation to notions of 'me' and 'not-me', self and other which forms part of my reassessment of the question of the specificity of the modern subject. For the present, I simply want to foreground the radical or counter-history of modernity which enables us to take a critical stance in relation both to the account of modernity as an history of the progress of reason and liberty and to the critical elements within Western thought which ambivalently inform the rewriting of modernity. The settling of accounts that I have in mind implicates neither unconscious forgetting nor an obsessive return to the imagined memory of an irenic past. For, whilst the spectres that have haunted modernity – logocentrism, Eurocentrism, masculinism, and the exclusions they invoke – continue to haunt the 'scripts' and the narratives of 'identity' and community, the disjunctions indicated by the 'post' of postcoloniality and postmodernity make it possible for us to refigure the history of modernity and of the present as part of the work we must do upon ourselves in order to rethink what might come after modernity.

Figuring out the Enlightenment

Perhaps we should preface Foucault's examination of the Zeitgeist of the Enlightenment with the briefest sketch of the conditions in which the provocative and sometimes revolutionary ideas we associate with the Enlightenment emerged in the course of the eighteenth century. The methodological protocols of genealogy insist that these conditions of possibility be specified. The period of the Enlightenment, as we should expect, is a complex and rich mixture of events and discourses that set the course for the history of Europe and the colonized world until well into the nineteenth century. I would like to begin with the reminder that the longish eighteenth century is marked by the emergence for the first time in history of a global system of colonization, dominated by Spain, France, England, with significant roles played by the Dutch, by Portugal, and even by Russia in Alaska. Spain continued to expand its empire in both North and South America. The English gradually established naval superiority and extended their subjugation to India – the East India Company was established in 1600 – and Australia, following Cook's voyages. The French similarly extended their interests in America (Louisiana, 1682; Canada), gaining a foothold in ports in India – Compagnie des Indes, 1664 – and, later, extended their trade routes and possessions to the Pacific after the travels of Bougainville (1766–8). The consolidation of the slave trade and plantation economy formed the basis for the great wealth in English ports and the expansion of commerce in everything connected with the triangular trade.[1] Colonial expansion multiplied the trade routes and the routes for travel and exploration. Accounts of European adventures inaugurated travel history and fed into anthropology and early social science, for instance Montesquieu's *Lettres Persanes* (1977 [1721]), Raynal's *Histoire des deux Indes* (1781 [1770]), Bougainville's account of his travels (1771). The enormity of the stock of knowledge accumulated in the process gave impetus to the effort of classification and collection of knowledge and attempts to systematize them which were one of the mainsprings for the Enlightenment. The fact that the main collective work of the Enlightenment is titled the *Encyclopédie* (1751) is symbolically significant; the *Encyclopédie* itself follows in the wake of *Chambers Cyclopedia* (1728), and is followed by the *Encyclopedia Britannica* (1768), adding to the astonishing number of lexicons and dictionaries pertaining to every major discipline. They were all primarily concerned with the task of drawing together the knowledges produced globally, seeking the completion of understanding, aiming to produce an educated, cosmopolitan public. The 1751 frontispiece of the *Encyclopédie* depicts a male Reason, whose sovereignty is symbolized in the crown he wears, pulling the veil away from truth, a demure woman whose nakedness is apparent beneath the veil. The clouds are torn apart to throw a revealing light on the assembled company of similarly veiled women. Thus does masculine Reason gather its harem of truth, the spoils of its conquests.

Another theme affiliated with Enlightenment is that of political economy. Adam Smith's *Wealth of Nations* (1812 [1776]) is one of the great achievements of the age, developing some ideas from Quesnay, who linked the prosperity of the nation to the prosperity and liberty of the poorest citizens. The accounting of wealth by reference to the concept of nation reveals much about the relation between the development of a macro-economic system of accounting and the construction of the nation-state. The conditions of possibility for this discourse include the establishment of national banks – for example, the Bank of England in 1694 – and the notion of the national debt, the emergence of stock markets in England and

France (in spite of the fiasco of John Law's spin-doctoring the South Sea Bubble), in other words, the emergence of the principle of aggregating wealth with respect to the entity: 'nation', and the invention of the regulative and statistical means for doing so. I would also like to highlight the view of Europe that was beginning to be constructed as a system constituted by inter-dependent parts, both in relation to internal trans-actions, and in relation to colonialism as a network of economic, political and military relations (see Wallerstein, 1980).

Thus the becoming-West of Europe, which I began to examine in the previous chapter, develops into a geo-political and cultural system in the period of the Enlightenment, operating at the level of conceptualization as well as at the level of political and economic interests, determining, for instance, shifts in alliances and conflicts. Colonialism cannot be regarded as simply background to all these developments. It was intrinsic to it.

It is particularly in the domain of culture that a cosmopolitan imaginary is constituted which is truly European, joining different sites – for example, in classical music, Mozart, Bach, Beethoven, Vivaldi, Rameau, Telemann, provided the musical experience which could be shared by the 'educated' person anywhere in Europe at the end of the eighteenth century. There clearly were 'national' inflections. Perhaps the French intellectual domina-tion from the late seventeenth century provided a certain degree of cohe-sion, but one would have to reconcile this possibility with the antagonistic stakes which split even Enlightenment from within, for example Herder, Vico and (ambivalently) Rousseau arguing against some of the basic principles of Enlightenment, whilst retrospectively belonging to the spirit of critique which animated intellectual endeavour at the time.

Foucault, for good reason, cuts through the massive archive of discourse and the wealth of historical detail relating to that period by the strategic positioning of Kant's text on the Enlightenment as a symptomatic state-ment. One must admit it would be easy to immerse oneself in the historical detail and the endless disputes and miss out on the immanent or liminal feature of the period, the sign of a desire or a will for a transcendent good, which might still animate human beings today. The interest in Kant's text, apart from its iconic place in the philosophy of modernity, arises from its tactic of answering the question of *Aufklärung* by way of a detour, namely, by specifying what it is that, against the taken-for-granted background of the economic, cultural, political, social, administrative changes and events that circumscribe Enlightenment as a period, one may detect as indicative of its ethos. Foucault, as I have noted, characterizes it as an attitude, the vagueness of the term itself appearing as a challenge. There are, though, crucial departures in Foucault's refiguration of the Kantian problematic of becoming which oblige us to locate his discourse in a different space, inside/ outside the discourse of modernity, acting as a theoretical 'jetty'.[2] When Foucault directs our attention to the problem of 'self-creation', framed within what he calls 'an ontology of ourselves', the creative aspect is not located within the framework of a project and does not privilege epistemology, even if in the last instance. Yet it could be argued that the turn to an ethics and an aesthetics of existence is not new, that it is an eminently Kantian gesture, more explicitly expressed in the later Third Critique, and is, in any case, repeated in the artistic history of the vicissitudes of the modern subject, expressing a 'Baroque Reason', that Buci-Glucksmann (1994) examined, shadowing the bright lights of Enlightenment's vision.

Within the Kantian problematic, self-becoming is ambiguously tied to the narrative of the progress of reason and of the coming to maturity of humanity as a whole. The story is a complex one, upsetting the neater stories of the purity and autonomy of a Reason that would sweep all before it. For instance, for Kant, the 'sign of history'[3] that nourished the hope of progress is enthusiasm for the revolution. It was not necessarily a matter of participation in the process of revolution, or its relative success or failure, but that enthusiasm itself is prioritized as the sign that humanity desired to dig itself out of the dark cave of its 'immaturity'. In other words, the measure of humanity's progress is not to be decided at the court of Reason, but is adjudicated in the permanent reactivation of an ethical imperative, that is to say, by reference to an ontology in which judgement, thus the operation of a principle of justice, occupies a central place. This means that, even in Kant, the trace of the other refuses to vanish, although pains have been taken to reduce it to invisibility. I am relying for this inference on Levinas, who describes his project in *Totality and Infinity* as

> The establishing of the primacy of the ethical, that is, of the relation of man to man – signification, teaching, and justice – a primacy of an irreducible structure upon which all other structures rest (and in particular all those that seem to put us primordially in contact with an impersonal sublimity, aesthetic or ontological). (1969: 79)

Ethics cannot seek refuge in the self-referentiality of a logocentric Reason, though, clearly, the history of modernity testifies to the attractions of such a stratagem.

Foucault's ontology does not avoid the question of desirable social transformation, but the relation between self-transformation and the transformation of history is not clearly worked through, with the result that the suspicion of voluntarism and universalism remain attached to his concept of an 'ontology of ourselves'. The concept comes to stand in the place of the absent theorization between the two levels and kinds of transformation, an absence symptomatically revealed by the absence of the concept of justice amongst the stakes – power, autonomy, freedom, the growth of capabilities – of the work of critical ontology. The term 'ourselves' is made to join 'self' and 'other' in the seeming commonality of an undifferentiated 'us'. But what purposes unite 'I' and my others for a common historical project? What underlying principles could supposedly underwrite the shared goals intimated in the term 'ourselves'? Is there, on the other hand, no future outside 'difference'? It is time to take a closer look.

One first approach to these questions is to examine the relation between Foucault's reflection on the Enlightenment and his elaboration of an 'aesthetics of existence' and the ethics bound up in the notion of the 'care of the self'.[4] His summary of Kant's view of the Enlightenment picks out the latter's understanding of enlightenment as the measure of man's 'release from his self-incurred tutelage' (Kant, 1992 [1784]: 90). It is here a question of humanity's long journey from immaturity to maturity, from relative imprisonment in the state of nature to mastery over the forces of nature as part of the historical process of self-actualization. The key to this process is the public use of one's reason, which 'must be free, . . . [for] it alone can bring about enlightenment among men' (1992 [1784]: 92). For Kant, the exercise of reason alone liberates us from dependence on the authority of books, priests and scientists, that is, from submission to epistemological, ethical and politico-social forms of authority. Tutelage, he tells us, 'is man's inability to make use of his understanding without direction from another' (1992 [1784]: 90). What is needed is courage – *sapere aude* – and the labour of understanding, based on the hard work of acquiring knowledge. Each 'man' must become his own authority, he must abandon the shackles of routines and the comforts of relinquishing responsibility to those in authority, our 'guardians' who thus become our guards. To deny reason the autonomy it requires in order for critique to be effective in hastening enlightenment, for instance by imposing upon it some illegitimate constraint, would wilfully hold back the immanent goal of humanity's emancipation through the progress of the understanding, a goal which is both moral and rational. For Kant, the problem here was the conflict between the private and the public use of reason, for, while the publicly conducted critique of the present was an obligation, and was essential if the state of affairs were to change at all, there was equally a duty to obey the law, at least until the maturity of all of humanity. The public use of reason is entrusted to the scholar – Foucault's 'universal intellectual' – who must be guaranteed the right to point out errors and injustices, so that the public might be able to exercise reason in judging policies and the rules of morality. It is clear that, for Kant, the process of enlightenment requires reason to occupy centre stage, though, when we turn to the *Critique of Judgment* (1987 [1790]), things are not as clear as all that.

The text of Kant deals also with the problem of the power of the monarch and ecclesiastical power, in relation to the general will and to the degree of religious freedom of belief, pointing to the view that the authority of the monarch rests on uniting the general will with the will of the sovereign, and that dogmas should not be allowed to bind future generations to contracts that would impede further enlightenment. The expectation is that 'men work themselves out of barbarity' (1992 [1784]: 95), provided they are not artificially restricted by illiberal laws and powers. This process has a universal reach, for the 'spirit of freedom' gradually spreads across the world. An unresolved problem is the relation between law and reason, for a tension exists between the view that law can be founded in reason and the recognition nevertheless that power, ever allied to law, is not grounded in sufficient reason. The aporia on the one hand keeps open the possibility of dialogue whilst, on the other hand, it allows power to appropriate reason on its side in a totalitarian fusion of the two, as Mladan Dolar (1991) has argued.

Given Foucault's critique of reason throughout his work, one would hardly expect him to propose or defend a rationalist ontology. Indeed, he uses the aporias in Kant's text in order to rewrite modernity not as a history of reason but as a history of a 'practice of liberty ', specifically in the freedom exercised through the critique of the present and the critical engagement with oneself which participates in self-actualization. His reading of Kant emphasizes the question of 'the present as a philosophical event . . . [that] sees philosophy . . . problematizing its own discursive present-ness' (Foucault, 1986: 89). Philosophy's self-questioning becomes re-centred in modernity on the problem of the relation between law and philosophy expressed in the search for the permanent cause operating in history that activates the possibility of a constant progress of humanity. This cause, as I indicated earlier, shows up as a moral disposition, signified in the enthusiasm for revolution. What is important for Foucault about this discourse of the Enlightment is 'What is to be made of this will to revolution?' (1986: 95).

The query brings into the picture the historicity of the two moments of being: what Foucault indicates in the term 'present-ness' and its universality signalled in the notion of a permanent cause. They repeat the split in the subject of modernity divided between the cognitive and the emotional, mind and body, which is refigured in Kant's 1784 essay in the distinction between the public and the private use of reason. The interesting departure in the later Kant is the attempt to reconcile the two parts of subjectivity in the notion of the aesthetic, formulating a thematic of the relation between subjectivity and the aesthetic which Foucault reformulates. His engagement with Kant leads him to rephrase the relay in the following terms:

> I have been seeking, on the one hand, to emphasize the extent to which a type of philosophical interrogation – one that simultaneously problematizes man's relation to the present, man's historical mode of being, and the constitution of the self as an autonomous subject – is rooted in the Enlightenment. On the other hand, I have been seeking to stress that the thread that may connect us with the Enlightenment is not faithfulness to doctrinal elements, but rather the permanent reactivation of an attitude – that is, of a philosophical ethos that could be described as a permanent critique of our historical era. (1984c: 42)

It is this attitude that characterizes modernity, that is, 'a mode of relating to contemporary reality, a way of thinking and feeling . . . of acting and behaving that at one and the same time marks a relation to belonging and presents itself as a task . . . what the Greeks called an ethos' (1984c: 39). Foucault draws from Baudelaire, who described modernity as 'the ephemeral, the fleeting, the contingent', in order to develop the view that the attitude to modernity is exemplified in the search for 'something eternal' within the passing moment. We can detect here a repetition of the venerable theme of the desire for a permanence that would abolish the instability and finitude of being, a craving for ontological security. For Baudelaire, there is something behind the costume of the present that the modern painter reveals as its 'poetic beauty' and as the 'essential, permanent, obsessive relation that our age entertains with death' (1984c: 40). The being of modernity searches for the 'passion', the 'strange beauty', the 'swift joys' that dwell in the evanescent reality of the present, working upon them in an effort to transfigure the world. Christine Buci-Glucksmann has pointed out that with Baudelaire there appears 'a new definition of "modern beauty" bound up with the uncanny and horrifying; a new consciousness of temporality and memory' (1994: 75). The Baudelairian aesthetics is allied to a critique of the idea of progress, working upon the tension between 'a will to see everything and a will to see something different in a different way, to interrupt through spleen the flow of time and to operate what Agamben calls an "appropriation of unreality"' (Buci-Glucksmann, 1994: 75). Benjamin understands spleen as 'catastrophe in permanence', as Buci-Glucksmann points out (1994: 76), thus associating it with the idea of the 'state of emergency' which Benjamin develops in the *Theses on the Philosophy of History* in speaking about the destabilizing impulse in modernity, and which we can further associate with Foucault's idea of the permanent 'insurrection of subjugated knowledges'. The terms of the modernist aesthetics – uncanny, memory, strangeness, death, unreality – suggest that when tied to the project of subjective becoming, it is a process similar to 'working through' in analysis, a point to which I alluded earlier.[5]

A tactic central to modern aesthetics has been to locate art as the material that makes possible subjective transfiguration. Foucault extends the idea of the creativity of artistic practice when he proposes that one should work on oneself in an attempt to fashion one's body, one's feelings and actions, one's whole existence, into a work of art. It is a *poiesis* directed at oneself. Emancipation is not a matter of discovering the secret, hidden truth of oneself – as in some liberation theology – but the task of inventing oneself. The attitude commensurate with the task of self-production is contained in the philosophical ethos that problematizes our mode of being as historical beings and our constitution as autonomous subjects through the exercise of a freedom that looks for a 'way out' of the present, namely, by seeking in the singular, the contingent and the arbitrary event the signs or the experience of what dislocates the given reality.

Once again the agenda for subjective transformation summons the problematic of the relation between aesthetic experience, ethical relation and critique. But we are still not very clear about some of the key terms and mechanisms. For instance, how does power function in the processes involved? Is this a variation on a self-centred stratagem for fulfilment? And what are the practical stakes?

I will try to disentangle the issues after examining the guide for practical existence that Foucault suggests. While recognizing that we are all to some extent historically determined by the Enlightenment, he wants to avoid taking sides for or against its project by refusing the 'blackmail' contained in the demand that one must take a stand on the question of its rationality. This blackmail covers humanism within its tactic, since, as we know, the polemic that has engaged with modernity and postmodernity has linked rationalism with humanism in the critique of the foundations that have supported the universalizing and totalizing and totalitarian ambitions of a certain Western despotic *logos*.[6] Foucault, however, considers the Enlightenment and humanism to be 'in a state of tension rather than identity' (1984c: 44).

Foucault's disengagement from the blackmail of the Enlightenment draws, besides, from his earlier work to argue that the philosophical critique of modernity finds support in the genealogical and archaeological analysis of modernity which demonstrate that there are limits to analysis, determined by the historicity of the agent of knowledge and the discursive horizon within which s/he necessarily operates which makes the search for universal structures speculative, relying on transcendental guarantees for thought. The rejection of this problematic implies the rejection of 'global' or 'radical' projects and positions in favour of 'practical critique' and the lessons they could reveal about the possibility of transgressions, that is to say, 'the possibility of no longer being, doing, or thinking what we are, do, or think. It is not seeking to make possible a metaphysics that has become a science; it is seeking to give new impetus, as far and wide as possible, to the undefined work of freedom' (1984c: 46).

These arguments, developed in the paragraphs where Foucault summarizes the positive implications of the notion of a philosophical ethos, implicit in Kant's essay, are crucial both for the ambiguities they contain concerning terms like 'freedom' and for challenging us to abandon the familiar grounds of critique for more adventurous forms of engagement that do not so easily yield to the temptations of totalitarianisms or to the invention of more subtle forms of control and repression. This is a point which Bernstein (1991) convincingly makes in the course of his interrogation of Foucault's text for signs of an 'ethical-political' perspective that appears to be implicit in Foucault's prescription of an ethos and his warnings about the dangers of further normalizations and repressions. This warning is coupled with the valorization of local against global theories and strategies, and of 'subjugated knowledges'. As Bernstein points out, 'the appeal to specificity and locality doesn't help us to elucidate the ethical-political question of how one is to act' (1991: 161). My point is that the fundamental problem arises from the fact that the analysis of instabilities and points of resistance, and the valorization of counter-discourses, does not indicate the ethical principles for preferring one type of resistance, say, women against forms of paternalist subjugation, to another, say, local Islamic fundamentalist defence of 'traditional' Sharia laws. A dilemma such as this one, a matter literally of life or death in some parts of the world, would have to rely on extraneous ethical principles or principles of justice that the 'undefined work of freedom' leaves equally undefined. It cannot be that Foucault refers the decision to individual conscience.

Indeed, Foucault counters the 'empty dream of freedom' with the specification of an experimental side to the 'historico-critical attitude'. This means that for him the work of the critical ontology of ourselves 'has its generality, its systematicity, its homogeneity, and its stakes' (1984c: 47). Presumably the point is meant as a defence against accusations of advocating a political practice that is vulnerable to more coherent, more globalized, more organized forms of power and discourse. One must admit that his explanations have a certain pragmatic force in acknowledging the historicity of the reality in which we want to intervene and the political and intellectual instruments that are at our disposal. And Foucault never loses sight of the fact that power is permanently at stake in all our actions and that the dilemma concerns the ways in which 'the care of the self' can be uncoupled from the intensification of power relations. The problem is formulated in the following questions: 'How are we constituted as subjects of our own knowledge? How are we constituted as subjects who exercise or submit to power relations? How are we constituted as moral subjects of our own actions?' (1984c: 49).

So, the right questions are there, but can we find in Foucault the bases for an ethics or a theory of power or for deciding between competing regimes of truth? And why are capitalism and newer forms of imperialism absent from this analysis of power? A wealth of commentary exists that disputes that his work provides us with the criteria we seek or with the theories that would answer the objections implied in my questions.[7] Charles Taylor has detailed the inconsistencies in Foucault's conceptualization of key terms like 'power', 'purposes', 'will', 'truth', 'freedom', evidenced in his talk of 'strategies without projects' and his 'failure to recognize the ambivalence of modern disciplines, which are the bases both of domination and self-rule' (1986: 95). Fraser points to the 'lack of any bipolar normative contrast comparable to, say, Jürgen Habermas's contrast between a partial and one-sided instrumental rationality, on the one hand, and a fuller practical, political rationality, on the other' (1989: 32). His notion of power is too undifferentiated, since it fails to distinguish between the forms of power that involve domination and those that do not. This is echoed in Said's criticism when he remarks: 'The problem is that Foucault's use of the term *pouvoir* moves around too much, swallowing up every obstacle in its path (resistance to it, the class and economic bases that refresh and fuel it, the reserves it builds up), obliterating change and mystifying its microphysical sovereignty' (1984: 245). Exploitative power is not morally commensurate with the power that supports resistance to oppression. Bernstein highlights the inconsistencies in reactivating a 'self' – 'What precisely is a self?', he wonders (1991: 163) – that Foucault himself has been at pains to deconstruct in his earlier studies. Equally, Foucault's work on the constitution of subjects casts a shadow on the issue of agency: 'Who or what is left to transgress historical limits?' (Bernstein, 1991: 164). The only echo of an answer appears in a statement made shortly before his death in 1984 when he declared that 'a whole morality is at stake, the morality that concerns the search for the truth and the relation to the other' (cited in Bernstein, 1991: 165). So the other finally appears on the scene.

Modernity, autonomy and the double seance of Reason

These criticisms of Foucault, valid as they are, do not dispose of the more intractable problems around the question of subjectivity that I think Foucault was trying to address. Take, for example, the issue of autonomy, ambivalently problematized in some parts of the lecture on the Enlightenment, yet reinscribed in the references to the self and to free moral subjects, as well as to the theme of an ethics of the self, so that we are led to other kinds of interrogations. The thematic of autonomy occupies such a crucial place in the conceptualization of the modern subject that it should alert us to expect some deep elements touching the core of our being lying under the surface that autonomy both protects and exposes. It would be easy to dismiss it by invoking Marx's argument that autonomy is the necessary illusion of the capitalist mode of production, an ideological counter that, among other things, makes subjects available on the market as 'free' agents, free to enter into forms of capitalist exchange. Equally, one could repeat Althusser's proposition that autonomy is an ideological effect in the process of constitution whereby subjects appear 'as if' they were constitutive rather than constituted. One could add Foucault's own analysis of the construction of docile and disciplined bodies, normalized subjects. But we know the difficulties which these approaches have encountered when dealing with the question of the who of agency and resistance and with regard to the neglect of difference – gender and 'race', for example – in theorizing subjectivity.

Autonomy is by no means a modern concept, though its functioning is historically variable, as, indeed, Foucault argued concerning classical Greek culture. A practice of liberty and the exercise of freedom in the process of formation of subjects was just as determining for the Greeks of that period as it is claimed to be for the man of modernity. Autonomy there was understood in relation to an apprenticeship whereby 'a man' learned to be master of himself and of others in relation to pleasures and to good governance, that is to say, it was part of an economy of pleasure and a political economy, instituted in a *techne*, understood here as the art of accomplishing and making present what a (social) technology institutes. Autonomy was inscribed in the dynamic of the power one exercised over oneself whereby mastery was achieved, a mastery expressing a victory over the natural forces inside every individual which threatened to rule over him. For the free man – it was, after all, a masculine philosophy – could not really be free unless he could domesticate the brute forces inside him, precisely in the same way as he was meant to command over those in his household: wife, servants, slaves, children. Whoever has succeeded in conquering his own impulses and tamed his passions, whoever has freed himself of the binds of youthful immaturity, can be trusted to dispense a virtuous justice. Foucault draws out the similarity between the economy of pleasure and domestic economy and the economy of the polity for the precise reason that self-mastery and mastery over others have the same form in classical Greek discourse. This is very clearly so in the code whereby the virtuous man was seen *ipso facto* to be the man most deserving of the exercise of authority over others and of enjoying a high status in the political life of the city.

One further correlation of autonomy was with the notion of liberty. Freedom was understood as a kind of relation to oneself conditioned by the degree of mastery over oneself, the degree to which a man could free himself from the shackles of desires that bound the man to a form of slavery: 'the worst servitude is that of the intemperate' (1984a: 93). Freedom, then, was allied to power: 'it is a power that one exercises over oneself in the power that one exercises over others' (1984a: 93). It is a liberty-freedom, which entertained a specific relation to knowledge to the extent that one needed knowledge in order to be able to practise temperance and to practise a virtuous authority.

I have pointed out elsewhere (Venn, 1985) that it is important to relate all this to the fact that Greek society at the time was conditioned by a culture of slavery. Freedom was experienced as a condition of not being a slave to oneself and to others; it was a positive conceptualization, something fought for in the mastery of oneself and in the face of the danger of servitude to the excessive, to what escaped the just measure. It is not the judicial freedom of the free agent of modernity, although both are allied to a morality. What was at stake is implicated in the rule that he who wished for or was worthy of dominion over others – fellow-citizens, wife, children, servants, slaves – must be capable of exercising a perfect authority over himself. The concept of autonomy, inscribed in a practice of self-actualization for free men, was clearly part of a political economy and thus inseparable from power relations and delimiting the relations a man could entertain with others. It is more than simply an intrinsic good that we should strive for or defend as part of a personal ethos.

In the modern discourse of the subject, the narrative of autonomy belongs to a problematic that binds it to notions of freedom and of reason, the three concepts supporting each other, for example, in the problematic of the emancipation of humanity developed in Kant's 1784 essay. In the eighteenth century, individual autonomy was asserted against existing tyrannies and the arbitrary exercise of an unimpeacheable power, demanding unconditional obedience from subjects. The classic instance from the point of view of 'the desire for revolution' is the political system in France before 1789; power was effectively monopolized by the clergy and the nobility, two of the three Estates, who claimed rights and privileges based in traditional authority, including arbitrary arrest and detention under the secrecy and impunity of the *lettres de cachet*. As Kant argued, reason cannot be free in such circumstances. Today, regimes of terror around the world, backed by the use of the systematic torture and murder of dissenters, force similar servitudes; in these circumstances autonomy is a clear political stake in economies of power which systematically distort the balance of justice, rights, obligations, freedoms.

My problem is not with this problematic of autonomy, which often stands in for that of liberty. The problem, from the point of view of the search for a philosophy which breaks with egology in its various forms and which refuses the 'forgetting' of the trace of the other, is that of reconciling the claims of individual autonomy and freedom against the claims of heteronomy and the implications of the intrinsic inter-subjectivity of lifeworlds. Other fundamental issues attach to this line of questioning. For instance, what does this mean for the refiguration of ethics? How can one uncouple notions of freedom and autonomy from the individualism with which it has become affiliated in the course of the history of modernity? The Kantian as much as the Foucauldian understandings of Enlightenment do not provide unambiguous indications for this different problematic of subjectivity. In Foucault, there are too many slippages between intimations of heteronomy and validations of a possibly solipsistic process of self-becoming; we cannot yet assume we have left behind the problematic of the subject constructed by the Enlightenment.

The postcolonial settling of accounts with that problematic obliges us to interrogate the extent to which that discourse, and the privilege it grants to the subject as centre and as agency of history, was conditioned, as much as that of classical Greek culture, by a slave culture and by an exploitative culture which systematized and naturalized inequality and difference – on the basis this time of universalizing principles and 'truths', precisely those that found the project of modernity. We can then return to the question of the 'critical ontology of ourselves' and to the question of the role of the aesthetic experience in the transfiguration of the subject.

What this means is that we need to extend the critique of a particular notion of rationality beyond the Derridean deconstruction of the meta-physical underpinnings of logocentrism, and beyond feminist demystifica-tions of its homocentrism[8] and postcolonial demonstrations of its complicity with colonialism and imperialism (Venn, 1993).

I will examine what I shall call the 'double seance' of Reason. The problem is that of understanding why it is reason and not something else which occupies the pivotal or nodal point in the great re-centrings and displacements that announce the modern era, suitably called the 'ego's era' by Lacan. Benhabib has defined four 'presuppositions' that constitute the grounds of the 'philosophy of the subject', namely, the unitary model of activity, the model of a transsubjective subject, history as the story of transsubjectivity, and the identity of constituting and constituted subjec-tivity (1986: 54). The global context of the constitution of the subject within such a philosophy in terms of the singularity of a self-centred entity whose agency is founded in Reason, freedom and individual autonomy is the expansion of Europe, inflated by slavery and New World colonialism, and the emergence of what Weber characterized as rational capitalism. I dealt with this complicated birth in the last chapter. It is clear that despite the world-transforming changes, this early modern period, from the end of the fifteenth century, was characterized by a social system, in Europe and most other places, in which the degree of freedom of every human being was dependent upon property relations and was strictly determined by culturally constituted attributes like gender and race. Social relations were locked within the nexus of property, biology, power, at a time when the degree of mobility and flexibility in the system was still very limited.

I have discussed too the crisis in hegemony during that period which threw into doubt the foundation of the normative principles regulating the domain of the social, inscribed in narratives that naturalized inequalities of power, status and property on the basis of divine providence and will. I argued that in the epistemic displacements that took place, the ancient theme of the anxiety of being confronting its finitude and the narratives which seek to secure the authority and legitimacy of power are reformulated within the *episteme* characterizing modernity, especially from Descartes. The foundation of truth and the narratives of legitimation shift away from the problematic which had its anchorage in the absolute certainties that God had whispered to His chosen scribes and which authorized a discourse of being in which one's spiritual needs and worldly desires were conjoined. This was not without its problems. We need to remember that already the discourse of reason from Augustine to Montaigne had tried to contain within its horizon the doubts and ambiguities, the tensions between the life of the spirit and the life of the body, between, on the one hand, the abnegations involved in the purification of the soul and, on the other hand, the will to knowledge that desired to narrow the odds of contingency in the midst of a very uncertain world. In the Christian problematic of being, the discourse of reason was allied to a narrative that banished doubt and incoherence only through the agency of grace, already placing itself outside scepticism by vesting the guarantee of its truth in what must, by definition, be beyond doubt, namely, God. Only divine intervention in an enchanted world reconciled Jerusalem and Athens, that is to say, reconciled the ethos founded in the law revealed in sacred texts and the ethos constructed on the provisional judgements of a critical secular reason.

We have seen that the modern discourse of reason before Kant attempts to reconcile the Christian and the secular narratives of being through a re-centring that installs the logocentric subject at the heart of the whole system. The Cartesian specular stratagem, as we know, fixes the subject as the place of origin (of consciousness, of knowledge and of will), the centre without trace, present to itself and sufficient unto itself. The Cartesian subject is burdened with the obsessional forgetting of the trace of the other, though the Big Other – God – is given His due: as transcendental condition for the subject and the faculty of reason. As Lacan has demonstrated, it is driven by the desire for mastery.

With modernity, then, the dilemmas dividing law and ethics, necessity and freedom, power and authority, self-interest and the general good become uncoupled from the revelatory discourse that reconciled them.[9] Gradually, particular concepts of reason and of individual autonomy come to function as the core principles organizing the coherence of the modern *episteme*. Kant explicitly demonstrates their mutual conditioning. More generally, both concepts are articulated in terms of the notion of the subject framed within the paradigm specified by the 'philosophy of the subject' such that the modern form of subjectivity becomes the *'point de capiton'*, suturing the different narratives that construct the conceptual framework of modernity. Theology is exchanged for the metaphysics of presence.

A genealogy of the modern subject, as I pointed out in the previous chapter, would have to account for the birth of the notion of the 'self' as mobile, open to a practice of self-fashioning, as Greenblatt (1980) has explored. It would need to take account of the conditions in which the fiction of a unified self emerged, inscribed in narratives in which self-presence functions as the mode of the recovery in the here and now of the life that constantly flies from us. Underlying Foucault's 'ontology of ourselves' lies the history of a discourse that from Augustine to Montaigne refigures an economy of the soul that desires to reconcile 'the time of the soul and the time of the world'.[10] This genealogy would have to include the more worldly discourse that from Machiavelli moves towards the new economy of power that Foucault (1979) has called governmentality.

The point of recalling the broad context of the birth of the modern subject and in emphasizing the *agon* of modernity is to locate the arguments and the principles that, in the midst of the diremptions that cross these discourses, came to justify the inequalities of property and power without having to refer to a notion of divine will and a narrative of redemption. I am leaving out the forms of legitimation of oppression that rely on Machiavellian, dog eat dog, principles. A disturbing thought is that most empires before modernity were built on economies of power that did not agonize over the ethical dimension of the relation to the other. Another genealogy of the relation to the other needs to be written; it would pay attention to the longer cross-cultural history of empires and colonizations, encompassing Japanese, Chinese, Egyptian, Inca, Roman, Yoruba, and many more cases of expansion and subjugation. One would have to examine the moral injunctions that limited what could legitimately be done to the other. What did the encounter with the other mean from the point of view of the relation to oneself? In an important sense, the very question of a relation between the economy of power and ontology and ethics arises within Western philosophical discourse itself and within the discourse of modernity in particular, inflected as it is by Christian theology.[11] From the point of view of a critique of modernity, the question is: what secular philosophy provides the founding narratives that could authorize systematic exploitation and expropriation? What philosophy erases the trace of the other?

I would like, at this stage, to add two other elements to the genealogy of the subject of modernity which I am pursuing. First, the logic of supplementarity in the logocentric discourse of the unitary subject which dictates that the other must be placed under erasure; yet the other must, by that same logic, appear, inscribed as the uncanny double in the logocentric subject's discourse of self-actualization. In other words, the other appears thus: ̶o̶t̶h̶e̶r̶: crossed out, yet remaining a spectral presence – with the burden of mourning and forgetting that is implicated in my imagery. Another 'hauntology' beckons in this respect, to make visible and to narrate differently the secrets buried beneath ontology. Additionally, the view that the other functions as supplement in this stratagem has implications for the view of the aesthetic experience as the means for reconciliation with the ethics of responsibility for the other, that is to say, the standpoint of the aesthetic as the liminal space of the recovery of the trace of the other. The implications disrupt the boundaries between the aesthetic and the ethical domains; thus, they call for their refiguration within a different problematic of being.

The second element concerns the question of terror in its many guises: ontological anguish and insecurity, or the terror of 'black bodies and darkness' and the 'terror of freedom' that Morrison (1992) explored by reference to American literature in the eighteenth and nineteenth centuries, and the terror which is inscribed in the 'mythic density of the space of death' (Taussig, 1987: 5), created by power to force obedience and acquiescence, which Taussig exposed in his study of the oppression of the poor and the Indians in Latin America. Morrison speaks of the abiding presence of a darkness haunting the formative texts of the American imaginary. For those living various forms of oppression in Europe in the seventeenth and eighteenth centuries, the New World was the 'clean slate' waiting to be inscribed with the dreams of freedom. It would be the place where control over one's destiny, that is, power and autonomy, 'would replace the power-lessness felt at the gates of class, caste, and cunning persecution. One could move from discipline and punishment to disciplining and punishing' (Morrison, 1992: 35). Yet the literature betrays a troubled and frightened spirit, confronting the contradictions in the disturbing realities of America, beset by the fears of 'boundarylessness', of 'savage' Nature and a people that could only be made docile by being violently bound and silenced, their unfreedom and serfdom validating the insecure freedom of the white masters. On the broader canvas of the colonized world, the values of auto-nomy and freedom are not deployed against tyrannies, but are validated in the lived relation between the 'masters' and the unfree or dispossessed.

I indicated earlier how the lived aspects of social reality and the underlying interests and investments inscribed in the lifeworld motivated and secreted the particular privilege granted to autonomy in the Greek ethos. The analytical standpoint which relocates the discursive and material constitu-tion of Europe as Western and modern within the complex space of world colonialism has similar implications for the specificity of the Enlightenment concepts of freedom and autonomy. The background for their emergence is a complex brew, mixing the confidence born out of the achievements and wealth-creating developments that I summarized earlier, with the fears tied to continuing serfdom and terror in Europe and the threats – of contamination with 'feminine' irrationality and weakness – which the logic of a masculine reason entailed. This agonistic and polymorphous imaginary is projected onto the space of 'Europe's others', where the intensity of hopes and fears, of terror and inhumanity is amplified on a universal scale, and returns in the themes of the noble savage of Rousseau, of the incommensurability of cultures in Herder, or in the arrogant denigration of non-European rationalities and cultures. In particular, the centredness of Europe with respect to other cultural spaces and the centredness of the subject in the metaphysics of presence relay each other in the dominant discourse of the Enlightenment, overdetermining a discursive closure with regard to the location of the other in the narratives of modernity which it is difficult to disrupt. There are important implications for the task of the reconciliation of the three value spheres and the refiguration of the 'subject' of postmodernity.

I am suggesting that in the circumstances attending the co-emergence of modernity, rational capitalism and colonialism, the concept of individual autonomy became the place-holder for the Law of the Master, the sign of control over destiny and over the non-white and the non-masculine 'other'. It conceals the contingency of being behind the willed acts of the free rational subject. Autonomy requires its (phallic) marker and guarantee: a (masculine) Reason, the possession of which signalled the possibility of mastery over contingency. The thought that motivates my suggestion is the idea that the fragility of human existence, balanced over the void opened up by splitting (the corporeal rift of birth and the vicissitudes of identification and (mis)recognition), intensified by the intimations of our mortality – the two are clearly not unconnected, as Lacan (1992) and Laplanche (1976) have established – drives the Enlightenment subject to seek ontological comfort and security in the promise of emancipation inscribed in narratives of mastery, of oneself and of others. For Lacan, splitting opens up difference and lack in a process of formation of subjectivity whereby the subject is barred from entry into the place of the lost object and embarks on the search for 'the part of himself, lost forever, that is constituted by the fact that he is only a sexed living being, and that he is no longer immortal' (Lacan, 1979: 205). What I have been trying to establish is the proposition that the alignment of autonomy with notions of self-sufficiency, the unitariness of the subject, individualism and narcissism is overdetermined by the conditions of emergence of modernity, particularly the contingent and correlated emergence of colonialism and capitalism. In these specific circumstances, the temptation of modernity has been to seek redemption by way of mastery – over oneself, over others, over nature and history – played out in the theatre of a universal, global project. The hope of emancipation and redemption of the self as understood in Christian onto-theology is thus made to dovetail into the project of universal and global transformation according to the world-historical process of the progress of Reason. For Europe at least, theology is thus reconciled with secular philosophy, so that the Christian mission which underwrote early colonialism – as in the ideology of Columbus – is aligned with the notion of a civilizing mission. This solidarity, from the nineteenth century, constitutes a central plank of imperialist ideology, although in practice there arose historically specific differences between the evangelist enterprise and the discourses and technologies of subjectification/subjection, to do with disjunctive calculations of the appropriate strategies for Westernization which I noted in Chapter 1. So, rephrasing Foucault's critical ontology, we can pose the question that confronts modernity thus: what is the desire of this subject who must understand himself by reference to self-autonomy and reason?

It seems to me that the historical context of the emergence of the phallogo-Eurocentric subject and its privilege with respect to occidentalism compels us to account for the effects of slavery and of colonialism on the founding narratives of the Enlightenment. We can then relocate the canonical narrative of self-formation in the discourse of modernity within an economy of power which subordinated the conditions of existence of the subjugated to the greater power and authority of those who lived their difference in the form of individual autonomy. Autonomy must make an accommodation with the socially 'instituted heteronomy' (Castoriadis, 1991: 163) of the cultural lifeworld. Those whose survival depended on the greater recognition of reciprocal dependence inside the shelter constituted by community – the poor and the oppressed – placed greater store by the values of solidarity and belonging.

In the discourse of modernity, it is philosophy that functions as the discourse establishing the principles of the thematic of identity; its articulation mortgaging it to the founding narratives legitimating the forms of exclusion of the other. In particular, philosophies of the subject theorize, among other things, a system of inequalities and exclusions, including a system for silencing certain knowledges and voices on the basis of an apparatus of the production of statements rooted in the soil of Reason. In the guise of a humanism centred on the self-as-identity, that is to say, in the discourse of the *cogito* that universalizes the form of the subject as the unified, singular being of Reason, it has authorized the 'worlding of a world' adequate to its totalizing ambition. Central to the analysis of the conditions of the emergence of and specificity of the autonomous, self-centred subject is the fact that this project was part of Europe's consolidation 'as sovereign subject by defining its colonies as "others", even as it constituted them, for purposes of administration and the expansion of markets, into near-images of that very sovereign self' (Spivak, 1985: 128). The irony is that Hegelian philosophy acknowledges the logic of supplementarity at work in the master–slave theme, for only the acknowledgement of the master as master by the slave confirms the master's self-identity. I will turn once more to Morrison, who is not at all surprised that the Enlightenment accommodated slavery: '[I]t would be a surprise if it did not. The concept of freedom did not emerge in a vacuum. Nothing high-lighted freedom – if it did not in fact create it – like slavery' (1992: 38).[12] My analysis problematizes the discourse of the Enlightenment beyond the logic at work in Morrison's remark, pointing to the agonistic terrain of its production and highlighting the counter-narratives of the Enlightenment that undermined it from within, a significant step if one is to think through the postmodern in its potentiality for emancipation.

From the point of view of conceptualizing the relation to the other, there is a stratagem in the emergence of the narrative of a sovereign reason and its self-centred subject that needs to be exposed. Let us call it the double seance of reason. Before the modern logocentric narrative of being and the narratives that institute the modern form of sociality, inequality and difference are attributed to divine will and order, or to the contingency of fate. In the classical *episteme*, the world is a domain of 'signatures' (Foucault, 1966) that register how every thing occupies its ordained place; the good order of society and justice depended not on notions of universal rights and liberties, but on custom and tradition which inscribed the supposition of hierarchy as natural and normal, as I noted in the previous chapter. Within this *episteme*, the ordered and just world need not be one in which all are equal. Radical thinking, however, erupting in periodic peasant or slave uprisings, surfacing in songs and sayings, or drawing from the egalitarian spirit in Christian teachings, could discover the basis of inequality in property and power. In other words, inequality, in the modern period, has often been grounded in socially instituted differences that are his-torically specific outcomes of processes which a democratic polity should be free to abolish. To that extent, the Enlightenment debate between natural law and the discourse of the economy is the theoretical counterpart of the struggle which had as stake different foundations for justice (see Hont and Ignatieff, 1983).[13]

Logocentric discourse displaces the basis of inequality onto something else, namely, reason itself. For instance, the cunning of Locke (1963 [1690]) was to argue that the possession of reason determines the possession of other things;[14] property can then appear as the metonym of reason, the natural result of its proper exercise, namely, through the efficient use of one's labour. We know that it is America that offers the stage for Locke's demonstration of the rationality and greater benefit for 'mankind' of the institution of private property and the invention of money. The displace-ment shifts the gaze from the contingent and socially established reality of inequalities to apparently unchanging and universal features intrinsic to human subjectivity. The discursive stratagem produces narratives in which reason and property come to refer to and relay each other in a specular signifying system. It is difficult to see the join since the differential dis-tribution of power and of property appears to correspond neatly to the (assumed to be natural) differential distribution of rationality; each instance performatively validates the 'truth' of the other. The double seance performs two simultaneous substitutions: it naturalizes inequality and difference, either as the consequence of what was intended by divine providence, or as the necessary result of 'man's' use of his rational powers, and it secularizes them, in the form of rational necessity, and thus brings them within the intentionality of subjects and their action. Reason is made to support all forms of oppressive relations and exploitation – colonial, 'patriarchal', class – while the 'Man of Reason' is installed as the centre of a new *logos*, namely, as the free, autonomous agent of History, the 'I' who decides the future. In the game-plan of reason the weaker of two powers cannot win.

In an admirable meditation on La Fontaine's fable 'The Lamb and the Wolf', Michel Serres reveals the strategy whereby, in the absence of justice, 'the reason of the stronger is always the best' (1982: 15). The story tells of a hungry wolf – wolves are always hungry – who comes to quench his thirst upstream in a river from which a lamb already drinks. The wolf accuses the lamb of muddying his water. There proceeds a form of trial, a truth game, in which, at every move, the wolf brings up new accusations – if it wasn't you it was your brother – to which the lamb counters using the logic of inno-cence – it cannot be me since I drink downstream, or, but I have no brother – as his only move in the game. It is clear from the start that the wolf means to be victorious and devour the lamb, as 'punishment', for 'It is always a wolf, and not a lamb, who quenches his thirst in the pure stream of reason' (1982: 18). The wolf, it is clear, has no superior force to challenge him; he is sovereign and autonomous. The outcome of such a game of truth is the death of the weaker party. Justice, in the figure of the shepherd, is invoked, but is absent; he is not playing.[15] If, in the court of Reason, no other regime of discourse is admissible, it is because this particular Reason is not interested in an equitable settlement of any '*différend*'. And so it is that, when justice is kept out of play, '"The reason of the strongest is *always* the best". The best reason *always* permits a winning game. The foundation of modern science is in this word, *always*' (Serres, 1982: 21, original emphasis). My argument is that the victory of a particular line of reasoning at the beginning of modernity means that the 'I' of Reason takes the place of the wolf; this 'I' occupies a place by itself, autonomous and rational: 'It has taken the wolf's place, its true place. The reason of the strongest is reason *by itself. Western man is a wolf of science*' (Serres, 1982: 28, original emphasis). So long as autonomy finds its guarantee in Reason, so long as rationality finds its proof in the action of the self-centred, self-sufficient, autonomous subject, it is not possible to break free from the mesmeric power of the double seance.

By locating the colonial project within the horizon of the articulation of the conceptualization of modern reason and its subject, I want to broaden the arena of insurrection that contributes to the critique of modernity by emphasizing the crisis implicated in the 'end of empire' today. The insur-rection of subjugated knowledges which Foucault talks about must cover critical thought as well as the narratives of the subordinated and memories of oppression. The broadening of the base of insurrection provides a leverage to lift the yoke of the 'truth' of a totalizing Reason that had immobilized critical thinking.

I do not wish to give the impression that the history of the foundation of the narrative of the autonomous, rational, unitary subject is a simple cover-up of the fact of self-advantage and self-preservation. Kant, indeed, breaks with the bourgeois philosophical anthropology of Locke and Hobbes, that is, with their privilege of self-preservation and self-interest as the founding principles of social order. He recognizes the conflict between self-interest and the common good, but in converting the (postulated) opposition between nature and reason into the metaphysical dualism of phenomenal and noumenal world, his analysis operates on the terrain of the 'forgetting' of the primacy of the other in the constitution of both the private and the public domains of subjectivity. To adduce moral self-reflexivity as a way out, that is, the capacity to put aside our self-interest in the interest of a universal law that has the force of an imperative, is to rely on a notion of autonomy that reinscribes within it the unitary, rational assumptions of the unmediated, non-heteronomous subject.

Hegel's apparent recognition of heteronomy, as Adorno (1990) has argued, wastes the promise contained in the conceptualization of autonomy as the capacity of the subject to express its freedom in the form of 'being-by-oneself-in-otherness' because he delivers this freedom and the other to the logic of World-Spirit (*Weltgeist*); the other, and its 'otherness', becomes the means, as dialectical pole, for the self-actualization of World-Spirit (through the historical process of becoming of Being). Real subjugated others disappear in the ethereal abstractions of idealism, or, better, in the imaginary of a fantasized reconciliation that leaves unchanged the conditions of exploitation (see also Honneth, 1995).

Adorno's own exit in considering how the subject can live its autonomy in a non-repressive form is to point to an aesthetic experience, a manoeuvre which is deeply embedded in the soul of Western thought, and that courts a variety of dangers. My point would seem to add to the arguments, developed in, say, the work of the Frankfurt School, that evaluate the balance of domination and emancipation in the history of modern reason to have favoured domination.[16] Yet the issue is not as simple as this view indicates. For the history of Enlightenment overlaps with the history of a counter-narrative of subjectivity which begins to be more fully elaborated in Romanticism and in 'Baroque Reason', heralding the emergence of a secular narrative of emancipation which promises the possibility of recon-ciliation with the other. It is an aspect of the dilemmas of modernity repeated in the oppositions of body and mind, law and ethics, the intelli-gible and the sensible, virtue and happiness, that is to say, they are repeated in the tropes of the doubling of the subject, tropes that are the indices of the deep fractures and vacillations of the self-centred subject. Additionally, they indicate another thematic that requires a fuller exploration than I will pursue in this chapter, namely, the effect of the metaphysics of presence in erasing the difference between Being and beings: 'the very thing that would have been "forgotten" in the determination of Being as presence, and of presence as present – this difference is so buried that there is no longer any trace of it. The trace of difference is erased' (Derrida, 1982: 65).

The sublime object of desire

The question of reconciliation, mimetic or otherwise, opens up in a different way the problem of the correlations of ethics and aesthetics and an 'ethos of existence' that have a purchase for the problem of the transfiguration of the subject. Reconciliation is meant in several senses. First, indicating a recovery of the other in the 'we' of community, echoing the Kantian *sensus communis* or universal feeling (Kant, 1987 [1790]: 87–8; para 20–1) which the 'I' of subject-centredness splits up in its individualization of being. Furthermore, reconciliation is implicated in the dissolution – but not by reducing the one to the other, that is, not by the tactic of identity – of dualisms of mind and body, the intellect and the senses, the phenomenal and the transcendental which have their specificities in the discourse of modernity. Third, there is the recovery of the different temporalities of being through a rememoriza- tion, thus, a renarrativization that both preserves and transfigures them. Reconciliation for Kant has a different purpose, burdened and ultimately constrained within the presuppositions of the unitariness of the subject which the aim of establishing the unity of philosophy confirms by impli- cation: the unity of philosophy and the unitariness of the subject summon up each other. The *Third Critique* sought reconciliation by way of the aesthetic, which thus functions as the site for restoring the unity of philosophy splintered by the critique of reason and the critique of the moral–practical in his earlier work, that is, for restoring the unity of the theoretical and the practical. These themes are woven into the discourse of modernity from Kant onwards; the first three are replayed in Foucault's discussion of an ethos of being. Their interrogation by way of the underside of reason, that is to say, through a genealogy of the aesthetic[17] from the Enlightenment, presents more than a critique of instrumental reason, since it opens up the question of subjectivity for a fundamental problematization and so contri- butes to the refiguration of the problematic of subjectivity after modernity, namely, by allowing the possibility of grounding the subjective project in principles that eschew the notion of a despotic rationality or of self-centred philosophies that erase the difference of the other.

Walter Benjamin showed an early awareness of this possibility in pointing to the importance for Romanticism of Fichte's view that the subject could not be reduced to objectivity. Bowie, in his discussion of Benjamin, reminds us that 'the attempt of modern subjectivity to grasp itself goes hand in hand with the genesis of aesthetic theory' (1990: 196), the point of articulation being the intractability of reflexivity in the theorization of consciousness. The point goes to the heart of the problem of foundation in Western philosophy, once the ground of theological foundation is abandoned. As I have argued in the previous chapter, the way the problem of foundation is formulated in the discourse of modernity has depended on the privilege of Reason and the *cogito* in the 'philosophy of the subject', that is to say, the privilege of epistemology in the search for the guarantees of the 'truths' that could serve human beings in the conduct of life and the search for meaning. The dilemma for thought is that, on the one hand, the 'I think' cannot establish itself in the space of consciousness, since reflective thought, in taking itself as the object of its own reflection, slips into an infinite regress. On the other hand, given that thought does not exist as a sensuous object of the real world, philosophy cannot find an objective domain of natural necessity to ground consciousness, as it can do concerning the sensuous world, namely, in the sciences. Instead, reflective thought attempts to deal with something outside or beyond the phenomenal world, thus, an un(re)presentable entity, which one approaches only by a detour. The fact that cognition can have these thoughts at all, and can separate itself from a domain of natural causality, for example in following moral imperatives, indicates the gap between Being and things which the term 'freedom' is meant to designate. Kant already elaborated this problematic of the subject which arises when the Cartesian stratagem of a self-present subject is rejected, pointing out that self-consciousness must be pre-supposed (Kant, 1933 [1787]: 168–9; para. 25B). We saw in the previous chapter how Descartes pulled off the trick by arguing that the reliability of the mind and its rational powers was underwritten by God; he makes God pick up the tab of epistemology that renders the *cogito* insolvent. Interestingly, in Kant's discussion in the *First Critique*, in the passage where he claims that 'the determination of my existence can take place only in conformity with the form of inner sense', he adds this in a footnote to explain the determination of existence:

> The 'I think' expresses the act of determining my existence . . . but the mode in which I am to determine this existence . . . is not given. In order that it be given, self-intuition is required; and such intuition is conditioned by a given a priori form, namely, time, which is sensible and belongs to the receptivity of the determinable. (Kant, 1933 [1787]: 169)

The recognition – more of an intimation in Kant – of the underlying primacy of the dimension of temporality, when pursued along different avenues, leads to other, post-Kantian, conclusions that I shall explore in the next chapter. This problematic of self-consciousness is refigured in Heidegger through the relationship between Being and *Dasein*; *Dasein*, he argues, 'is an entity which does not just occur among other entities. Rather it is ontically distinguished by the fact that, in its very Being, that Being is an *issue* for it . . . *Understanding of Being is itself a definite characteristic of Dasein's Being*' (Heidegger, 1962: 32; H. 11–12, original emphasis). In the nineteenth century, the development of such ideas through the problematic of time and of the temporality of being had to wait for phenomenology. Kant did not, or could not, pursue it, but sought a different route, one

already broached by the initial separation between the spheres of epistemology and ethics; the aporias in this conceptual enframing of modernity
invisibly shape the attempt to reconcile them at a higher level, where the
value of Reason would count for more than the value of Understanding.
Let us examine how far this higher principle concerns aesthetic judgement.

It is important to bear in mind that Kant had a rather conventional view
of art; for him, art is a static category, having limited purchase on the issues
of the development of humanity and of emancipation, in contrast with the
sciences, as Bowie (1990) has noted. Beauty and art were important because
'they made something "infinite", Reason, sensuously available' (Bowie,
1990: 36). The special place of the artistic experience in philosophy since
Kant has to do with the fact that the artistic product – music, a visual
object, dance – is sensuous, and so does not simply exist in thought as an
object of thought.[18] Yet its apprehension, for instance in the judgement of
taste (according to Kant), involves reflective judgement, that is, a judgement which tries to reveal a generality or a universality to the objects of the
world or to the freedom immanent in reason. In other words, there is a
transcendental dimension to the faculty of judging since nothing authorizes
it except the faculty of judging itself. Aesthetic judgement, then, appears
uniquely to combine the two levels, phenomenal and transcendental, of our
engagement with reality, hence the central role it has played in the search
for the reconciliation of truth, the good and beauty and the search for
(transcendent) unity.

In the 'Analytic', Kant makes a crucial distinction between the beautiful
and the sublime: 'we regard the beautiful as the exhibition of an indeterminate concept of the understanding, and the sublime as the exhibition of
an indeterminate concept of reason' (1987 [1790]: 98). One implication is
that the communication of taste tied to the beautiful, *sensus communis* (1987
[1790]: 162; para. 40), is different from that of the sublime. He reserves the
sublime for an experience of nature alone, an 'absolutely large' emotion
which 'agitates' us and is experienced as 'displeasure'; it is the experience of
the 'monstrous' and the 'colossal' that leaves aesthetic judgement bereft of
concepts to describe it; it is an experience of the infinite, beyond the power
of reason to comprehend teleologically, although the sublime is an 'intellectual feeling'.[19] However, the very violence of the disruption is proof of
the power of the mind to expand to cover the power to think the sublime.
When thinking about the model of nature in Kant, we need to remember
that he remains within the conventional concept of nature located by reference to the duality nature/culture, such that the subject appears external to
it, whereas I would rather problematize these categories by hybridizing
both, and by examining the 'experience' of 'natural' phenomena by reference to the fact that they are always-already culturally marked, say a storm
(to refer to an example used by Kant), and therefore must include semiotic
considerations and questions of memory, history, embodiment.[20]

Lyotard believes that the importance of the 'Analytic of Aesthetic
Judgment' derives not so much from the analysis of reflective judgement as

from its functioning as 'a propaedeutic to philosophy . . . [because] aesthetic judgment conceals . . . a secret more important than that of doctrine, the secret of the "manner" (rather than the method) in which critical thought proceeds in general' (1994: 6). The manner has only the 'feeling of unity in presentation' to guide it. What seems to support this sense of unity is what Lyotard calls the 'tautegorical' character of aesthetic reflection, using the term to draw attention to the 'fact that pleasure and displeasure are at once both a "state" of the soul and the "information" collected by the soul relative to its state' (1994: 5). This feature of aesthetic reflection is more pronounced when we examine the (Kantian) sublime, as opposed to the beautiful, for the latter promises the 'happiness of a subjective unity' (1994: 25), whilst the former's sense of unity is revealed only in the wake of the ruins of subjective unity provoked by the disruption of the experience of the sublime. Aesthetic judgement shares with critical thought the openness to receive the concept or the pleasure that it does not seek in a teleological manner, or that it does not appropriate for instrumental purposes, but receives 'passively'. It is in this attitude of passivity that critical as well as reflective judgement do their work. For Lyotard, the *Third Critique* unifies the field of philosophy precisely 'by making manifest, in the name of the aesthetic, the reflexive manner of thinking that is at work in the critical text as a whole' (1994: 8). Passivity, interestingly, appears in the work of Ricoeur when discussing responsibility and in Levinas and Merleau-Ponty, as I will discuss in relation to the refiguration of the ethical in the final chapter.

Within the Kantian problematic, aesthetic experience, because it relates to an intrinsic feeling of pleasure, and because it can command universal assent, at least for Kant (1987 [1790]: 85–90; paras 18–21), is not motivated by self-interest or by a desire to control; its 'disinterested interest' escapes instrumental rationality. The analogy between the beautiful and the good shows that aesthetic judgement has an affinity with the ethical. One should not infer from this that the experience of the beautiful leads to the moral feeling, a point Lyotard is keen to make in his analysis of the distinct faculties involved in listening to the law and in the experience of the aesthetically pleasing – the use of pleasure? – so that the 'principle of the heterogeneity of the faculties prevents one from confusing the beautiful with the good' (Lyotard, 1994: 165–6). The ethics and the aesthetics of the self are not the same thing, though there is a bridge, or even a ladder, between the two that one may use with caution. The sublime, however, threatens to destroy the bridge, for it requires the sacrifice of one of the faculties, as Kant pointed out: 'It is only through sacrifices that this might [of moral law] makes itself known to us aesthetically' (Kant, in Lyotard, 1994: 188). Sacrifice in the Kantian problematic belongs to a chain of terms – usage, interest, benefit – which, argues Lyotard (1994), reveals their economic provenance. The economy of the faculties is modelled on that of the economy. One may well wonder if there is a different conceptualization of the sublime which would align the violence of sacrifice not with an economic loss but with a different economy of being, a non-economy of being, for which loss is a necessary price for overcoming egology, yet not equivalent to the loss involved in self-sacrifice (and not to be thought in terms of Bataille's notion of *dépense*). The analysis of the sublime beyond the Kantian problematic would furnish us with a different way of relating the aesthetic to the ethical, beginning with the break with the Kantian privilege of law with respect to the good.[21]

I pose the problem in this way because in Kant the exploration of the possibility of uniting the cognitive and the ethical on the terrain of the aesthetic remains bound to a position which places a premium on the interiority of the subject as the site of their union, appearing to close the subject upon itself. The aesthetic of the beautiful, in promising the union of the faculties, by the same token promises the birth of the subject, that is, its birth as the unitary and originary ground upon which consciousness grasps itself. However, the process of self-consciousness, when conceptualized in this manner, promises the birth of the subject *to itself*: an endlessly deferred promise, for the moment of union does not come.

One of the key problems with the analytic of the aesthetic is the suspicion that the conceptual apparatus deployed to deal with reflective thinking, and the search for the categories that would enable philosophy to think through the problem of the gap or abyss between the objects of thought and thought itself, is beholden to the presupposition of one mind, one thought, one subject. The Enlightenment context of a European universalizing project centred on a unitary concept of Europe is not irrelevant to the intelligibility of this whole problematic of subjectivity. If, on the other hand, thought and the subject are decentred with respect to consciousness, then mind could be seen as a 'dwelling place' for the presence – through interiorization and because of the narrative character of the self (as I have discussed in Chapter 2) – of the other in oneself. Passivity, from that standpoint, would have a different meaning, namely, openness to the thought/thinking of the other mediated in communicative action. Intimations of this different trajectory are found in the (Kantian as well as post-Kantian) view that the aesthetic experience yearns to be communicated, that is, that it desires, seeks, or opens towards an heteronomy.

If, bracketing the distinction between the beautiful and the sublime, we think of art as the space in which the artist tries to make the invisible visible, to present the un(re)presentable or unfathomable, we could say that it tackles a problem similar to the epistemological conundrum of the self-presence of consciousness to itself – which Cartesianism and logocentrism resolved through the subterfuge of the metaphysics of presence. One could say that aesthetic reflection functions as an heuristic method in guiding the subject to feel her or his way towards grasping the secret concealed in the saying of the work of art, a secret that cannot be told except in the artwork, or that cannot be revealed except by way of the work that art urges us to do. Which means to say that an hermeneutics of the artistic act or product is necessary for one to learn to decipher or listen to the work, a work which is at once reflexive and therapeutic (in the psychoanalytical sense). This hermeneutics is not separable from the apprenticeship whereby we learn to become ethical beings, and learn the meaning of being-with, a point I shall discuss in the next chapter: they are part of the same signifying practice.

Perhaps Benjamin's storyteller has learned to combine the two functions in the practice of telling. We recall that in the storyteller, Benjamin (1973) looks for the mysterious gift which the storyteller conceals in his craft, the art of restituting to the memory of the living the immemorial tales of the lives whose passage leaves for us a treasury of wisdoms and lessons that the storyteller discloses in the telling. I shall pick out two aspects in the analysis of Benjamin. First, the self-forgetful attitude of the listener, who must give herself over to the telling, listening for the saying in the tale which transmits something inscrutable about the world that dwells in the happening of the life narrated. It is a form of remembrance, a memory of the forms of hope. The second element is woven around the discussion of the novel and extends into the question of what is disclosed in the narration that so enthralls us. The novel, he tells us, is significant not for the story itself, but because the stranger's fate, narrated to us, 'by virtue of the flame which consumes it yields us the warmth which we never draw from our own fate. What draws the reader to the novel is the hope of warming his shivering life with a death he reads about' (Benjamin, 1973: 101). He borrows from Paul Valéry this reflection about the work of a woman embroiderer:

> Artistic observation can attain an almost mystical depth. The objects on which it falls lose their names. Light and shade form very particular systems, present very individual questions which depend on no knowledge and are derived from no practice, but get their existence and value exclusively from a certain accord of the soul, the eye and the hand of someone who was born to perceive them and evoke them in his own inner self. (1973: 108)

The passage evokes the sense of the unpresentable in the work of art that the work itself liminally secretes. The storyteller captures an echo of this secret, letting 'the wick of his life be consumed by the gentle flame of his story . . . [he] is the figure in which the righteous man encounters himself' (1973: 108–9).

Gift, sacrifice, memory, death, loss, the unpresentable: we find again the traces of these terms in Baudelaire and in Foucault's engagement with the Enlightenment and modernity. They are faintly echoed in Kant's notion of the sublime. They suggest a different economy of being in which the sublime stands for the recognition of excess and violence, the disproportions of desire in its will to grasp the fleeting flame of life. The sublime renews the experience of the thrownness of being, its dehiscence or gaping when faced with the anguish of loss and finitude, and the disturbing thought of an unconditioned freedom. The sublime is not exceptional, though there are ways of closing oneself off from the ecstasies it provokes and that drive us to seek it. So can the experience of the aesthetic, or, more accurately, can art in the sense of a creative and poetic figuration and transfiguration of subjectivity as lived, provide, by itself, the leverage for breaking with the modern problematic of emancipation which rescues the sense of promise?

A number of references in Foucault's text seem to hold out the possibility of finding a number of openings there in spite of the traces of narcissism in the notion of 'care of the self' that Thacker (1993) and Bernstein (1991) have noted. The terms he repeats from Baudelaire – strange beauty, swift joys, an echo of poetry – suggest an experience and the thought that 'derealizes' the world, to borrow a term from Bachelard. They resonate with the Freudian concept of the uncanny (*unheimlich*), and, at an ontological level, with Lacan's discussion of *jouissance* in *The Ethics of Psychoanalysis* (1992). It is possible therefore that the problematic of the aesthetic experience latent in Foucault's analysis, when read in the light of Lyotard's (1988a, 1994) reflections on the Kantian Analytic, could help clear the ground of a number of obstacles to thinking the 'post' of the postmodern and the postcolonial in terms of the 'who' rather than in terms of truth or reason and their substitutes.

Lyotard's analysis attempts to link the work of 'working through' involved in writing the kind of history that leads to refiguration with the project of emancipation and with something similar to the aesthetic experience. Let me explain. He at first makes the important point that there is something in the process of emancipation that works in a manner similar to the work of the imagination in the aesthetic experience. Imagination exceeds the conceptual framework of the understanding (in the Kantian problematic). It is able to apprehend time beyond the logocentric ruse which aims to contain the temporal within the horizon of conscious cognition. This is because its attitude is one which is open to the data of experience and not one which seeks to tame or dominate the object. Aesthetic pleasure is not the result of a command, it 'falls on the spirit like a grace' (Lyotard, 1988a: 201). For reasons that will become clearer later, I will propose that we can understand it as a form of giving oneself over to the Thing (*das Ding*, in the Lacanian sense).[22]

Lyotard notes that the work of 'working through' is not the same as that of the aesthetic, because, to begin with, analytic work is driven by an 'unbeareable suffering' and has no end since '[t]he dispossession of the subject, its subjection to an heteronomy, is constitutive of the subject' (Lyotard, 1988a: 201). It is a thought that calls up another discourse of dispossession, that which is involved in the pain and frustration of recognition and misrecognition intimated by Lacan in his discussion of working through. Referring to the discourse of the analysand, he asks:

> Does it not embroil the subject in an ever greater dispossession of that being of his whereby . . . he ends up recognizing that that being has never been anything other than his construct in the imaginary and that this construct disappoints all his certainties? For in the work he does to reconstruct it for an other, he recovers the fundamental alienation which made him construct it in the image of an other, and which has always destined it to be stripped from him by an other. (1966a: 125)

Following Kant, Lyotard argues that the aesthetic relation is both a 'promise of joy', as Baudelaire had originally put it, and the promise of a community of feeling (*sensus communis*) instituted in the reconciliation of the subject 'with itself and with others' (1988a: 201). For him, the difference between the aesthetic of the sublime and that of the beautiful can be understood by analogy with the difference between primary repression and secondary repression, between what belongs to the domain of the Thing and escapes representation in the symbolic and what can find access to forms of representation, as in dreams, the symptom, and so on. On that basis, 'rewriting . . . concerns the anamnesis of the Thing . . . the Thing which haunts "language", tradition, the material with, against, and in which we write. Thus, rewriting belongs to the problematic of the sublime as much as to . . . that of the beautiful' (1988a: 203).

This view opens up the question of the relation of the aesthetic and the ethical, by introducing a way in which we can reinscribe subjectivity within that relationship without having recourse to the mediating function of the epistemic, intrinsically split subject. The background issue remains the project of emancipation through critique.

I would like to try to connect several things that would help to rethink the connection between law, ethics, desire and subjectivity that the question of aesthetics throws up. In modernity, art is the space where a certain excess of the subject is given expression, precisely what moves beyond the epistemic subject. It is an experience of the limit: beyond the domain of comprehension, located in the non-linear temporality of the imagination, when the imagination works 'at a glance' rather than by 'progression', when it works 'regressively' (Lyotard, 1994: 142). I propose that we under-stand this 'regression' in the sense of a retroactive working, linking it up analogically with the retroactive effect of the '*che vuoi*' in Lacan's dis-cussion of the 'fading of the subject' (1966b: 176–7). It is the place where the subject loses itself in 'the mixture of fear and exaltation that constitutes sublime feeling' (Lyotard, 1994: 127) . Whether through the work of art or otherwise, the experience of the sublime, or what the term 'sublime' has come to designate, has profound implications for the problem of the transformation of subjectivity. Lyotard in his analysis of the concept in Kant to which I have just referred says that 'the "regression" of the imagination in sublime feeling strikes a blow at the very foundation of the "subject" . . . the sublime threatens to make him disappear . . . striking at the unity of an "I think"' (1994: 144). The disappearance, or what Lacan calls 'fading', of the subject occurs at the point of the repetition of the splitting of the subject – here between the subject of the 'I think' and the subject of the sublime feeling – the point where re-emerges the lack of the Other and thus the place where the dialectic of desire is played out in the form of the demand or the appeal in the '*che vuoi*' addressed to the Other.[23] The response to the demand about the desire of the Other intro-duces the theme of *jouissance* and that of fantasy, of ideology too, as Žižek (1989) has demonstrated, and, beyond that, the question of the primacy of the other, for 'Love itself is thus taken to be the satisfaction of a sublime hunger. . . . A desire without satisfaction which precisely includes [*entend*] the remoteness, the alterity, and the exteriority of the other' (Levinas, 1969: 34). So, is the sublime also the place of the Other, more specifically, the place of the *jouissance* of the Other, and, retroactively, the place of the *jouissance* of the subject? And is that the way to meet 'the necessity of supplementing the analysis of discourse with the logic of enjoyment' (Žižek, 1989: 125), that is to say, joining critical ontology with an aesthetics?

Let us consider the kind of work of art that exists at the limits of the sayable and of what can be thought, a work that attempts to communicate an experience at the edge of disintegration, carrying still the emotional charge that threatens to disrupt its coherence as signifying object. This experience of the fugitive and the nomadic, floating between the echo of death and the 'quiver of life', disturbs the certainties of the subject of reason. This work of art is an object in which the intelligible and the sensuous co-exist in a space between the 'not yet', 'nevermore' and 'now' (Lyotard, 1988a: 203) of a wild imagination. By transcending the specific moment yet 'capturing something eternal within it', the work of art becomes a 'sign of history' in Lyotard's (1983) sense. This points towards the domain of the uncanny, the disturbing space of the sublime. The sublime occupies the liminal space where the wound of the loss of the other is healed by the spear of lack in the 'saying' of the sublime.[24]

One could think of Picasso's *Guernica* as an example of the trans-mutation of the event into a 'saying' that transcends yet preserves within its timeless and figural space the rawness or 'grain' of the event, as Barthes (1977) might put it. Equally, Morrison's novel *Beloved* (1987), and par-ticular musics, force to the surface a buried pain and refigure the event in a form that facilitates the work of 'working through'; they are examples of a transfigurative experience. I would like to examine this in some detail.

It is remarkable that the themes I have been trying to gather and regroup in my discussion are expressed in their immediacy and poignancy in the work of a Black American woman. Speaking about her novel *Beloved*, Toni Morrison says: 'The book is not a historical novel . . . but it deals directly with the power of history, the necessity of historical memory, the desire to forget the terrors of slavery and the impossibility of forgetting' (1993: 179). Black American writers turn to history because 'we live in a land where the past is always erased and America is the innocent future in which immi-grants can come and start over, where the slate is clean. The past is absent or it's romanticized', yet the vital thing is 'to come to terms with the truth about the past' (Morrison, 1993: 179). Later she says: 'Black Americans were sustained and healed and nurtured by the translation of their experience into art, above all in the music' (1993: 181). It is this music, what dwells in it, that she tries to reactivate in her writing.

Beloved is described in the conventional canon − in thrall still to the sovereignty of the problematic of representation − as a 'magic realist' novel, a description Morrison spurns because it assumes that she 'has no culture to write out of' (1993: 181). It deals with the ghosts locked up at the heart of African-American history, yearning to be born again in the midst of the present. It is a story of an escaped slave woman, Sethe, who, at the point of losing her children to the slave agent, kills her daughter, Beloved, because she could not bear to let white men do to her children what they had done to her: 'dirty you so bad you forgot who you were and couldn't think it up . . . [they must not dirty] her best thing, her beautiful, magical best thing – the part of her that was clean' (Morrison, 1987: 251). The result is amnesia and repressive forgetting for those closely involved, until, years later, Beloved returns as a young woman, the 'becoming-body' of the spectre (Derrida, 1993: 25), to 'join' with her mother in response to the latter's desolate yearning and pain. It is a story of how the out-of-jointness of time as lived by those subjected to an excessive oppression locks the familiar events of existence – traumas and loss, birth and death – into an uncanny dreamtime that only cathartic violence or healing can release and reassemble. Violence binds both perpetrators and victims in the return of the past as the uncanny figure, the *revenant*, to whom justice must be rendered. Such unthinkable and unrepresentable violence already points to the economy of the sublime, dramatized in a narrative that binds passional and libidinal forces to sacrifice and gift and to an emancipation. In Beloved, the repressed and the unmourned return for real, demanding the recognition of their 'having-been', a recognition that the whole community must share in order for the refiguration of the living to take place. The last part of the story enfolds as a collective process of what Morrison calls 'rememory' and of rescue which counters the literal fading of Sethe as she gives herself to and is possessed by the object of loss, itself symbolic of unbearable other losses, their catalyst. A significant moment of healing comes when Beloved's sister calls for help from the women of the neighbourhood. They gather outside Sethe's house and sing, searching for the sound at the beginning when there were no words: 'the voices of women searched for the right combination, the key, the code, the sound that broke the back of words' (Morrison, 1987: 261). So reflexive activity and communicative action by themselves are not sufficient – for refiguration and for the anamnesis of the 'thing' – although the characters in the novel spend a good deal of time delving into their own and the community's history, and into their emotions and experiences to figure out their pain and their pleasures in relation to their identity. In the end it is the uncanny force of the music and the communal host, embodying and transmitting the shared suffering of generations and expressing the recognition of a repressed memory, that, working at a liminal level, sets to right the disjunctions of time that injustice had wrought. Its work belongs to the economy of the gift, freely given, expecting no restitution and responding to an immemorial ethical imperative.

There are many other instantiations of the sublime in the book, often in the form of music: Sixo, who sacrifices himself so that Sethe and his family could escape, singing while being burned to death by the slave agents; the chanting and dancing of slaves gathering in the 'Clearing' to get back in touch with the thing that humiliations and routine torture tried to beat out of them, the thing that puts back together the pieces of their humanity. Suffering, repeated in the endless beatings and humiliations, the hard labour and the wilful destruction of the soul, becomes inscrypted in the body, so that everything pours into and out of it; the body of the slave becomes the site, the figural place, where the plural history of the community and the singular story of the individual speak in the coded language of excessive loss and desire.

It is clear throughout the novel that music plays a central part: 'Black Americans were sustained and healed and nurtured by the translation of their experience into art, above all in the music' (1993: 181); it is this music, what dwells in it, that Morrison tries to reactivate. *Beloved* is more than a story of the everyday distress of slaves retold as vernacular history; it is about the bodily and collective re-enactment of the unpresentable, it is about the phenomenal world that circumscribes our existence and the liminal spaces in it where something beyond the bits and pieces of daily living are assembled in an interiority, and it is about modernity as lived by those once considered outside the modern. The novel makes present a dimension which remains in the background in many other narrations of suffering and emancipation. Slavery throws the slave into a permanent state of emergency, the lived reality of which the events in the novel depict, allowing us access through the narration to the most acute existential anguish that being may live: the proximity of death and the threatening loss of everything that gives meaning to living: love relations, filiality, clandestine liberties, creative activity. Morrison is Benjamin's storyteller and Lyotard's analyst, combining the presencing of the sublime with the work of 'working through', so that history and memory may give expression to the gaping of being, allowing the narrative, through the derealization of reality and the effects of the surreal, to function as a transfigurative text. Our own life is warmed for a while by the flame of the lives that burn in her stories, so that the questioning of our identity – who are we in the present? – is entangled in the recapitulation of a whole history of struggle and survival, activating the economy of debt and gift which is at work in rememoration. She is clear that in making present the 'having-been' of Black American history, in particular the terror that was slavery, she is giving voice to an experience of modernity. She argues that 'modern life begins with slavery . . . black women had to deal with "post-modern" problems in the nineteenth century and earlier. Certain kinds of dissolution, the loss of and the need to reconstruct certain kinds of stability. . . . These strategies for survival made the truly modern person' (Morrison, 1993: 178).

The stories that Morrison tells and the reasons she gives for telling them lend substance to the rather abstract issues that I have been trying to make visible. The themes I have picked out – of rememoration, in the sense of the reworking of memory and history that refigures our selfhood/identity, the recognition of the impossibility of forgetting and the need to come to terms with traumas and with the repressed and the displaced, the aporias of a critical ontology that uncovers the questions of debt and justice, the theme of a dimension to beingness irreducible to the abstractions of systems and theories – they are all the themes buried at the heart of the two series of the refiguration of modernity with which I have been concerned, namely, the postmodern philosophical critique of our presentness and postcolonial interrogations.

The argument about the transfiguration which the work of art makes possible relates directly to the fact that it is itself, ideally, the product of *poiesis*, the activity that transforms the event into a statement that congeals within it the anxiety of our being in the face of an overwhelming emotion, the proximity of the dissolution of the subject in the intensity of its passion, the taste of death in the moment of the body's most ecstatic experience. This is what the sublime tries to restitute or 'unconceal'. If death stalks the sublime, it is because it is in the face of our dissolution in the ecstatic moment that we are the most fully alive and the most free, dwelling in a space that transcends the horizons of ordinary reality and temporality: '*jouissance* implies precisely the acceptance of death' (Lacan, 1992: 189). The theme of *jouissance* reappears here because this space where we both lose and find ourself, this fantasized space of the plenitude of the subject beyond the loop of the symbolic, is the place of the Thing. It is also, as Lacan suggests, the place of the Other.

So ecstasy and epiphany of the subject instantiate the dimensions of transfiguration. The concern with change means we should shift the focus away from an obsession with the object[25] to the analysis of the experiential, and therefore rethink the sublime, understood in relation to ecstasy and epiphany, by reference to other experiences of embodiment in addition to the 'work of art': the spectacle and the carnivalesque, collective forms of 'art' played out in some ceremonies and rituals, the 'abject',[26] 'swift joys' that invoke *jouissance*. But is it enough to stay on the terrain of the aesthetic, of *jouissance* and pleasure, of death?

The question of ethics

Lacan, in his discussion of the ethics of psychoanalysis, connects the paradox of the Law, founded as it is in the Other who provides the ultimate guarantee for the Law, with the paradox of *jouissance*. He does so by inserting between them the meaning of the myth of the death of God. Christianity coupled the death of God with the problem of what must happen to the Law if God must die, finding an answer in the trans-formation of the Law that does not destroy it but commutes it into the commandment 'Thou shalt love thy neighbour as thyself' (1992: 193). For Lacan, the demand of this commandment is that the subject must renounce access to *jouissance*; it forces the subject to seek *jouissance* in transgression: the Sadean option.

There is another option, for which some other remarks of Lacan provide an opening, interestingly, in his reference to Kant. Lacan thinks that psychoanalysis leads us to reconsider ethics in terms of 'the relationship between action and the desire that inhabits it' (1992: 313). The standpoint for rethinking ethics beyond convention is 'that of a Last Judgment: have you acted in conformity with the desire that is in you?' (1992: 314). Traditional ethics is opposed to this 'pole of desire'; it is a 'morality of the master' founded in 'human – all too human – power'. At its opposite pole we discover the place where signifiers are unbound from the rule of Law, where 'gods and beasts join together to signify the world of the unthinkable' (1992: 314).

The reference to the unthinkable and the unrepresentable returns us to the question of the liminal space of the sublime. But there is a sense in which the rethinking of ethics reconnects the problematic of *jouissance* and the Law with Kant for whom 'moral imperative is not concerned with what may or may not be done' (Lacan, 1992: 315). In a sense, then, the imperative is the degree zero of judgement; it refers to an infinite measure, beyond the place and time of sensible human interests, thus to the place of desire, but a place which remains 'a space where accounts are kept' (Lacan, 1992: 317). I take this to mean that this space harbours the trace of the Other by way of the underlying reference to accounts, that is to say, to justice.

I will return to the issue of the keeping and settling of accounts in my conclusion. For now I will turn again to Lyotard, who points to the options that have divided thought since the Renaissance, highlighting the opposition between a specific concept of rationality and other ways of thinking and writing that culminate in the opposition between, on one side, logical positivism and, on the other, a poetic ontology, or, rephrasing this opposition, between, on one side, an 'ordering of the orderable' (Heidegger, 1977) allied to instrumental rationality and cybernetic logic and, on the other, the thought which is turned to being and the life of the spirit. Two lines of thought can be uncovered in the polarity. One is directed to minimize contingency and risk in the global extension of a cognitivist discourse that appropriates everything within its 'enframing'.[27] The other line of thought is motivated by the desire to keep open a discourse 'turned towards the incessant, interminable listening to and interpretation of a voice', obeying an imperative which enjoins us to 'preserve and reserve the coming of the future in its unexpectedness' (Lyotard, 1989: 20). This discourse grounds its legimacy not in the past but in the open temporality of the future; it is 'prepared to receive what thought is not prepared to think' (1989: 17). But, asks Lyotard, 'who is the author of the commandment [to resist totalizing thought]? What is its legitimacy?' (1989: 20).

Lyotard's discussion of (post)modern times brings us back to the territory of ethics and the space of the unthinkable. The attitude consistent with the ontological option he defends is that of a listening to the phenomenon, to interpret it without the expectation of being able to reveal its ultimate 'truth'. Interpretation in that sense can be seen as an 'enigmatic' and 'marvellous' practice, to use Levinasian language, involving a repeated deferral of meaning, the working upon the illegible trace that we must try to restitute to the present. Trace, for Levinas, refers to the 'unthinkable'; it can be thought as 'the presence of whoever, strictly speaking, has never been there, of someone who is always past' (1974: 201).

We can imagine the trace of the other to be marked by the 'a' of *différance*, this unrepresentable spacing which, nevertheless, makes all thought possible. It has the anteriority of the already said which wells up in the interstices of the said. The liminal character of trace suggests that it functions in a manner analogous to the functioning of the sublime, at least understood in the way I am trying to redefine it. We could imagine its presence in the flash of the face of the other in the saying of a statement or of the work of 'art', that is to say, the other behind the work, the other concealed or withheld from presentness by the force of the immediacy, the here-and-nowness, of the work. Grasping the work in its sublime aspect is a form of 'unconcealment', the revelation of a 'truth' that cannot be told in any other form or language, the voice of someone who is always past. The attitude to the sublime requires a kind of passion, both a grasping and an abandonment of the 'self', a form of giving oneself over to the Thing which I mentioned earlier. I mean by this an attitude combining the readiness to 'receive what thought is not prepared to think', the attention to the phenomenon that respects its 'enigmatic' and 'marvellous' and temporally open character, and an ethical relation to the other which neither reduces alterity to identity nor abolishes the concreteness of being in onto-theological abstractions. This ethical attitude is summarized by Levinas in the notion of the face, that is, an openness to the reality of the other that I would express in the Augustinian principle: *Volo ut sis* – I wish you to be.

The face stands in for a number of concepts and values in Levinas, all attempting to capture the essence of the ethical relation that I must have with my other. The face, he tells us, is 'a fundamental event . . . it is not a representation, not a given of knowledge. . . . It is an irreducible means of access, and it is in ethical terms that it can be spoken of' (Levinas, 1988: 168–9). Furthermore, 'The face is not a force. It is an authority' (1988: 169), that is, it is a commandment without force, an imperative to recognize alterity (not reducible to difference in Levinas) and respond to the silent demand in the saying of the face. The face calls for a response and a responsibility, but 'responsibility is a love' (1988: 174), which is the only attitude I must have to the uniqueness and singularity of the other. In this manner there emerges a familiar and venerable theme, for, 'The idea of the face is the idea of gratuitous love' (1988: 176): the giving of oneself without the expectation of a return – saintliness of the '*sinthome*'?[28] Responsibility, love, authority, these are the paradoxes of the primacy of the relation to the other which lead to another aporia, that of justice, because whilst 'justice is the way in which I respond to the face . . . it is ethics which is the foundation of justice' (1988: 174–5). Both concepts implicate the possibility of the improvement of justice towards an ideal or Idea: 'There is no moral life without utopianism' (1988: 178).

It is to Derrida that we can turn for a politically pertinent rephrasing of the Levinasian principle of responsibility for the being of the other. He proposes a notion of justice inherent in the unconditional dignity, surpassing any form of exchange, owed to 'those who are not present, those no longer or not yet present and living' (1993: 16). This notion of justice is not a 'calculable or distributive justice . . . but justice as the incalculability of the gift and singularity of the non-economic ex-position toward the other. "The relation to the other – in other words justice", writes Levinas' (1993: 48–9). It is interesting that Derrida develops his discourse on justice starting with the question of responsibility that arises because of the ghosts that now haunt modernity in the shape of those who have been 'victims or not of wars, political or other violences, nationalist, racist, colonialist, sexist or other exterminations, the oppressions of capitalist imperialism and of all forms of totalitarianism' (1993: 16). Their past and our future are joined in the question of justice.

The line of thought I have been developing has moved from Foucault's ontology of 'ourselves' via Derrida's 'hauntology' (1993: 24, 43) to the position summarized in the notion of being-towards-the-other which implicates a narrative of subjectivity at odds with the narrative inscribed in the 'philosophy of the subject' and in occidentalism. What is implicated is a different history of the subject of modernity, a different story of modernity that allows the imagination to dream of alternative projects of the becoming of being. The theme of history ushers in another element that needs to be added to the problematic of subjective transfiguration: it is that of mourning, raised by Derrida in his 'hauntology', and discussed by reference to the Holocaust and the postmodern by Santner (1990).

Space prevents me from dealing with the many important issues implicated in the necessity and the ability or inability to mourn and grieve. Mourning relates to rememoration and 'working through' (and nostalgia and fantasy); it involves a keeping of accounts which is also a coming to terms with a new reality while preserving a history in a presentness of the past. The process of mourning works beyond repressive forgetting. Though critical ontology and critical history have their part to play, it is more than genealogy. Through mourning, debts are settled or acknowledged or cancelled that enable the 'angel of history'[29] to face the future in its unexpectedness.

Ricoeur too speaks of debt, regarding the distinction between history and fiction, for 'we are not only inheritors, we are equally debtors to a debt which in some way renders us insolvent' (1991: 186). We have a 'duty of restitution' towards the dead, the victims of past injustices and oppressions which triumphalist history 'forgets'; the historian 'must "render" what has happened, that is to say, figure it at the same time as returning it to the dead; [it is] the task of doing justice to the world' (1991: 186).

The flight into postmodernity or the fantasized return to fundamentalist identities repress or misrecognize the resilience of the modern and its legacies, for the violences we associate with modernity twinned with capitalism have not disappeared, nor have the traumas. Critique needs the supplement of working through so that we may settle accounts with that history too if we are to put an end to the cycles of repetition. I noted earlier that the settling of accounts is not a matter of restitution, but a process of renunciation, especially the violences that have accompanied the history of occidentalist modernity so far.

Conclusion

We have seen how in his reassessment of what the Enlightenment might still mean for us, Foucault gestures towards a pragmatic politics of the possible, allied to the ethos of self-actualization. His analysis repeats the interdependence of the cognitive, the moral–practical and the aesthetic – agreeing in this with Habermas – and makes clear that critique is a central element in both the political dimension and the ethical and aesthetic dimension of the practice of liberty that for him defines modern subjectivity. I have been arguing that without a notion of a project and without clear new ethical principles the talk of an aesthetics of the self is open to any kind of politics. After all, still predominant in corporate, global capitalism are the conditions that supported systematic exploitation, in the form of Europe's imperial project, those that continue to support patriarchal oppression and the wilful extermination of others for self-interest, as in many kleptocracies, and those that validated subject-centredness. For instance, the discussion of aesthetics cannot ignore the claims of the aestheticization of the commodity in the context of the seductions of an hyper-real world of simulacra, and the implications of this hallucinatory culture for the possibility of disengagement from existing forms of sociality. Nor can we forget that the aestheticization of politics has been intrinsic to Nazism and totalitarian thought, as Lacoue-Labarthe (1990) has shown in his interrogation of Heidegger. The closures operated in the cultural stratagems of postmodernity imply that the 'practice of liberty' would be confined to a privatized domain, limiting ethical life and aesthetic pleasures to narcissistic forms of self-actualization, consistent with the concept of autonomy inscribed in individualism or fantasized by the political economy of liberalism.

This is not to say that one must instead privilege alterity in some self-sacrificial communitarianism, for, the guarantee of something like autonomy is necessary for the process of critique to work in making a difference in the present. As Castoriadis has argued, 'autonomy, social as well as individual, is a project' located in a society that can be lived as 'instituted heteronomy' (1991: 163). In any case, autonomy cannot be tied to freedom alone, for, as Levinas (1987: 53) asks, does freedom precede justice? And how does one reconcile justice with power?

It is clear that as soon as we introduce the standpoint of the 'other', the rewriting of modernity must supplement the analyses that depart from philosophies of the subject with critiques of Eurocentrism and homocentrism, and critiques of the brutality of oppressions which today have been amplified by modern technology; we need to attend to their co-articulation in the history of our era. This involves making visible the primacy of the relation to the other in the process of formation of the self and of the lifeworld. For example, the different conceptualization which recognizes the polysemic and narrative character of the 'who' of action developed in the work of Ricoeur implies that '(t)he autonomy of the self will appear then to be tightly bound up with *solicitude* for one's neighbour and with *justice* for each individual' (1992: 18, original emphasis). This new 'subject' is a host, welcoming the other in its interiority. There are, of course, problems that are thrown up in the attempt to establish the different founding principles of a non-oppressive form of sociality, to do, for example, with notions of trust, of justice itself, of self-actualization. Their resolution belongs to the same problematic of being which obliges us to think the re-ethicalization of politics in line with the view that: 'Ethics redefines subjectivity as this heteronomous responsibility in contrast to autonomous freedom' (Levinas, 1984: 63).

Oppression and exploitation of any kind are, in principle, incompatible with such an ethics. I think that this means, principally, equalizing the conditions in which each of us is able to practise a liberty which remains within the ethical and aesthetic frame of a vision of a subjective becoming which combines the project of the transformation of society as a whole with the commitment to give to the reality of living a quality that redeems the fragility and contingency of existence. It is the difficult task, full of danger, that the Enlightenment, in its own way, placed on the agenda, but which, as Fanon long ago pointed out, the history of modernity, in the 'West' and elsewhere, has failed to deliver for the majority of people.

Notes

1 A vast literature exists which establishes the extent to which colonization and the slave trade benefited Europe and the West. What Europe derived from the trade cannot be reduced to a balance sheet alone. One must take account of the effects on demand and confidence, on the development of industries that would otherwise not have flourished, for instance the clothing sector, or take account of the numerous discoveries and imports that changed life in Europe, for example those of rubber or tobacco. It would take volumes to detail the things that do not fit into accounting practices, yet made a whole new world. For classic sources, see Blackburn (1988), Fryer (1984) and Williams (1961).

2 See Chapter 1 for an explanation of the concept of jetty.

3 See the discussion by Lyotard (1983).

4 The intriguing connection to be pursued is that between Foucault's title for the third volume of his history of sexuality and the central theme of care in Heidegger (1962).

5 Even so, I think the constitutive elements of psychoanalysis need to be recast in the light of a different understanding of embodiment, that is, not mortgaged to the libidinal – whilst recognizing its primacy – and recognizing equally the inter-subjective and cultural character of the process of formation of subjectivity, imbricated as it is in the narrative and temporal forms in which a self understands itself. I established this in the second chapter.

6 There is a very lucid summary in Young (1990).

7 See, for example, Bernstein (1991) for a discussion of the ethical issues. Also, the following analyses: Coles (1991); Fraser (1989); Thacker (1993).

8 The work of Luce Irigaray and Julia Kristeva has paved the way for a rich body of explorations that establish the phallocentric credentials of the logocentric subject.

9 Gillian Rose (1992) has produced a challenging examination of the diremptions of law and ethics, arguing that totalizing discourses attempt to resolve them on the side of oppressive, normalizing power.

10 I take my cue from one of the chapters in Ricoeur (1988).

11 What differences are there between the Semitic religions concerning these issues? In what different ways is the question posed, if it is posed at all, in, say, the *Mahabharata*?

12 It is possible that her view could apply equally to other imperialisms based on slave cultures, for example the Roman empire.

13 This debate continues today in different terms and on different terrains. The transcendental functioning of Reason has been replaced by the norm of performativity whereby the rationality of economic process slips under the established practices of accounting and exchange to acquire the immanence of the natural. Efficiency has become the transitive norm: a process, such as, for example, the distribution of incomes is rational if it is efficient. The market is the mechanism which is supposed to decide; it is also the last court of appeal. The market judges its rationality according to its own criteria of the rational. The market today is the wolf of reason. Lambs can only hope that the shepherd is watching. But who is the shepherd today? Does not a realist cynicism threaten to snatch from the poor the husk of hope on which they suck?

14 See the Second Treatise on Government, written in 1690, para. 34, and the chapter on property generally.

15 Not only is the shepherd of justice absent, he never shows up, though we know that, like Godot, he hangs around somewhere, and his coming would change everything.

16 Benhabib (1986) has introduced a line of thinking, working through critical theory and feminist theory, that helps to rethink the contribution of the work of the Frankfurt School for the transfiguration of the subject.

17 A genealogy of the aesthetic would pass through Kant, Schelling, Baudelaire, Nietzsche, Benjamin, Adorno, Lyotard, Derrida, Lacan, Foucault, Kristeva. Elements contributing towards such a vast task are developed in, amongst others, Bowie (1990), Buci-Glucksmann (1994) and Eagleton (1990).

18 Writing and oral forms of narratives have a special status from that point of view, invoking a social reality but working more directly at the level of the imagination through mimetic and poetic practices. The issues that open up here are too complex to be summarized in a note. I can only say that since my analysis of the aesthetic is moving in the direction of the work of *poiesis*, the literary form can be included without causing too many problems. Kristeva's *Revolution du langage poétique* (1974) and Ricoeur's work on narrative and time will stand as indications of the kinds of arguments I would invoke in support.

19 See *Critique of Judgment*, para. 26, and Lyotard's discussion of the sublime (1994: 181–7).

20 For instance, the experience of a storm recalls previous ones, or imagined or fictional storms described in news reports or in some literary text, or storms seen in a film or a painting to which particular feelings and emotions still cling because of the specific context of these varied experiences: who we were with, what was said, what were the effects, what emotions were attached to these encounters. The later experience of a storm invokes or taps into this chain of significations and the jumble of feelings associated with the previous ones – real, literary, filmic, iconic, and so on – so that the experiential, generally, is only in a specific sense 'personal'. The experience of nature is mediated by culture to such an extent that it becomes

impossible to separate out the one from the other when it is a question of describing our lived relation to 'nature'.

21 Kant says: 'The concept of good and evil is not defined prior to the moral law, to which, it would seem, the former would have to serve as foundation; rather, the concept of good and evil must be defined after and by means of the law' (in Lyotard, 1994: 168).

22 The complete discussion is in Lacan (1992).

23 I am reconstructing a number of filiations to be found in Lacan's *Écrits* (1966b), in the chapter 'Subversion du sujet et dialectique du désir dans l'inconscient freudien'.

24 I am taking some liberties with the text of Žižek (1993).

25 For example, in debates about whether the avant-garde is or isn't transgressive and subversive of the present, or which particular art object qualifies as sublime in the sense I am discussing.

26 I use the term 'abject' to signal the fruitful correlations that Kristeva's work brings to mind between the emotions bound and unbound in the primal scene and the emotions that require to be worked through, and which are reopened by 'artistic' experiences, or experiences that bring into play the same signifying mechanisms. See particularly Kristeva (1982) and (1983).

27 I use the concept in the sense that Heidegger gives it in 'The Question Concerning Technology' (1993: 330).

28 *Sinthome* in Lacan is a pun conjoining the meaning of *saint homme* (saintly man) and *symptome* (symptom).

29 My allusion is to Walter Benjamin's meditation on Klee's painting *Angelus Novus*, pointing to the 'the storm we call progress . . . [which flings] the angel of history . . . into the future to which his back is turned', 'Theses on the Philosophy of History', in Benjamin (1973: 259–60).

5

HETERONOMY, ALTERITY, EMBODIMENT: ON BECOMING OTHERWISE

Relocating the problem of the 'post'

The exploration of the question of modernity that I have pursued has constantly stumbled upon another question: that of what being is. The way that I have examined the latter has moved away from the terrain of a fundamental ontology, that is to say, a terrain where the question of being is posed by reference to itself, enclosed in a discourse which proceeds by reflection on being as such, drawing from a corpus of work within the European tradition – of metaphysics, ontology, onto-theology – that has not thought it relevant to pose the question by reference equally to history. Several displacements have enabled me to shift the question onto that of the genealogy of being and a critical phenomenology, putting to work the critiques that have disclosed the cultural and historical specificity of the discourses of being, for instance from the point of view of difference, and from the point of view of the relation to the other. To the initial ontological problem, other questions have been added concerning, namely, the history of being, the conditions, discursive and material, that enable particular forms of being to appear and change, and the forms of being that await in the future[1] I have addressed some aspects of this issue in Chapter 4, and I shall extend my discussion in what follows. If modernity is the period in which a particular – logocentric, Eurocentric, phallocentric, rationalist – form of subjectivity has been instituted as normative, one can argue that the problem of 'who comes after the subject' and after modernity is but another form of posing the question of the transformations that would provide the conditions of possibility for a post-occidentalist way of being. These transformations clearly implicate a politics, in much the same way that modernity, to the extent that it was a project, and to the extent that that project sought to institute both a form of sociality and a form of subject congruent with it, inaugurated a modern politics around ideas of autonomy, liberty, the sovereignty of the state, democracy, progress through the rational calculation of the future, and so on.

My intention in this chapter is not to proceed to an exposition of the conditions of a postmodernity, except to emphasize again the inscription of modernity in the contemporary lifeworld, even in postcolonial conditions, as I have discussed. The longer genealogy of modernity and of the West which I have pursued, connecting with the idea of the historicity of the present, has tried to reveal two things: an older preoccupation embedded in human cultures, to do with what it means to be human at all, instituted differently in different cultures and epochs, and the modernity and openness of the question of 'who comes'. By way of a reflection on the existential conditions of beingness, I have suggested that through the different modes of being in the world one can detect a common anguish about finitude and about the temporality of being, tied to the notion of suffering expressed in terms of lack and loss which motivates the characteristic imagination of the future in the form of a promise or an anticipation: of redemption, of emancipation, of *jouissance*. Equally, because human beings are 'desiring machines', the experience of joy and ecstatic states drives us to seek and to anticipate their repetition in the future.

I now want to examine the question of an emancipatory narrative in the shadow of the postmodern, starting with the conflicting approaches in Lyotard and Habermas in order to eliminate the attempt to rescue the project of modernity which neglects the question of rethinking the foundational issues. I shall explore these issues by drawing some lessons from Levinas, the later Merleau-Ponty, Ricoeur and others who have gone some way in the direction in which I am venturing. In Chapter 1, in my discussion of the modern project of universal emancipation and liberation, I picked on the attempt by Habermas to shift the emphasis from the rationality of cognitive–instrumental discourse to that of communicative action. I indicated the limitations for a proper grounding of the ethical which residual Eurocentric suppositions and the inadequate theorization of difference produce in his work.

Lyotard examines another option, posed in the form of a question: 'Can we today continue to organize events according to the Idea of a universal history of humanity?' (1988b: 45). In other words, how are we to judge our competence or our capability to so organize events? Lyotard says that we have to be sceptical in view of the failure of the post-Keynesian management of democratic liberalism and the bankruptcy of the project of modernity symbolized by events like Auschwitz. We are left with an ethical option, namely, what we ought to do. Here Lyotard counsels us to undertake 'the apprenticeship of the proper names . . . names of those close to us, heroes in the wider sense, of places, of dates, and . . . the units for measuring space, time, exchange value' (1988b: 49). He adds that names can be learned not in isolation but in the context of little narratives, located in named places, distinct from national categories, but now constantly threatened with colonization by global capitalism. Appeals to the category Foucault called the 'universal intellectual' are no longer adequate because this kind of intellectual work today has no authority: it does not conform to the criterion of good or efficient thinking, which is to gain time, whereas the older kind of thinking 'makes one lose time' (1988b: 55).[2] If we give up on universal forms of legitimation, are questions of what is ethically acceptable reduced to judgements circumscribed by local forms of legitimation, that is, by local narratives? There is a problem with this option, first examined by Lyotard (1983) by reference to the Cashinahuas' strategy for legitimating the authority of a narrative, whereby the positioning of a named narrator in the telling of the stories authorizes both the narrator and the narration. There is a circularity in the mechanism of this form of narration of legitimation, the effect of which is to produce closure, immunizing the process from the application of external criteria and principles in reaching judgement about particular narrativizations of events. The self-referential character of the mechanism confirms the homogeneity and authenticity of the community as an effect of doubling, delegitimizing any genre of discourse that falls outside its space. Radical difference cannot be accommodated within this discursive stratagem. Scientism and essentialism operate in much the same way. So, does the answer to what we ought to do, and what we ought to be, reduce to a matter of how we are to constitute the community, given that it is the latter that grants legitimacy to a people? The choice we face, for Lyotard, divides between an appeal to an originary founding moment of the imagined community – the race, the true believers, the *ethne*, and so on – an appeal which is ultimately despotic, or the making of the people according to an idea of republican liberty that keeps open the issue of popular unity and identity (1988b: 71).

The idea of universalism, then, is not thrown out but construed to be the stake in its own definition. In highlighting the grand narratives' claim to universality and their tendency to totalize history in the idea of a rationally ordered project, Lyotard makes the point that this form cannot accept competing claims, and must erase difference in the unitariness of the 'we' in whose name the project is authorized. It does not accept the existence of differends, in epistemology as much as in the practice of everyday life. The task of Habermas, from that point of view, appears to be on shaky ground. One may well ask who is the 'we' of universalism now, what is humanity today? Previous projects of the emancipation or happiness of the people have tended to use criteria of inclusion in constituting the 'we' that were also criteria for exclusion: the tribe, the nation, the chosen people, the believers, the master race, the West, and so on. Such forms of exclusion have been used to justify every crime, and continue to work to the same ends today.

In the wake of debates about the politics of difference and the politics of identity, there is talk today of a new pluralist cosmopolitanism. Kant and Diderot spoke about a cosmopolitan culture a long time ago, though the version now is supposed to be less Eurocentric, deriving from the recognition of the 'hybridity' and heterogeneity of cultures, driven by the translations and crossings of peoples and cultures thrown together by modernization. A variation, perhaps latent in 'third way' political discourse, might imagine the community to be constituted by the 'we' of the new middle classes, sharing an orientation towards the goals of self-realization and the maximization of autonomy, occupying the new plural spaces in cities. In this picture, we would all in the end join, or aspire to join, together under the united colours of this new universal community. Leaving aside the issues of continuing exploitation – which neo-liberalism would like to naturalize – can one run with the hare of universality and hunt with the hounds of difference, while avoiding the jaws of ethical relativism? In other words, what relationship – of convergence, of relay, of opposition, of solidarity – exists between the normative content of positions like feminism and 'postcolonialism' and that of the modernist universalism of communicative ethics?

The example of the customary sexual mutilation of girls in some Muslim communities, which I introduced in Chapter 1, will serve once more as a case for examining the stakes in the different language games, and a way of approaching the theoretical differends. Those who defend the practice tend to invoke traditional values and customs in support, customs to do with the particular construction of sexuality in the communities: what men desire, how women should behave, what they should expect of themselves, the value of virginity, what service to a husband means in terms of sexual pleasure, the place of paternity and blood-lines in relation to kinship, and the idea that respect for parents and men, and for the community, should be expressed through respect for the traditions. At another level the 'little narratives', telling the lives of particular persons and families, are placed under the greater signifier of Islamic beliefs and law, that is, their local normativity is guaranteed by appeal to an idea of divine sanction founded in religion, that is to say, by reference to an explicit universalist discourse and a transcendent authority. The issue of justice is tied up with the question of responsibility and expectation, so that, for instance, many mothers feel that they would have failed in their responsibility towards their daughters if they do not act according to customary expectations, genuinely believing that they are acting in the best interest of their daughters.

Feminist opposition to the practices points to patriarchal forms of oppression, arguing that everything connected with these practices institutionalizes attitudes to women and gender differences that systematically deny women equality, liberty and autonomy. The 'little' or local narratives, tied to the context of the community, legitimize the real violences inflicted which have permanent consequences concerning pleasure and health, and turn women into sexual objects for men. The issue is refigured as one to do basically with power and exploitation and the intrinsic injustice of an oppressive practice which denies women basic rights.

A universalist critique of the practice could not deny that the participants are communicatively competent, or that they can find arguments in support of their action which are valid in terms of the kinds of claims to authority that obtain in the community, or in terms of the appropriateness of action, the correctness of the speech acts inscribed in the practice, or in relation to the norms and values that are upheld in the community. There is no doubt either that actors in the situation understand their identities by reference to the arguments and the acts involved in sexual mutilation and to a domain of intersubjectivity that puts into play the variety of beliefs, values, expectations, attitudes, knowledges, that are communicatively instituted within the relevant lifeworld. There is nothing wrong here with the pragmatics of meaning displayed by participants. In order to judge genital mutilation unacceptable and unjust, one would need to appeal to the universality of truth-claims about autonomy, liberty, justice and individual rights. Yet it has been the point of 'postmodernist' critiques of the hegemonic discourse of modernity, and of critiques from those marginalized or excluded by it, to establish the partiality and ideological character of such claims. Does that mean that there is no option but to support the line that Habermas proposes? Or does the confusion arise from 'categorial distortions' (Benhabib, 1992: 13) within theories of universalist morality? Let us examine if there is a way out.

Benhabib counters what she sees as the excessively rationalistic perspective of Habermas in the emphasis he places on a rationally motivated consensus, proposing instead that the universalizability procedure in ethics should be in line with 'the open-ended procedure of an "enlarged mentality"' (1992: 145). This Arendtian procedure would be consistent with the principle of 'reversibility of perspectives' central to Kohlberg's cognitive-developmental moral perspective. Communicative ethics, Benhabib argues, must take account of the situated character of meaning-generating action and the 'contingent cultural, institutional and emotive presuppositions of the ability to take the "standpoint of others"' (1992: 145). Borrowing from Carol Gilligan, she argues in favour of thinking of the moral self as a composite of a 'generalized' and a 'concrete' other. She agrees with her that communicative ethics must break with the 'juridical' bias in the standpoint of the universalist morality which informs the divide between justice and the good life. Benhabib supports a 'post-Enlightenment project of interactive universalism . . . without metaphysical props and historical conceits' (1992: 3). Such a universalism would be interactive rather than legislative, it would recognize gender difference rather than privilege a 'disembedded autonomous male ego' (1992: 3), and be sensitive to context. The moves in the elaboration of this project involve first of all a 'shift from a substantialist to a discursive, communicative concept of rationality' (1992: 5). This view relies on the understanding that the process of 'socialization' happens through interaction with others in a speech community, whereby one 'acquires language and reason, develops a sense of justice and autonomy' (1992: 5). I expect Benhabib is assuming the process to take place in an ideal speech community, or at least in a democratic, republican community, as undestood by Lyotard. For it seems to me that neither a commitment to justice nor respect for autonomy is an automatic outcome of 'socialization' in most communities.

This, I think, is where Benhabib's elaboration of a feminized Habermasian position comes unstuck. Reason, for her, would be a linguistically and communicatively contingent achievement, suggesting an 'interactive rationality' that implicates an ability to make judgements on the basis of their 'hypothetical validity from the standpoint of some standard of justice, fairness, impartiality' (1992: 6). Benhabib's position leads her to the idea of a post-metaphysical, interactive universalism based on

> the universal pragmatic reformulation of the basis of the validity of truth claims in terms of a discourse theory of justification; the vision of an embodied and embedded human self whose identity is constituted narratively, and the reformulation of the moral point of view as the contingent achievement of an interactive form of rationality rather than as the timeless standpoint of a legislative reason. Taken together, these premises form a broad conception of reason, self and society. (1992: 6)

Now, this is all very well, but such an approach to what she calls 'interactive rationality' describes how, in spite of the claims of positivist and cognitivist psychology, and the assumptions of logocentrism, subjects generally, in any community, come to be integrated members of the community, accepting the norms of moral conduct and so on that are normative there. It applies to the traditional Muslim community as well as to cults and to the Mafia. Besides, the assumption that the process leads to the development of a sense of justice and autonomy begs many questions about the particularism of context-specific standards and norms; autonomy, for instance, is not a universally accepted social good. Benhabib does discuss the issues by reference to Rawls's 'political' conception of justice, restricted to the context of liberal democracies, but she wants to overcome these restrictions on the grounds that 'conceptions of self, reason and society and visions of ethics and politics are inseparable' (1992: 7); they are conceptions that are ever open to challenge. Again, this openness, presumably, assumes a community in which each member has equal power and equal access to the sites of deliberation, in which case, there would be no problem. What is it that keeps open the conceptualizations of reason or justice? Is it resistance and counter-narratives of the community? So the question of power, though recognized, for example, by reference to gender difference, is surprisingly underdeveloped.

The problems arise from the desire to reformulate a universalist discourse ethic whilst rejecting the illusion of consensus or the assumption of uniform rational moral autonomy, as in Habermas. Benhabib is able to pursue her project by holding on to the possibility of a 'phenomenology of moral judgement' that would reconcile universalist morality and context-sensitive moral judgement within situations in which situatedness can be challenged 'in the name of universalistic principles, future identities and as yet undiscovered communities' (1992: 8). In support of these commendable goals, she relies on a series of concepts and propositions, principally, Arendt's 'enlarged way of thinking' – constituted by the self's interiorization of an imagined community of interlocutors, so that thinking is never a solipsistic activity – which supports the (Arendtian) model of 'reversibility of perspectives'. Tied to this is the claim that every human being is 'worthy of universal moral respect' (1992: 10), and the thesis of a continuum linking the generalized and the concrete other, so that, at the level of the generalized other, one can assume a public sphere embodying the Habermasian principles of communicative ethics, whilst at the level of the private sphere, one can assume the predominance of values of 'care, solidarity and solicitude' inscribed in the relation to the concrete other. The 'postconventional *Sittlichkeit*' which Benhabib proposes would be characterized by a dynamic and reciprocal relationship between the public and the private spheres, so that the norms of 'freedom, equality and reciprocity' and those of care and solicitude would interpenetrate. It would nevertheless uphold as universal 'the legal, moral and political norms of autonomy, choice and self-determination' (1992: 16).

It is clear, therefore, that Benhabib's refiguration of the project of modernity remains partly within the conceptual framework of modernity, drawing some comfort from Habermas, but occupying equally the terrain of feminist interrogations of the grand narratives, especially in proclaiming the death of the Subject, the death of History and the death of Metaphysics. Up to a point she finds grounds for a feminist alliance with Lyotard's analysis of the destruction of the *episteme* of representation which had dominated the epistemic order of modernity. She disagrees with Lyotard that the only option left supports a 'polytheism of values' and an 'agonistics' of language, arguing instead for the alternative of a 'proceduralist' and 'interactive' concept of rationality and a 'pragmatic conception of language' (1992: 209). Additionally, and quite consistently, she parts with the postmodern narrative when it celebrates the 'superliberal values of diversity, heterogeneity, eccentricity and otherness' (1992: 16). Now these are also the values which many 'postcolonial' intellectuals want to support as part of validating the cultures and the ways of being that a particular, occidentalist, discourse of modernity has systematically denigrated or marginalized. Furthermore, disputes like the one in Palestine pose a problem from the point of view of arriving at any consensus, in spite of the fact that the parties in conflict occupy the same spaces and would support ideals of justice and autonomy. The history of the *différends* separating those in conflict there, inscribing incommensurable narratives founding the nation and the *ethne*, work against the possibility of finding universalist principles capable of establishing a negotiating space for deciding between the contending interests and visions of the future. Reliance on terms like 'autonomy', 'liberty' and 'justice' leaves the process open to the 'distortions' which the reality of unequal power produces for the communicative process. Benhabib's haste in taking a distance from Lyotard's standpoint of an agonistics of language, whilst expressing optimism about the values of solidarity and solicitude, values that in principle, or ideally (if we assume conditions of intimacy and love), operate in the private sphere, and extend to the public sphere in specific circumstances, allows her to by-pass all the questions relating to the effects of power on the constitution of subjectivity.[3] At least, Lyotard's analysis faces up to these issues and keeps open the space for pursuing questions around new subjectivities and heterogeneity, and it is far from being superliberal, or, indeed, neo-conservative.

There are several issues here that require clarification before I deal with the question of a different understanding of being that might indicate the different grounding for the kind of polity – clearly desirable – that Benhabib advocates. In the attempts to rephrase the project of modernity, there exists the temptation to replace the project of emancipation through the progressive development of reason with that of the construction of a consensus, making it the goal that would unify all parties. Tied up with this move are the problems of communitarian ethics versus liberalism that involves degrees of commitment to versions of a universalism. Much of the philosophical debate is pitched at the level of generality, so that when it comes down to an issue like, for example, the rightfulness or otherwise of the pro-life anti-abortion campaign, it is difficult to see how the principles can be unproblematically applied. Such issues force contending parties to make visible the underlying assumptions, both about the facts of the case and about the metaphysical or philosophical principles that sustain the intelligibility of particular positions. One of the major problems in reworking a postmodern, secular, grounding for an ethics that could command universal assent is that judgement of local action now often relies explicitly or implicitly on religious authority, as in the case of the anti-abortion campaign. It is not a matter of the rationality of deliberation, but a matter of incommensurability in Lyotard's sense. Nevertheless, the question of justice remains, and, thus, a problem about what is admissible as grounds in the court of a postmodern ethics.

In his Wittgensteinian analysis of the *agon* of language games, Lyotard relates the idea of their incommensurability to the heterogeneity of 'regimes of phrases', depending on whether their intent is cognitive, prescriptive or declarative, and so on, which makes it difficult to find the same law or purpose to which they could all be submitted and thus compared. One would need to assume a common purpose for it to be possible to join up different regimes of sentences in pragmatic conditions. The question of common purpose implicates the problem of a 'we', as well as problems relating to the different types of discourse and intentions, whether, for instance, 'we' are trying to 'persuade, seduce, convince, be in the right, make believe, cause to question', and so on, tied to discourses that are 'dialectical, erotic, didactic, ethical, rhetorical, "ironic"' (1983: 197). A communicative or discursive ethics must deal with these pragmatic differences, which always implicate and hypothesize the 'we', so that its status is always conditional and indeterminate. The conflicts that arise and are implicated in the different types of discourse produce *différends*, in that the goals are in competition, and there is no rule of all rules to which one can appeal for their reconciliation. There are different language games in town and we can only play one at a time. This is far from the desire, in Benhabib, to specify an 'interactive universalism' founded on the 'universal pragmatic reformulation of the basis of the validity of truth claims in terms of a discourse theory of justification' (1992: 6). There is a circularity in the self-referential form of this kind of legitimation which is similar to the way mythic narratives work, via the metalepsis of whoever and whatever do not fall within the parameters of consensus, in this case, those who refer to quite other grounds for the legitimation of their goals or values, as in the examples I have noted. After all, the obligation to listen to the narrative of the other is not motivated by epistemological or cognitive interests, but by an unconditioned ethics, or by a will or by a love. This willing is itself not directly presentable, and must be read in signs, or events which function as the index of the desired future, that is to say, which function as what Lyotard designates as the 'sign of history' (Lyotard, 1983). For him, following Adorno, Auschwitz is the (negative) sign of speculative discourse, the discourse which resolves conflict into a higher unity, discursively dissolving differences or wiping them out in the name of a speculative 'we': the French people, the Aryan race, the people of Zion. Within speculative dialectics, 'The "we" has been mistaken for the subject of the autonomy legitimizing obligation' (1983: 151).

One could add that in the political discourse of populism today, the people's will is a ventriloquist will, a simulacral voice repeating the master's voice. The question of a general will authorizing the legislative apparatus, so central in the birth of democracy and its legitimation, is short-circuited in processes of mediatized simulation of popular deliberation. But, one may well ask, who is the master in this masquerade of seduction? The options for Lyotard are starker: we have a choice between heterogeneity – under-stood by Lyotard in terms of the open republic dedicated to an indeterminate search for liberty – and events of the type 'Auschwitz'. To broaden the understanding of totalitarian discourse, I will point to the argument that capitalism too requires the suppression of the heterogeneity of discourse, so that only its type of economic discourse can prevail and become hegemonic; capitalism is therefore on the side of totalization and closure, a tendency which discourses of the type 'Fukuyama' indicates only too well. Lyotard, we know, concludes that one has to be on the side of the *différend*, accepting the unknowable future it opens up. Are we back in the territory of the wager on a sublime good, this time refigured as an aestheticized ethics? Is the question of a 'we' not answerable on the terrain of ontology, or does it, in the light of the postmodern objection to founding narratives, signal the irrelevance of an authorizing voice and the irrevocable plurality of agency?

Being more than one

I want to explore how far the work of Levinas provides elements for displacing the problem onto the terrain of historicity. It is useful before proceeding briefly to complete my examination of the attempts to rescue or refigure modernity by holding on to the ethical dimension in its promise of emancipation and liberty. The dispute between communitarianism and liberalism has lately become the site of this rethink. The core issue revolves around the notion of the limits to individual freedom. Bauman directs attention to the core of the matter when he says that the bone of contention depends on the fact that

> The difference the liberals esteem and hold dear is external to the human individual; 'difference' stands here for the profusion of choices between the ways of being human and living one's life. The difference for which the communitarians clamour is of the internalized kind; 'difference' stands here for the refusal, or inability, to consider other forms of life as options – for being determined or fated to remain what one is, to stay this way whatever happens, and resist all temptation to the contrary. To put it in a nutshell, the liberal 'difference' stands for individual freedom, while the communitarian 'difference' stands for the group's power to limit individual freedom. (1996: 81)

Communitarian theory, in Bauman's view, is a modern ideology; it regards the modern condition as one in which the individual is '"sentenced" to the life-time of choosing' (1996: 81), yet condemned to a shallow and risky existence, devoid of 'meaningful' identity. Some supporters of a communitarian position express concern at the demise of minority communities which cannot survive under the stresses of present modern conditions, which have produced what Beck (1992) calls the 'risk society', namely, when the routines of everyday life lose their taken-for-granted, self-evident quality, and the attempts to control the social provoke unexpected and unthought consequences that undermine and feed back into regulative power. Responsibility is increasingly thrown onto the individual and away from the collectivity. For communitarians, communities and forms of life or Tradition have a right to survive, even if that means the curtailment of certain kinds of freedom in the interest of the community as a whole, for the survival of the community benefits all, securing the forms of life in which identities are inscribed and enacted. Taylor's or MacIntyre's arguments are more complex than Bauman allows, having to do centrally with the recognition that human beings are fundamentally oriented towards signification and that meaning-giving activity is embedded in a background of inter-subjectivity and tradition such that it makes problematic a clear separation between truth and value. For instance, Taylor's (1992) notion of a 'strong hermeneutics' leads him to recognize 'difference' as a problem to be addressed seriously.[4]

Bauman's particular take on communitarianism is to refer the argument in favour of 'natural community' to the yearning for neo-tribes, claiming that 'such neo-tribes are products of multiple choices and are no more durable than the choices which made them' (1996: 87). The view that a community arises out of the choices its individual members make assumes a view of subjects – individualist, rational, unitary, constitutive rather than constituted, autonomous and self-willing – which flies in the face of all the work which establishes the extent to which subjectivity is the effect of complex socially situated mechanisms. The kind of choosing he speaks about suggests a legal-rational subject, whereas the point of view of being-in-the-world and being-with refers, in addition, to psychic and 'spiritual'/

liminal economies of being that cannot be reduced to contractual processes. Maybe these are matters that he would leave to the privacy and mysteries of personal biographies, an approach that would retain the duality of a public versus a private/privatized domain which Benhabib questions. The problem with the liberal approach is that, as Bauman rightly points out, whilst it might appear that choosing has become a common fate in the postmodern consumer society, only those with the means can exercise it without the humiliations and indignities which the poor suffer. In Rio or New York or Manila the poor can only fantasize choosing from behind the security windows of the palaces of consumption. So, unchecked freedom plus basic inequality equals greater inequality. For Bauman, the dilemma that exists between communitarianism and liberalism comes down to the judgement that 'community without freedom is a project as horrifying as freedom without community' (1996: 89).

Bauman's attitude of 'a plague on both your houses' may leave him with the space to propose that we look for some other way of securing the durable qualities in people's transient lives and of living out the risks which are the inevitable condition of human existence, but it does not dissolve the questions of the 'we' that could authorize the normative framework of existence, nor, indeed, the ontological problems of foundation. Benhabib's position tries to steer a course between communitarianism and liberalism, recognizing, on the one hand, the groundedness of the self in that human beings become human only by virtue of an apprenticeship into the community – which additionally provides the conditions for satisfying the human need for belonging and for communication – and, on the other hand, recognizing that the goal of autonomy requires the exercise of a number of basic freedoms that must be guaranteed through a consensual mechanism grounded in 'communicative ethics'. But communicative ethics, either transcribed in the value of community and belongingness in communitarianism, or guaranteed by something called 'interactive rationalism', does not get us out of the quandary. The qualifiers: 'interactive', 'communitarian', 'communicative', all hover around the idea that human beings are constituted as particular subjects – gendered, racialized, and so on – as a result of a range of technologies, a range of normative discourses and a web of narratives and what Lyotard calls 'proper names'; these exist in the form of cultural mechanisms and forms of life. Such mechanisms cannot themselves stand for some independent order functioning as the ground for foundational narratives. They only appear to do so because of the abstract and contentless manner in which much of the debate refers to the mechanisms and processes instituting the social and subjectivities. As I pointed out earlier, the domain of representation and signification cannot be examined without centrally considering the effects of power, including what Foucault has called pastoral power, which I examined in the context of postcolonialism. The problem, as I see it, is twofold. There are the circularities that operate in the arguments of both communitarianism and liberalism in their different reformulations of the problems of 'identity' and of a *sensus communis* in postmodern conditions. One of the most immediate circularities is that the appeal to an interactive or communitarian rationality and to communicative ethics would work only if all parties were already convinced by the arguments, a situation which would not apply to the case of sexual mutilation I discussed. That is to say, it only works if one were to exclude precisely all those whose inclusion would make 'undistorted' communication amongst all parties begin to be possible. There is clearly no space for fundamentalists of whatever variety to join in. This is probably a good thing, but it does not resolve the political or the ontological issues.

Then there are problems to do with shifts in the process of constitution of subjects arising from the changes in the culture of postmodernity, namely, the effects of new media, noted by Lyotard and unevenly explored in Baudrillard's work, and the reality of constant migrations and crossings, producing cultural 'translations' and hyphenated identities – in conditions of dedifferentiation – that challenge orthodox as well as reconstituted views of tradition and community. Is there a way of avoiding these impasses? Would a critical phenomenology break the circularity? My line of inquiry will examine whether the question of foundation has to operate in a philosophical space outside or to the side of practices and forms of life, an ungrounded space, in order to problematize the conditions for any ethics at all.

This approach, it is clear, has been directed towards the thought of the foundation of a new 'ethics of existence'. My interest, though, is not the problem of ethics as such – or the problematic reinvention of an ethics – but the problem of the grounds that could authorize new forms of life after modernity. Yet every project of becoming is at the same time, and inevitably, an ethical one too, since behind the question of what I am to be lies another question: what it is good for me to be, and thus, in its wake, the problem of a universal good. The history of being is at the same time an ethical history. My discussion so far shows that there have been three options available in answer to the problem of how to decide between competing normative discourses. One could, as Habermas does, propose a reason transcending the games of truth in particular communities and cultures, a critical reason which would judge and legislate by working through deliberation. Another option is to accept the incommensurability of normative frameworks in different cultures and periods, and return the activity of judgement to the procedures operating within communities, accepting a procedural or weak ethics. Or one can search for the a priori, but post-metaphysical, conditions for the possibility of any ethics, that is, one could re-examine the transcendental, universalist grounds for ethics. The issue is then how to make such an orientation practical, to ensure its relevance for the politics of difference and recognition and for politics generally, and to guide action in everyday practice. The first option in the end cannot avoid the privilege of epistemological grounds; the second upholds relativism and the autonomy of communities as ultimate values;

the third is open to the kind of strictures against fundamental ethics which Heidegger and Derrida have expressed.

Another reflection, drawn from my analysis of the postcolonial, directs my questioning, namely, that the question of who we are in the present appears at the end of a complex history of the subject that cannot be undone and must not be forgotten. This history passes through the traumas of subjugations of every kind and the imperialism of Reason, taking in the epistemic, ontological and psychic and physical violences which have accompanied occidentalism. The analyses which refigure these events for us today make us think of the 'we' in a way that could not have been possible a century ago, when the 'we' of humanism and of the universal subject of the grand narratives could be taken for granted, and could function to quite different effects. My way of problematizing the 'we' (of *sensus communis*) now appears at the end of a whole series of previous questionings, with their different stakes and lessons, that stand as the conditions of possibility of a refigured discourse of being. For instance, in thinking about the 'we' today, one must add to the problems associated with difference those which postmodern thought has revealed concerning the relation to the Other and the transcendent which I examined in previous chapters. Behind the grand narratives of modernity and other narratives of emancipation or redemption is a question concerning the who of beingness: who speaks? who knows? who wants? and the recognition of the historicity of this who.

A third line of thought that I am taking into consideration is the conclusion that Lash (1996) comes to in his examination of postmodern ethics, namely, that such an ethics would have to be an ethics of practice premised on the recognition both of the 'groundedness' of being in forms of life and of a certain 'groundlessness', that is to say, premised on the necessity both of 'roots and routes', as Gilroy (1993a) famously puts it, repeated in Lash's text. For reasons which I explained in previous chapters, my aim is to return time to a phenomenological horizon, that is to say, that of being-in-the-world and being-with-the-other, but after the misadventures of the philosophy of presence and the philosophy of the Same, and after that other mode of living temporality and postponing finitude which religion has always provided.

The Levinasian route

I am drawn at first to the Levinasian discourse about the unconditional responsibility for the other in these times when this idea of responsibility is not cultivated even amongst self-proclaimed revolutionaries who announce the coming of a better world and meanwhile sacrifice the living in dead slogans. The neo-liberal right proclaims such a responsibility to be at best naïve or romantic, at worst 'unnatural' and harmful even for those who are meant to benefit. In the new order, busily inventing its newness in the old guise of modernization, to be responsible means to look after one's own interest, perhaps extending to one's family, and let the market look after the rest. Not many in the 'real world' will think the idea of an unconditional responsibility 'realistic' even in these times of hyper-reality and simulation, and an illusionist political rhetoric. It just does not fit in. I am not proposing that this principle should determine political action; in any case the relation of theory to politics is not, or should not be, one of determination.[5] Rather, the idea of ethical responsibility should inform the grounds of a last court of appeal, but outside the law, in some way acting counter-politically. In any case, the direction of my analysis is to find a space beyond or to the side of Levinas, though a space which can be reached by way of Levinas and the other positions I have put to work throughout the book. My engagement with this work is thus strategic.

The approach of Levinas is balanced between two 'givens' of being: on the one hand, a phenomenology which is a way to 'recover the origin of meaning in our lifeworld' (Levinas, 1984: 51), and, on the other hand, the irreducibility of a dimension in which '"Being" [is] disengaged from the phenomenon in an "otherwise than being"' (1985: 28), between the intentionality of our relation with the world and the 'irreducible intentionality' (1985: 32) which frames the relationship with the Other (*Autrui*). I am at every moment tending towards an object even if that object is sometimes imaginary or an hallucination, as the infant towards the absent mother's breast. Tending towards is an instance of the will or of desire, seeking out an object, either real or virtual, for we are creatures hooked on fantasy. We cobble our sense of our self from the multitude of objects of the phenomenal world stitched together by the invisible thread of lack. Anguish and solitude mark the experience of a desire beyond satisfaction, the yearning for plenitude or *jouissance*, sought through the caress which 'seeks what is not yet . . . remaining in the no man's land between being and not-yet-being' (Levinas, 1969: 258–9). There is in Levinas the sense of a waiting and a wanting in the happening of being, a deferral lived as the not-yet, perhaps the sublime space of the trace and of anticipation within temporality. It is the space of the 'there is', 'neither nothingness nor being' (1985: 48), but not the void, rather a 'murmur', a 'rumbling' or trembling of being, waiting for the Other who dethrones the ego, yet gives meaning to the verb 'to be'.

This view of being breaks with the (Greek) idea of presence as the intelligibility of what can be 'gathered or synchronized into a totality which we would call the world', tied to the idea of Being as 'essentially this presence' (Levinas, 1984: 55). It is affiliated with a concept of history which 'totalizes time into a beginning or an end, or both, which is presence' (Levinas, 1984: 55). It breaks too with the Heideggerian ontology in which presence is transmuted into 'the coming-into-presence of Being' (Levinas, 1984: 56). Although Levinas acknowledges the debt to the Heideggerian notions of, for instance, finitude, being-there, being-towards-death, and the importance of the philosophical breakthroughs in *Being and Time* for his own analysis of being, he argues that 'Heideggerian ontology subordinates the relation to the other to the relation with the neuter, Being, and it thus continues to exalt the will to power' (Levinas, 1987: 52). For Levinas 'ontology presupposes metaphysics' (1969: 48), whilst 'ethics is not derived from an ontology of nature; it is its opposite, a meontology which affirms a meaning beyond Being' (Levinas, 1984: 61). Meta-physics and ethics both call to a transcendent dimension, but a dimension which folds back into or touches the phenomenal world through the modalities of the relation to the Other (Levinas, 1969). It follows that Levinas cannot share with Heidegger the privilege accorded to finitude or to the anguish before death in the determination of being: 'the fundamental relationship with being, in Heidegger, is not the relationship with the Other, but with death, where everything that is non-authentic in the relationship with the Other is denounced, since one dies alone' (1985: 58).

If the relation to the Other is central to the problematic of being which Levinas elaborates, how do the different concepts relay each other in his discourse? And what lessons are there for renewing the ethical promise in narratives of emancipation? A central theme around which we could organize the conceptual structure of the problematic is that of the rela-tionship between the inter-human and time and responsibility; I will want later to reconnect this apparatus to history, memory, narrative, the sublime and the idea of project. Levinas has this to say:

> I am trying to show that man's ethical relation to the other is ultimately prior to his ontological relation to himself (egology) or to the totality of things which we call the world (cosmology). The relationship with the other is *time*: it is an untotalizable diachrony in which one moment pursues another without ever being able to retrieve it, to catch up with it or coincide with it. . . . This means that the other is forever beyond me, irreducible to the synchrony of the same. . . . But because there are always more than two people in the world, we invariably pass from the ethical perspective of alterity to the ontological perspective of totality . . . we are obliged to ask who is the other . . . the ethical relationship with the other becomes political and enters into the totalizing discourse of ontology. (1984: 57–8, original emphasis)

From early on, in *Le Temps et l'autre* (1983 [1948]), Levinas has posed the question of time in terms of limits: whether time is the horizon within which being is contained or whether it is the modality of the relation to God. This way of questioning is not so much concerned with the ontological level of the problem of being, for instance as a way of thinking through the oppo-sition between a self-sufficient being and the sentiment of a lack or a need for something that would complete being. Time is thought as the 'modality of the beyond-of-being, as the relation of "thought" towards the Other and – through the diverse figures that sociality takes in the encounter with the face of the other: eroticism, paternity, responsibility for the other – as relation to the Absolute Other, to the Transcendent, to Infinity' (1983 [1948]: 8). The relation to time thus is the invisible trace of the fundamental 'inadequacy' of knowledge to grasp the 'Infinity of the absolutely Other' (1983 [1948]: 10). This relation enters signification for being by way of the ethical relation. There is a sense in the language of Levinas of a movement from the 'most high' – concepts of infinity, transcendence, the absolutely Other, and so on – to the phenomenal and the existential, but not so much the other way round, though the moments of the existent and the transcendental – that is, the I and God, or the finite and the infinite – are not kept separate, but figured by way of the face relation.

The connections are made in the following manner. The concretization of the infinite in the finite produces Desire, not a desire that can be satisfied through possession, but 'the Desire for the Infinite which the desirable arouses rather than satisfies. A Desire perfectly disinterested – goodness' (1969: 50).[6] This idea of the desirable and of desire, tied to goodness – in contrast to the urge of the ego to possess the desired other or have power over the object – suggests to Levinas the 'possession of a world that I can bestow as a gift to the Other – that is as a presence before a face', where face is understood as 'The way in which the other presents himself, exceeding *the idea of the other in me*' (1969: 50, emphasis in the original). Generosity and (vigilant) passivity, readiness to receive what exceeds the I, the welcoming of the Other, a kind of dispossession of the ego: these are the modalities of the face relation. It is in that sense that the relation with the Other is an ethical relation. And since heteronomy precedes autonomy, 'Ethics redefines subjectivity as this heteronomous responsibility in contrast to autonomous freedom' (1984: 63). Levinas claims to avoid the pitfalls of both the 'philosophy of transcendence that situates elsewhere the true life' (1969: 52) – for example, implicated in thaumaturgical practices – and the philosophy of immanence for which being finally realizes its potential when every 'other' will have been abolished in the totalizing ambition of the philosophy of the Same. He proposes a history in which the other remains transcendent with respect to the self, indicating 'a relationship with the other that does not result in a divine or human totality, that is, not a totalization of history but the idea of infinity. Such a relationship is metaphysics itself' (1969: 52). This account of the inaccessibility of the other who is nevertheless the being desire seeks, but without hope, since the other remains beyond me, locked in alterity, indicates a different view of history, that is, not as a history of the relationships between men, but as something outside history: 'When man truly approaches the Other, he is uprooted from history' (1969: 52). And it is in that space beyond the data of existence that ethics finds its hold; as Derrida summarized it: 'No phenomenology can therefore account for the ethical, for speech and for justice' (1967: 157). So is the answer to all the violences associated with the adventures of the ego the cultivation of an other-worldly attitude? After the end of ontology and onto-theology, logocentrism, History, and philosophies of the Same, is there no way out but metaphysics? Let us examine how far Levinas opens up possibilities which enable us to leave behind the baggage of occidentalism.

Let us first be clear about what is left behind. Lash (1996) summarizes the stakes very neatly. He points out that the I of Levinas is not the abstract I of Enlightenment, but a concrete being, interpellated by name. Levinas, for that matter, says: 'The I is a privilege and an election. To utter "I" means . . . to possess a privileged place with regard to responsibilities for which no one can replace me and from which no one can release me' (1969: 245). The I of responsibility is rooted in suffering, inescapable, to do with the impossibility of retreat, with the I caught in the hold of the other yet seeking to grasp the ungraspable, the way in which subjectivity is caught between the ambivalences and aporias of will and of freedom, so that 'the supreme ordeal of freedom (and of the will) is not death, but suffering' (1969: 239). The way out is the cultivation of 'patience': 'in patience the will breaks through the crust of its egoism and as it were displaces its center of gravity outside of itself, to will as Desire and Goodness limited by nothing' (1969: 239). The I of subjectivity is pulled in two directions. Its freedom takes the form of the will which seeks to master the dread of the 'there is' by constituting institutions and fabricating tools. In this way, it 'fixes the powers of its future action in transmissible and receivable things. Thus a political and technical existence ensures the will its truth' (1969: 241–2). But this expression of the will does not open towards goodness, does not escape the illusion of the sovereignty of the ego.[7]

The other direction is the path of patience, the passivity of the will, the state of attending to the need of the other in a 'dis-inter-ested relation': 'responsibility for the other, being-for-the-other . . . [stop] the rumbling of being. It is in the form of such a relation that the deliverance from the "there is" appeared to me' (1985: 52).[8] In assuming responsibility for the other, an infinite responsibility, the I opens itself to the judgement of the other, 'it is given over to risk and to the moral creation of the I' (1969: 246). So it is not formal reason or the reason inscribed in contractual relations which guides the creation of the moral agent, but the vulnerability and suffering of the I (and the other, since, for the other, I am an other). Lash, in this connection, points out that if 'the institutions of totality, including law, politics and history, can only judge the individual as a universal I', then it cannot address the 'other as marginal – as the "beggar", "stranger", "widow", "orphan" – . . . [who] "overflow" the categories of totality' (1996: 93). The I of singularity can only be addressed in 'aesthetic–expressive' (pace Habermas) or 'evaluative' discourse.

The centrality of the idea of the singularity of the 'who' as the named or interpellated I is evident in Levinas's discussion of justice. For him, 'justice would not be possible without the singularity, the univocity of subjectivity' (1969: 246), that is, justice is owed to the interpellated 'who' of subjectivity. The force of this claim is most clearly evident in his arguments against an opposition between freedom and justice, locating freedom on the side of the will to power of the ego or the I of a totalizing consciousness. It appears, for instance, in his argument against Heidegger when he says

the well-known theses of Heideggerian philosophy – the pre-eminence of Being over beings, of ontology over metaphysics – end up affirming a tradition in which the same dominates the other, in which freedom, even the freedom that is identical with reason, precedes justice. Does not justice consist in putting the obligation with regard to the other before obligations to oneself, in putting the other before the same? (1987: 53)

The opposition between freedom and justice, when freedom in Western rationalist thought is weighted on the side of the will to power of the ego or the *cogito* of a totalizing consciousness (as in Hegel too), recalls the opposition between law and ethics which Gillian Rose examines by reference to the reconfigurations of the trinity of universal, particular and singular in terms of the broken-back dualities 'between inner morality and outer legality, individual autonomy and general heteronomy, active cognition and imposed norm' (1992: xii), and the attempts to mend the disjunctions with love. But, one could ask, does justice not also promise a certain freedom to the who of being, the freedom to be? Does not an heteronomy, in which the I is not dissolved in a Thou to constitute a 'we', suggest a share of freedom which in a sense is unaccountable?[9] I would like to tie this thought with another which I will later connect with the question of historicity as responsibility, encountered in Chapter 2: 'For me to know my injustice, . . . someone has to call me to account . . . [justice] comes from the outside, . . . appeal is nonetheless made to an ideal conscience' (Levinas, 1987: 40). The calling to account, which suggests that justice does not arise from a spontaneous interiority, implies an apprenticeship, as I have been arguing in the book, and the functioning in the domain of the social of narratives that guide judgement, but not on the basis of a rationalism, not on the basis of law and contract, but on the basis of the responsibility provoked by the face of the other and of something which is immanent to what I have called historicity. Apprenticeship is thus allied to the choreography describing the relation of I and thou. Levinas, however, does not follow this implication of an apprenticeship in the calling to account.

The way in which Lash deals with the dilemma between the freedom of the 'individual' and the normative grounding of action in communal ethics – repeated in the opposition between the positions 'communitarianism' and 'liberalism' – is to propose grounding 'forms of ethical life' in the recognition of the 'plurality of worlds or fields of practices in which ethical life can be lived' (1996: 95). The grounded dimension of ethical life is crucial. Yet, as I noted earlier, this does not by itself show a way out of the troublesome problem of relativism, for instance in legitimating intervention on the side of any particular form of oppression even when local narratives and practices can claim normative authority and consensual support for these practices, as, for example, in the case of Sharia laws concerning the custody of children after the separation of the parents, or in the case of companies claiming ownership of particular knowledges and techniques through the patenting laws.[10] The prior issue concerns the basis upon which one decides that a particular practice or state of affairs constitutes oppression in the first place. Universalist reason had thought it had a right to claim the absolute superiority of its values and truths; postmodern ethics now says that this is an illusion and part of an ideological discourse which itself supports oppressive and totalizing power relations. So the question is whether a way can be found of grounding judgement, outside religion and metaphysics, yet avoiding falling back onto the old terrains.

Levinas searches for a meta-physical grounding of the sublime elements of experience and of the temporality of being – the relation to the Other – which would not derive the understanding of being from the data of sociology, that is, from existing forms of sociality, but then attempts to ground the ethical relation in the idea (and ideal) of being-for-the-other and the theme of Eros, a conjugation of the 'other-worldly' Other with the 'this-sidedness' of a named and loved other, a conjugation that conjures the epiphany of the self. Let us look at this.

I think there is an opening in Levinas that suggests the possibility of a displacement away from the conventional terrain of ethics towards a historicization, although this is not immediately apparent. In his discussion of the temporality of being in *Le Temps et l'autre* he notes at the beginning that 'time is not the accomplishment of an isolated and and lone subject, but it is the subject's very relation with the Other' (1983 [1948]: 17). The thesis requires the development of the concept of solitude to show that it is a category of being, entering into a dialectic whereby one can overcome the limitations of 'the definition of solitude in terms of sociality and sociality in terms of solitude' (1983 [1948]: 18), and so reach a notion of pluralism which avoids abolition of difference in a unity but instead fills out the notion of being-with. Solitude, in his discourse, is not the existential isolation of the I, not the assertion of a solipsistic subject, but the fact that I am unable to communicate existence, though 'I can tell about it' (Levinas, 1985: 57). The exit from solitude is in 'terrestrial nourishments: the enjoyments through which the subject eludes his solitude' (1985: 59). For Levinas, the escape can only be through a 'dispossession', for 'time is not a simple experience of duration, but a dynamism which leads us elsewhere than toward the things we possess' (1985: 61). The destiny of being is not to be found in the model of knowledge, which absorbs the other into the Same, but the erotic relationship in which 'alterity and duality do not disappear. . . . The pathos of the erotic relationship is the fact of being two, and that the other is absolutely other' (1985: 66). Eros, though, 'goes beyond the face' (Levinas, 1969: 264). It tends to something which is not graspable and cannot be universalized, for the relationship between lovers does not admit third parties; it is closed upon itself enclosing a dual solitude, as lovers seek a voluptuosity driven by its own hungers. The theme of Eros in Levinas is elaborated in terms of a range of concepts: paternity, fecundity, caress, filiality – terms standing for a renewed deferral whereby the desired object always slips away, keeping itself inaccessible, even in the case of the caress: 'And the caress is the anticipation of this pure future without content' (1985: 69). They are curiously set against 'the alterity of the feminine' (1985: 61). (I say 'curiously', but this is less so when we bear in mind the ambivalent relation to Judaism which Levinas's work entertains, and the place of the feminine there.) So does the only concrete proximity happen in the 'saying' inscribed as trace of the Other in the face relation, answering to the presence of the other, or does proximity too – for example, in the erotic love relation – contain within it a measure of the infinite, that is to say, a relation to Desire? Is ethical responsibility the only form in which I can express solidarity with the other?

The theme of Eros as developed in Irigaray's reflections on Levinas reveals other aspects of the relation between lovers, extending the face relation to include the bodily: 'The face relation of lovers is not circumscribed by their face but their whole body' (1984: 179). Writing in the shadow of the terms that Levinas displays, like 'caress', 'voluptuosity', 'fecundity', when he analyses what he calls the erotic relationship,[11] she draws attention to the different, embodied exchange between lovers by which they 'engender each other in the genesis of their immortality' (1984: 177). For her, the caress would seek a kind of transcendence in the irreducibility of the desire for the other, and in the vertigo into which the 'sensing–sensed' entity loses its will to know and its separate identity, seeking to discover the other in the other's alterity, but through the 'touching–touched' aspect of bodies, to borrow some terms from Merleau-Ponty. The emphasis on the tactile, on the plasticity of bodies attempting to transgress the threshold of the ego in the indefinite presence of being-with-the-other, suggests the possibility of a dispossession which is at once ethical and incarnate, in-between groundedness and the ungrounded, and therefore touching on the sublime. So Eros, as much as 'art', gives a passable imitation of infinity, suspending time for a moment, in the economy of the gift and of desire, in the risk of a communication which is not 'the risky search for consensus' that Habermas talked about, but the risk of vulnerability and a loss: 'loss is legion', Gillian Rose confessed in *Love's Work*, surveying the gathering of other losses that the end of a sublime love affair assembles (1995: 67); loss is calculable not in terms of conscious reckonings, but in the insufficiency of the gaping of being.

Levinas, 'holy' thinker that he is, dilutes the intensity of being-with with the thought of the intransitivity of being and deferring and displacing the presencing of being in the 'love' relationship to the futurity of fecundity and paternity, for example when he says: 'the relationship of paternity going from me to another who, in a certain sense, is still me and nevertheless is absolutely other: temporality brought near to the concreteness and logical paradox of fecundity' (1985: 62). This 'near to' forgets that lack – of the other, and the lack that drives paternity and maternity – is lived not only as the unbridgeable distance separating being from the Other, or the immeasurable gap which designates the inaccessible alterity of the other, or not as this abyss alone, but is hollowed out of other separations and other excessive expectations, born from intimacies and dependencies that bind a being to an other so that, under some circumstances and for a moment, each is 'more than one and less than two', as Irigaray would express it, for instance in the infant–mother relationship.

(In)visibilities, folds, hollows

I am going to draw from the 'Working Notes' of Merleau-Ponty – intimations and fragments that they are – to indicate ways in which the ethics
of Levinas – unconditional responsibility for the other, passivity, and so on
– can be tethered to some attachments in the lifeworld and to the fact of
embodiment. Let us begin with the remarks about the relation to the other
which he begins to develop after reflections on notions of being, science,
consciousness, language, philosophy, and so on, commenting on the works
of, principally, Husserl, but also Descartes, Bergson, Sartre, Heidegger,
Kant. He points to the inadequacy of the I-other relation as perceived in
philosophy and says:

> The I–other relation to be conceived . . . as complementary roles one of which
> cannot be occupied without the other also: masculinity implies feminity, etc.
> Fundamental polymorphism by reason of which I do not have to constitute the
> other *in face of* the Ego: he is already there, and the ego is conquered from him.
> Describe the pre-egology, the 'syncretism', indivision or transitivism. What is it
> that *there is* at this level? There is the vertical or carnal universe and its
> polymorphic matrix. (1968: 221, original emphasis)

He adds that the I–other problem is a Western problem.

I wonder what he meant by that last remark, left undeveloped in the rest
of the 'Working Notes'. One is struck too by the terms used, like 'face',
'egology', 'there is', and the emphasis on the relation to the other, located
within phenomenology but reminiscent of Levinas, although there are no
references to him in the text. However, the problematic of subjectivity in
Merleau-Ponty is different in significant ways, especially by reference to the
embodiment of being in its relation with the other, for instance when he
says: 'The experience of my own body and the experience of the other are
two sides of the same Being . . . the other is the horizon or other side of this
experience' (1968: 225). Or again, when speaking about the manner in
which the inter-human and the world are inter-related so that 'we may
rediscover as the reality of the inter-human world and of history a surface
of separation between me and the other which is also the place of our
union' (1968: 234). There is an articulation of the other's body with mine
which 'does not empty me . . . but on the contrary redoubles me with an
alter ego' (1968: 233). We need to understand this kind of statement by
refiguring the analytical apparatus that he is suggesting.

The thought that weaves in and out through the sketch for a 'concrete
ontology' which is offered in the 'Working Notes' is the idea of an
intertwining of the world and the human, of interiority and exteriority, of
body and of soul, of the I and the other as a curve to its hollow, a
relationship repeated in every aspect, suggesting a non-transcendental
transcendence, or 'constitutive transcendence', to use Merleau-Ponty's ter-
minology, whereby being relates to Being not as figure to ground, but
rather as the disclosure of what, in the relationship of figure to ground,
escapes figuration, belonging to the relation itself. It is not a question of the

projection of Being into the infinite time of a plenitude that must remain inaccessible, and with regard to which the lightness of being is weighed. With Merleau-Ponty, Being participates in the world as the happening in the relation of the invisible to the visible. Let us unpack some of the main themes that, I think, enable me to concretize the face relation in Levinas without losing the ethical dimension.

Merleau-Ponty distances himself from a number of concepts and positions as part of constructing his different *analytique* of being, for instance in extending the Husserlian critique of Cartesianism, the critique of a *cogito* as self-constitutive agency, a notion tied to the 'mythology of a self-consciousness to which the word "consciousness" would refer – there are only *differences* of significations' (1968: 171, original emphasis). Consciousness does not exist before language, since language is the foundation of the I think/*cogito*. Merleau-Ponty rejects any notion of the body and the mind or the soul as bounded categories, proposing the dissolution of the division between biology, psychology and philosophy. Ideas of the in-itself and the for-itself, including the Sartrian refiguration of these terms, are problematized when his discourse moves towards the thought of transcendence as 'a world seen within inherence in this world, by virtue of it, of intra ontology, of a Being encompassing–encompassed, of a vertical, dimensional Being, dimensionality' (1968: 227). Within this perspective, the 'fold or hollow of Being' has an outside, that is, is constituted as the field of fields in intersection, each of which conditions the existence of the other, establishing in their union a 'vertical world' (1968: 228). The model for the relation is the male–female relation for which each is the copula of the other, in which each is the fulfilment or realization of the other. The metaphor for the idea of co-presence, or compossibility, which this way of making sense of intra ontology suggests, is contained in the relation of the visible to the invisible, where the invisible is not the non-visible, but what is 'behind' the visible, itself understood not as the positive term of the couplet, but as 'dimensionality of Being' (1968: 257). Visibility, besides, is not for-itself, but for the other. The connections that Merleau-Ponty is trying to establish are admirably expressed in a passage when he says: 'the invisible is a hollow in the visible, a fold in passivity, not pure production' (1968: 235), and when he links this thought to the setting to work of mind:

> the mind quiet as water in the fissure of Being. We must not look for spiritual things, there are only structures of the void – But I simply wish to plant this void in the visible Being, show that it is its reverse side – in particular the reverse side of language. (1968: 235)

The void, clearly, is not nothingness or emptiness, but something like the 'there is'. The notion of transcendence too acquires its specificity within the problematic which Merleau-Ponty is trying to put in place. Thus he says that 'the invisible is there without being an object, it is pure transcendence, without an ontic mask' (1968: 229), proposing a relation between invisibility and transcendence which is not immediately clear. The theme of the corporeity of being can be used to reconstruct a sense that returns the discussion to the question of the way we are in the world and the implication for a history of being.

Merleau-Ponty suggests that the body 'is made of the same flesh as the world . . . this flesh of my body is shared by the world, the world reflects it, encroaches upon it and it encroaches upon the world . . . they are in relation of transgression and overlapping' (1968: 248). We need to bear in mind here that the flesh of the world is itself thought in terms of 'segregation, dimensionality, continuation, latency, encroachment' (1968: 248), so that we would have to relocate the concept away from a simple notion of a sensing materiality and place it instead within two thematics of being: first, the problematic of visibility and invisibility, that is to say, within a frame of intelligibility that inscribes the body on the side of the 'verticality' of being, in other words, on the side of the transcendent unicity of disjunct elements of the lifeworld; second, we need to locate it in relation to the idea of the inscription of the subject in the thickness of the world in relation to which one derives one's sense of one's own body. Furthermore, in elaborating a problematic of the body, Merleau-Ponty severs any connection with dualism, proposing that we understand the relationship between the body and the 'soul' according to the bond between the convex and the concave: 'The soul is planted in the body as the stake in the ground . . . the soul is the hollow of the body, the body is the distension of the soul' (1968: 233). Additionally, Merleau-Ponty thinks of the body as the other side of the mind, in the sense of every mind being doubled with the body in which it is anchored: 'There is a body of the mind and a mind of the body and a chiasm between them' (1968: 259). Such a formulation of the relationship between mind and body could easily be thought to form a closed, solipsistic system. This impression is undermined if we remember their compossibility as an event in the clearing of the chiasm. Additionally, for Merleau-Ponty, 'to feel my body is also to feel its aspect for the other' (1968: 245), so that when I perceive the visibility of my body, I do so in terms of its visibility for the other. Besides, my being in the world as 'sharing the same flesh' prolongs my awareness of myself as body and as embodied into the materiality of the inter-human and the world of objects. Thus, he says: 'it is necessary that a body perceive bodies if I am able to be not ignorant of myself' (1968: 233); what it sees is not the obvious materiality but the apprehension of the non-visible 'the presence of the imminent, the latent, or the hidden' (1968: 245). I should add to this conceptualization the reflexive aspect of the body which Merleau-Ponty develops in the 'Working Notes', and more fully in his discussion of painting and the gaze in his last complete work, *L'Oeil et l'esprit* (1964). He argues against the view which regards vision to be an operation of the mind, pointing to the interpenetration of body and the world, whereby my being immersed in the world of things is another aspect of this world. My perception of the world must be referred back to the way my body is sutured to the world, and must bring into view its doubleness, for

> my body is at one and the same time what sees and visibility . . . it sees itself
> seeing, it touches itself touching, it is visible and sensitive for itself. . . . Visible
> and mobile, my body is numbered amongst things, it is one of them, it is caught
> up in the web of the world. (1964: 18–19)

I must emphasize that the drift of the argument supports the view that the reflexivity of the mind–body is a kind of doubling which is not the repetition of the same; it is rather the process whereby the self opens itself to itself, not to discover itself, but in order to escape itself, for reflexivity 'terminates in the invisible' (1968: 249), that is to say, reflexivity awakens in the self an echo of the liminal aspects of the world that my experiential engagement with the world has kept as a trace.

Corporeity, therefore, is a guardian of time – alongside narrativity, which, for Ricoeur, is also a guardian of time, as I showed in Chapter 2 – in that it is the field or clearing in which space and time interpenetrate – another sense of the chiasm – to produce 'a historical landscape and a quasi-geographical inscription of history' (1968: 259). How is this field activated and sedimented? asks Merleau-Ponty, rhetorically, since he proposes no answer. Let us examine how notions of memory and of the event can fill out the indications left unelaborated at this point.

We could, first, examine the case of painting – Merleau-Ponty elsewhere (1964) refers to the Lascaux paintings, and to Cézanne and Klee amongst others. It could be argued that what the eye sees transcends what is painted, that it wanders inside the image, giving itself to the trace and to the memory of the invisible dimension inscribed in it, so that 'I see according to it or with it rather than I see it' (1964: 23). The vision in a painting 'gives visible existence to what profane vision believes to be invisible. . . . This devouring vision, beyond the "visual data", opens upon a texture of Being' (1964: 27). We could relate the transcendent dimension implied in these lines to the reflexivity of the body, its attentiveness to the happening of Being in the works produced by the techniques of making and revealing which produce the world for us. If I add to this Merleau-Ponty's view that 'every technique is a "technique of the body". It figures and amplifies the metaphysical structure of our flesh' (1964: 33), it becomes possible to envisage the conditions and the mechanisms for the presencing of the transcendent dimension of our beingness in the world. I have in mind two levels of articulation of the problem. First, by reference to the (aesthetic) experiences that harbour the dimension of the sublime, in the arts and in artistic practices like dance and singing, or in the rituals enacting the core beliefs of a community, religious or ideological. We could take as examples the place of dance in constituting the community amongst tribal societies and making flesh the memory of the community, or, at a different level, the presencing of the divine in the mysteries of the Eucharist, or, from the point of view of the mythical dimension of originarity and authenticity brought to presence in rituals of belonging, we could think of the spectacular staging of the 'master race' in Nazi rallies. In other words, the liminal, invisible dimension of being-in-the-world is

revealed in all the forms of the ex-stasy of the self, that is to say, in the
emptying of the self as it readies itself for being-towards-the-other, an
ecstasy which is lived as both self-presence and an ex-centredness of the
self. The indications in Levinas support the idea that the erotic love relationship and the filial relationship also promise such ecstasies of being. I
would not think it solely in terms of the (Lacanian) fading of the subject in
the transcendence of the relation to the other. For, although this promise is
lived within the economy of desire, and is therefore ever deferred because
of the excessive demand which desire makes of our expectation, projecting
the fulfilment of its fantasized *jouissance* into the infinite insistence of the
lost object, a taste remains of what it seeks. I would emphasize too the
fantasized aspect of this promise, since it is located within an economy of
desire, thus relaying the investment of something unattainable, which we
must yet incessantly search for.[12]

The second level of the articulation of technique brings up the question
of the cumulative mutation and sedimentation of the historicality of being
in the lifeworld. The lifeworld is a fold of what Merleau-Ponty calls
'vertical Being' or, rather, 'vertical Being' is folded in the lifeworld, whilst
'constitutive transcendence' is inscrypted in the here and now of the
present. What I mean by this is that transcendence would refer to what, in
the lifeworld, is unpresentable, the invisibility which is folded in the visible,
on the understanding that what is folded are the ripples of the events which,
in their dispersion in the world, constitute history. In a sense, what is folded
in the lifeworld is time itself. Technique sets to work and extends previous
techniques through an apprenticeship, through exemplars and through the
(Arendtian) initiation of action. Apprenticeship concerns learning a particular language game and an (alchemical) practice, that is, it involves at the
same time a discursive and a material, transformative and transmutative
practice.[13] Technique relates to Heidegger's 'revealing' (*aletheia*) and to
techné, and so recalls the Heideggerian implications about the 'happening
of truth' in the setting to work of technology, though I would leave out the
strong version of unconcealment, preferring a weaker version affiliated with
Bachelard's and Canguilhem's notions of the technical elaboration of truth
by the 'workers of the truth' which I have discussed elsewhere (Venn, 1982);
such an approach is more in keeping with the phenomenological standpoint
I am developing. Technique, therefore, is also a deeply social activity,
conveyed in Arendt's notion of work, that is, the result of action and the
labour of creation. Consider, for example, an ordinary task or skill like
painting a wall, cooking. While performing the activities involved in the
practice, I am immersed in a world both physical and imaginary. I recite in
my head the rules of good performance, my body already knows what to
do, repeating well-rehearsed movements; it feels its way among objects. I
replay conversations with those who taught me or advised me or com-
mented on my previous activity of painting or cooking. At the same time I
remember, in the form of an interior monologue, those involved at the time
of learning – *X* always told me to do it this way – as well as later repetitions

of the activity, and the social relations they were woven into. I have in my head a picture of the finished work, I anticipate responses; in this way, my activity in the present re-enacts the cumulative learning of generations before me, makes slices of my own past visible to me in the imaginary, locks me into a complex of relations with significant others, and allows me to anticipate the continuity or discontinuity of these relations. I recite and enact my self into the fabric of the world, at once material and discursive/social. My temporality and my body are enveloped in a wider temporality, as, and in, the 'flesh of the world'. I am a knot in the present, whose threads extends in a spatio-temporal space in which the two, dissonantly, rhizo-mically, criss-cross each other. This would be the way in which I would understand Merleau-Ponty's remark that corporeity is a guardian of time. Thus, it is possible to understand the entwinement of being in a body and in the lifeworld by reference to the suturing function of temporality, acting both at the synchronic level of the world as ready-to-hand and at the diachronic level of the historicity of being, open in principle to an indeter-minate future. Responsibility for the other, debt, agency, notions of what living well means, as ethical life and as fulfilment, are all woven into this complicated fabric.

The critique of cognitivism and objectivism implicated in Levinas and Merleau-Ponty adds weight to the rejection of the position which sets the world of things over against the world of the subject, repeated at the epistemological level in the subject/object dualism that itself supports the idea of the possibility of the truthful representation of social and material phenomena. The strong version of the claim of representation to truth takes the form of the privilege of realism in the nineteenth century, also the period when the subject – logocentric, occidentalist – assigned to itself the role of the autonomous agent of universal history. This attitude, though now less confident, still prevails when it comes to the objectivity of scientific knowledge, and stands in the way of a decisive shift away from the project of masterly domination towards which the stratagems of objective reason still gravitate. The work of Haraway (1991) in undermining the duality of nature and culture, 'man' and machine, adds concrete instances to back up the theoretical generalities about corporeity in the thought of Levinas, Merleau-Ponty or Ricoeur. Furthermore, the relation of mind and body, which the phenomenology of Merleau-Ponty proposes, undermines in a fundamental way the mentalist prejudice of the standpoint that reduces the world to discourse. One could incidentally make the point that the privilege of discourse over the 'real' betrays its epistemological location on the terrain of representation and of dualism. For if I am both mind and body, and if my body belongs both to the world and to the apprehension of a self in the 'I think', then I am at once an object of the world acting upon and in the world, as well as the being acted upon by the world, who labours to gather its action into the polysemic identity of a conscious self. I cannot set out my belonging to the space of discourse over against the world which discourse discloses. This view finds support in Ricoeur, who declares that, concerning the

manner in which the self belongs to the world, our body is 'the very place –
in the strong sense of the term – of this belonging' (1992: 319).

An interesting case, analysed by Knorr-Cetina (1997), provides a number
of insights concerning the further de-centring of the *cogito* with respect to
the body and to the world which I think add a different dimension to the
question of embodiment and being-in-the-world. She proposes the emergence of object-centred forms of sociality in response to the expansion in
object-centred environments and the disembeddings produced in contemporary processes of 'socialization' due to the development of 'postsocial', de-traditionalized lifeworlds.[14] Individuals, increasingly, have to
rely to a greater extent on their own resources to construct coherent
identities and forms of togetherness, as Beck and Beck-Gernsheim (1994)
have argued. Objectual relationships have come to form an important part
of these new mechanisms for establishing new stable spaces for re-
embeddings of identity. 'Postsocial' cultures have become 'creolized' or
hybrid, interweaving other cultures, including expert systems, so that social
and knowledge processes are now inter-related. Knorr-Cetina's analysis
emphasizes the special quality of objects of knowledge, namely, their provisional character as objects in that they are constantly enfolding in tandem
with changing knowledge. Borrowing from Heidegger, she argues that one
comes to them with a '"theoretical attitude" which entails the withholding
of practical reason' (1997: 10). Objects of knowledge are 'question-
generating', 'never quite themselves', such that the relationship the expert
has with them is homologous with the 'structure of wanting' attaching to
lack in the Lacanian sense. There are further elements and analogies – the
non-identity of objects of knowledge, their textual or signifying character,
the pleasures and expectations of a form of solidarity associated with the
relationship – which introduce a libidinal and an ontological dimension to
the relationship. To that extent such objects – and Knorr-Cetina suggests
the possibility of extending the range of these objects and object-relations to
include, for example, some objects of leisure such as PCs – cannot be
regarded as inert means outside sociality, but should be thought as integral
elements of 'postsocial' cultures. Whilst remaining agnostic about some of
the arguments, I think the broad line of thought and the example she
develops – the case of the biologist Barbara McClintock – undermine the
conventional view of our relationship to the material objects of the world as
one of externality and thingness.

One of the problems that I have been trying to address via Merleau-
Ponty arose because of the seeming 'groundlessness' into which being is cast
in Levinas's theorization of being. Lash (1996), as we saw, argued for the
complement of a certain groundedness, the here and now of human
experiential reality that binds us to existing institutional practices, and
refers, besides, to technologies of the constitution of subjectivity. Human
beings are inescapably worldly, and the urgent problems facing society, like
systematic exploitation and ethnic and gender conflicts, require solutions
that have their feet firmly planted in complicated historical and material

reality. The emphasis on the embodiment of subjectivity which we encounter in Merleau-Ponty allows us to figure the face relation as also an
embodied relation, having the value of an existential. It is, of course, not a
matter of an opposition – indeed, in Merleau-Ponty, groundedness and
groundlessness, or, better, ungroundedness, relay each other – in the
clearing of the chiasm – as the metaphors of visibility and invisibility are
meant to indicate. Thus, it is possible to concretize the other-worldly basis
of ethics in Levinas not only by reference to embodiment – the face, sight –
but also in terms of the inter-human thickness of sociality, and in terms of
historicality, revealed as the cumulative, rememorized temporality invested
in the facticity of the world which we encounter as the ready-to-hand:
temporality with knobs on.

As I discussed in the second chapter, following the analysis developed by
Ricoeur, the inter-human world is the world fashioned by narrative; it is a
storied world, splicing phenomenal time, or temporality as lived, into the
cosmological time of history and of the sublime, that is, into the 'the time of
the soul', to use a phrase from Ricoeur (1992). Corporeity and narrativity
and the poetics of the sublime: these are the threads whereby groundedness
and ungroundedness are sutured into each other – or folded into each
other; they are the *points de capiton*. The liminality of what is not grounded
keeps open the boundaries that groundedness tends to close up or envelop
inside the lifeworld; it stands for the dehiscence or gaping of being. The two
can be thought analogically as the link-up between the saying and the said,
or, to think of it in a more down-to-earth analogy: on the one side,
vulnerability and the gift in the love and the filial relation, and, on the
other, the *agon* of language games with clear strategies for winning something from the adversarial other.

The 'there is' can then be seen to invoke both the inhospitable world into
which being is thrown and the world as the homely shelter for being-in-the-
world. Thus, to the idea of the thrownness of being, already living the
anguish of finitude and loss, one must counterpose the view that the facticity
of the world offers anchorage and hospitality for being-in-the-world, the
place, or *domus*, where we feel at home; it is therefore lived also as a
welcome in the intimacy of a relation which is enveloped–enveloping, social
and material. We are part of the 'flesh' of the world, if we understand 'flesh'
in the Husserlian or Merleau-Pontian sense, that is, underlining its non-
spatiality, its openness to the invisible, and relating it to the category of
inter-subjectivity. The impulse towards either plenitude or *jouissance* is
embedded in these existential conditions, as is the dilemma between the
risky exhilaration of an indefinite openness against the comfort and security
of closure. Both tendencies have been equally at work in the discourse and
in the history of modernity. On the one hand stands the figure of being-
towards-death or of *ressentiment*, and, on the other, that of being-with and
of desire.

At another level, we find the indeterminacy of becoming and of history set
against the closures that totalizing systems of thought operate, containing

and returning to themselves all the forces that threaten to disrupt the wishful unicity of being. Violence is inevitable, whether as the effraction of the newness that erases traditionality or as the force of the closures that cancel difference. How is one to live with or manage these destructive forces – outside solutions that project them, and encrypt them, in the metaphysics of Transcendence, cashed out in the form of God or gods and their secular substitutes: the Subject, History, Will, Reason, Desire? Can one, on the other hand, escape the need to anchor the foundations of ontological security in some (non-totalizing) transcendental moment or Being?

This latter question is probably the most difficult one to resolve, except by accepting that there are no transcendental guarantees, but only a wager and a (ludic rather than Nietzschean) throw of the dice. The discourse of philosophy and, even more so, that of politics have few resources for dealing with this kind of issue, leaving us to look to a poetics, say, in some of the indications in Agamben (1998) and Lacoue-Labarthe (1999). For instance, the apparatus that Merleau-Ponty constructs sometimes threatens to contain every difference and resolve every conflict within a system in which their functioning always-already promises a reinscription within the lifeworld. One might well ask, how do things change? And how are we to conceptualize agency within its framework, extending the notion of the 'I can'? Is there a way out of the choice between the ethical imperative of the face relation, which urges us towards the excessive demands of an infinite (and unfulfillable) goodness, and the non-transcendent monad that locks us into a lifeworld conceptualized as unicity?[15]

Who comes?

Suffering

Many other questions rush into the breach created by the deterritorializations within classical narratives of being which my analysis has tried to operate, loosening their anchorage in the terrain of ontology and onto-theology, or that of conventional epistemology, ethics and metaphysics. Since one of my central themes concerns the interrogation, from the location of the 'postcolonial as theoretical jetty', of the being which modernity has sought to institute, I suppose I should end with the issues which relate to the question of who is to come after this subject. The longer genealogy of the subject that I have sketched indicates that there is no already delineated terrain on which to seek an answer. What is left after the subject has been stripped to the vulnerability of the face relation and the fragility of finitude, without the props which narratives of transcendence provide, or after it has been inflated with traditionality and historicity, is temporality itself. It remains as the one constant factor when describing the being of a critical hermeneutic phenomenology, and it remains not as residue, but as the primary fundamental element. I want to develop this in relation to the ideas that I have examined in the course of my explorations, namely, narrative, debt, suffering, gift, responsibility, the 'I can' of agency.

In earlier chapters, I have indicated the relation of temporality to responsibility and to narrative, borrowing from Derrida, Lyotard and Ricoeur to examine how the birth to historicity is at the same time the birth to responsibility, and to establish that narrative is the form in which our experience of existing as beings in time can become communicable. Even more, not only is narrativization the process enabling human beings to apprehend and communicate temporality as a specifically human dimension, it is the means whereby we are able to attest to the happening of being in its different modes and moments, and it is the form in which we appropriate for the present, and remember in the present, the accumulated history which we live as inheritance and burden, without which we would be cast back into the darkest of times, condemned each time to start from time zero again. This is in part why it is possible to relate the narration of the past, that is, history, to the notion of debt, especially the incalculable debt owed to those who have existed before us, victims of one form of oppression or another, whose testimony makes a demand of recognition which we must live as a call to justice and to responsibility.[16]

But what of suffering? I am not thinking of physical pain, or ordinary suffering (which is not properly suffering in the ontological sense) arising from a present emotional pain, for instance the experience of a temporary loss or absence or humiliation, or bound up with sympathy for another's suffering, directly winessed or narrated in a text or discourse, such as the suffering of the starving poor or of the victims of atrocities of war we watch on the television. Perhaps one should push the argument beyond the thought of the ontological suffering tied to the consciousness of finitude and the proximity of death – life is always too short – or the recognition of the vanity of individual lives in the longtime of humanity, that is, measured against the infinity of time.[17] I assume, furthermore, that we can take as 'already said' the suffering tied to the idea of lack that one could connect either with the notion of fallenness or with the gaping of being, or with the Lacanian discourse of insufficiency and the impossibility of *jouissance*.[18]

Whilst these aspects of suffering are important, I want to focus on a dimension in suffering which is not immediately obvious, and that could, additionally, be related to the question of agency. Let us assume as taken for granted that loss and lack as well as injustice are at the core of the experience of suffering.[19] If we were to take, for instance, the death of a loved other, or the oppression one suffers because of racism or masculinism, it could be argued that what transforms the experience connected with the relevant event or action is the realization that the loss or absence or humiliation or hurt will continue in the future (though see the discussion of the 'I can' below). Similarly, for example, the loss of youthful hopes and pleasures pour into the abyss of ontological suffering not because of their loss or pastness alone – ordinary suffering – but because we know already that such loss is irrevocable and can therefore anticipate their absence in the future. It is the anticipation and expectation of a future in which an injustice or a loss will endure that gives to suffering its intensity and extends it beyond the ontic dimension, and thus projects it into the domain of the imagination or towards a transcendent space. It is this knowledge itself, inseparable from the ability of human beings to anticipate and imagine the future in its becoming, even in the absence of appropriate cues or stimuli, which makes of suffering an aspect of the temporality of being. So it is the aspect of duration enframing the experience of suffering that makes of it a category of a critical phenomenology of being.

To the extent that temporality is lived in the form of narration, suffering is conditioned by a background of narratives that instruct human beings about how they are to give a meaning to the feelings which are lived in the modality of suffering. It remains that without the ability to imagine the to-come – for instance, as a time of emancipation from a recognized oppression – and without narratives which speak of the destiny or condition of being, suffering would remain within the perimeter of the present, that is, within the horizon of ordinary suffering.[20]

The temporal dimension in suffering, whether at the ontological or the political level, enables us to analyse it by reference to responsibility by way of the 'I can' of action. The third term which connects the two is that of historicity, my analysis of which, in Chapter 2, indicated the ethical basis upon which historicity implies a responsibility. The decisive point is that human beings are able to decide to initiate action in order to bring about a change in the expectation of the future. For instance, we know already the conditions which produce and sustain neo-slavery among the poor and are inflicted upon countless children in many 'Third World' countries. We can envisage a different future for these victims of postcolonial and global capitalisms and can decide to take action to bring about such a future. One can link this possibility with one meaning of the 'I can', for example as a promise to act in such a way as to put an end to an injustice.[21] This is where the point made by Ricoeur about power is relevant, when he associates acting with the power-to-act and to *praxis*, and when he correlates the self and being-in-the-world so that the who can be aligned with both an existing self and a potentiality. It is this correlation of facticity and (a refigured) *energeia* that makes it possible to say that 'human acting and suffering are rooted in being' (Ricoeur, 1992: 315). The embodied anchorage of the self in the world, when set alongside the notion of the who as potentiality, that is to say, as an entity to be realized, that is, as futurity, and when set in the context of the entanglement of the who in (inter-subjectively grounded) narrative identity, provokes a number of thoughts which together lead to the proposition that suffering, from the point of view of narrative, can take the form of the 'incapacity to tell a story, the refusal to recount, the insistence of the untellable' (Ricoeur, 1992: 320). Those who are not allowed or who are unable to tell their stories, those, therefore, who experience oppression precisely, or additionally, in the form of this prohibition of attestation are thereby denied the means to expose the injustice of their plight and to demand redress. It goes without saying that those who are prevented from initiating action to end an injustice which they suffer belong to the category of the oppressed. But 'decrease in the power of acting [is] experienced as a decrease of the effort of existing' (Ricoeur, 1992: 320), which implies that the inability to tell one's story because of some injunction or obstacle, and the inability to end an injustice because of a constraining force, is evidence of ontological violence. Given what I have said about suffering in relation to the expectation of a loss or an injustice continuing in the future, we can extend the 'I can' of agency to include the power to act to make a difference in the future, responding to the fragility of the other, for instance the infant, the destitute, or acting to end an injustice – for instance, the case of sexual mutilation or the denial of basic rights – or to realize a particular (non-oppressive) self-identity. It is clear that suffering, ethical responsibility, historicity, initiation, in the (Arendtian) sense of an action that changes the future (Arendt, 1959, 1994), are terms which relay each other in my problematic of being-in-the-world.

The gift of time

The analysis of suffering and responsibility that I have undertaken demonstrates the overly pessimistic implications of understanding temporality and being negatively, by reference alone to being-towards-death. The other side of this notion of the temporality of being is the side which expresses the sense of being-with-the-other and accommodates the idea of the ecstasy and epiphany of being. It is necessary, for a start, to eliminate from the analysis the substitutes for loss or lack that arise from misrecognitions of the infinite excess inscrypted in the economy of desire, bearing in mind that what being lacks is the other.[22] A different kind of content for the temporality of being can be promoted which seeks the presencing of the relation to the other and tries to express the historicity of the world. This content requires the presence of the other, the other's gaze or the other as interlocutor, and therefore requires a communicative action which is at the same time a communion. This can take the form of what is communicated in the approximation or the liminality of poetic discourse or music, that is, in 'art' in the generic sense I developed in the previous chapter; equally, it concerns what is communicated in Eros and its metonymies: the caress, love, voluptuosity, and in filiality. In what follows I will examine the consequences of thinking temporality in this positive sense, whilst holding on to the consciousness of the finitude of being.

To begin with, I think it is possible to hold that time is the gift of greatest value, the incalculable good that being may have, and the thing deserving of the greatest respect. The 'gift' of time is the other face of the 'gift' of death. Responsibility for the other can then be understood as responsibility for the time of the other; solicitude means giving one's time to or for the other, beyond reciprocal expectation, as gift, holding nothing back, not qualifying it with contractual understandings, that is to say, when the gift is not reduced to a token exchanged for some other good.[23] The notion of gift here is clearly far from the ethnographic scope of the term, developed by Mauss in *The Gift*, which involves customary rules of reciprocal obligation that are inscribed in rituals of the enactment of differential power relations: who is allowed to give, what kind of gift, to whom, in what measure.

Derrida has given us an extended analysis of the gift relation in *Given Time*, developing ideas that are dispersed in his earlier works. A central focus for him concerns the paradox of the impossibility of the gift, namely, 'For there to be a gift, it is necessary that the gift not even appear, that it not be perceived or received as gift' (1992: 16). The implication is that the gift must be absolutely forgotten, beyond recall, so that it cannot at some future time activate a sense of debt or exchange. Such a forgetting is possible only if the gift is such that it does not appear as gift and is meant to be forgotten. Thus, 'The gift would also be the *condition* of forgetting', but in the sense that 'forgetting would be in the *condition of the gift* and the gift in the *condition of forgetting*' (1992: 17–18, original emphasis). For Derrida, it is this sense of condition and of forgetting which discloses the connection between the question of the gift and the question of time, and so introduces the Heideggerian analysis of Being beyond the metaphysics of presence, that is, beyond the interpretation of Being as 'being-present/ present-being'. Time too, since it is not a thing that can be grasped as an object, has the quality of an entity that exists in the intuition of the 'there is'. It is well to remember that the way that Heidegger reflects upon the facticity of Being and of time, that is, the recognition that the starting point is simply that *there is* Being and *there is* time, is to think of their givenness in terms of 'It gives' (Heidegger, 1972: 4–5). Thus, we could say that time and being are linked or placed in the way of each other by way of the notion of gift, but it is a gift which is not properly given, for the giving is tied to the unconcealment of Being, to its presencing, thus also to the play of trace and *différance*, since presence never simply is, but is a moment of duration, caught between the having-been and the coming-towards. According to my analysis, the giving – of time, of Being – would belong to the *epoché* in which Being appears.

Derrida uses the aporetic character of the relation between time, being and the gift in order to make two propositions: that 'What there is to give, uniquely, would be called time' (1992: 29), and that what matters is that one 'knows how to give' (1992: 30). He retells Baudelaire's story 'Counterfeit Money', as the basis for a reflection on the economy of the gift, drawing from Mauss's essay on the gift in order to question the gift-giver about this knowledge, and the consequence of not knowing how to give.

The story, in brief, is the account by the narrator of an episode in which his friend deliberately gives to a beggar a counterfeit coin of rather large nominal value in order to enjoy the pleasure of surprising the man 'by giving him more than he hopes for' (in Derrida, 1992: 32). The friend had previously carefully selected the coin, and it was possible in the narrator's mind that he slipped the beggar the counterfeit coin out of some criminal pleasure arising from the imponderable outcome of the gift, in the knowledge that the coin may turn out to benefit him greatly for a few days but could just as well land the poor man in serious trouble. However, it is clear from the explanation that his friend gives – 'there is no sweeter pleasure than to surprise a man by giving him more than he hopes for' (Derrida, 1992: 32) – that he candidly thought the pleasure he gave, and obtained, was worth the danger in which he had put the beggar. The narrator was prepared to forgive his friend had his motive been knowingly an unethical one, but not when it is clear that the evil he did was committed 'out of stupidity' (Derrida, 1992: 33). Forgiveness is made conditional on the ability or inability to account for oneself in the giving of the gift, specifically, the condition of knowing that the gift is a test of one's self-knowledge, in particular, that it calls for the forgetting of oneself in the giving. There is the implication in the tale that forgiveness is premised on the condition that one knows what one does, and therefore on the possibility that one can recognize the harm one has inflicted and thus on the possibility of confessing to a wrong. What is not forgivable is the harm which is done out of thoughtlessness.

There is not much point in rehearsing the many issues that Derrida teases out of the tale, grounding his arguments in the work of Heidegger and Mauss. A key element I want to retain is the an- or non-economic point of view of the gift, that is, the view that it must not involve any calculation or notion of contract or exchange, or any assumption of a promise. Although it is something which is given, the gift must not trigger obligation and debt, but must annul itself in the giving. So what is there to give if one must give outside the economy of exchange, and if one cannot give directly? And what giving, in putting into question our sense of self or identity, compels us to question ourselves as to our way of being?

Through the gift, then, we return to the discussion of the questioning of being and of putting oneself in question. This questioning takes two forms, namely, the consciousness of existing as a being in time, and the questioning of oneself as ethical being, that is, by reference to the judgement of our conduct from the point of view of an ethics (or of an Idea regulating judgement.)[24] It is not so much a matter of acting according to one's conscience, but, more precisely, a matter of allowing our conduct to be the occasion to think anew the meaning of the ethical, so that the ethical does not allow itself to be reduced or circumscribed by convention, that is, by morality, or by the Law, but participates in the questioning of being, and therefore in the determination of being as possibility.[25]

For Levinas, the determining gesture in thinking about the ethical is the 'welcoming of the Other' (1969: 88). It means not regarding the other as fact or threat to the self, and it refuses any notion of knowledge centred on oneself. To understand knowing by reference to the welcoming of the other, and as the condition of language, is to break with the foundation of the self in the self. Knowing, in that sense, becomes the articulation of the desire for the other, and the recognition of the presence of the other: 'The essence of reason consists not in securing for man a foundation and powers, but in calling him in question and in inviting him to justice' (1969: 88). The calling of being into question which inaugurates ontology is tied up in Levinas with the idea of justice so that the question of being turns towards 'seeing in justice and injustice a primordial access to the Other beyond all ontology' (1969: 89). But the recognition of the Other already implicates the generosity of the subject, so that the subject comes to the Other 'across the world of things, but at the same time to establish, by gift, community and universality. . . . The relationship between the same and the other, my welcoming of the other, is the ultimate fact, and in it the things figure not as what one builds but as what one gives' (1969: 76–7).

I have put several elements in relation to each other in the preceding arguments, so that recognition, generosity, hospitality, justice, call to each other across the questioning of being. All of this is disclosed when the primacy of the ethical is seen to be correlated to the primacy of temporality in the determination of being. This standpoint about being uproots the discourse of the subject from the terrain of philosophical anthropology. It clearly breaks with the privilege of epistemology in the foundation of the subject. It grounds the theorization of subjectivity differently, specifically, away from cognitivism, with significant implications for reconstituting a psychology or a sociology.

The giving of a gift without return, the excess of the pure '*dépense*' in the economy of the gift which I am considering, indicates instead that the questioning of being is tied to the economy of desire.[26] The alignment of the problematic of desire alongside that of being directs attention to the question of lack and of affect. For, it could be argued, desire is motivated by lack. However, what the subject lacks is the Other, that is, the transcendent Being whose recognition of the subject confers presence, as an existent, by a process of doubling. Thus, we can understand lack to be the trace of what is unpresentable or what has never been present, that is, the trace of what would cancel lack, for instance the presence of the Other, or ownership of the Phallus in Lacanian theory, or the lack of being in the sense of the experience of 'nothingness' in existentialist thought. Lack, thus, is an intimation of an immemorial loss. For this reason, lack is bound up with presence: it motivates the desire for presence. Lack, from this reading, is what drives desire, whilst desire is the desire for the Other and for presence. It is in that sense that gift, at the ontological level, relates to lack: it derives from it whilst seeking to move beyond its horizon, for instance in wanting to establish, through the act of giving, community, friendship.[27]

The way that the question(ing) of being is tied to the economy of desire can be grasped at several levels. At the level of the everyday and of affect, there is the giving which enters the relation to the beloved, when the gift is of oneself, or, rather, the gift of what the other does not have, that is, what must be given in order for the other to be, at the basic level, recognition.[28] At another level it relates to the attempt in 'art' to make present what is unpresentable but liminally or sublimely present in the lifeworld or at the level of the experiential. Both these instances of 'giving', which do not appear as gift, inscribe temporality in their action or in their saying, in that they unconceal the relation of the present to a memory and to the anticipation of a 'to-come' and ground the present to an immemorial and immanent archive. Thus, the questioning of oneself which takes place in, or by way of, these instances of giving, relocates it within a process of remembering and, thus, within a process of the reconstitution of subjectivity.

If we agree with Derrida about the impossibility of a gift which does not trigger an economy of exchange, and if we agree that what there is to give is time, then the gift of time must appear in a passive mode, as given-time. The givenness of time, given at the beginning with finitude and all that it harbours, echoes with the 'there is' and the ungrounded character of beingness. The importance of passivity in given-time is demonstrated, when we recognize it is at work in the 'tautegorical' manner characterizing the openness and reflexivity which aesthetic judgement and critical thought share towards artistic experience and the concept, discussed in Chapter 4, and the idea of the welcoming of the Other in my analysis of Levinas, where generosity and vigilant passivity are revealed to be modalities of the face relation. Let us transcribe this view into the discourse of a critical phenomenology – to avoid sliding into metaphysics – and shift the terrain to the lifeworld, taking into account the corporeity of beingness, in line with the dissolution produced by Merleau-Ponty of the dichotomy between mind and body. Given-time can then be refigured in a form which the other can incorporate in the self. Two examples: the disclosures of oneself in the (idealized or fantasized) relation to the beloved – as threshold of the I– Thou relation, not reducible to the They, but a way of being 'more than one but less than two', to recall once more Irigaray's rephrasing of filiality (and alterity) – the giving of time to and for the other so that the other's time becomes more fulfilling: these are the modalities of given-time. Its quality could be called friendship – for Levinas, filiality and so on, as I have noted – the exemplar of hospitality and care. Equally, my analysis of the aesthetic experience in the previous chapter, for example in my analysis of *Beloved*, indicates that artistic products and poetic discourse are other modalities because they inscribe temporality in forms which make present the having-been of a community and of the 'who', and promise its safekeeping in the future, as a monument that can be folded in being, and so as a gift which is bestowed and received in the form of a memorization. Memorization here turns attention to apprenticeship, a process which institutes the inheritance of a practice through recapitulation and the formation of subjectivities, and prepares the subject for the future as possibility. 'Art', or, more precisely, poietic activity, gives history and biography in its lived form, and thus, by the same token, it gives the future to individual subjects and to a community, without reducing either one to the other. It belongs to historicity.

The other side of the standpoint of temporality which I am developing in terms of giving time and given-time implies that time must not be reduced to property; it cannot be owned or appropriated. It follows that every form of exploitation and oppression ultimately reduces to the appropriation or the theft of someone else's time, and/or the community's time. This standpoint implies, for example, that the exploitation and oppression of women in patriarchal cultures, and capitalism's and possessive individualism's systematic and rationalized mechanisms for appropriating time through unequal exchange, and through the legalization of property in the form of capital, is fundamentally unethical and destructive of humanity.[29] The legitimacy of buying someone else's time itself becomes questionable, for how can one place a monetary value on a person's time, or reduce the temporality of being to the value of a commodity? How can it be ethical to abolish the value of existential time, returning it in the small change of the commodity form? At one end of the scale, we find slavery as the pure form of the theft of someone else's time, whilst, at the other end, we encounter the mundane dispossessions in everyday relationships, the time we take from those closest to us, and forget to return in enjoyment and forms of the (aneconomic) gift of oneself.

The other sense of giving time which I want to signal is tied to the idea of historicity as the ready-to-hand, that is, the fact that the works of a culture, the knowledges and technologies, are the legacy, discursive and material, which every generation inherits in the form of its conditions of formation and which it puts to work in instituting itself.[30] Historicity, from that point of view, that is to say, as the archival and monumental space of the institution of subjects, is bound up with the fact that human beings make themselves by constituting a world from the taken-for-granted ready-to-hand materiality in which traditionality has been deposited. A sense of indebtedness is implicated in the view of historicity that I am using, intimating an immemorial and incalculable debt which the narativization of history must keep alive as one of the conditions for ethical judgement, as I noted in relation to Curtis (1998) (see note 24). So the (re)constitution of the lifeworld involves the inscription of subjects within such a narrative or historicization of the past, as well as within a material world.[31] It is included as an element of apprenticeship in the process of subjectivity. History-as-lived, the history in the streets, is temporality writ large, the imprint of those who have been before, the resource which is unlocked, transformed and redistributed in the process of instituting. At the imaginative level, it relates to the 'structure of feeling' which directs how we get in touch with the embodied character of subjectivity, in the strong sense of 'flesh', that is, beyond the materiality of the habitus but coupled to it, for instance in the cobbled streets of a medieval town, in the Arcades.[32]

A test of the gift of time concerns the relation to the stranger. In contemporary conditions of the heterogeneity of cultures, the polyphony of identity prompts the question that Levinas asked: who is my neighbour? And behind that question, the issue of the limit and sphere of application of the law, and the problem of the just war as the limiting case of the judgement I may pass on my neighbour. The who, in any case, is polysemic, and this presents a problem from the point of view of what secures trust in the public domain. Is this where we need to turn to deliberative, communicative rationality? The stranger, typically, is the one who disrupts the already said of the commonality of community. Today, she is the anonymous person about whom we warn our children. Or else he or she is the *flâneur* in the city chasing after the shadows of authenticity, if not the tourist of vicarious pleasures, passing through. More pertinently, the stranger is the immigrant, the exile and the refugee, the outsider imprisoned in 'otherness', the one pointed out by the child: 'Look, a Negro' – the example from Fanon I used in the second chapter – or picked out by a glance, by bodily stratagems, a tone of voice: the multiple ways in which the other is named in the iterability of strangeness. From a distance, the 'Third World' stranger is the exoticized other whose difference is reduced to the habits of the everyday, soon appropriated by consumer culture in the form of style, or for the 'tourist gaze' (Urry, 1990). In the context of the emergence of new or modified forms of governance, new figures of the threatening other are appearing to extend the metonymies of the stranger. They are figures like the drug addict, the single parent, the homeless beggar, the illegal immigrant, and those who can be categorized as fakers and tricksters, that is, whoever can be thought to be 'dysfunctional units' from the point of view of normality and efficiency, those whom the dominant form of accounting practice can quantify as a net cost to the community, the burdensome surplus which the post-welfare state increasingly excludes from its responsibility. The stranger provokes an uncomfortable interrogation of one's own responsibility for the other, as in Baudelaire's story 'Counterfeit Money'. The discomfort becomes acute if we recognize the appeal to responsibility to be directed at each person, as the named individual – you, Abraham must do this – that it is a duty I cannot delegate or transfer to some general body, like a state apparatus – the legalistic option – or that I cannot annul on the grounds of a fateful/fatal strategy beyond my control – somebody else's karma: the cynical option, or: nothing we do can change anything: the pessimistic option.[33] Responsibility is a love, says Levinas, or responsibility is the price of belonging, say the communitarians. Between the prudent inclusiveness of communitarian responsibility and the judicial estrangement of the generalized other, we find the epiphany of the face of the other, and a difficult question: is there some way of adjudicating between the share of agape and the share of the law? Do we settle for the incommensurability of *différends*, as in Palestine? And at the level of political discourse, who are 'we' today who must decide?

Conclusion

My approach has been not to seek the compromise of a middle way, but to look for a way of being that recognizes, at one level, the common humanity of all on the basis of the experience of suffering and fragility, the withintimeness of being and the responsibility – of hospitality, care – triggered in the face relation, and, at the other level, in spite of the radical alterity of the other, a way of being which acknowledges the impossibility of an I by itself existing: 'To say self is not to say I. The I is posited – or is deposed,' says Ricoeur (1992: 18). This means recognizing the investments and imbrication of every self in a particular polymorphic matrix of relationships and narratives. This sense of recognition, incidentally, can act as the shared experiential condition for the kinds of disembeddings that make imaginatively possible (the result of a dialogical form of *'prise de conscience'*), through the reflexivity of mimesis, the 'reversibility of perspectives' which Arendt advocated. It implies too the embodied character and locatedness or rootedness of difference which motivate the need for a sense of belonging. Thus, at one level, we have the idea of some permanent but unpresentable, liminal features of beingness everywhere which come to be inscribed in the sublime products and experience of a culture and inscripted in specific transcendental principles or objects, and, at the other level, the particular and transient fate of individual subjects played out in the web of a particular inter-subjective nexus, yet subjects who nevertheless constantly desire to transcend the limits and limitations of subjectivity because of the trace of the sublime buried in each life.

The cosmological and the phenomenal dimensions of being both have time for their horizon. The time of Being and the time of being-in-the-world relay each other by way of the I as *epoché*, not (a mathematical) punctum, so that the self, as singularity, is a punctuation – rather than point – in the narrative of being, the place whence Being is revealed as the 'there is', that is, as an-archic openness. If we accept that time implicates the relation to the other, that corporeity is the guardian of time and that we apprehend existential time in the form of narratives, that is, an inter-human textuality, we can imaginatively construe how the phenomenal and 'transcendental' dimensions of being are folded into each other as an aspect of the folding of the I into the other: at once an embodied, ontic, relation and a relation that harbours the trace of Being. It makes no sense to try to reduce the one to the other, for instance by favouring the law – relation to the generalized other, Halakah – against the ethical relation – the relation to the Other, Haggada – or by pitting reason against ethics, a point Gillian Rose (1993) has challengingly made. It is a matter of listening to the saying in the face relation as well as to the other kind of saying concealed in the immemorial voice immanent in the phenomenological history of being, a saying inscripted in the dwelling of being-in-the-world.

What is at stake here is the rejection of otherness in favour of alterity, the respect of difference in the awareness of 'oneself as another' (Ricoeur, 1992), not the occidentalist privilege of Oneness and the Same or the imperialism of *Logos*. The historicality and temporality of being, understood according to my analysis, means that the politics of difference can be grounded in the recognition of shared elements of beingness, historically constituted as well as expressing the experience of suffering and belongingness which enable each being to be considered as the other to whom responsibility is owed. This is the meaning of recognition which my line of argument indicates. The project of becoming can then be conceptualized as an heteronomous adventure and as inheritance of historicity. This project is tied with the guiding idea throughout the book that the becoming-responsible of humanity is the result of a difficult apprenticeship, requiring explicit critical narratives of being, implicating an ethics of responsibility and solicitude for the other, extending to the natural world in which being exists as 'flesh' of the world. Modernity itself has been a crucial stage in that apprenticeship.

I have ended up with only one condition for rethinking the 'to-come', namely, that whatever is decided must be conditioned by one principle, grounded in the analysis of being in terms of temporality that I have developed: the principle that time is the primary value, as the time of the other and as the time stored up in historicity. Because of its relation to indebtedness, it is incalculable, and is owed unconditional respect. What is derived from this thought is a negative ethics, that is to say, a non-prescriptive ethics, but one which frames the judgement of goodness and justice regarding human acting and is applicable to every concrete practice. It could be seen as a way of rephrasing Rawls's (1971) idea of an 'original position'. It will be recalled that Rawls argued that the conditions for justice should be, first, the supposition of a 'veil of ignorance', whereby we do not know in advance what is our position in society, and so cannot know in advance what social arrangements will be to our benefit. Additionally, he proposes that deliberation should accord priority to maximizing formal equal rights and freedoms, and should aim to benefit the least advantaged people.[34] My version of the original position would make illicit the instituted theft of the time of the other. In that sense it is not so much an original position as a terminal or projected one, functioning as a regulative Idea (and ideal) directing judgement in local situations. It opens towards an ethos. It relates back to the claim that all forms of exploitation, such as feudalisms, capitalisms, masculinism, patriarchalism, are fundamentally unethical. Furthermore, the delegitimation of oppressive power relations, implied in the conditions I have specified, means that the political can then be reconstructed in the (counterfactual) absence of conditions that give rise to systematic distortions – of communicative action and so on. Instead of the 'veil of ignorance', one would have the idea of an apprenticeship into this reconstituted political field as basis for making judgement about particular cases. This modified notion of an 'original position' guiding justice shows up the ethical insufficiency of every form of sociality so far – Western, modern, ancient, 'Asiatic', and so on. My view supports the possibility of a non-egological form of subjectivity, envisaging a subject which assumes responsibility for its own judgement, without recourse to the old transcendentalisms or to the new occult entities of the Market, Money, Efficiency, the Consumer. The history of modernity, its discourse of subjectivity and what it has materially accomplished, brings us to a fateful crossroad: we can choose to continue down the path of a careless postmodernity towards a catastrophic and inhuman destiny, or we can decide to bring about a post-occidentalist, postcolonialist, transmodern future which modernity itself had glimpsed.

Notes

1 The generality of the terms in which I am posing these questions suggests the fruitfulness of working with a number of universals; in the light of my critique of universalism, this need not revive the issue of the Eurocentric assumptions that universalism, given its modernist history, trawls behind it.

2 See also Bauman's (1987) view of legislators, and Sennett's (1976) analysis of the changed role of 'public man'.

3 Themes which have been extensively explored in Henriques et al. (1998 [1984]).

4 See Smith (1994) for a discussion of Taylor which takes in the thought of Habermas.

5 We have ample evidence of the excesses to which politics is driven when it derives its policies directly from a domain of theory.

6 Note that Levinas understands Infinity thus: 'The idea of Infinity is neither immanence of the *I think* nor the transcendence of the object' (1969: 86, original emphasis).

7 The affinities of this idea of the will are with the Nietzschean concept of the will to power rather than the willing which we find in the idea of the 'I can' that I have examined by reference to Ricoeur.

8 Levinas uses the term 'being-for-the-other' because he distrusts the 'compromised' term 'love'.

9 Levinas says 'I must always demand more of myself than of the other; and this is why I disagree with Buber's description of the I–Thou ethical relation as a symmetrical co-presence' (1984: 67).

10 I deliberately use this latter example to enlarge or generalize the meaning of local, especially in the context of 'globalization'.

11 The erotic here is not reducible to sexual encounter, though it may include it.

12 The lived aspect of this search, conscious of the fragility of its tempestuous passions, is eloquently expressed in Gillian Rose's (1995) reflections on love and mortality, the story of the rootless exposure of something we may wish to call spirit to the abyss of unconsolable losses, renewed in the name of love's work.

13 I use the term 'alchemical' advisedly, to invoke the relation to the old sense, that is, what is preserved of the old sense of a magical or unaccountable dimension in the process whereby the mundane conceals the possibility of overcoming the limitations to which ordinary practice binds us.

14 I would take the 'postsocial' claim with a pinch of salt.

15 Deleuze, in his discussion of the monad, points out that in Leibniz it is 'ascribed to the soul or the subject as a metaphysical point' (1993: 23), the point in relation to which two other points are enveloped into a fold: the physical point of the body and the metaphysical point of the spatial location of the body. Deleuze argues that today 'nomadology' has overtaken monadology, that is to say, we can no longer enfold the multiplicity of the world in the unicity of a singularity, wrapping up the chaos of events in the closed circle of a totality. The world is now made up of divergent series, the 'chaosmos': 'crapshooting replaces the game of Plenitude . . . [although] we all remain Leibnizian because what matters is folding, unfolding, refolding' (1993: 137). Dicing with mathematics can be instructive for exploratory journeys, yet the fragility of hope urges us to ask what new narrativizations allow us a glimpse of a different world to come, and what promise incites us to desire an other way of being?

16 I would add the speculative proposition that the relation of temporality and language/ narrative is tied to the emergence of the consciousness of temporality from the earliest moment of human history, as consciousness of a movement linking the having-been to the making-present and to the becoming-future. Human beings are the only living creatures to know they

are beings in time and can anticipate the future as futurity, that is, as undecidable 'to-come'. One could imagine that the acquisition of language in the earliest humans developed as an aspect of the complexification of mental processes, requiring the capacity to learn from one's own past experience and from others, that is, to communicate a memory. Reflexivity as a capacity of the mind, indispensable for learning and for imagining the future as difference, could then be thought to have been, from the beginning, bound up with the consciousness of oneself as a being in time. I venture that it could not have emerged without the co-emergence of language, that is, a fundamentally social inter-subjective capability and an infinitely flexible system for communicating and transforming experience. The proposition suggests that the linguistic process, self-consciousness and the consciousness of temporality can be understood as co-articulated developments in the genealogy of being, the one functioning as condition of possibility for the other. The development of complexity, then and now, depends on the tripartite relationship between language, (self)-consciousness and time. In that respect, I am reminded of Teilhard de Chardin's views of increasing complexity in the world and in human consciousness, though he theologizes the relationship. It follows too that the experience of loss and anguish tied to the pastness of the past and to the anticipation (of absence and death) in the future, particularly the knowledge that one is destined to die, emerged at the same time. And with it the urge to recover or communicate such an experience of lack or loss and an ineffable desire. The communication of the unpresentable requires that it be transcribed in some form like music or a graphic medium – for instance, 'cave painting', carvings – which preserves it in the form of a communication, as a gift and as a knowledge, an instance of sociality and a memory. The apprehension of an excessive dimension to existence fills being with the 'time of the soul'. Art too begins there. Indeed, it may well be that the first human being proper was born with the first artistic, mimetic act of memorization and the first recognition of a transcendent or liminal or unpresentable dimension to existence. Human beings are the only species which has invented 'art' and makes music. The 'wild boy' dancing to the moon in the scene from the film *L'Enfant Sauvage*, expressing joy and loss in the same moment and gesture, the body speaking for the soul.

17 It is interesting that Laplanche suggests that the idea of death in psychoanalysis has a place 'in a dimension which is more ethical than explanatory' (1976: 6).

18 I will not enter into the issue of existential angst arising from the presumed unfixity of the I or the experience of 'nothingness', the nausea of unbeing and unbelonging.

19 One would have to distinguish the loss attached to nostalgia from other kinds of losses. Nostalgia is usually prompted by a remembered pleasure, now irrecoverable in the form of the original experience and the psychic energies invested in it, or attached to situations and conditions that no longer obtain, for instance relating to one's youth, or to a period gone by, and so on. So loss is intrinsic to nostalgia but there is in nostalgia the reactivation of a pleasure or its aura, which distinguishes nostalgia from melancholia and from mourning.

20 Such narratives speak about general, universal features of human existence; they address the 'big' questions, as, for instance, in the Enlightenment discourse about humanity and history, or in Buddhist or Christian discourse about the destiny and place of human beings in the eternal scheme of things. Without these metanarratives, the scope of action to put an end to suffering would also be limited to the present, or to the narrowly political.

21 I do not imagine that suffering can be eliminated. What would be the right conditions in which human beings will cease to be beset by existential realities? Injustice, however, is not ethically tolerable. Which does not mean that it is obvious what constitutes injustice, and what just actions are available to eliminate it, as the example of Nato's intervention in Kosovo illustrates. It remains that the refusal to act or to speak out, that is, to testify in some way, is an abnegation of responsibility. My analysis does not begin to examine the political problems to do with choosing appropriate action, or with the (differential) allocation of blame. There are too many intractable issues here: who participates? In what measure? Who knows what is happening? I am more concerned with the principles, like indebtedness, responsibility for the other, and so on, that should inform the political deliberations.

22 I am omitting any content that relies on religious or mystical assumptions. Equally, the non-egological character of subjectivity that I have stressed throughout the book implies that

any content which can be thought in terms of the metonymies of the objects of secondary narcissism – for instance, the objects of desire in contemporatry consumer culture – would fall outside the scope of my analysis. See Featherstone (1990) for details.

23 The model of the ultimate gift is the disinterested sacrifice of one's own life: Christ on the cross, the abnegation of Buddha. Perhaps the heroic surrendering of one's life to save the life of the community or the loved one may not be thought sufficiently disinterested to qualify.

24 I am thinking of the reworking of the Kantian problematic which the work of Lyotard makes possible, examined in Curtis (1998). Curtis argues against Kant's idea of autonomy as the regulatory principle in settling differences. He proposes an Idea of justice based in 'heteronomous anarchy', tempering the recognition of difference with the 'pragmatics of obligation'. On the one hand, it rejects any notion of foundation in some origin – so that anarchy means without beginning – but maintains a multiplicity of origins, keeping alive the *agon* of difference whilst submitting all differences to the obligation of an immemorial debt and the subject's state of indebtedness. Notions of responsibility – especially regarding that which is silenced – of justice and of bearing witness are tied up with his analysis of the ethical conditions for judgement.

25 The drift of my argument, it is clear, is towards a non-prescriptive 'ethics', that is to say, a process of judgement which is not based on a set of rules, thus, by extension, circumscribed by laws, but a process which is each time a test of judgement, an unavoidable test, since we cannot avoid having to judge, and, thus, we cannot evade the obligation to take responsibility for our decision.

26 See also Bataille (1988) for a discussion of the non-productive and aneconomic expenditure of energy in relation to giving.

27 An implication of my argument in Chapter 2, that I and my other belong to the same *epoché*, is that the gift as event belongs to the determination of being as *epoché* (see Heidegger, 1972: 19ff., for the meaning of event in the context of my discussion).

28 See also Lacan's discussion of lack in relation to Being in *Écrits* (1966a, 1966b).

29 Take the case of the privatization of wealth that once belonged to the community, for instance roads, or the water system, which has been constituted as work and as monument as a result of the collective labour of a whole community. Such appropriations amount to the dispossession of the community of a collective good, valued not in monetary terms but in terms of the time given up by generations to establish, so that the good stands as monument to their time, and as inheritance, belonging to the lifeworld. They determine what a community is able to do and experience; they function as the ready-to-hand store of knowledge and instruments that enable the community to re-enact itself as community. The appropriation of any part of it as private property is a theft of collective time and an injustice.

30 It is not a direct way of giving time, indeed only retrospectively can this legacy be thought of as a gift, for example in enabling particular know-hows and techniques to become the raw materials for further transformation, or, for example, when particular buildings and so on become icons for a nation's identity and culture.

31 Constituting is a form of bricolage since little is ever invented from scratch.

32 The communitarian sense of historicity is implicit when communities undertake works which are meant to survive for generations, or provide benefit in the future, such as in attempts to limit environmental damage. The commodification of history in postmodernity – in diverse forms: heritage industry, sampling, the simulation of the past for the tourist gaze, even the packaging of the vestiges of the slave trade for African-American consumption – reinvented as nostalgia or pastiche, flattens temporal depth and erases the past; it is ambiguously complicit with the modernist impulse periodically to 'set the clock back at zero'; it disrupts temporality and traditionality, with consequences that are still unclear. Jameson's (1991) prognosis of the cultural logic of late-capitalism provides a number of (problematic) lines of inquiry. The discussion of this issue does not belong to this moment in my analysis. One question arises though, namely, if the temporal depth of history is flattened in 'postmodernism', yet people cannot help but locate themselves as beings in time, how is 'history' folded into biographies in the constitution of selves? Is history privatized too, reduced to family history? Is the result a specific form of amnesia – social amnesia? Or do people live in a distorted, simulated historical

time? Or live nomadic and simulacral subjectivities in the hyper-real world of mediatized forms of narrative identity? Is fundamentalism one response to the erasure of the past? Should one displace the discussion onto the terrain of a nebulous globalization? See Featherstone (1990) and Featherstone et al. (1995).

33 Those who are being daily destroyed in ethnocidal wars or in bandit capitalism have no options but to resist and to call us to responsibility. In any case, the situation today is that no one can be absolved since affluence and poverty are dynamically related, as I noted in Chapter 1. Consumer capitalism means that one person's surplus enjoyment is the result of the theft of someone else's time and well-being.

34 This 'difference' principle states that social and economic inequalities, or differences, should be so arranged that they can be expected to be to everyone's advantage, indeed, to maximize the advantage of the worst-off category of people (Rawls, 1971: 60–83).

REFERENCES

Adorno, Theodor (1990) *Negative Dialectic*. Trans. E.B. Ashton. London: Routledge.

Adorno, Theodor and Horkheimer, Max (1979) *Dialectic of Enlightenment*. Trans. John Cumming. London: Verso.

Agamben, Giorgio (1991) *Language and Death: The Place of Negativity*. Trans. Karen Pinkus. Minneapolis: University of Minnesota Press.

Agamben, Giorgio (1998) *The End of the Poem: Studies in Poetics*. Trans. Daniel Heller-Roasen. Stanford: Stanford University Press.

Amin, Samir (1974) *Accumulation on a World Scale. A Critique of the Theory of Under-development*, Vols 1 and 2. Hassocks: Harvester Press.

Amin, Samir (1976) *Unequal Development*. Hassocks: Harvester Press.

Appiah, Kwame Anthony (1992) *In My Father's House: Africa in the Philosophy of Culture*. Oxford and New York: Oxford University Press.

Aquinas, Thomas (1945 [1259–73]) *The Basic Writings of St Thomas Aquinas*, ed. Anton C. Pegis. New York and London: Random House.

Arendt, Hannah (1959) *The Human Condition*. Anchor Books in assoc. with The University of Chicago: Chicago.

Arendt, Hannah (1977) *The Life of the Mind*. 2 vols. Michael McCarthy (ed.) New York: Harcourt Brace Jovanovich.

Augustine, St (1961) *Confessions*. Trans. R.S. Pine-Coffin. Harmondsworth: Penguin.

Bacon, Francis (1859 [1620]) *Novum Organum*. Trans. Andrew Johnson. London: Bell & Daldy.

Bacon, Francis (1975 [1620]) *The Advancement of Learning, Book 1*. Ed. Willliam Armstrong. London: Athlone Press.

Bakhtin, Mikhail (1981) *The Dialogic Imagination*. Trans. Caryl Emerson and Michael Holquist. Austin: University of Texas Press.

Barker, Francis (1984) *The Tremulous Body*. London and New York: Methuen.

Barthes, Roland (1977) *Image-Music-Text*. Trans. Stephen Heath. London: Fontana Press.

Bataille, Georges (1988) *Inner Experience*. Trans. Leslie Anne Boldt. Albany: State University of New York Press.

Bauman, Zygmunt (1988) *Legislators and Interpreters: On Modernity, Post-Modernity and Intellectuals*. Cambridge: Polity Press.

Bauman, Zygmunt (1996) 'On communitarians and human freedom: or, how to square the circle', *Theory, Culture & Society*, 13 (2): 79–90.

Beck, Ulrich (1992) *Risk Society*. London: Sage.

Beck, Ulrich and Beck-Gernsheim, Elisabeth (1994) *The Normal Chaos of Love*. Cambridge: Polity Press.

Beck, Ulrich, Giddens, Anthony and Lash, Scott (1994) *Reflexive Modernization*. Cambridge: Polity Press.

Benhabib, Seyla (1986) *Critique, Norm and Utopia*. New York: Columbia University Press.

Benhabib, Seyla (1992) *Situating the Self*. Cambridge: Polity Press.

Benjamin, Walter (1973) *Illuminations*. Trans. Harry Cohn. London: Fontana.

Benton, Ted (1993) *Natural Relations*. London: Verso.

Bergson, Henri (1991) *Matter and Memory*. Trans. N.M. Paul and W.S. Palmer. New York: Zone Books.

Berman, Marshall (1983) *All That Is Solid Melts Into Air: The Experience of Modernity*. London: Verso.

Bernal, Martin (1987) *Black Athena: The Afroasiatic Roots of Classical Civilization, Vol 1*. New Brunswick, NJ: Rutgers University Press.

Bernstein, Richard. J. (1991) *The New Constellation*. Cambridge: Polity Press.

Bhabha, Homi (ed.) (1990) 'DissemiNation: time, narrative, and the margins of the modern nation, *Nation and Narration*. London: Routledge. pp. 291–322.

Bhabha, Homi (1994) *Location of Culture*. London: Routledge.

Bhabha, Homi (1996) 'Culture's In-Between' in Stuart Hall and Paul du Gay (eds), *Questions of Cultural Identity*. London: Sage.

Blackburn, Robin (1988) *The Overthrow of Colonial Slavery, 1776–1848*. London: Verso.

Bougainville, Louis Antoine (1771) *Voyage autour du monde par la frégate du roi la Boudeuse, et la flute l'Étoile en 1766, 1767, 1768, 1769*. Paris.

Bowie, Andrew (1990) *Aesthetics and Subjectivity: From Kant to Nietzsche*. Manchester: Manchester University Press.

Braidotti, Rosi (1994) *Nomadic Subjects: Embodiment and Sexual Difference in Contemporary Feminist Theory*. New York: Columbia University Press.

Braudel, Fernand (1974) *Capitalism and Material Life, 1400–1800*. Trans. Miriam Kocham. London: Fontana.

Buci-Glucksmann, Christine (1994) *Baroque Reason: The Aesthetics of Modernity*. London: Sage.

Butler, Judith (1990) *Gender Trouble: Feminism and the Subversion of Identity*. New York and London: Routledge.

Butler, Judith (1993) *Bodies that Matter*. New York and London: Routledge.

Butler, Judith (1999) 'Revisiting bodies and pleasures', *Theory, Culture & Society*, 16 (2): 11–20.

Capra, Fritjof (1976) *The Tao of Physics*. Bungay: Fontana.

Cascardi, Anthony (1992) *The Subject of Modernity*. Cambridge: Cambridge University Press.

Castoriadis, Cornelius (1991) 'Power, politics, autonomy', in David Curtis (ed.), *Castoriadis: Philosophy, Politics, Autonomy*. Oxford: Oxford University Press.

Chakrabarty, Dipesh (1988) 'Conditions for knowledge of working-class conditions', in Ranajit Guha and Gayatri C. Spivak (eds), *Selected Subaltern Studies*. Oxford: Oxford University Press.

Clavelin, Maurice (1974) *The Natural Philosophy of Galileo*. Trans. A.J. Pomerans. Cambridge, MA: MIT Press.

Coles, Roman (1991) 'Foucault's dialogical artistic ethos', *Theory, Culture & Society*, 8 (1): 99–120.

Columbus, Christopher (1930 [1492]) *Select Documents Illustrating the Four Voyages of Columbus*. 2 vols. Ed. Cecil, Jane. London: The Hakluyt Society.

Columbus, Christopher (1988 [1492]) *The Four Voyages of Christopher Columbus*. Ed. J.M. Cohen. London: Century Hutchinson.

Critchley, Simon (1997) *Very Little . . . Almost Nothing*. London and New York: Routledge.

Crollius (1624) *Traité des Signatures*. French trans. Cited in Michael Foucault 1966.

Crombie, A.C. (1961) *Augustine to Galileo. Vol. 1*. London: Mercury Books.

Curtis, Neal (1998) 'Against Autonomy: Lyotard, Justice and the Idea'. Unpublished. PhD thesis, Nottingham Trent University.

Dangarembga, Tsitsi (1988) *Nervous Conditions*. London: Women's Press.

Deleuze, Gilles (1993) *The Fold: Leibniz and the Baroque*. Trans. Tom Conley. Minneapolis and London: University of Minnesota Press.

Deleuze, Gilles and Guattari, Félix (1985) *Anti-Oedipus: Capitalism and Schizophrenia*. Trans. H.R. Lane and Robert Hurley. Minneapolis: University of Minnesota Press.

Deleuze, Gilles and Guattari, Félix (1994) *What is Philosophy?* Trans. Hugh Tomlinson. New York: Columbia University Press.

Derrida, Jacques (1967) *L'Écriture et la différence*. Paris: Éditions du Seuil.

Derrida, Jacques (1972) *La Dissémination*. Paris: Éditions du Seuil.

Derrida, Jacques (1982) *Margins of Philosophy*. Trans. Alan Bass. Brighton: Harvester Press.

Derrida, Jacques (1990) 'Some statements and truisms about neo-logisms, newisms, postisms, parasitisms, and other small seismisms', in David Carroll (ed.), *The States of 'Theory'*. Stanford, CA: Stanford University Press.

Derrida, Jacques (1992) *Given Time: 1: Counterfeit Money*. Trans. Peggy Kamuf. Chicago: University of Chicago Press.

Derrida, Jacques (1993) *Les Spectres de Marx*. Paris: Éditions Galilée.

Derrida, Jacques (1995a) *Points . . . Interviews, 1974–1994*. Ed. Max Weber. Stanford, CA: Stanford University Press.

Derrida, Jacques (1995b) *The Gift of Death*. Trans. David Wills. Chicago: University of Chicago Press.

Derrida, Jacques (1997) *Le Droit à la philosophie du point de vue cosmopolitique*. Paris: Éditions Unesco.

Derrida, Jacques (1999) 'Hospitality, justice and responsibility: a dialogue with Jacques Derrida', in Richard Kearney and Mark Dooley (eds), *Questioning Ethics*. London and New York: Routledge.

Descartes, René (1968 [1637]) *Discourse on Method and the Meditations*. Trans. F.E. Sutcliffe. Harmondsworth: Penguin.

Dickson, David (1979) 'Science and political hegemony in the 17th century', *Radical Science Journal*, 8: 7–37.

Diderot, Denis (1955) *Supplément au Voyage de Bougainville*. [1773] edn. Geneva and Lille: Herbert Dieckmann.

Dolar, Mladan (1991) 'The legacy of the Enlightenment: Foucault and Lacan', *New Formations*, 14: 43–56.

Eagleton, Terry (1990) *The Ideology of the Aesthetic*. Oxford: Blackwell.

Easlea, Brian (1980) *Witch-hunting, Magic and the New Philosophy*. Brighton: Harvester Press.

Eco, Umberto (1983) *The Name of the Rose*. Trans. William Weaver. London: Secker & Warburg.

Elias, Norbert (1982) *The Civilizing Process: State Formation and Civilization*. Trans. Edmund Jephcott. Oxford: Blackwell.

Elias, Norbert (1984) *Power and Civility*. New York: Pantheon.

Elliott, J.H. (1970) *The Old World and the New, 1492–1650*. Cambridge: Cambridge Unversity Press.

Elton, G.R. (1963) *Reformation Europe: 1517–1559*. London: Fontana.

Fabian, Johannes (1983) *Time and the Other: How Anthropology Makes its Object*. New York: Columbia University Press.

Fanon, Frantz (1967) *The Wretched of the Earth*. Trans. Constance Farrington. Harmondsworth: Penguin.

Fanon, Frantz (1970) *Black Skin White Masks*. Trans. Charles L. Markmann. London: Paladin.

Farrington, John (1970) *The Philosophy of Francis Bacon*. Liverpool: Liverpool University Press.

Faye, Jean-Pierre (1972) *Théorie du récit*. Paris: Herman.

Featherstone, Mike (ed.) (1990) *Global Culture: Nationalism, Globalization and Modernity*. London: Sage.

Featherstone, Mike, Lash, Scott and Robertson, Roland (1995) *Global Modernities*. London: Sage.

Foster, Hal (1983) *Postmodern Culture*. London and Sydney: Pluto Press.

Foucault, Michel (1966) *Les mots et les choses*. Paris: Éditions Gallimard.

Foucault, Michel (1970) *The Order of Things*. Trans. Alan Sheridan. London: Tavistock.

Foucault, Michel (1979) 'On governmentality', *Ideology & Consciousness*, 6: 5–21.

Foucault, Michel (1982) 'The subject and power', in Hubert Dreyfus and Paul Rabinow (eds), *Michel Foucault: Beyond Structuralism and Hermeneutics*. Brighton: Harvester Press.

Foucault, Michel (1984a) *Histoire de la sexualité: L'Usage des plaisirs*. Paris: Éditions Gallimard.

Foucault, Michel (1984b) *Histoire de la sexualité: Le Souci de soi*. Paris: Éditions Gallimard.

Foucault, Michel (1984c) 'What is Enlightenment?', in Paul Rabinow (ed.), *The Foucault Reader*. Harmondsworth: Penguin.

Foucault, Michel (1986) 'Kant on Enlightenment and revolution', *Economy and Society*, 15 (1): 88–96.

Frank, André Gunter (1969) *Capitalism and Underdevelopment in Latin America*. New York: Monthly Review Press.

Fraser, Nancy (1989) *Unruly Practices*. Cambridge: Polity Press.

Friel, Brian (1981) *Translations*. London: Faber and Faber.

Fryer, Peter (1984) *Staying Power: The History of Black People in Britain*. London: Pluto.

Galileo, Galilei (1962 [1632]) *A Dialogue Concerning the Two Chief World Systems*. Trans. Stillman Drake. Berkeley and Los Angeles: University of California Press.

Gatens, Moira (1996) *Imaginary Bodies: Ethics, Power and Corporeality*. London and New York: Routledge.

Giddens, Anthony (1990) *The Consequences of Modernity*. Cambridge: Polity Press.

Giddens, Anthony (1994) 'Living in a Post-Traditional Society', in Ulrich Beck, Anthony Giddens and Scott Lash (eds), *Reflexive Modernization*. Cambridge: Polity Press.

Gilroy, Paul (1993a) *The Black Atlantic: Modernity and Double Consciousness*. London: Verso.

Gilroy, Paul (1993b) *Small Acts*. London: Serpent's Tail.

Gilson, Étienne (1930) *Études sur le role de la pensée mediévale dans la formation du système cartésien*. Paris: Vrin.

Graus, Frantisek (1971) 'The crisis of the Middle Ages and the Hussites', in Steven E. Ozment (ed.), *The Reformation in Medieval Perspective*. Chicago: Quadrangle Books.

Greenblatt, Stephen J. (1980) *Renaissance Self-Fashioning: From More to Shakespeare*. Chicago: University of Chicago Press.

Grosz, Elizabeth (1994) *Volatile Bodies: Towards a Corporeal Feminism*. Bloomington: Indiana University Press.

Habermas, Jürgen (1983) 'Modernity – an incomplete project', in Hal Foster (ed.) *Postmodern Culture*. London and Sydney: Pluto Press. pp. 3–15.

Habermas, Jürgen (1987) *Philosophical Discourse of Modernity*. Trans. Frederick Lawrence. Cambridge: Polity Press.

Habermas, Jürgen (1992) *Postmetaphysical Thinking*. Trans. William M. Hohengarten. Cambridge, MA: MIT Press.

Habermas, Jürgen (1996) *Between Facts and Norms*. Trans. William Rehg. Cambridge, MA: MIT Press.

Hall, Stuart (1996a) 'Introduction: Who needs identity?', in Stuart Hall and Paul du Gay (eds), *Questions of Cultural Identity*. London: Sage.

Hall, Stuart (1996b) 'When was "the post-colonial"? Thinking at the limit', in Iain Chambers and Lidia Curti (eds), *The Post-colonial Question*. London and New York: Routledge.

Hall, Stuart and Gieben, Bram (1992) *Formations of Modernity*. Cambridge: Polity Press.

Hall, Stuart, Held, David and McGrew, Tony (eds) (1992) *Modernity and its Futures*. Cambridge: Polity Press.

Haraway, Donna (1991) *Simians, Cyborgs, and Women: The Reinvention of Nature*. London: Free Association Books.

Hegel, Georg W.F. (1995) *Lectures on the Philosophy of History*, 3 vols. Trans. E.S. Haldane and Frances Simson. Lincoln: University of Nebraska Press.

Heidegger, Martin (1962) *Being and Time*. Trans. John Macquarrie and Edward Robinson. Oxford: Blackwell.

Heidegger, Martin (1972) *On Time and Being*. Trans. Joan Stambaugh. New York and London: Harper and Row.

Heidegger, Martin (1977) *The Question Concerning Technology and Other Essays*. Trans. William Lovitt. New York: HarperTorchbooks.

Heidegger, Martin (1993) *Basic Writings*. Ed. David F. Krell. London: Routledge.

Henriques, Julian, Hollway, Wendy, Urwin, Cathy, Venn, Couze and Walkerdine, Valerie

(1998 [1984]) *Changing the Subject: Psychology, Subjectivity and Social Regulation*. London and New York: Routledge.

Herder, Johann Gottfried (1997) *On World History*. Ed. H. Adler and E.A. Menze. Trans. E.A. Menze and B. Palma. New York: M.E. Sharpe.

Hill, Christopher (1975) *The World Turned Upside Down*. Harmondsworth: Penguin.

Hobsbawm, Eric (1962) *The Age of Revolution*. London: Weidenfeld and Nicolson.

Honneth, Axel (1995) *The Struggle for Recognition. The Moral Grammar of Social Conflicts*. Trans. Joel Anderson. Cambridge: Polity Press.

Hont, Ivan and Ignatieff, Michael (1983) 'Need and justice in the *Wealth of Nations*', in Ivan Hont and Michael Ignatieff (eds), *Wealth and Virtue*. Cambridge: Cambridge University Press.

Horkheimer, Max and Adorno, Theodor (1979) *Dialectic of Enlightenment*. Trans. John Cumming. London: Verso.

Hulme, Peter and Jordanova, Ludmilla (1990) *The Enlightenment and Its Shadows*. London: Routledge.

Humboldt, Alexander von (1846) *Cosmos: Sketch of a Physical Description of the Universe*. Trans E. Sabine. 4 vols. London.

Hume, David (1882) 'On national characters', *Essays, Moral, Political and Literary*, 2 vols, eds T.H. Green and T.H. Grose. London (in Anthony Pagden 1993).

Husserl, Edmond (1960) *Cartesian Meditations*. Trans. Dorian Cairns. The Hague: Martinus Nijhoff.

Husserl, Edmund (1970) *The Crisis of European Sciences and Transcendental Phenomenology*. Trans. David Carr. Evanston, IL: Northwestern University Press.

Irigaray, Luce (1979) *Et l'une ne bouge pas sans l'autre*. Paris: Éditions de Minuit.

Irigaray, Luce (1984) *Ethique de la différence sexuelle*. Paris: Éditions de Minuit.

Jalée, Pierre (1965) *Le Pillage du tiers monde*. Paris: Maspéro.

James, C.L.R. (1938) *The Black Jacobins: Toussaint L'Ouverture and the San Domingo Revolution*. London: Alison and Busby.

Jameson, Fredric (1991) *Postmodernism or the Cultural Logic of Late Capitalism*. London: Verso.

JanMohamed, Abdul (1983) *Manichean Aesthetics: The Politics of Literature in Colonial Africa*. Amherst: University of Massachusetts Press.

JanMohamed, Abdul (1986) 'The economy of Manichean allegory: the function of racial difference in colonialist literature', in Henry Louis Gates Jr (ed.), *'Race', Writing and Difference*. Chicago: University of Chicago Press.

Kamen, Henry (1976) *The Iron Century: Social Change in Europe 1550–1660*. London: Sphere Books.

Kant, Immanuel (1933 [1787]) *Critique of Pure Reason*. Trans. Norman Kemp Smith. London: Macmillan Press.

Kant, Immanuel (1987 [1790]). *Critique of Judgment*. Trans. Werner S. Pluhar. Indianapolis: Hackett Publishing Company.

Kant, Immanuel (1992 [1784]) 'An answer to the question: What is Enlightenment?', in Patricia Waugh (ed.), *Postmodernism: A Reader*. London and New York: Edward Arnold.

Kearney, Richard (1988) *The Wake of Imagination*. London: Hutchinson.

Kepler, Johannes (1596) *Mysterium Cosmographicum*.

Knorr-Cetina, Karin (1997) 'Sociality with objects: social relations in postsocial knowledge societies', *Theory, Culture & Society*, 14 (4): 1–30.

Koyré, Alexandre (1971) 'Paracelsus', in Stephen E. Ozment (ed.), *The Reformation in Medieval Perspective*. Chicago: Quandrangle Books.

Koyré, Alexandre (1978) *Galileo Studies*. Trans. John Mepham. Hassocks: Harvester Press.

Kristeva, Julia (1974) *La Révolution du langage poétique*. Paris: Éditions du Seuil.

Kristeva, Julia (1982) *Powers of Horror*. New York: Columbia University Press.

Kristeva, Julia (1983) *Histoires d'amour*. Paris: Denoël.

Lacan, Jacques (1966a) *Écrits, Vol. 1*. Paris: Éditions du Seuil.

Lacan, Jacques (1966b) *Écrits, Vol. 2*. Paris: Éditions du Seuil.

Lacan, Jacques (1979) *The Four Fundamental Concepts of Psychoanalysis*. Trans. Alan Sheridan. Harmondsworth: Penguin.

Lacan, Jacques (1992) *The Ethics of Psychoanalysis*. Trans. Dennis Porter. London: Routledge.

Lacoue-Labarthe, Philippe (1990) *Heidegger, Art and Politics*. Trans. Chris Turner. Oxford: Basil Blackwell.

Lacoue-Labarthe, Philippe (1999) *Poetry as Experience*. Trans. Andrea Tarnowski. Stanford, CA: Stanford University Press.

Ladurie, Emmanuel Le Roy (1978) *Montaillou*. Trans. Barbara Bray. London: Scholar Press.

Laplanche, Jean (1976) *Life and Death in Psychoanalysis*. Trans. Jeffrey Mehlman. Baltimore and London: Johns Hopkins University Press.

Lash, Scott (1994) *Reflexive Modernization*. Cambridge: Polity Press.

Lash, Scott (1996) 'Postmodern ethics and the missing ground', *Theory, Culture & Society*, 13 (2): 91–105.

Lévi-Strauss, Claude (1987) *Race et histoire*. Paris: Denoël.

Levin, David Michael (1985) *The Body's Recollection of Being: Phenomenological Psychology and the Deconstruction of Nihilism*. London: Routledge and Kegan Paul.

Levinas, Emmanuel (1969) *Totality and Infinity*. Trans. Alfonso Lingis. Pittsburgh: Duquesne University Press.

Levinas, Emmanuel (1974) *La Trace de l'autre: en découvrant l'existence avec Husserl et Heidegger*. Paris: Vrin.

Levinas, Emmanuel (1983 [1948]) *Le Temps et l'autre*. Paris: Presses Universitaires de France.

Levinas, Emmanuel (1984) 'Ethics of the infinite', in Richard Kearney (ed.), *Dialogues with Contemporary French Philosophers*. Manchester: Manchester University Press.

Levinas, Emmanuel (1985) *Ethics and Infinity*. Trans. R.A. Cohen. Pittsburgh: Duquesne University Press.

Levinas, Emmanuel (1987) 'Philosophy and the idea of infinity', in *Collected Philosophical Papers*. Trans. Alfonso Lingis. Dordrecht: Martinus Nijhoff.

Levinas, Emmanuel (1988) 'The paradox of morality: an interview with Emmanuel Levinas', in Robert Bernasconi and David Wood (eds), *The Provocation of Levinas*. London: Routledge.

Lloyd, Genevieve (1984) *The Man of Reason: 'Male' and 'Female' in Western Philosophy*. London: Routledge.

Lloyd, Genevieve (1993) *Being in Time*. London: Routledge.

Locke, John (1963 [1690]) *Two Treatises of Government*. New York: Cambridge University Press.

Lortz, Joseph (1968) *The Reformation in Germany*. London and New York: Routledge and Kegan Paul. (In 'Introduction' in Steven Ozment 1971, pp. 3–11).

Luria, Alexander (1982) *Language and Cognition*. Ed. James Wertsch. New York: Wiley.

Luther, Martin (1971 [1517]) 'Disputations against scholastic theology', in Paul Vignaux.

Lyotard, Jean-François (1983) *Le Differend*. Paris: Éditions de Minuit.

Lyotard, Jean-François (1984) *The Postmodern Condition: A Report on Knowledge*. Trans. Geoff Bennington and Brian Massumi. Manchester: Manchester University Press.

Lyotard, Jean-François (1988a) 'Reécrire la modernité', *Cahiers de Philosophie*, 5. pp. 193–203.

Lyotard, Jean-François (1988b) *Le Postmoderne expliqué aux enfants*. Paris: Éditions Galilée.

Lyotard, Jean-François (1989) 'Time today', *Oxford Literary Review*, 11 (1–2): 3–20.

Lyotard, Jean-François (1993) *Un trait d'union*. Sainte-Foy: Le Griffon D'argile.

Lyotard, Jean-François (1994) *Lessons on the Analytic of the Sublime*. Trans. Elizabeth Rottenberg. Stanford, CA: Stanford University Press.

McClintock, Anne (1995) *Imperial Leather: Race, Gender and Sexuality in the Colonial World*. New York and London: Routledge.

Macey, David (1993) *The Lives of Michel Foucault*. London: Vintage.

Macnaghten, Phil and Urry, John (1998) *Contested Natures*. London: Sage.

Merleau-Ponty, Maurice (1964) *L'Oeil et l'esprit*. Paris: Éditions Gallimard.

Merleau-Ponty, Maurice (1968) *The Visible and the Invisible*. Ed. Claude Lefort. Trans. Alfonso Lingis. Evanston, IL: Northwestern University Press.

Montaigne, Edmond de (1987 [1580]) *An Apology for Raymond Sebond*. Harmondsworth: Penguin.

Montaigne, Michel de (1958 [1580]) *Essays*. Trans. J.M. Cohen. Harmondsworth: Penguin.

Montesquieu, Charles (1977 [1721]) *Persian Letters*. Trans. C.J. Betts. Harmondsworth: Penguin.

Morrison, Toni (1987) *Beloved*. London: Chatto & Windus.

Morrison, Toni (1992) *Playing in the Dark: Whiteness and the Literary Imagination*. New York: Vintage Books.

Morrison, Toni (1993) 'Living memory: a meeting with Toni Morrison', in Paul Gilroy (ed.), *Small Acts*. London: Serpent's Tail.

Nancy, Jean-Luc (1990) 'Finite History', in David Carroll (ed.), *The States of Theory*.

O'Gorman, Edmundo (1961) *The Invention of America*. Bloomington: Indiana Universty Press.

Osborne, Peter (1995) *The Politics of Time*. London: Verso.

Ozment, Steven (ed.) (1971) *The Reformation in Medieval Perspectives*. Chicago: Quadrangle Books.

Pagden, Anthony (1993) *European Encounters with the New World*. New Haven and London: Yale University Press.

Parry, Benita (1997) 'The postcolonial: Conceptual category or chimera?' *Yearbook of English Studies, Vol. 27*, pp. 3–21.

Pasquino, Pasquale (1978) '*Theatrum politicum*: the genealogy of capital – police and the state of prosperity', *Ideology & Consciousness*, 4: 41–54.

Patterson, Orlando (1982) *Slavery and Social Death*. Cambridge, Mass: Harvard University Press.

Petty, William (1682) *Political Arithmetic*. London.

Porta, Giordano (1650) *Magie Naturelle*. Paris.

Pratt, Mary Louise (1992) *Imperial Eyes: Travel Writing and Transculturation*. London: Routledge.

Prigogine, Ilya and Stengers, Isabelle (1984) *Order out of Chaos*. London: Heinemann.

Procacci, Giovanna (1978) 'Social economy and the government of poverty', *Ideology & Consciousness*, 4: 55–72.

Rabasa, José (1985) 'Allegories of the altlas', in Francis Barker, Peter Hulme, Margaret Iverson and Diane Loxley (eds), *Europe and its Others, Vol 2*. Colchester: University of Essex.

Rawls, John (1971) *A Theory of Justice*. Oxford: Oxford University Press.

Raynal, Abbé (1781 [1770]) *Histoire des deux Indes*. Paris.

Ricoeur, Paul (1984) 'The creativity of language', in Richard Kearney (ed.), *Dialogues with Contemporary Continental Thinkers*. Manchester: Manchester University Press.

Ricoeur, Paul (1988) *Time and Narrative, Vol. 3*. Trans. Kathleen Blamey and David Pellauer. Chicago: University of Chicago Press.

Ricoeur, Paul (1991) 'Discussion: Ricoeur on narrative' and 'Narrative identity', in David Wood (ed.), *On Paul Ricoeur*. London and New York: Routledge.

Ricoeur, Paul (1992) *Oneself as Another*. Trans. Kathleen Blamey. Chicago: University of Chicago Press.

Ricoeur, Paul (1996) 'Reflections on a new ethos for Europe', in Richard Kearney (ed.), *Paul Ricoeur. The Hermeneutics of Action*. London: Sage.

Riley, Patrick (1986) *The General Will Before Rousseau: The Transformation of the Divine into the Civic*. Princeton: Princeton University Press.

Rodney, Walter (1972) *How Europe Underdeveloped Africa*. Harare: Zimbabwe Publishing House.

Rose, Gillian (1992) *The Broken Middle*. Oxford: Blackwell.

Rose, Gillian (1993) *Judaism and Modernity*. Oxford: Blackwell.

Rose, Gillian (1995) *Love's Work*. London: Chatto & Windus.

Rose, Nikolas (1989) *Governing the Soul*. London: Routledge.

Rose, Nikolas (1996) 'Identity, genealogy, history', in Stuart Hall and Paul du Gay (eds), *Questions of Cultural Identity*. London: Sage.

Rose, Stephen (1997) *Lifelines: Biology, Freedom, Determinism*. Harmondsworth: Penguin.

Said, Edward (1978) *Orientalism*. London: Routledge and Kegan Paul.

Said, Edward (1984) *The World, the Text, the Critic*. London: Faber & Faber.

Said, Edward (1993) *Culture and Imperialism*. London: Chatto & Windus.

Santner, Eric (1990) *Stranded Objects: Mourning, Memory and Film in Postwar Germany*. Ithaca, NY: Cornell University Press.

Sartre, Jean-Paul (1967) 'Preface', in Frantz Fanon (ed.), *The Wretched of the Earth*. Trans. Constance Farrington. Harmondsworth: Penguin.

Searle, Chris (1992) 'Unlearning Columbus: A review article', *Race and Class*, 33 (3): 67–77.

Sennett, Richard (1976) *The Fall of Public Man*. Cambridge: Cambridge University Press.

Serres, Michel (1982) *Hermes: Literature, Science, Philosophy*. Baltimore: Johns Hopkins University Press.

Shohat, Ella and Stam, Robert (1994) *Unthinking Eurocentrism: Multiculturalism and the Media*. London and New York: Routledge.

Smith, Adam (1812 [1776]) *The Wealth of Nations*. London.

Smith, Nick (1994) 'Charles Taylor, strong hermeneutics and the politics of difference', *Radical Philosophy*, 68: 19–27.

Spivak, Gayatri Chakravorty (1985) 'The Rani of Sirmur', in Francis Barker, Peter Hulme, Margaret Iverson and Diane Loxley (eds), *Europe and its Others, Vol. 1*. Colchester: University of Essex.

Spivak, Gayatri Chakravorty (1990) *The Post-colonial Critic: Interviews*. Ed. Sarah Harasym. New York and London: Routledge.

Suleri, Sara (1992) *The Rhetoric of English India*. Chicago: University of Chicago Press.

Taussig, Michael (1987) *Shamanism, Colonialism and the Wild Man: A Study in Terror and Healing*. Chicago: University of Chicago Press.

Taussig, Michael (1993) *Mimesis and Alterity*. New York and London: Routledge.

Taylor, Charles (1986) 'Foucault on freedom and truth', in David C. Hoy (ed.), *Foucault: A Critical Reader*. Oxford: Blackwell.

Taylor, Charles (1989) *Sources of the Self: The Making of the Modern Identity*. Cambridge: Cambridge University Press.

Taylor, Charles (1992) *Multiculturalism*. Ed. Amy Gutman. Princeton: Princeton University Press.

Thacker, Andrew (1993) 'Foucault's aesthetics of existence', *Radical Philosophy*, 63: 13–21.

Thomas, Keith (1971) *Religion and the Decline of Magic: Studies in Popular Beliefs in Sixteenth- and Seventeenth-century England*. London: Wiedenfeld & Nicolson.

Todorov, Tzvetan (1992 [1982]) *The Conquest of America*. Trans. Richard Howard. New York: HarperPerennial.

Trinh Minh-ha (1989) *Woman, Native, Other*. Bloomington: Indiana University Press.

Tuchman, Barbara (1979) *A Distant Mirror: The Calamitous Fourteenth Century*. London: Macmillan.

Urry, John (1990) *The Tourist Gaze*. London: Sage.

Vattimo, Gianni (1988) *The End of Modernity*. Trans. Jon Snyder. Cambridge: Polity Press.

Venn, Couze (1982) 'Beyond the Science/Ideology Relation'. Unpublished PhD thesis. Colchester: University of Essex.

Venn, Couze (1985) 'A subject for concern: sexuality and subjectivity in Foucault's *History of Sexuality*', *PsychCritique*, 1 (2): 139–54.

Venn, Couze (1993) *Occidentalism and its Discontents*. London: University of East London.

Venn, Couze (1996) 'History lessons: formation of subjects, (post)colonialism, and an Other project', in Bill Schwarz (ed.), *The Expansion of England: Race, Ethnicity and Cultural History*. London: Routledge. pp. 32–60.

Venn, Couze (1997) 'Beyond Enlightenment? After the subject of Foucault, who comes?', *Theory, Culture & Society*, 14 (3): 1–28.

Venn, Couze (1999) 'Narrating the postcolonial', in Mike Featherstone and Scott Lash (eds), *Spaces of Culture: Nation, City, World*. London: Sage.

Vico, Giambattista (1982) *Selected Writings*. Ed. and trans. Leon Pompa. Cambridge: Cambridge University Press.

Vignaux, Paul (1971) 'On Luther and Occam', in Steven E. Ozment (ed.), *The Reformation in Medieval Perspective*. Chicago: Quadrangle Books.

Viswanathan, Gauri (1989) *Masks of Conquest: Literary Study and British Rule in India*. London: Faber and Faber.

Volosinov, Valentin (1973) *Marxism and the Philosophy of Language*. Trans. Ladislav Matejka and I.R. Titunik. London: Seminar Press.

Vygotsky, Lev (1986) *Thought and Language*. Trans. Alex Kozulin. Cambridge, MA: MIT Press.

Wallerstein, Immanuel (1980) *The Modern World-System, Vol. 2*. New York: Academic Press.

Wallerstein, Immanuel (1984) *The Politics of the World-Economy*. Cambridge: Cambridge University Press.

Wallerstein, Immanuel (1991) *Geopolitics and Geocultures: The Changing World-System*. Cambridge: Cambridge University Press.

Watson, James (1970) *The Double Helix*. Harmondsworth: Penguin Books.

Watson, Sean (1998) 'The New Bergsonism: Discipline, Subjectivity and Freedom', *Radical Philosophy*, 92: 6–16.

White, Hayden (1978) *Tropics of Discourse: Essays in Cultural Criticism*. Baltimore and London: Johns Hopkins University Press.

Williams, Eric (1964) *Capitalism and Slavery*. London: Andre Deusch.

Winnicott, David (1963) 'The devleopment of the capacity for concern', *Bulletin of the Menninger Clinic*, 27: 167–76.

Wood, David (1988) *The Deconstruction of Time*. Atlantic Highlands: Humanities Press.

Yates, Frances (1964) *Giordano Bruno and the Hermetic Tradition*. London: Vintage Books.

Yates, Frances (1983) *The Occult Philosophy in the Elizabethan Age*. London: Ark Paperbacks.

Young, Robert (1990) *White Mythologies: Writing History and the West*. New York and London: Routledge.

Žižek, Slavoj (1989) *The Sublime Object of Ideology*. London: Verso.

Žižek, Slavoj (1993) *Tarrying with the Negative*. Durham, NC: Duke University Press.

INDEX